Forget Not God's Benefits (Psalm 103:2):
A Festschrift in Honor of Leslie J. Hoppe, OFM

CATHOLIC BIBLICAL QUARTERLY IMPRINTS
No. 3

EDITORIAL BOARD

Richard J. Bautch, General Editor

ASSOCIATE EDITORS

Bill T. Arnold
Mary Rose D'Angelo
Thomas B. Dozeman
Peter Dubovský
Joachim Eck
Beverly Roberts Gaventa
J. Todd Hibbard
Amy-Jill Levine

Francis M. Macatangay
Dominik Markl
Roberto Martinez, OFM Cap.
Margaret M. Mitchell
Anathea E. Portier-Young
Deborah C. Prince
Susanne Scholz

Forget Not God's Benefits (Psalm 103:2): A Festschrift in Honor of Leslie J. Hoppe, OFM

Edited by
Barbara E. Reid, O.P.

CBQ Imprints
The Catholic Biblical Association of America
Washington, D.C.

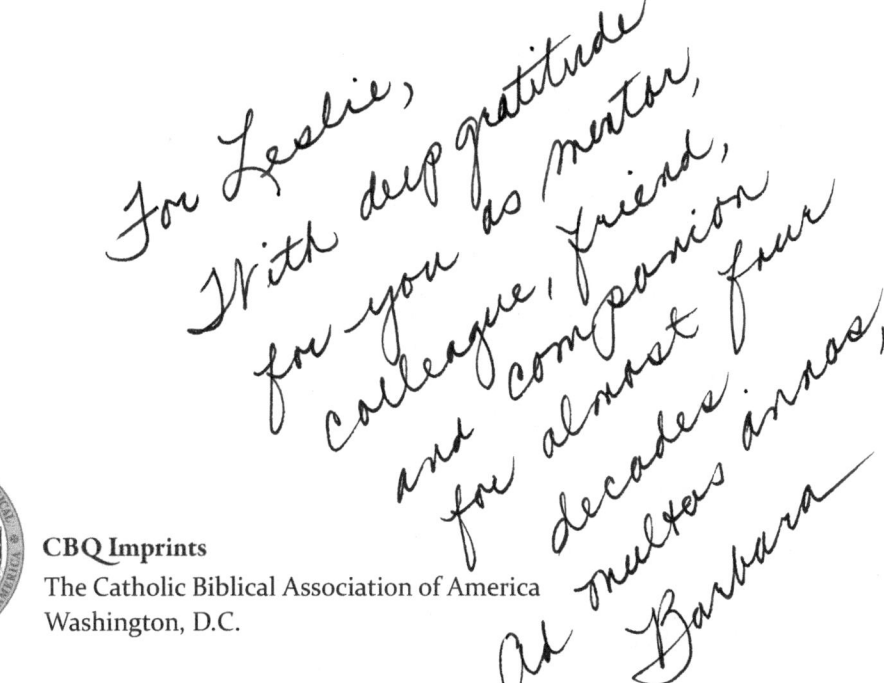

© 2022 The Catholic Biblical Association of America,
Washington, DC 20064

All rights reserved. No part of this book may be reproduced in any form or by any means without permission in writing from the Catholic Biblical Association of America.

Produced in the United States of America

Library of Congress Cataloging-in-Publication Data

Names: Hoppe, Leslie J., honoree. | Reid, Barbara E., editor.
Title: Forget not God's benefits (Psalm 103:2) : a festschrift in honor of Leslie J. Hoppe, OFM / edited by Barbara E. Reid.
Description: Washington, D.C. : The Catholic Biblical Association of America, [2022] | Series: Catholic Biblical quarterly imprints ; no. 3 | Includes bibliographical references and index. | Summary: "A collection of essays written by Leslie Hoppe's present and former colleagues of the Department of Biblical Literature and Languages at CTU and colleagues from the Old Testament Colloquium that meets annually at St. John's Abbey in Collegeville, Minnesota. The essays range over a wide variety of topics and span both Old and New Testaments. They reflect both the interests of the authors and those of Leslie Hoppe and are arranged in canonical order"— Provided by publisher.
Identifiers: LCCN 2022003077 (print) | LCCN 2022003078 (ebook) | ISBN 9780915170609 (paperback) | ISBN 9780915170616 (ebook)
Subjects: LCSH: Hoppe, Leslie J. | Bible—Criticism, interpretation, etc.
Classification: LCC BS511.3 .F66 2022 (print) | LCC BS511.3 (ebook) | DDC 220.6/1—dc23/eng/20220408
LC record available at https://lccn.loc.gov/2022003077
LC ebook record available at https://lccn.loc.gov/2022003078

Leslie J. Hoppe, OFM

Carroll Stuhlmueller, C.P., Distinguished Professor Emeritus of Old Testament Studies

1962	Entered the Assumption BVM Province of the Order of Friars Minor
1971	Ordained a Roman Catholic priest
1971	M.A. in Theology, Aquinas Institute of Theology
1978	Ph.D. in Religion, Northwestern University
1976–1979	Faculty member, Aquinas Institute of Theology
1979–1981	Faculty at Mundelein Seminary
1981–2005, 2011—2020	Professor of Old Testament Studies, Catholic Theological Union at Chicago
2005–2011	Provincial Minister of the Assumption BVM Province of the Order of Friars Minor

Contents

Abbreviations	ix
Contributors	xv
Introduction *Barbara E. Reid, O.P.*	1
"In the Image of God"—but What Is the Image? *Dianne Bergant, CSA*	10
Dinah at Shechem (Genesis 34): The Narrator's Point of View *James Chukwuma Okoye, C.S.Sp.*	25
Tamar and Judah (Genesis 38) in Early Jewish and Christian Traditions *John R. Barker, OFM*	45
Tamar, Delilah, and a Nameless Timnite: Women as (De)constructions of Social Landscape *Mahri Leonard-Fleckman*	60
Historiography across the Book of Judges *Mark S. Smith*	77
The Exact Same Thing Only Different: "Hebrews" and "Israelites" in 1 Samuel *John L. McLaughlin*	90
The End of Humiliation in LXX Isaiah 40 *Andrew R. Davis*	111
My, What a Big Ship You Have! Ezekiel's Jealousy of the Favored Minority *Corrine Carvalho*	125

Ezekiel 17: Zedekiah's Idolatrous Invocation of the Divine Name as a Capital Crime
Dale Launderville, OSB   140

The Diaspora as a Word and Concept in Early Judaism
Malka Zeiger Simkovich   153

"An Evangelizing Church": The Ecclesiology of Matthew's Gospel
Donald Senior, C.P.   171

There Shall Be No Poor among You: The Lucan Solution
Barbara E. Reid, O.P.   185

Reconstructing the Cultural Horizon for Lucan Soldiers: Texts and Artifacts in Conversation
Laurie Brink, O.P.   199

Who Was Holy and How Did They Get That Way?
Carolyn Osiek, RSCJ   219

Greco-Roman καλοκαγαθός in the Pauline and Pastoral Letters
Ferdinand Okorie, CMF   230

The Answer Lies Beneath
Barbara E. Reid, O.P.   247

Publications by Leslie J. Hoppe, OFM: A Partial List   248

Indexes
   Ancient Sources   252
   Authors   264

Abbreviations

ÄAT	Ägypten und Altes Testament
AB	Anchor Bible
ABD	David Noel Freedman, ed., *The Anchor Bible Dictionary* (6 vols.; New York: Doubleday, 1992)
ABRL	Anchor Bible Reference Library
ABS	Archaeology and Biblical Studies
AfO	*Archiv für Orientforschung*
AGAJU	Arbeiten zur Geschichte des antiken Judentums und des Urchristentums
ANRW	Hildegard Temporini and Wolfgang Haase, eds., *Aufstieg und Niedergang der römischen Welt: Geschichte und Kultur Roms im Spiegel der neueren Forschung*, Part 2: *Principat* (Berlin: de Gruyter, 1972–)
AOAT	Alter Orient und Altes Testament
AOS	American Oriental Series
ASOR	American Schools of Oriental Research
ATANT	Abhandlungen zur Theologie des Alten und Neuen Testaments
ATD	Das Alte Testament Deutsch
ATSAT	Arbeiten zu Text und Sprache im Alten Testament
AYB	Anchor Yale Bible
AYBRL	Anchor Yale Bible Reference Library
BA	*Biblical Archaeologist*
BARev	*Biblical Archaeology Review*
BASOR	*Bulletin of the American Schools of Oriental Research*
BDB	Francis S. Brown, S. R. Driver, and Charles A. Briggs, *A Hebrew and English Lexicon of the Old Testament* (Oxford: Clarendon, 1907)
BETL	Bibliotheca Ephemeridum Theologicarum Lovaniensium
BHS	*Biblia Hebraica Stuttgartensia*
Bib	*Biblica*
BibInt	*Biblical Interpretation*
BibInt	Biblical Interpretation Series
BJS	Brown Judaic Studies
BKAT	Biblischer Kommentar, Altes Testament
BNTC	Black's New Testament Commentaries

BO	*Bibliotheca Orientalis*
BR	*Biblical Research*
BSac	*Bibliotheca Sacra*
BTB	*Biblical Theology Bulletin*
BZAW	Beihefte zur Zeitschrift für die alttestamentliche Wissenschaft
CAT	Commentaire de l'Ancien Testament
CBC	Cambridge Bible Commentary: New English Bible
CBET	Contributions to Biblical Exegesis and Theology
CBQ	*Catholic Biblical Quarterly*
CBQI	Catholic Biblical Quarterly Imprints
CBQMS	Catholic Biblical Quarterly Monograph Series
CEB	Common English Bible
CEV	Contemporary English Version
CHANE	Culture and History of the Ancient Near East
CIG	August Boeckh, ed., *Corpus Inscriptionum Graecarum* (4 vols; Berlin: Reimer, 1828–77)
CIL	*Corpus Inscriptionum Latinarum* (Berlin: Reimer, 1862)
ConBOT	Coniectanea Biblica: Old Testament Series
CSCO	Corpus Scriptorum Christianorum Orientalium
CSHJ	Chicago Studies in the History of Judaism
CTH	Emmanuel Laroche, ed., *Catalogue des textes hittites* (Etudes et commentaires 75; Paris: Klincksieck, 1971)
DCH	David J. A. Clines, ed., *Dictionary of Classical Hebrew* (9 vols.; Sheffield: Sheffield Phoenix, 1993–2014)
EBR	Hans-Josef Klauck et al., eds., *Encyclopedia of the Bible and Its Reception* (Berlin: de Gruyter, 2009–)
ECC	Eerdmans Critical Commentary
EJL	Early Judaism and Its Literature
EST	Esarhaddon's Succession Treaty
ExpTim	*Expository Times*
FAT	Forschungen zum Alten Testament
FC	Fathers of the Church
GKC	*Gesenius' Hebrew Grammar* (ed. Emil Kautzsch; trans. Arthur E. Cowley; 2nd ed.; Oxford: Clarendon, 2010)
GNS	Good News Studies
Greg	*Gregorianum*
HALOT	Ludwig Koehler, Walter Baumgartner, and Johann J. Stamm, *The Hebrew and Aramaic Lexicon of the Old Testament*, trans. and ed. under the supervision of Mervyn E. J. Richardson, 4 vols. (Leiden: Brill, 1994–99)
HAT	Handbuch zum Alten Testament
HBM	Hebrew Bible Monographs
HBT	*Horizons in Biblical Theology*
HdA	Handbuch der Archäologie

HdO	Handbuch der Orientalistik
HeBAI	*Hebrew Bible and Ancient Israel*
HKAT	Handkommentar zum Alten Testament
HNTC	Harper's New Testament Commentary
HS	*Hebrew Studies*
HSM	Harvard Semitic Monographs
HSS	Harvard Semitic Studies
HThKAT	Herders Theologischer Kommentar zum Alten Testament
HThKNT	Herders Theologischer Kommentar zum Neuen Testament
HTR	*Harvard Theological Review*
HUCA	*Hebrew Union College Annual*
IBC	Interpretation: A Bible Commentary for Teaching and Preaching
ICC	International Critical Commentary
IEJ	*Israel Exploration Journal*
IGR	R. L. Cagnat, J. F. Toutain, V. Henry, and G. L. Lafaye, eds., *Inscriptiones graecae ad res romanas pertinentes* (4 vols.; Paris: E. Leroux, 1911–27)
Int	*Interpretation*
JAJ	*Journal of Ancient Judaism*
JANES	*Journal of the Ancient Near Eastern Society*
JAOS	*Journal of the American Oriental Society*
JBL	*Journal of Biblical Literature*
JETS	*Journal of the Evangelical Theological Society*
JHebS	*Journal of Hebrew Scriptures*
JHNES	Johns Hopkins Near Eastern Studies
JHS	*Journal of Hellenic Studies*
JJS	*Journal of Jewish Studies*
JNES	*Journal of Near Eastern Studies*
JPSV	Jewish Publication Society Version
JRS	*Journal of Roman Studies*
JSJ	*Journal for the Study of Judaism in the Persian, Hellenistic, and Roman Period*
JSJSup	Journal for the Study of Judaism Supplement
JSOT	*Journal for the Study of the Old Testament*
JSOTSup	Journal for the Study of the Old Testament: Supplement Series
JSPSup	Journal for the Study of the Pseudepigrapha: Supplement Series
KHAT	Kurzgefasstes exegetischer Handbuch zum Alten Testament
KJV	King James Version
LAI	Library of Ancient Israel

LCL	Loeb Classical Library
LHBOTS	Library of Hebrew Bible/Old Testament Studies
LXX	Septuagint
MT	Masoretic Text
NAB	New American Bible
NABRE	New American Bible Revised Edition
NCB	New Century Bible
NCBC	New Century Bible Commentary
NEA	*Near Eastern Archaeology*
NEB	New English Bible
Neot	*Neotestamentica*
NETS	Albert Pietersma and Benjamin G. Wright, eds., *A New English Translation of the Septuagint and the Other Greek Translations Traditionally Included under That Title* (New York: Oxford University Press, 2007)
NIB	Leander E. Keck, ed., *The New Interpreter's Bible* (12 vols.; Nashville: Abingdon, 1994–2004)
NICNT	New International Commentary on the New Testament
NICOT	New International Commentary on the Old Testament
NIDB	Katharine Doob Sakenfeld, gen. ed., *The New Interpreter's Dictionary of the Bible* (5 vols.; Nashville: Abingdon, 2006–9)
NIGTC	New International Greek Testament Commentary
NIV	New International Version
NJB	New Jerusalem Bible
NKJV	New King James Version
NRSV	New Revised Standard Version
NTT	*Nederlands theologisch tijdschrift*
OBO	Orbis Biblicus et Orientalis
OCD	Simon Hornblower and Antony Spawforth, *Oxford Classical Dictionary* (4th ed.; Oxford: Oxford University Press, 2012)
OrChrAn	Orientalia Christiana Analecta
OTE	*Old Testament Essays*
OTL	Old Testament Library
OTP	James H. Charlesworth, ed., *The Old Testament Pseudepigrapha* (2 vols.; New York: Doubleday, 1983–85)
PA	Palaestina Antiqua
PEQ	*Palestine Exploration Quarterly*
PG	Jacques-Paul Migne, ed., *Patrologiae Cursus Completus: Series Graeca* (162 vols.; Paris, 1857–86)
PL	Jacques-Paul Migne, ed., *Patrologiae Cursus Completus. Series Latina* (217 vols.; Paris, 1844–64)
PRSt	*Perspectives in Religious Studies*
RSV	Revised Standard Version

Abbreviations   xiii

SAA	State Archives of Assyria
SacPag	Sacra Pagina
SBLABS	Society of Biblical Literature Archaeology and Biblical Studies
SBLDS	Society of Biblical Literature Dissertation Series
SBLWAW	Society of Biblical Literature Writings from the Ancient World
SBS	Stuttgarter Bibelstudien
SBT	Studies in Biblical Theology
ScrHier	Scripta Hierosolymitana
SEÅ	*Svensk exegetisk årsbok*
SHBC	Smyth & Helwys Bible Commentary
SHCANE	Studies in the History and Culture of the Ancient Near East
SIG	Wilhelm Dittenberger, ed., *Sylloge Inscriptionum Graecarum* (4 vols.; 3rd ed.; Leipzig: Hirzel, 1915–24)
SMNIA	Tel Aviv University Sonia and Marco Nadler Institute of Archaeology Monograph Series
SO	*Symbolae Osloenses*
ST	*Studia Theologica*
SubBib	Subsidia Biblica
SVTQ	*St. Vladimir's Theological Quarterly*
SWBA	Social World of Biblical Antiquity
SymS	Symposium Series
TAPA	*Transactions of the American Philological Association*
TBT	*The Bible Today*
TDNT	Gerard Kittel and Gerhard Friedrich, *Theological Dictionary of the New Testament* (trans. Geoffrey W. Bromiley; 10 vols.; Grand Rapids: Eerdmans, 1964–76)
TDOT	G. Johannes Botterweck and Helmer Ringgren, eds., *Theological Dictionary of the Old Testament* (trans. John T. Willis et al.; 17 vols.; Grand Rapids: Eerdmans, 1974–2018)
TNK	Tanak
TSAJ	Texte und Studien zum antiken Judentum
TWAT	G. J. Botterweck and Helmer Ringgren (eds.), *Theologisches Wörterbuch zum Alten Testament* (10 vols.; Stuttgart: Kohlhammer, 1973–2016)
TWOT	R. Laird Harris et al., eds., *Theological Wordbook of the Old Testament* (2 vols.; Chicago: Moody, 1980)
TynBul	*Tyndale Bulletin*
UF	*Ugarit-Forschungen*
VT	*Vetus Testamentum*
VTSup	Supplements to Vetus Testamentum
WBC	Word Biblical Commentary
WCS	Wisdom Commentary Series
WGRWSup	Writings from the Greco-Roman World Supplements

WUNT	Wissenschaftliche Untersuchungen zum Neuen Testament
ZAW	*Zeitschrift für die alttestamentliche Wissenschaft*

Rabbinic Writings
Ag. Ber.	*Aggadat Bereshit*
b. Meg.	Babylonian Talmud, tractate *Megillah*
b. Soṭah	Babylonian Talmud, tractate *Soṭah*
Gen. Rab.	*Genesis Rabbah*

Other Writings

Ambrose of Milan
Exp. Luc.	*Expositio Evangelii secundum Lucam*

Aristotle
Eth. nic.	*Ethica nicomachea*

Augustine
C. mend.	*Contra mendacium*

Clement of Alexandria
Strom.	*Stromateis*

Cyprian of Carthage
Test.	*Ad Quirinum testimonia adversus Judaeos*

Ephrem of Syria
Comm. Gen.	*Commentarium in Genesim*
Hymn. nat.	*Hymni de nativitate*
Hymn. virg.	*Hymni de virginitate*

Jerome
Comm. Matt.	*Commentariorum in Matthaeum libri IV*

John Chrysostom
Hom. Gen.	*Homiliae in Genesim*
Hom. Matt.	*Homiliae in Matthaeum*

Josephus
Ant.	*Antiquitites*
War	*Jewish War*

Origen
Hom. Luc.	*Homiliae in Lucam*

Philo
Leg.	*Legum allegoriae*

Tertullian
Cult. fem.	*De cultu feminarum*
Pud.	*De pudicitia*

Contributors

JOHN R. BARKER, OFM, is a Franciscan friar of the Province of St. John the Baptist (Cincinnati). He received his Ph.D. in Biblical Studies from Boston College and served on the Bible faculty at Catholic Theological Union in Chicago from 2012 to 2020. He is the author of *Disputed Temple: A Rhetorical Analysis of the Book of Haggai* (Fortress, 2017) and has contributed articles and book reviews for *The Bible Today, Emmanuel Magazine, The Jerome Biblical Commentary for the Twenty-First Century,* and *The Oxford Handbook of Minor Prophets.*

DIANNE BERGANT, CSA, is Carroll Stuhlmueller, C.P., Distinguished Professor Emerita of Old Testament Studies at Catholic Theological Union. She is past President of the Catholic Biblical Association and Rev. Robert J. Randall Distinguished Professor of Christian Culture, Providence College, Providence, Rhode Island. She holds honorary doctorates from the Jesuit School of Theology of Santa Clara University, Santa Clara, California; Marian University, Fond du Lac, Wisconsin; and Australian Catholic University. She has authored thirty-six books as well as several book chapters and numerous articles. She has taught and lectured extensively in the United States, Europe, Asia, the Caribbean, and the South Pacific.

LAURIE BRINK, O.P., is a Dominican Sister of Sinsinawa, Professor of New Testament Studies at Catholic Theological Union in Chicago, and an associate editor of *The Bible Today*. Her publications include *What Does the Bible Say about Friendship* (New City Press, 2019); "New Testament Archaeology," in *The Jerome Biblical Commentary for the Twenty-First Century* (Bloomsbury, 2022); "The History and Archaeology of the New Testament," in *The Catholic Study Bible,* 3rd ed. (Oxford University Press, 2016); and *Soldiers in Luke-Acts: Engaging, Contradicting, and Transcending the Stereotype* (Mohr Siebeck, 2014).

CORRINE CARVALHO holds a Ph.D. from Yale University and is Professor in the Theology Department at the University of St. Thomas, Saint Paul, Minnesota. Her main area of focus is Israelite poetic and prophetic texts related to the exile. Her publications include *Reading Jeremiah* (Smyth & Helwys, 2017) and "Ezekiel" in *The Paulist Biblical Commentary* (2018). She is currently the editor of *The Oxford Handbook on the Book of Ezekiel* (online publication, 2021) and co-editor with John McLaughlin of *God and Gods in the Deuteronomistic History* (Catholic Biblical Association, 2021).

ANDREW R. DAVIS is Associate Professor of Old Testament at the Boston College School of Theology and Ministry. He holds an M.T.S. from the Weston Jesuit School of Theology and a Ph.D. from the Johns Hopkins University. His research interests include the prophetic literature (especially the books of Isaiah and Amos), biblical historiography, literary approaches to biblical narrative, and the Hebrew Bible in its ancient Near Eastern context.

DALE LAUNDERVILLE, OSB, is Professor of Old Testament and Dean of St. John's University School of Theology and Seminary, Collegeville, Minnesota. He earned his Ph.D. at The Catholic University of America in 1987. He is a member of the Editorial Committee on Revision of the New American Bible and is past President of the Catholic Biblical Association (2018–2019). His publications include *Piety and Politics: The Dynamics of Royal Authority in Homeric Greece, Biblical Israel, and Old Babylonian Mesopotamia* (Eerdmans, 2003); *Spirit and Reason: The Embodied Character of Ezekiel's Symbolic Thinking* (Baylor University Press, 2007); *Celibacy in the Ancient World: Its Ideal and Practice in Pre-Hellenistic Israel, Mesopotamia, and Greece* (Liturgical Press, 2010).

MAHRI LEONARD-FLECKMAN is Assistant Professor of Hebrew Bible in the Religious Studies Department at the College of the Holy Cross. Her books include *The House of David: Between Political Formation and Literary Revision* (Fortress, 2016) and *Ruth*, co-authored with Alice Laffey (Wisdom Commentary; Liturgical Press, 2017).

JOHN L. MCLAUGHLIN is Professor of Old Testament/Hebrew Bible and Interim Dean of the Faculty of Theology at the University of St. Michael's College, Toronto, and an Associate Member of the Graduate Faculty, Department of Near and Middle Eastern Civilizations, University of Toronto. His recent publications include *An Introduction to Israel's Wisdom Traditions* (Eerdmans, 2018); *What Are They Saying about Ancient Israelite Religion?* (Paulist, 2016); *The Ancient Near East: An Essential Guide* (Abingdon, 2012); and entries on "Amos" and "Wisdom Literature" in *The Jerome Biblical Commentary for the Twenty-First Century* (Bloomsbury, 2022).

FERDINAND OKORIE, C.M.F., is a Claretian Missionary priest and Assistant Professor of New Testament and Early Christianity and Director of Bible Study and Travel Programs at Catholic Theological Union, Chicago. He is the Editor-in-Chief at *U.S. Catholic*. His peer-reviewed articles have appeared in scholarly journals including *NACATHS Journal of African Theology*. In addition, he writes pastoral reflections on various New Testament topics, notably on theological and pastoral issues in the letters of Paul and book reviews in *U.S. Catholic*. His book *Favor and Gratitude: Reading Galatians in Its Greco-Roman Context* was published by Lexington Books in 2020.

JAMES CHUKWUMA OKOYE, C.S.SP., earned an L.S.S. at the Pontifical Biblical Institute in Rome (1975), an M.A. in Biblical Languages at Oxford, England (1977), and D. Phil., Targums, at Oxford (1980). He is Director of the Center for Spiritan Studies at Duquesne University, Pittsburgh, Pennsylvania. He was a member of the International Theological Commission (1986–1991) and held the Carroll Stuhlmueller, C.P., Distinguished Professorship in Old Testament at Catholic Theological Union, Chicago. His latest publications include *Genesis 1–11: A Narrative Theological Commentary* (Cascade, 2018); *Genesis 12—50: A Narrative Theological Commentary* (Cascade, 2020); *Scripture in the Church: The Synod on the Word of God and the Post-Synodal Exhortation Verbum Domini* (Liturgical Press, 2011); *Israel and the Nations: A Mission Theology of the Old Testament* (Orbis Books, 2006). He is General Editor of the *African American Catholic Youth Bible* (St. Mary's Press, 2015) and is the current editor of *Spiritan Horizons*. He has published over sixty peer-reviewed articles and chapters in books.

CAROLYN OSIEK, RSCJ, was Professor of New Testament at Catholic Theological Union for twenty-six years before becoming Charles Fischer Catholic Professor at Brite Divinity School, Fort Worth, Texas. She retired in 2009 and is now provincial archivist and canonical treasurer for the Society of the Sacred Heart, U.S.-Canada Province. She is General Editor of the Anselm Academic Study Bible (2013), for which Leslie Hoppe is Old Testament editor.

BARBARA E. REID, O.P., is a Dominican Sister of Grand Rapids, Michigan, and holds a Ph.D. in Biblical Studies from The Catholic University of America in Washington, D.C. She is President of Catholic Theological Union and Carroll Stuhlmueller, C.P., Distinguished Professor of New Testament Studies. She has taught at Catholic Theological Union since 1988 and served as Vice President and Academic Dean from 2009 to

2018. She is past President of the Catholic Biblical Association (2014–2015) and served as Associate Editor and Book Review Editor of the *CBQ*. She is one of the general editors of *The Jerome Biblical Commentary for the Twenty-First Century* (Bloomsbury, 2022). Her most recent publication is the two-volume commentary on *Luke*, co-authored with Shelly Matthews in the Wisdom Commentary series (Liturgical Press, 2021), for which she is also General Editor.

DONALD SENIOR, C.P., is President Emeritus and Professor of New Testament at Catholic Theological Union in Chicago. He is a past President of the Catholic Biblical Association and of the Association of Theological Schools of the United States and Canada. He has served on the Pontifical Biblical Commission under three popes, most recently with Pope Francis. He has taught and traveled extensively in the Middle East and maintains an interest in the connection between archaeology, geography, and biblical exegesis. His most recent work is an award-winning biography of the noted Catholic biblical scholar Raymond E. Brown.

MALKA ZEIGER SIMKOVICH is the Crown-Ryan Chair of Jewish Studies and Director of the Catholic-Jewish Studies program at Catholic Theological Union in Chicago. She earned a doctoral degree in Second Temple and Rabbinic Judaism from Brandeis University and a master's degree in Hebrew Bible from Harvard University. Her first book, *The Making of Jewish Universalism: From Exile to Alexandria* was published in 2016, and her second book, *Discovering Second Temple Literature: The Scriptures and Stories That Shaped Early Judaism*, was published in 2018 and received the 2019 AJL Judaica Reference Honor Award.

MARK S. SMITH is Helena Professor of Old Testament Literature and Exegesis at Princeton Theological Seminary and Skirball Professor Emeritus of Bible and Ancient Near Eastern Studies at New York University. A past President of the Catholic Biblical Association and recipient of the 2020 Johannes Quasten Medal from the Catholic University of America, Smith is the author of sixteen books and over 120 other publications. With the archaeologist Elizabeth Bloch-Smith (to whom he is married), Smith has written the first of two volumes of a commentary on the book of Judges for the Hermeneia series (Fortress, 2021).

Introduction

BARBARA E. REID, O.P.
Catholic Theological Union
Chicago, Illinois

Many times I have heard Leslie Hoppe recite the beginning of Psalm 103, especially when he is asked to lead a spontaneous prayer:

> Bless the LORD, O my soul,
> and all that is within me,
>   bless God's holy name.
> Bless the LORD, O my soul,
> and do not forget all God's benefits. (Ps 103:1–2)

An extraordinary scholar, teacher, preacher, leader, and humble friar, Leslie knows that the myriad gifts he has been given are from God, and he voices his thanks often. In this year of his seventy-fifth birthday and his retirement from full-time teaching at Catholic Theological Union (2019–2020), it is fitting that his colleagues also give thanks for his giftedness in the form of this festschrift.

Leslie entered the Assumption BVM Province of the Order of Friars Minor in 1962 and completed his M.A. in Theology at Aquinas Institute of Theology in 1971, the same year he was ordained. He then earned his Ph.D. in religion from Northwestern University in 1978. From his initial doctoral work on the Book of Deuteronomy and Deuteronomistic literature, Leslie's interests have ranged over many areas of the Scriptures, including intertestamental literature, the prophets, biblical geography, history, archaeology, fundamentalism, and biblical perspectives on poverty (see a partial list of his publications at the end of this volume). Since he began his teaching career at Aquinas Institute of Theology (1976–1979), he has inspired countless students to love the Scriptures and to long to learn more. He enjoyed teaching at Mundelein Seminary (1979–1981) before being appointed to the faculty of Catholic Theological Union at Chicago in 1981. He has also been visiting professor at Garrett-Evangelical Theological Seminary, Seabury-Western Theological Seminary, and the Studium Biblicum Franciscanum in Jerusalem. For many summers he enjoyed teaching at St. Michael's College in Vermont.

With his passion for archaeology and for the lands of the Bible, Leslie helped develop and has led a great many of CTU's study programs and retreats in Israel, the Palestinian territories, Jordan, Egypt, Greece, and Turkey. His *Guide to the Lands of the Bible* (Collegeville, MN: Liturgical Press, 1999) has enabled countless others to learn about and enjoy the Holy Lands with him. Leslie's vast knowledge, quick wit, and genuine care for students has made him a highly sought-after teacher throughout his career. His colleagues have repeatedly sought his wisdom and insights that flow from his many years of commitment to the formation of ministers for the Church. In 2012, Leslie was named the Carroll Stuhlmueller, C.P., Distinguished Professor of Old Testament at CTU, an honor that he cherished as he carried on the legacy of one of CTU's beloved founders.

Leslie is one of those unique scholars who have made outstanding contributions in every arena. He researches and writes for other scholars, breaking new ground and advancing the discipline. He has served on almost every committee of the Catholic Biblical Association of America and has been General Editor of its flagship journal, the *Catholic Biblical Quarterly*, for nine years. He served as President of the CBA (2015–2016) and as President of the Chicago Society of Biblical Research (2007–2008). Leslie is equally attentive to helping nonspecialists understand the Bible. One example is his regular column entitled "Biblical Landscapes" for *The Bible Today*, a publication he has shaped as past General Editor and member of its editorial board. Leslie also writes for ministers, preachers, and teachers, helping them make connections between current situations and the biblical text.

In addition to his teaching and writing, Leslie also exercises his priestly ministry weekly, bringing the word alive through his presiding and preaching at several parishes in the Archdiocese of Chicago. Especially dear to him is St. Rosalie Parish in Harwood Heights (a northwest suburb of Chicago), where he served weekly for more than twenty-four years.

Leslie is a natural leader and it was no surprise when he was tapped to serve as Acting Vice President and Academic Dean at CTU in 1995–1996. In 2011, his congregation, the Franciscan Friars of the Assumption BVM Province, called him forth to be their Provincial Minister. He served as their leader for six years, after which he returned to the faculty at CTU. Upon his retirement from CTU in May 2020, he was granted the title

Professor Emeritus. CTU is delighted that he is continuing to teach part-time.

The essays in this collection are written by Leslie's present and former colleagues in the Department of Biblical Literature and Languages at CTU and colleagues from the Old Testament Colloquium that meets annually at St. John's Abbey in Collegeville, Minnesota. There are a number of other scholars who very much wanted to contribute and whose good wishes accompany this tribute. We offer these essays in gratitude to our extraordinary colleague, friend, mentor, and brother.

The essays in this volume range over a wide variety of topics and span both Old and New Testaments. They reflect both the interests of the authors and those of Leslie Hoppe and are arranged in canonical order.

Dianne Bergant leads the way with an exploration of how new science is challenging us to rethink our faith categories and biblical understandings. A prime example is how to understand the metaphor "image of God" in Gen 1:26–28. Using historical-critical analysis, Bergant first analyzes the metaphor in the context of the monarchy's responsibility for subduing dangerous chaotic situations and for exercising dominion over the realm, acting as God would act to guarantee the flourishing of creation. Then, using an ecological hermeneutic, she shows that the human creature is *sui generis* and that humans' identity as "image of God" derives from having dominion over nature, not the other way around. Recognizing that both of these approaches are anthropocentric, she then explores how "image of God" might be interpreted in a cosmological context. Pierre Teilhard de Chardin's insight that humankind is an "arrow of evolution" opens the way to understanding humankind as an integral part of the evolutive process, but not above the rest of the natural world nor over it. Humanity's uniqueness resides in the direction it sets for this ongoing process.

Next, James Chukwuma Okoye seeks to "throw new light on old stories" (alluding to the title of one of Leslie Hoppe's books)[1] through a narrative investigation of Genesis 34. He begins by noting contemporary questions raised in feminist exegesis of the passage. He then inquires into the narrator's goals to ascertain the message that the narrator was trying to convey and to whom it was directed. Okoye identifies conflicting intentions as the narrator employs the story in constructions of identity. After reviewing some early Jewish retellings of the story, he explores the ethical implications and repercussions of the narration, noting that

---

1. Leslie J. Hoppe, *New Light from Old Stories: The Hebrew Scriptures for Today's World* (New York: Paulist, 2005).

"responsible exegesis must see to it that the word of God be not co-opted for violence of any type."

The next essay, by John Barker, explores interpretations in rabbinic and early Christian traditions of the actions of Tamar in Genesis 38. He first looks at retellings of the chapter in *Jubilees* and the *Testament of Judah,* both of which give primary attention to Judah. Then he turns to the targums and later rabbinic literature, which present Judah and Tamar in a positive light, as their behavior is interpreted in terms of divine purposes. Early Christian interpretations also view the behavior of Judah and Tamar positively. After analyzing texts from Eusebius of Caesarea, Ambrose of Milan, Ephrem the Syrian, and John Chrysostom, Barker concludes that, in both rabbinic and early Christian traditions, although some of Tamar's actions are seen as morally problematic, she is lauded because her actions lead to the birth of David and, from his line, the Messiah. Both traditions see Tamar as a heroic cooperator with the divine plan.

Mahri Leonard-Fleckman takes us into the topic of the connections between social landscape and geography. She notes that biblical texts vary in their constructions, or deconstructions, of social landscape, including identities and boundaries between people or social groups and that geography is a powerful tool in these varied (de)constructions. For example, Joshua's land allotments utilize geography to construct clear literary idealizations of borders, while the Samson stories use Shephelah geography to deconstruct borders. Yet geography is not the only tool in such portrayals; women are also used in particular ways to help construct or deconstruct landscape. The question Leonard-Fleckman poses is, Do these remarkably creative (often remarkably problematic) literary depictions of women hold any historical value? Or: what ideologies and goals might they reveal about scribes, or the ancient world? She focuses on three stories in the Shephelah: Tamar in Genesis 38 and the tales of Delilah and the unnamed woman in Timnah (or from Timnah?) in Judges 13–16 as test cases to examine the intersection of archaeology, anthropology, and literary-historical and historical tools of investigation as viewed through a feminist lens on the Bible.

Next, Mark S. Smith examines historiography across the Book of Judges, showing that the process of collecting the various accounts issued in a larger historiographical vision, one particularly framed in terms of geography and chronology. The book's geographical order shows a doubly circular route, giving the impression of the past as a repeating cycle involving individual leaders. It represents the period of Judges not only as a repeating cycle but also as a downward spiral, as the major judges move generally from better to worse. The book's women offer a parallel progression to the men, largely in how they fare at the hands of men. The book also shows a concern for chronology, which serves to depict the period of the Judges as an era of Israelite suffering, analogous to the times of the Israelites in Egypt and in exile. These two axes of geography and chronology create a historiography that is sermonic in force; prescriptions for the present are rooted in the religious vision of the past.

In "The Exact Same Thing Only Different," John L. McLaughlin explores the terms "Hebrew" and "Israelite" in 1 Samuel. Normally these terms are understood to be synonymous except that "Hebrew" is used by foreigners or by Israelites interacting with foreigners. McLaughlin demonstrates, however, through a close reading of the relevant sections of 1 Samuel in light of the archaeological evidence for the intersection of Philistines, Canaanites and Israelites in the late premonarchical period, that this is not the case in 1 Samuel. Israelite characters and the narrator use the term for at least two different non-Israelite groups. Philistines do use the term "Hebrew" for Israelites, but not always knowingly. At the same time, their Canaanite subjects avoid "Hebrew" even when the Philistines employ it. The term has a social meaning comparable to the ʿapiru, and this nuance predates the composition of the Deuteronomistic History. Thus, the individual texts probably contain a historically accurate memory of actual Philistine and Israelite usage.

Moving to prophetic literature, Andrew R. Davis, in "The End of Humiliation in LXX Isaiah 40," presents a test case that can be instructive for creative interaction with the Hebrew Bible. His analysis of ταπείνωσις in Isa 40:2 LXX shows that, although the word differs from its Hebrew *Vorlage*, its departure should be seen as an effort to convey more clearly the meaning of the Book of Isaiah as a whole and its connection to the Greek Pentateuch. The translation updated the Hebrew text of Isaiah by employing a Greek word that resonated with Isa 53:8 and other occurrences of ταπείνωσις in the Greek Pentateuch. In this way, this translation, like most of the Septuagint, strikes a balance between adapting the verse for a new audience and remaining faithful to the unity of its source text. The way Isa 40:2 was translated in the Septuagint is but one example of how the Septuagint can provide a model of actualization such as was urged by the Pontifical Biblical Commission's *The Interpretation of the Bible in the Church* (1993).

The next two essays deal with Ezekiel. In "My, What a Big Ship You Have! Ezekiel's Jealousy of the Favored Minority," Corrine Carvalho examines references to Tyre in Ezekiel's oracles against the nations (chaps. 26–28) through an economic lens, revealing the literary function of this material. She shows that the prophet's engagement with the economic status of Tyre serves larger rhetorical purposes in the book. In Ezekiel, Tyre is depicted as an ally who failed Judah, and who, therefore, would only temporarily survive the Babylonian encroachment. Judah's jealousy of Tyre's booming trade reflects the archaeological record from the Assyrian period. Although the oracles in Ezekiel 26–28 predict the collapse of Tyre, the city did, in fact, remain intact, although its trade ventures abruptly ceased. The jealousy on the part of Jerusalem's elite of Tyre's less disastrous fate is preserved in the social memory of these poems.

Dale Launderville, in "Ezekiel 17: Zedekiah's Idolatrous Invocation of the Divine Name as a Capital Crime," takes up a different question in Ezekiel: Zedekiah's invocation of the divine name in a vassal treaty with Nebuchadnezzar. Zedekiah can be seen as a royal symbol for the Judean community whose forging of multiple treaties with other lands is like "wife Jerusalem" who seeks out numerous lovers (Ezek 16:15–43). Zedekiah's rebellion against Nebuchadnezzar in Ezek 17:15–21 is equated with a rebellion against the LORD, since his solemn pronouncement in the LORD's name in an oath or covenant transfers the ownership of the covenant to Yhwh. When seen in this light, Yhwh's carrying out of the curse on Zedekiah is justifiable. Zedekiah's opportunistic forging of multiple treaties and casually invoking the divine name is an idolatrous act; Yhwh takes seriously the pronouncing of his divine name in an oath.

Malka Zeiger Simkovich turns our attention to "The *Diaspora* as a Word and Concept in Early Judaism," where she explores the dissonance between texts in the Septuagint that use the term διασπορά with a predominantly negative connotation and texts that speak positively about the lived reality of diaspora as a place where Jews can thrive as practitioners of their ancestral customs. She concludes that this dissonance caused later Jewish authors writing about the diaspora in the late Second Temple period to avoid using the term διασπορά. She analyzes the usage of διασπορά both in the LXX and in other late Second Temple texts, showing that overwhelmingly, it is associated with punishment for abandoning the covenant. Simkovich then shows the shift in meaning that occurs in the New Testament, where διασπορά designates a community bound to one another in faith rather than in attachment to Judea as a homeland. This redefinition of διασπορά allows Jesus's followers outside of Judea to see themselves as participating in the scriptural promises of a divine plan in which dispersion will end in reward and restoration. Consequently, Jews likewise began to speak of their contemporary dispersion as the fulfillment of Scripture, reimagining dispersion as a punishment presently endured by all Jews, even those living in Judea. Simkovich concludes, "The earlier dissonance between the negative use of διασπορά and widespread positive attitudes toward the diaspora would dissolve into a cohesive view that allegorized the dispersion into a temporal rather than a spatial state of being that pushed a messianic restoration into the distant future."

Donald Senior opens the section of essays on New Testament texts and topics with his exploration of "'An Evangelizing Church': The Ecclesiology of Matthew's Gospel." He analyzes Matthew's vision of church and shows its continuing relevance for ecclesiology today. Christology is Matthew's "guiding star" in navigating the time of transition when the extension of the mission to the gentiles is seen as the fulfillment of Israel's own destiny, actualized through Jesus. A first characteristic of the ἐκκλησία ("church") is that followers of Jesus imitate him by engaging in authentic teaching and compassionate healing. The question of authority surfaces in the two key passages where the term ἐκκλησία occurs: 16:13–20 and 18:15–20. For Matthew, both the authority of the community's leaders (exemplified by Peter in chap. 16) and that of the whole ἐκκλησία (chap. 18) are important. In Matthew 18, there is an egalitarian dimension of ecclesiology, one that is reaffirmed in chap. 23. Also illustrated in chap. 18 are two other primary characteristics of the Matthean church: pastoral care for those who are vulnerable and endless forgiveness for those who miss the mark. Senior concludes with a comparison to the vision of church put forth by Pope Francis in *The Joy of the Gospel*.

In my own essay, "There Shall Be No Poor among You: The Lucan Solution," I build on Leslie Hoppe's monumental study *There Shall Be No Poor among You: Poverty in the Bible* (Nashville: Abingdon, 2004)[2] focusing on the approach taken by Luke in his Gospel and Acts. I first present an overall sketch of the emphasis that Luke places on the poor and on the danger of riches and the variety of ways in which he shows disciples of Jesus dealing with their possessions. Some leave everything to follow Jesus; others place their resources at the service of Jesus's mission; still others hold all their possessions in common and distribute to each according to their need. I then explore six Lucan parables that illustrate the need for solidarity among believers, which is the key to ensuring that there will be no poor. Three parables present positive examples: A Friend in Need (11:5–8); All Are Invited to the Table (14:15–24); All Count (15:8–10); and three reveal the perils of isolation and greed: A Solitary Rich Man (12:13–21); Not My Brother (16:19–31); Despising Others

---

2. This is a revision of his previous work, *Being Poor: A Biblical Study* (GNS 20; Wilmington, DE: Michael Glazier, 1987).

(18:9–14). All six parables invite the hearer to a conversion of heart that can lead to eradication of poverty.

Laurie Brink's essay, "Reconstructing the Cultural Horizon for Lucan Soldiers: Texts and Artifacts in Conversation," draws on her passion for correlating the findings of archaeology with study of the biblical text, an interest sparked by her studies with Leslie Hoppe. She analyzes archaeological evidence—coinage and inscriptions—as well as contemporaneous literature to reconstruct the horizon of cultural knowledge of the Lucan audience concerning imperial soldiers. She explores the passages in Luke and Acts in which soldiers appear and what the ancient auditor could be expected to know about soldiers and their lives and roles from "the extra text," that is, archaeological findings and extrabiblical texts. As Luke constructs military characters, he relies on the audience's capacity—both ancient and modern—to fill in the gaps by making inferences from their cultural knowledge acquired from "the extra text."

In "Who Was Holy and How Did They Get That Way?," Carolyn Osiek explores the biblical grounding for the universal call to holiness articulated in *Lumen Gentium* and how this call was received in times past. She shows how Paul advanced the notion that holiness resided in individual members of the Christian community by virtue of their baptism. This contrasts with earlier ideas of the holy and holiness—that it resides primarily in God, in sacred objects, and in the collective group. Paul speaks of the believers as holy and able to convey holiness into their families. Holiness is not dependent on virtuous behavior but is a free gift from God. By accepting this gift, believers are holy and consequently must act in ways that reflect divine holiness. In Paul's letters, we find specific instances of what kinds of behavior promote or inhibit the flow of holiness. A shift in the ideal of holiness came with the rise of the cult of the martyrs, whose heroic struggle and giving of their lives became the model for sanctity, a trend later replicated in the movements that exalted the ascetic life. Thus, the focus shifted from ideas of holiness centered on the transcendent power of God to the qualities of character shown by faithful followers of Jesus. Osiek concludes with Pope Francis's renewed call to holiness in his Apostolic Exhortation *On the Call to Holiness in Today's World*.

Finally, Ferdinand Okorie, in "Greco-Roman καλοκαγαθός in the Pauline and Pastoral Letters," examines the Greco-Roman virtue of doing what is good and noble, namely, the appeal to the cultural appreciation of the good person (καλοκαγαθός) in the Pauline and Pastoral Letters. He analyzes how the Greco-Roman virtue of doing noble and good deeds, which is commonly associated with the sociopolitical and economic elite of the Greco-Roman world, is recommended to the auditors of the Pauline and Pastoral letters. His investigation of how this virtue (ἀρετή) is used in the Pauline and Pastoral Letters reveals that, in the Greco-Roman world, the one who does noble and good deeds, namely, the good person (καλοκαγαθός) is usually rewarded with honorific inscriptions by beneficiaries. But in the Pauline and Pastoral Letters the reward is given in the eschatological age to the one who does noble and good deeds in the Christian community, a recompense that is given only by God.

A postscript by me, "The Answer Lies Beneath," and a partial list of Leslie Hoppe's countless books, articles, and electronic publications conclude the volume. While this collection is quite disparate, the unifying thread is deep appreciation for a colleague who has touched all our lives and so many others, inspiring our own love of the Bible and of God's people. We hope not only that this volume offers a fitting tribute to Leslie Hoppe but also that many other scholars and students of the Bible will find these essays a help to their own study and for deepening their faith life.

"In the Image of God"—but What Is the Image?

DIANNE BERGANT, CSA
Catholic Theological Union
Chicago, Illinois

It is with long-standing professional respect that I add this essay to the collection gathered to honor my colleague Leslie Hoppe, OFM. His commitment to both biblical scholarship and its pastoral implementation has benefited us all these many years he has taught Scripture and committed his thinking to writing. As is so often the case with ministry, one never knows how one's efforts will take root and flourish. Only God knows how Leslie's influence has taken hold in the minds and hearts of the ministers of the word he has helped to fashion.

Biblical interpretation is on the cusp of a revolutionary step into the unknown. Perhaps it is more correct to identify it as an evolutionary step, for it is a step forced upon us by the radical concept of an evolving universe.[1] Since all of the writing of both biblical testaments developed in the context of an ancient, static, three-tiered cosmology, a radically different cosmology is bound to challenge the suitability of some of the metaphoric expressions of the Bible, many of its predominant anthropological presuppositions, and some of the long-standing theological testimonies.

---

1. According to Zachary Hayes, OFM, creation theology was the subject of considerable study in the 1950s and early 1960s. However, the secularity movement of the late 1960s and 1970s with its focus on the "death of God" shifted theological concern to the question of God. Environmental problems have reawakened the need for a solid creation theology; see Hayes, *A Window to the Divine: A Study of Christian Creation Theology* (Quincy, IL: Franciscan Press, 1997) ix.

This is not the first time fundamental religious beliefs have been challenged by innovative scientific insights. Throughout the history of human enlightenment, significant revolutionary scientific discoveries have forced new cosmological renderings, and theological revisions have followed these renderings. Sometime around 500 B.C.E., Pythagoras concluded from his study of lunar eclipses that Earth is a sphere and not flat. This challenged literal belief that God is enthroned in the heavens above us, as so many of the psalms claim (Pss 33:13–14; 80:1; 99:1; 123:1). This position also challenged the claim that Jesus literally ascended into heaven (Mark 16:19; Luke 24:51). To this day, such a three-tiered concept remains part of the religious cosmology of many people. Copernicus, a Renaissance-era mathematician and astronomer, advanced a heliocentric model of the universe. Copernicus himself, however, credited the ancient Greek astronomer Aristarchus of Samos (310–230 B.C.E.) with an earlier version of this insight. Perhaps the name that comes immediately to mind when one thinks of heliocentrism is Galileo (1564–1642). He championed Copernicus's claims and suffered greatly for this at the hands of the Church, which insisted on geocentric models. Condemned by the Roman Inquisition, Galileo was finally reinstated in 1991 by Pope John Paul II, 359 years later. Most likely it was the writings of Darwin, the nineteenth-century English naturalist, geologist, and biologist whose insights into evolutionary processes dispute the notion of the direct creation of humankind (Gen 2:7), that constituted the greatest threat to prominent theories of anthropology.

The Church was not the only institution that stood against such groundbreaking and world-shattering scientific thinking. People of all walks of life resisted the implications of such new scientific insights. This included historians of science, philosophers, theologians, and scientists, as well as the general population across the world. Since science and religion[2] often claim jurisdiction over questions concerning the origin of the universe and humankind's place within and relationship to that universe, conflict was inevitable. Science and religion, both very complex social and cultural areas of interest and knowledge, soon became antagonists, insisting on the veracity of the principles that undergirded their respective cosmologies. From the scientific point of view, religion's intransigence in clinging to a literal reading of various biblical texts and the

---

2. When the phrase "science and religion" is used, "science" usually precedes "religion." This has nothing to do with importance. Rather, a new scientific insight usually precedes any religious interpretation; seldom does religion prompt scientific discovery.

interpretations that these texts generated as well as its insistence that the scientific method of inquiry fails to consider the supernaturalism of traditional religion has made any form of reconciliation between the two impossible. Religion, on the other hand, denounced scientific claims that challenged the adequacy of what was considered the unalterable word of God and insisted that there are transcendent and immaterial forces in the world that are beyond the scope of scientific examination and categorization. Lines were drawn, and, though over the years adherents of both approaches have entered into dialogue that has profited both participants, many people have still not crossed those lines. This conflict between science and religion is still found in many traditional or evangelical religious circles where the literal reading of texts pertaining to creation of the universe and/or humankind continues to be the norm.

One way the chasm between science and religion has been resolved has been by not crossing it. From this point of view, science and religion are understood to be discrete, sometimes even parallel, disciplines, each interested in different aspects of reality, each with very well-defined, distinct methods of approach. Some have said that science is attentive to the *how* of the natural world, while religion is concerned with the *why*. This has allowed scientists and religious thinkers to pursue their respective interests making sure that boundaries of distinction are respected and not crossed. In this way science and religion are thought to have no right to meddle in each other's undertakings.

Today we face a new scientific revolution the scope of which has led some to claim that we are living in a second Axial Age, facing a new transformation of society. The term Axial Age was coined in 1949 by the German philosopher Karl Theodor Jaspers. The first age was "a time between approximately 900 and 200 B.C.E. when the spiritual foundations of modern humanity were established. It was a pivotal time in early human history when human beings began to reflect for the first time on human existence and the meaning of life and death."[3] This first axial consciousness gave birth to a new, self-reflective character that resulted in human beings perceiving themselves as subject rather than object, partially determining their own fate. This new way of thinking developed almost simultaneously in four major areas of the world: Confucianism and Daoism in China; Hinduism, Buddhism, and Jainism in India; Persian Zoroastrianism and the Hebrew prophets in the Middle East; and Greek philosophy in northern Mediterranean Europe.

---

3. Ilia Delio, OSF, *Making All Things New: Catholicity, Cosmology, Consciousness* (Maryknoll, NY: Orbis Books, 2015) 5.

New science's notions of an evolving universe; open systems rather than well-defined, static, closed systems; relatedness or entanglement; complexification; increasing consciousness; and emergent probability all tell us that we are on the threshold of a new way of thinking. These concepts upset our clearly defined Newtonian notion of the cosmos. The idea that the universe is always coming into being in an emergent fashion disputes the assurances found in our time-honored creation traditions. The apparent disinterest of the natural world toward us throws into question our faith in a personal God who is committed to each individual in a unique way. Any assault on our cosmology or our anthropology will be felt by every other tenet of our faith. Long-held views of teleology and eschatology will appear inadequate. Precise statements about sin and redemption will have little meaning. Finally, carefully framed definitions of God will appear to be empty formulations.

■ I. Faith Seeking Understanding

Anselm, the renowned theologian of the eleventh century, wrote that theology is faith seeking understanding. Many contemporary theologians have given evidence of the enduring truth of that statement as they stepped into the realm of evolutive cosmology and produced noteworthy theological interpretations and reconstructions. In the English-speaking world, two names come immediately to mind here, Pierre Teilhard de Chardin, S.J., and Thomas Berry, C.P. Both men were professionally trained, Teilhard in paleontology and Berry in cultural history. Both men spent the bulk of their lives interpreting theology through the lens of contemporary science or within the categories of science. They were the trailblazers who inspired today's ecotheologians. Not far behind them were groundbreaking theologians like Karl Rahner and Bernard Lonergan.[4] Following them is a new brand of theologians who reside in various branches of theology. Some develop what might be considered a theology of creation.[5] Others moved into issues like the character of

---

[4]. See Denis Edwards, "Teilhard's Vision as Agenda for Rahner's Christology," in *From Teilhard to Omega: Co-creating an Unfinished Universe* (ed. Ilia Delio; Maryknoll, NY: Orbis Books, 2014) 53–66; and, in the same volume, Patrick H. Byrne, "The Integral Visions of Teilhard and Lonergan: Science, the Universe, Humanity, and God," 83–110.

[5]. John F. Haught, *God after Darwin: A Theology of Evolution* (Boulder, CO: Westview, 2000); idem, *Deeper than Darwin: The Prospect for Religion in the Age of Evolution* (Boulder, CO: Westview, 2003); John Polkinghorne, *Science and Religion in Quest of*

God,[6] Trinitarian theology,[7] pneumatology,[8] divine action in creation and redemption,[9] christology,[10] catholicity in the new cosmology,[11] ecclesiology,[12] Christian life,[13] Christian ministry,[14] ecology and issues of justice[15] to name but a few areas.

In developing new insights, these authors employed what has come to be known as the "hermeneutic of suspicion," a reference traced back

---

Truth (New Haven: Yale University Press, 2011); Mary L. Coloe, ed., *Creation Is Groaning: Biblical and Theological Perspectives* (Collegeville, MN: Liturgical Press, 2013); Elizabeth A. Johnson, *Ask the Beasts: Darwin and the God of Love* (London: Bloomsbury, 2014); Delio, *Making All Things New*.

  6. Thomas E. Hosinski, *The Image of the Unseen God: Catholicity, Science, and Our Evolving Understanding of God* (Catholicity in an Evolving Universe; Maryknoll, NY: Orbis Books, 2017).

  7. Denis Edwards, *The God of Evolution: A Trinitarian Theology* (New York: Paulist, 1999); idem, *Partaking of God: Trinity, Evolution, and Ecology* (Collegeville, MN: Liturgical Press, 2014); Heidi Russell, *The Source of All Love: Catholicity and the Trinity* (Maryknoll, NY: Orbis Books, 2017).

  8. Denis Edwards, *Breath of Life: A Theology of the Creator Spirit* (Maryknoll, NY: Orbis Books, 2004).

  9. Denis Edwards, *How God Acts: Creation, Redemption, and Special Divine Action* (Theology and the Sciences; Minneapolis: Fortress, 2010).

  10. Denis Edwards, *Jesus and the Cosmos* (New York: Paulist, 1991); idem, *Jesus and the Wisdom of God: An Ecological Theology* (Maryknoll, NY: Orbis Books, 1995); Cletus Wessels, *Jesus in the New Universe Story* (Maryknoll, NY: Orbis Books, 2003); Celia Deane-Drummond, *Christ and Evolution: Wonder and Wisdom* (Theology and the Sciences; Minneapolis: Fortress, 2009); Ilia Delio, *The Emergent Christ: Exploring the Meaning of Catholic in an Evolutionary Universe* (Maryknoll, NY: Orbis Books, 2001).

  11. Ilia Delio, *Christ in Evolution* (Maryknoll, NY: Orbis Books, 2008); Edwin E. Olson, *And God Created Wholeness: A Spirituality of Catholicity* (Catholicity in an Evolving Universe; Maryknoll, NY: Orbis Books, 2018).

  12. Cletus Wessels, *The Holy Web: Church and the New Universe Story* (Maryknoll, NY: Orbis Books, 2000); Joseph A. Bracken, SJ, *Church as Dynamic Life-System: Shared Ministries and Common Responsibilities* (Maryknoll, NY: Orbis Books, 2019).

  13. Beatrice Bruteau, *The Grand Option: Personal Transformation and a New Creation* (Gethsemani Studies in Psychological and Religious Anthropology; Notre Dame, IN: University of Notre Dame Press, 2001); Denis Edwards, *Ecology at the Heart of Faith: The Change of Heart That Leads to a New Way of Living on Earth* (Maryknoll, NY: Orbis Books, 2006); Ilia Delio, *The Unbearable Wholeness of Being: God, Evolution, and the Power of Love* (Maryknoll, NY: Orbis Books, 2013).

  14. Donald C. Maldari, *Christian Ministry in the Divine Milieu: Catholicity, Evolution, and the Reign of God* (Catholicity in an Evolving Universe; Maryknoll, NY: Orbis Books, 2019).

  15. Leonardo Boff, *Ecology & Liberation: A New Paradigm* (Ecology and Justice; Maryknoll, NY: Orbis Books, 1995); idem, *Cry of the Earth, Cry of the Poor* (Ecology and Justice; Maryknoll, NY: Orbis Books, 1997).

to Paul Ricoeur's "school of suspicion" which included groundbreaking thinkers like Karl Marx, Sigmund Freud, and Friedrich Nietzsche. It seems that suspicion of the prevailing understanding precedes innovative insights. Not satisfied with serious and valid critique, such theologians reinterpreted many standard theological concepts within new scientific categories.

Biblical theologians too have ventured into this new area of research. Several of them, under the leadership of the Australian ecotheologian Norman C. Habel, have drawn up a list of what they call ecosensitive principles:

1. The principle of intrinsic worth, which honors the value of Earth and all of its components in themselves and not in their usefulness to human beings.
2. The principle of interconnectedness, which recognizes the interdependence of members of the "community of Earth."
3. The principle of voice, which appreciates the unique way each member of the "community of Earth" expresses itself.
4. The principle of purpose, which claims that all members of "community of Earth" have a part in the dynamic cosmic design.
5. The principle of mutual custodianship, which acknowledges the role played by each member of "community of Earth" in sustaining Earth's delicate balance.
6. The principle of resistance, which maintains that Earth itself struggles against its manipulation and exploitation.[16]

These principles have functioned as lenses through which various biblical passages have been interpreted. A critique of the biblical metaphor "image of God" as found in Gen 1:26–28 is an example of this approach.[17]

---

16. Norman C. Habel, ed., *Readings from the Perspective of Earth* (Earth Bible 1; Cleveland: Pilgrim, 2000) 24. Four more collections of essays written by scholars who employ these principles have appeared: *The Earth Story in Genesis* (ed. Norman C. Habel and Shirley Wurst; Earth Bible 2; Sheffield: Sheffield Academic, 2000); *The Earth Story in Wisdom Traditions* (ed. Norman C. Habel and Shirley Wurst; Earth Bible 3; Sheffield: Sheffield Academic, 2001); *The Earth Story in the Psalms and the Prophets* (ed. Norman C. Habel; Earth Bible 4; Sheffield: Sheffield Academic, 2001); *The Earth Story in the New Testament* (ed. Norman C. Habel and Vicky Balabanski; Earth Bible 5; Sheffield: Sheffield Academic, 2002).

17. What follows is a shortened version of what appears in Dianne Bergant, *God So Loved the Cosmos – But Do We?* (Los Angeles: Marymount Institute, 2017) 11–15.

■ II. Icon or Idol?

In the first creation account (Gen 1:1–2:4a), the fundamental character of the human couple is found in the expression "image of God" and in the twofold commission "subdue" and "have dominion" (1:27–28).[18] In the ancient world, people fashioned images of their gods, symbolic objects not considered to be the gods themselves but rather representations of the power and authority of the gods. This power and authority was usually jurisdictional. The reverence given these images was not unlike the way we revere national flags, which are symbols of the jurisdiction of the power and authority of the nation. To say that the human couple was made in the "image of God" is to say that they were meant to represent where and how God exercised power and authority. This was particularly true with regard to royalty, who, in most nations, were considered in some way divine. (This explains why the establishment of the monarchy was initially a religious threat to the sovereignty of the God of Israel.)[19]

In Israel, "image of God" clearly referred to human beings, not gods. There was, however, always the great temptation for royalty to begin to think of themselves as somehow divine. Genesis 3 tells us that this was precisely the sin of the first couple. They were not satisfied being "image of God," following God's directives and representing where and how God is sovereign. The serpent argued, "God knows well that the moment you eat of [the tree of the knowledge of good and evil] your eyes will be opened and you will be like gods who know what is good and what is bad" (Gen 3:5). It seems that being "image of God" was not enough when there was the possibility of being like a god. The serpent suggested something very attractive, and the couple chose to follow that attraction. This sin was certainly one of disobedience. However, the underlying reason for the disobedience was hubris, which is understood to be excessive pride in the face of or in defiance of the gods.

The prophet Ezekiel condemns the same kind of hubris. He reinterpreted elements of the Genesis story of sin in his condemnation of the prince of the ancient Phoenician city Tyre. The prince's successes in trading led him to think too highly of himself. This excessive pride resulted in violence and exploitation:

> Because your heart is proud
>   and you have said, "I am a god;

---

18. All biblical citations are from NRSV unless otherwise noted.
19. "... they have rejected me from being king over them" (1 Sam 8:7b).

> I sit in the seat of the gods,
> > in the heart of the seas,"
> yet you are but a mortal, and no god,
> > though you compare your mind with the mind of a god. (Ezek 28:2)

His hubris led to his downfall:

> Will you still say, "I am a god,"
> > In the presence of those who kill you,
> though you are but a mortal, and no god,
> > in the hands of those who wound you? (Ezek 28:9)

In the ancient Near Eastern world, the domain of the gods and societal reality were regarded as so interrelated that human royal rule usually played some role in the cosmic drama. For the Egyptians, whose experience of life was established by the regularity of the Nile, kingship was an essential part of the structure of creation. The activity of the creator found its natural sequel in the absolute rule of the pharaoh. The Mesopotamians did not seem to regard divine kingship as a natural concomitant of an ordered pantheon. Although they did believe that kingship descended from heaven, they did not perceive it as a divine reality. Unlike the Egyptians, who regarded their pharaoh as a god, Mesopotamians viewed their king as a mortal endowed with a singular responsibility. Clearly the Israelite notion of monarchy resembled the Mesopotamian view more than that of Egypt.

The difficulty in the interpretation of "image of God" lies not in the metaphor itself but in the verbs associated with it in Gen 1:28. The verb כבש (NRSV: "subdue") is an extraordinarily harsh word. It means "to tread down," if necessary, by force. It connotes the conquest of the Canaanites (Num 32:22) and rape (Esth 7:8). The second verb רדה (NRSV: "have dominion") also means "to tread" (Joel 4:13 MT). Its usual meaning, however, is "to rule." Interpretation of the metaphor influences how the verbs are to be understood. Here "subdue" and "have dominion" are royal language, indicating that the monarchy was responsible for subduing dangerous chaotic situations and for exercising dominion over the realm. In Israel, the monarchy did indeed have a special relationship with God;[20] it did indeed act as the agent of God in a certain way. Yet that relationship did not bestow divinity on the monarchy. As images of God, Israelite royalty were ambassadors of the sovereignty of God. They were

---

20. Through the prophet Nathan, God tells David that his heir will have a special relationship with God, not unlike the father–son relationship thought to exist in royal monarchies of the day: "I will be a father to him, and he shall be a son to me" (2 Sam 7:14).

commissioned to subdue or bring order into chaotic situations and to exercise dominion over all that existed in their realm, which included all aspects of natural creation. However, they were to act as God would act; they were to guarantee the flourishing of creation, not cause its exploitation.

This connection of humans with the monarchy is seen in Psalm 8:

> Yet you have made them a little lower than God,
>   and crowned them with glory and honor.
> You have given them dominion over the works of your hands;
>   you have put all things under their feet,
> all sheep and oxen,
>   and also the beasts of the field,
> the birds of the air, and the fish of the sea,
>   whatever passes along the paths of the seas. (Ps 8:5–8)

The expressions "lower than God" and "crowned . . . with glory and honor" suggest both dignity and limitation. While humans are not divine, they are characterized as royalty, and the close association of royalty and divinity has been discussed above. The word translated "dominion" is משל, which means "to rule." This is the same word used earlier in the Genesis story where the greater light (the sun) is said "to rule the day" and the lesser light (the moon) is said "to rule" the night (Gen 1:16). The meaning of the word in Ps 8:6 throws light on the possible meaning of the command given to the human couple "to have dominion" over the living creatures of Earth (Gen 1:26, 28). As the heavenly bodies were to exercise order in the skies so that all creatures could perform their respective functions within the ecosystem, so humans were to exercise power in a way that all creatures might perform their respective functions.

In summary: In this creation account, human beings are not autonomous sovereigns who were granted a license to exploit the earth or tyrannize other creatures, as a literal reading has sometimes claimed. Instead they were issued a mandate that included serious responsibility for the world of which they are a part, and accountability to the creator for the governance of that world.[21] This way of reading the creation narrative challenges any kind of excessive, tyrannical, distorted, or misguided anthropocentrism.[22] Ignorance of or unwillingness to acknowl-

---

21. Recently the notion of stewardship has come under serious critique. See, e.g., Richard Bauckham, *The Bible and Ecology: Rediscovering the Community of Creation* (Sarum Theological Lectures; Waco, TX: Baylor University Press, 2010) 1–12.

22. Excessive, tyrannical, distorted, or misguided are the words used by Pope Francis when, in his encyclical letter *Laudato Si'* (Libreria Editrice Vaticana, 2015), he

edge the limitations of human governance over the natural world may be at the heart of much of the arrogance many people exhibit today in their attitudes toward the rest of creation. Many still want to "be like God," boasting of unconditional authority and unlimited control over other people and over the rest of nature. Temptation to hubris is ever present.

Employing standard steps of historical-critical analysis, this interpretation has shown that the metaphor "image of God" does not support humankind's unbridled expenditure of Earth's natural resources. In fact, it argues for responsible oversight of human use of those resources and accountability to God in the exercise of that oversight. Furthermore, this approach argues strongly against an exaggerated sense of human power and authority within the natural world. While the words "subdue ... and have dominion" actually suggest harsh control, the representative character of "image" tends to soften that harshness. At least, this is how the interpretation of the above passage was originally meant to be read. This manner of interpretation was a common way of ameliorating the harshness of the verbs and attempting to show that the depletion or pollution of natural resources was never the intent of the original authors.[23] But what is enough?

■ III. A Creature *SUI GENERIS*

The fundamental weakness of the above interpretation or of any strictly historical-critical interpretation is its obvious and intended anthropocentric focus. Such a reading of the passage reinforces both a sense of superiority of humankind over all other Earth species and over Earth itself, and it depicts human beings as a very different kind of creature. Today, many ecotheologians espouse a position similar to the following: "The Bible . . . is ambivalent and ambiguous in terms of its ecological implications. Some texts are problematic for an ecological perspective, notably those which present humankind as rulers over the earth, or depict (or eagerly anticipate) a future cosmic collapse; while others offer an apparently more positive ecological contribution, notably those which

---

censures an anthropocentric attitude dominant in the West today, §§68, 69, 116, 119, 122.

23. Antoinette Collins, "Subdue and Conquer: An Ecological Perspective," in Coloe, *Creation Is Groaning*, 19–32; David G. Horrell, *The Bible and the Environment: Towards a Critical Ecological Biblical Theology* (Biblical Challenges in the Contemporary World; Oakville, CT: Equinox, 2010) 26–29. Horrell refers to such approaches as "readings of recovery."

relativize the importance of humanity and stress the inclusion of all creation in God's saving purposes."[24]

Might an interpretation that focuses on Earth rather than on humankind yield a different message? Norman Habel maintains that Genesis 1 is really "a 'geophany,' a manifestation or revelation of Earth. The secondary story of human entry onto the Earth scene (Gen 1:26–30) poses a conflict of orientation within the Earth story that remains unresolved."[25] Unlike other Earth species, humankind does not emerge from the very substance of Earth, as do "living creatures of every kind: cattle and creeping things and wild animals of the earth of every kind" that are brought forth by Earth (Gen 1:24), or the "swarms of living creatures" brought forth from the waters or the birds above the earth (Gen 1:20). As far as living creatures are concerned the human creature is a creature *sui generis*.

The Genesis 1 account of the creation of humankind has been identified as "a grey text—a text that is ecologically destructive, devaluing Earth and offering humans a God-given right to harness nature."[26] The innovative character of Habel's thinking cannot be denied. There are times, however, when he reads a ruthlessness into the meaning of the verbs of this text that might not actually be there. He states that "humans are created in God's image for the very purpose of exercising dominion."[27] In other words, their identity as "image of God" derives from having dominion over nature, not the other way around. He also links the injunction "fill" Earth with "subdue it." He holds that "[t]he act of filling Earth suggests that Earth is the domain where humans are to rule. . . . Filling Earth sounds like a takeover. This is confirmed with the final mandate: 'subdue Earth.'"[28] The text need not be read in this way. In fact, the mandate "Be fruitful and multiply, and fill the earth" (Gen 1:28) corresponds to a comparable mandate: "Be fruitful and multiply, and fill the waters of the seas" (1:22), which in no way grants a specific water creature dominion over other water creatures. The mandate "to be fruitful . . . multiply . . . and fill" deals with propagation of the various species in their respective habitats. Habel goes on to argue that the mandate for humans to dominate is reinforced in the story of God's directives after the flood, and then cele-

---

24. Horrell, *Bible and the Environment*, 117.
25. Norman C. Habel, "Geophany: The Earth Story in Genesis 1," in Habel and Wurst, *Earth Story in Genesis*, 35.
26. Norman C. Habel, *An Inconvenient Text: Is a Green Reading of the Bible Possible?* (Adelaide, SA: ATF, 2009) 2.
27. Ibid., 5.
28. Ibid., 6.

brated in Psalm 8.[29] The way these two passages are understood depends on how the Genesis 1 mandate is read, and it need not be read as Habel argues.

Habel offers an ecological hermeneutic that enables the interpreter to read the text in an Earth-friendly fashion. This hermeneutic consists of three steps: (1) a hermeneutic of suspicion that the passage under consideration is fundamentally anthropocentric and not Earth-friendly; (2) a hermeneutic of identification with characters in the text other than human beings, preferably with Earth itself; (3) a hermeneutic of retrieval of the voice or concerns of Earth.[30] This three-step approach certainly helps the interpreter to design a critical lens through which to read a text in order to uncover both the text's and the interpreter's biases. However, it may not offer a satisfactory reconstruction of the theological possibilities for interpretation. But then the reconstruction of theological principles was never Habel's goal. For those who espouse his approach, "authority effectively lies not with the Bible or the Christian tradition but with the ecojustice principles; it is these that present a set of norms to inspire and instruct human belief and action."[31]

How, then, are biblical interpreters to reconstruct possible new meanings of the text? In order for this to occur, careful attention must be paid to three areas of concern: (1) the actual text should be examined by means of thorough historical study and informed exegesis; (2) attention must be given to the broader theological tradition that is situated somewhere between the rigidity of conservative apologists and the overstatement of radical reconstructionists; and (3) the interpreter must engage with contemporary science in order to understand the ecological issues that confront us today.[32]

■ IV. Arrow of Evolution

In 1959, the English version of the writing of Pierre Teilhard de Chardin broke onto the theological stage.[33] Basic to his thinking is the argument that evolution did not cease at the appearance of *Homo sapiens*. Rather, it

---

29. Ibid., 7–10.
30. Norman C. Habel and Peter Trudinger, eds., *Exploring Ecological Hermeneutics* (SymS 46; Atlanta: Society of Biblical Literature, 2008) 1–8.
31. Horell, *Bible and the Environment*, 120.
32. Ibid., 121–27.
33. Pierre Teilhard de Chardin, *The Phenomenon of Man* (New York: Harper & Row, 1959).

moved from biogenesis to psychogenesis to anthropogenesis or what he called hominization. In fact, this unfinished universe continues to evolve —but how? With the appearance of humankind, Earth has produced a creature that is self-reflective. Quoting Julian Huxley, the evolutionary biologist, Teilhard states, "The person discovers that 'humankind is nothing less than evolution become conscious of itself. . . .'"[34] Teilhard shattered the prevailing anthropological understanding by insisting, "Humankind is not the centre of the universe as once we thought in our simplicity, but something much more wonderful—the arrow pointing the way to the final unification of the world in terms of life."[35] In other words, evolution does not end with humankind but takes a definite direction:

> [E]volution, from being initially *selective*, cannot but make itself *elective* in higher living beings, as a *direct effect of complexity*: until the time comes when, with the appearance of the faculty of *thought*, it reflects definitively upon itself and so "takes off" and suddenly opens out into planned invention (technology) and higher co-consciousness (civilization)."[36]

Might these revolutionary scientific insights provide a new way of understanding "image of God"?

Interpretation of biblical metaphors is always done within some context, whether that context be historical-critical, literary-critical, liberationist, or postcolonial—to name but a few. The two interpretations of "image of God" described above developed out of the context of historical reconstruction. The first interpretation (icon or idol) attempted to rescue the metaphor from "radical" anthropocentrism, while the second (*sui generis*) made no such effort at rescue but threw into question the revelatory value of that creation tradition. Neither reading, however, suggests a focus that is not anthropocentric. Biblical interpretation cannot rest at this stage of understanding, namely, the stage of critique. "The bible inserts the human being in the cosmos, but the way it does it must be translated into a more contemporary lexicon."[37] The next step in critical interpretation must now be taken. Contemporary cosmology challenges interpreters to do their work within contemporary cosmological contexts rather than within merely historical or anthropocentric ideological

---

34. Ibid., 220.
35. Ibid., 223.
36. Pierre Teilhard de Chardin, "The Transformation and Continuation in Man of the Mechanism of Evolution," November 19, 1951, written for Julian Huxley.
37. François Euvé, "Humanity Reveals the World," in Delio, *From Teilhard to Omega*, 77.

contexts. Within which cosmological context might "image of God" be interpreted?

Identifying humankind as the "arrow of evolution" lends itself to a new understanding of "image of God." Carrying Teilhard's thinking forward, ecotheologians have made some bold but exciting claims: "God evolves the universe and brings it to its completion through the instrumentality of human beings."[38] "There is a linkage, however, between the source of our being created and our own creativity. To the degree that evolving nature has created us, our own creating is taken up into that nature, so that we are nature's own creators, co-creators with the evolutionary process that has engendered us."[39] This co-creating is being accomplished through various forms of technology. The fruits of human consciousness have enabled nature to make the transition from biological evolution to technological evolution. According to Teilhard, "Abstraction, logic, reasoned choice, and inventions, mathematics, art, calculation of space and time, anxieties and dreams of love—all these activities of *inner life* are nothing else than the effervescence of the newly-formed centre as it explodes onto itself."[40] It is through technology that human beings transform their environment and in that way direct the very evolutionary process.

Here again, the importance of the metaphor "image of God" is found in its function. This understanding, however, focuses on the relationship between humans and the rest of the natural world rather than on the relationship between humans and God. It also offers a different understanding of the uniqueness of human creatures. First, as part of the evolutionary process, human beings are not separate from the rest of creation, as is the case in the first two approaches. Like all other creatures, humans have been brought forth by the same evolutive process. Furthermore, they are not simply products of that process; they are a very active part of it. Second, since their function is technological they act on the rest of creation in a way other aspects of creation do not act on them. They creatively transform aspects of the natural world through hoeing and planting and harvesting, through breeding and taming, through firing and tanning and manufacturing, through various forms of subduing and exercising dominion. The process of evolution is always fraught with violence, since within the process itself, what is new always breaks out of what

---

38. Delio, *Christ in Evolution*, 138.

39. Philip Hefner, "The Evolution of the Created Co-creator," in *An Evolving Dialogue: Theological and Scientific Perspectives on Evolution* (ed. James B. Miller; Harrisburg, PA: Trinity Press International, 2001) 399.

40. Teilhard de Chardin, *Phenomenon of Man*, 165.

already exists. In the very reshaping of the natural world through various forms of technology, humans do indeed subdue and exercise dominion, but they do so in the very act of co-creating.

This understanding of "image of God" has been well stated by Ilia Delio:

> The notion of a dynamic image of God leads to the deeper significance of cultivating science and technology. The human person has become transformed by his/her own initiative and artistic inventiveness which expresses in a new way both the divine image of its creator and the human image of its re-creator. The notion of the human as a dynamic image of God, with a vocation to develop this image by an evolving dialogue with the material cosmos, sets technology in a wider framework that provides strong religious, moral, and humanistic controls on its exploitation.[41]

According to this final interpretation of "image of God," humankind remains an integral part of the evolutive process, not above the rest of the natural world nor over it. Humankind's uniqueness resides in the direction it sets for this ongoing process. Its ability to set this direction springs from its highly developed consciousness, a consciousness that is shaped by the evolutive process itself. As Huxley so clearly stated, humankind is the consciousness of evolution reflecting on itself. The usefulness of this final interpretation of "image of God" will be seen in the manner in which contemporary women and men grasp the challenge placed before them and exercise "strong religious, moral, and humanistic controls" in their co-creating of the natural world.

41. Delio, *Christ in Evolution*, 159.

Dinah at Shechem (Genesis 34): The Narrator's Point of View

JAMES CHUKWUMA OKOYE, C.S.SP.
Duquesne University
Pittsburgh, Pennsylvania

Genesis 34 provokes diverse and competing agendas.[1] Feminist interpreters focus on the rape[2] and the silencing of Dinah. "Dinah's story has yet to be told. In it, the rape plays a center role";[3] "only if we reread Dinah's wordless absence as a scream can we do her justice."[4] Caroline Blyth admits that "to call Genesis 34 a story about a woman's rape is to say something about the text that the author himself takes measures to exclude from representation."[5]

In this article, I focus on the narrator's point of view. "Texts have agendas; they are attempts by the author(s) to persuade the audience to a particular way of thinking or behaving."[6] I inquire into the narrator's

---

1. I have thoroughly revised and extended a version of this essay that appeared in James Chukwuma Okoye, *Genesis 12–50: A Narrative Theological Commentary* (Eugene, OR: Cascade, 2020). Unless otherwise stated, I use the NABRE (New American Bible, rev. ed., 2010) translation for biblical passages.

2. The attention is justified, as 683,000 women are raped by men every year in the United States. See Susanne Scholz, "What 'Really' Happened to Dinah: A Feminist analysis of Genesis 34," *European Electronic Journal for Feminist Exegesis* 2 (2001) 13, www.lectio.unibe.ch/01_2/s.htm. The actual figure could be vastly more, as rape is underreported! It should be noted that men too and transgender persons suffer rape.

3. Scholz, "What 'Really' Happened to Dinah."

4. Caroline Blyth, "Terrible Silence, Eternal Silence: A Feminist Re-Reading of Dinah's Voicelessness in Genesis 34," *BibInt* 17 (2009) 483–506, here 499, citing Nehama Aschkenasy, *Woman at the Window: Biblical Tales of Oppression and Escape* (Detroit: Wayne State University Press, 1998) 52.

5. Blyth, "Terrible Silence," 485.

6. Kathryn M. Lopez, "Telling and Retelling the Story of Dinah: Violent Storytelling as Social Formation," *PRSt* 42 (2015) 275–82, here 276.

goals, why the narrator told this story at all, and why tell it in this way? What message was the narrator conveying to whom? I show that the narrator's message is accentuated in some Jewish retellings of the story. I inquire into the ethical implications of the narration as told. The repercussions and ethical implications of rape will be understood within the context of the story. The West and traditional societies, like ancient Israel, may construe it differently. Thus, I seek to throw new light on old stories.[7]

Narrative reading does not have to be a purely synchronic reading, for "diachronic reading may show how any synchronic reading of a text is a choice."[8] In fact, the synchronic often demands the diachronic, seeing that "awareness of the sources and redaction of biblical texts . . . far from obscuring or neglecting or denying literary art . . . makes possible the retrieval of the intentions of the biblical writers and redactors, which have been lost with the passing of the centuries and obscured by modern notions of the single-author book."[9]

■ I. THE ROLE OF THE NARRATOR

The narrator is the voice that tells the story. The biblical narrator usually tells the story, rarely breaking out of the narrative to comment on it. When he (I use the masculine since in context the narrator was probably male) does, this is significant. Sometimes he speaks through the characters but may also yield the perspective to a character to voice his or her feelings and interest in the story.

The narrator knows everything, even the future and what is in the mind of God, not just the thoughts of people, so scholars call him the "omniscient narrator." Such omniscience is, in the first place, understood in a literary, not a theological, sense: "[I]t is not necessary to consider such a statement 'historically reliable' and assume a prior phone call from the Holy Ghost to the writer."[10] Yet many scholars prioritize the narra-

---

7. I refer to my respected colleague Professor Leslie Hoppe's *New Light from Old Stories: Hebrew Scriptures for Today's World* (New York: Paulist, 2005). I am glad to join other friends in this festschrift in honor of his seventy-fifth birthday.

8. David M. Carr, *Reading the Fractures of Genesis: Historical and Literary Approaches* (Louisville: Westminster John Knox, 1996) 334.

9. Robert S. Kawashima, "Sources and Redaction," in *Reading Genesis: Ten Methods* (ed. Ronald Hendel; Cambridge: Cambridge University Press, 2010) 47–70, here 70.

10. Jan P. Fokkelman, *Reading Biblical Narrative: An Introductory Guide* (trans. Ineke Smit; Louisville: Westminster John Knox, 1999) 56.

tor: the narrator's statements, evaluations, silences, and manner of telling the story are believed to determine meaning.

The biblical narrator credits God with complete trustworthiness; some authors even opine that "both God and the narrator must be trustworthy and hence are the benchmark of trustworthiness for all other personae."[11] Surprisingly, some scholars speak of the narrator's knowledge as divine in origin. That is, it is unlimited in extent and compels with divine authority, for he "invests his dramatizations with the authority of an omniscience equivalent to God's own. . . . [T]his omniscience itself ultimately goes back to God."[12] How this can be when narration is sometimes in tension with other narration is not clear. It is even questionable whether there is just one consistent narrator or several:

> When Samuel–Kings is read alongside Chronicles, where is the reliable narrator? Where for that matter is the reliable narrator of the four Gospels? Or, to put it another way: Who among the four narrators is reliable? What *did* Jesus say?[13]

Meir Sternberg speaks of Scripture as "fool-proof" composition:

> By foolproof composition I mean that the Bible is difficult to read, easy to underread and overread and even misread, but virtually impossible to, so to speak, counter-read. . . . The essentials are made transparent to all comers: the story line, the world order, the value system. . . . The Bible always tells the truth in that its narrator is absolutely and straightforwardly reliable. . . . [T]he reader cannot go far wrong even if he does little more than follow the statements made and the incidents enacted on the narrative surface. For the narrator who conveys them to him cannot go wrong himself . . . nor is the narrator mendacious. . . . But follow the biblical narrator ever so uncritically, and by no great exertion you will be making tolerable sense of the world you are in, the action that unfolds, the protagonists on stage, and the point of it all.[14]

---

11. Yairah Amit, *Reading Biblical Narratives: Literary Criticism and the Hebrew Bible* (Minneapolis: Fortress, 2001) 95.

12. Meir Sternberg, *The Poetics of Biblical Narrative: Ideological Literature and the Drama of Reading* (Indiana Literary Biblical Series; Bloomington: Indiana University Press, 1985) 90.

13. David M. Gunn, "New Directions in the Study of Biblical Hebrew Narrative," *JSOT* 39 (1987) 65–75, here 71.

14. Sternberg, *Poetics of Biblical Narrative*, 50–51. He adds, "[T]he narrator does not tell the whole truth either." His statements about the world are rarely complete, fall much short of what his elliptical text suggests between the lines; "his *ex cathedra* judgments are valid as far as they go, but then they seldom go far below the surface of the narrative, where they find their qualification and shading."

My reading of the story of Dinah does not find a "foolproof" narrator. Anachronisms and sutures in the text lead in various directions. The narrator's message for his time redirects another message visible in the text. Some of his narrative decisions seem to conflict with others; he thus appears conflicted.

■ II. Shechem "Takes" Dinah (34:1–12)

How this narrative advances the plot of the patriarchal story is not clear. In fact, Genesis 35 continues the story directly from Genesis 33. After separating from Esau, Jacob lands in Succoth and builds a home there and booths for his livestock (33:17). He must have then settled over against Shechem (33:18–19). Following the Dinah incident at Shechem (Genesis 34), God has Jacob going up to Bethel, reminding him of his vow. The tale of Dinah is clearly an independent piece, an interlude.[15] After the initially tense meeting between Jacob and Esau comes to a good conclusion, Genesis 34 perhaps tells another story of confrontation that could have wiped out the line but for God's protection.[16] The narrator uses the story to give pointed messages to his audience.

Nomadic groups and city dwellers usually exchange wares. An incident leads to high tension.

> Dinah, the daughter whom Leah had borne to Jacob, went out to visit some of the women of the land. When Shechem, son of Hamor the Hivite, leader of the region, saw her, he seized her and lay with her by force. (Gen 34:1–2)

Dinah is identified as the daughter of Leah, the unloved wife, not as Jacob's daughter. Is the narrator foreshadowing Jacob's behavior in the matter? Dinah, Jacob's only daughter, needed female company. She was also grown up and ready for marriage. When Isaac grew up, Abraham sent a servant to Mesopotamia to fetch a wife for him from among his kindred. The ostensible reason for sending Jacob himself to Paddan-aram was to seek a wife from the kindred and so not to marry "a native of the land" (Gen 27:46). We do not hear of such arrangements for Dinah.

Dinah goes out "to see" the women of the land:[17] ותצא דינה בת־לאה אשר ילדה ליעקב לראות בבנות הארץ. The expression ראה ב- is unusual;

---

15. See also Alison L. Joseph, "'Is Dinah Raped?' Isn't the Right Question: Genesis 34 and Feminist Historiography," *JHebS* 19 (2019) 27–37, here 33.
16. Ibid.
17. Some readers blame her for going out without a male chaperon. The narrator thinks she should be safe with other women.

Victor P. Hamilton has her go out *to be seen among* the daughters of the land.[18] Nothing in the text suggests that she wanted to be seen by men. But Shechem saw her—a different type of seeing. In the previous chapter, Shechem was the city in which Jacob settled; its inhabitants were descended from an ancestor called Hamor (Gen 33:18–19). Here Shechem is a person, a Hivite, and his father is Hamor, the נשיא (prince or leader) of the area. There is conflation here between the individual and the tribe. The Hivites are one of the peoples of Canaan (Gen 10:17) whom Yhwh will wipe out before Israel (Exod 23:23) and whom Israel, upon entry into Canaan, must put under the ban of destruction (Deut 7:3; 20:17). These resonances are ominous.

In Hebrew, חמור means an ass. Is there name calling here? "Sons of Hamor" may also mean those bound together by treaty, members of a confederacy. In the Mari texts, killing the foal of a donkey signifies concluding a covenant.[19]

Shechem saw—took, lay with her, violated her; לקח ("to take") often signifies taking a woman as wife, though the usual expression is לקח אשה. In v. 4, Shechem will ask his father to "take me this girl for wife." In the meantime, he has Dinah in his private quarters. The usual term for sexual relations is שכב עם ("to lie with" someone, using the preposition עם), which is how the NRSV translates the expression in Gen 24:2. The narrator wrote וישכב אתה, which is pointed in *BHS* as the verb with the object marker את. Some interpreters see this as evidence of using Dinah as an object merely for Shechem's pleasure. There are resonances between this text and the rape of Tamar in 2 Sam 13:14.

Genesis 34:2:
וירא אתה שכם בן־חמור החוי נשיא הארץ ויקח אתה וישכב אתה ויענה
When Shechem, son of Hamor the Hivite, who was chief of the region, saw her, he seized her and lay with her by force.

2 Samuel 13:14:
ולא אבה לשמע בקולה ויחזק ממנה ויענה וישכב אתה
Not heeding her plea, he overpowered her; he shamed her and had relations with her.

In 2 Samuel 13, ענה clearly refers to forcible rape. Both the lack of consent and the element of force are explicit: ויחזק ממנה ויענה וישכב אתה (literally,

---

18. Victor P. Hamilton, *The Book of Genesis: Chapters 18–50* (NICOT; Grand Rapids: Eerdmans, 1995) 351; see also 353: "The active sense is possible only if one understands *bĕ* partitively, that is, 'to see *some* of the women.'"

19. Nahum M. Sarna, *Genesis* בראשית: *The Traditional Hebrew Text with the New JPS Translation* (JPS Torah Commentary; Philadelphia: Jewish Publication Society, 1989) 233.

"he was too strong for her: he forced her down and raped her"). In Genesis 34, however, ויענה occurs at the end of a string of verbs of action and what it adds to them is unclear. Claus Westermann believes that ויענה underscores a forceful violation[20]—the three verbs are of increasing severity and underscore the brutality of Shechem's assault. Sternberg concurs: "[The text] unrolls a series of three, whose apparent redundancy marks an ascending order of explicitness, violence, and denunciation: 'he took her and lay with ["laid"] her and abused her.'"[21] He speaks of the narrator's "unequivocal condemnation of the assault."[22] The versions struggle:

LXX: καὶ ἐταπείνωσεν αὐτήν ("humbled her")
NIV: "violated her"; Robert Alter renders: "debased her"[23]
NJB: "forced her"; NABRE, NRSV, TNK add the phrase, "by force"

The verb ענה does not always mean forcible rape. Sarah treated Hagar oppressively (Gen 16:6); Laban warned Jacob not to treat Laban's daughters badly (Gen 31:50). In Deut 21:10–13, the verb is used where force is absent. A man who takes a female captive as wife but later dislikes her may not sell her for money or enslave her, for he has dishonored or humiliated (עניתה) her.[24] Yet ענה is a verb used for exerting power over a people, oppressing or debasing them. In the West, rape requires force against one's consent. The West defines the person as solitary self, an individual, so rape is primarily a violation of a [person's] autonomy and bodily integrity.[25] Other cultures, like ancient Israel and many traditional societies, define personal identity in relationality. These cultures recognize personal injury but consider rape "a crime against men (husbands and fathers) and not women."[26] "Biblical rape is theft of sexual property."[27]

---

20. Claus Westermann, *Genesis: A Commentary* (trans. John J. Scullion; 3 vols.; Continental Commentary; Minneapolis: Fortress, 1984–86) 2:538. See also Sarna, *Genesis*, 234.

21. Meir Sternberg, "Biblical Poetics and Sexual Politics: From Reading to Counterreading," *JBL* 111 (1992) 463–88, here 475.

22. Sternberg, *Poetics of Biblical Narrative*, 446.

23. Robert Alter, *Genesis: Translation and Commentary* (New York: Norton, 1996) 190. For Alter, the chain of uninterrupted verbs—*saw – took – lay with – debased*—conveys the precipitousness of the action.

24. See Tikva Frymer-Kensky, *In the Wake of the Goddesses: Women, Culture, and the Biblical Transformation of Pagan Myth* (New York: Free Press, 1992) 274 n. 34.

25. See Robin Parry, "Feminist Hermeneutics and Evangelical Concerns: The Rape of Dinah as a Case Study," *TynBul* 53 (2002) 1–28, here 11.

26. Ibid., 21.

27. Susan Brooks Thistlethwaite, "'You May Enjoy the Spoil of Your Enemies'—Rape as a Biblical Metaphor for War," *Semeia* 61 (1993) 59–78, here 59.

Woman embodies the honor of the whole community; to violate her is to violate the entire community. Even if Dinah consented, it would still be rape. Shechem's act of laying Dinah before the required marriage negotiations and payment of the dowry debased her in the eyes of society and debased her father and brothers, whose duty it was to protect and uphold her honor, rendering them impotent nonentities in the eyes of society. In modern times, the families of some Chibok girls in Nigeria kidnapped by Boko Haram rejected them and their children after the young women's release. This extreme revulsion illustrates how intertwined the honor of the woman is with the honor of a traditional community.

In contrast to Amnon, whose hatred for Tamar surpassed the love he had for her, the narrator reports that

> [Shechem] was strongly attracted to Dinah, daughter of Jacob, and was in love with the young woman. So he spoke affectionately to her. Shechem said to his father Hamor, "Get me this young woman for a wife." (Gen 34:3–4)

Did Shechem fall in love with Dinah after he raped her, or did he rape her because he loved her? Frances Klopper sees this as "a classic case of acquaintance or date rape."[28] For Susanne Scholtz, love after rape is treachery; she renders the Hebrew as follows: "and he took her, and he laid her, and he raped her. And he stayed close to Dinah, the daughter of Jacob, and he lusted after the young woman, and he tried to soothe her."[29] This rendering does not stand. The narrator says explicitly that Shechem was in love: ותדבק נפשו בדינה בת־יעקב ("he was strongly attracted to Dinah, the daughter of Jacob"). The verb דבק means to "cleave to." In Gen 2:24 the man cleaved to his wife. Shechem was indeed in love, his very self clung to Dinah.[30] The narrator, in adducing this fact, suggests that the offer of marriage was genuine on Shechem's part. The piling up of phrases of love kindles some empathy for Shechem. Robin Parry suggests that the narrator is calling for a compromised but realistic solution.[31]

"*He spoke to her heart.*" David M. Gunn and Danna Nolan Fewell see this phrase as perlocution; that is, Shechem succeeded in soothing her, and she responded positively and stayed willingly.[32] Hermann Gunkel

---

28. Frances Klopper, "Rape and the Case of Dinah: Ethical Responsibilities for Reading Genesis 34," *OTE* 23 (2010) 652–65, here 655.
29. Scholz, "What 'Really' Happened to Dinah," 7.
30. Alter, *Genesis*, 190.
31. See Parry, "Feminist Hermeneutics," 7.
32. See David M. Gunn and Danna Nolan Fewell, "Tipping the Balance: Sternberg's Reader and the Rape of Dinah," *JBL* 110 (1991) 193–211, here 196.

opined that Shechem promised to set things right by marrying her,[33] thus restoring her honor in the eyes of all. Sternberg insists, however, that to "speak [*dbr*] to the heart of somebody" should not be confused with "the patient-oriented 'touch [or reach, *ngᶜ*] the heart of somebody.'"[34] We do not know. Dinah, unfortunately, utters no word all through the account, nor are her feelings ever expressed.[35]

> Meanwhile, Jacob heard that Shechem had defiled his daughter Dinah, but since his sons were out in the field with his livestock, Jacob kept quiet until they came home. (Gen 34:5)

Is this the narrator's viewpoint, or is he conveying a report that Shechem had defiled Jacob's daughter (טמא את־דינה בתו)? The term טמא evokes the language of Ezekiel, the Priestly Writer, and the Holiness Code; it recalls the impurity of the nations of the land (Ezra 6:21) and of the land made impure through idolatry.[36] The perspective glides from individual history to national identity. For this reason, Gunkel and Westermann consider the motif of defilement a late gloss. David Frankel asserts that most references to the "defiling" of Dinah can be recognized as removable additions.[37]

In biblical law, adultery refers to sexual relations between a man and a married or betrothed woman. In biblical law, טמא applies to married or betrothed women only, so it is inappropriately used here: "The seduction or rape of a virgin in the biblical milieu did not signify her being defiled."[38] Biblical law about unattached virgins makes no distinction between rape and consensual sex. "No laws require the death of the male, in stark contrast to such an act with either a betrothed virgin or married woman."[39] For attached women, the offense and the punishment of death are for "rape" seen as the violation of the rights of the father and the groom.

When Jacob heard, he kept silent; when his sons heard, they were indignant and extremely angry. The contrast is jarring. Could Jacob not

---

33. Hermann Gunkel, *Genesis* (trans. Mark E. Biddle; Mercer Library of Biblical Studies; Macon, GA: Mercer University Press, 1997; German original, 1901) 363.

34. Sternberg, "Biblical Poetics and Sexual Politics," 476.

35. Marriage decisions concerning a girl are made by the men in the family, her father and/or her brothers.

36. Alexander Rofé, "Defilement of Virgins in Biblical Law and the Case of Dinah (Genesis 34)," *Bib* 86 (2004) 369–75, here 371.

37. Gunkel, *Genesis*, 362; Westermann, *Genesis*, 2:543; David Frankel, "The Proto-Story of Shechem and Jacob's Daughter," https://thetorah.com/the-proto-story-of-shechem-and-jacobs-daughter.

38. Rofé, "Defilement of Virgins," 375.

39. Angela B. Wagner, "Considerations on the Politico-Juridical Proceedings of Genesis 34," *JSOT* 38 (2013) 145–61, here 153.

feel the pain of a daughter, even if she is the daughter of the unloved wife? The narrator tried to excuse Jacob: he kept silent until the sons, whose duty it was to avenge the honor of their sister, returned.

> Now Hamor ... went out to discuss the matter with Jacob. (Gen 34:6)

The father of the prospective groom asked the father of the prospective bride for her hand. Meanwhile, Jacob's sons arrived and showed great pain and anger at the news:

> for [כי] Shechem had committed an outrage in Israel by lying with Jacob's daughter; such a thing is not done. (Gen 34:7b)

The narrator and the sons of Jacob concur in this judgment. The outrage (נבלה) is a senseless and disgraceful act of folly. The anachronistic use of the term "Israel" illustrates the glide mentioned above. Jacob had yet to become the nation Israel. The phrase לשכב את ("to lie with") appears here, as in v. 2. The use of "Jacob's daughter" in a reported speech highlights ethnic difference and religious outrage. The sacred norms that constituted the moral underpinnings of the later people[40] were being read into the situation.

> Hamor appealed to them, saying: "My son Shechem has his heart set on your daughter. Please give her to him as a wife. Intermarry with us; give your daughters to us, and take our daughters for yourselves. Thus you can live among us. The land is open before you. Settle and move about freely in it and acquire holding here." (Gen 34:8–10)

Hamor makes a clever political speech. He not only asks for the betrothal of Dinah to his son Shechem, but proposes a supposedly advantageous political alliance, in which both sides would intermarry and the sons of Jacob would become full citizens (ישב, "to dwell," no longer as alien גר), able to acquire land and move about freely. Hamor can offer this because he is the ruler of the place. But he has overlooked the deep pain and shame caused by Shechem's deed. The talk about intermarriage resonates with the language of Deut 7:3, which forbids such. Compare the following texts:

> "Intermarry with us; give your daughters to us, and take our daughters for yourselves." (Gen 34:9)

> "You shall not intermarry with them, neither giving your daughters to their sons, nor taking their daughters for your sons." (Deut 7:3)

> Then Shechem appealed to Dinah's father and brothers: "Do me this favor, and whatever you ask from me, I will give. No matter how high

---

40. Sarna, *Genesis*, 234.

> you set the bridal price and gift, I will give you whatever you ask from me; only give me the young woman as a wife." (Gen 34:11–12)

The bride-price (מהר) is given to the father of the bride, the gift (מתן) to the bride. Shechem's first words, "let me find favor in your eyes," struck the wrong note. He needed to acknowledge the dishonor to Dinah and Jacob's family. Was his offer of a bride-price and gift in excess of what would be the normal amount a tacit recognition of the need to make reparation?[41] Or did the brothers view it as an attempt to buy them off?

■ III. Deceit and Massacre (34:13–29)

> Jacob's sons replied to Shechem and his father with guile, speaking as they did because he had defiled their sister Dinah. (Gen 34:13)

Here Jacob's sons reply; in v. 25 only Simeon and Levi begin the massacre.[42] Jacob's sons or the pair of brothers sideline their father and take over the negotiations. The narrator accepts that the brothers responded "*with guile*" (במרמה),[43] and justified the guile.[44] "Guile" points forward to hidden plans.

> They said to them, "We are not able to do this thing: to give our sister to an uncircumcised man. For that would be a disgrace for us. Only on this condition will we agree to that: that you become like us by having every male among you circumcised. Then we will give you our daughters and take your daughters in marriage; we will settle among you and become one people. But if you do not listen to us and be circumcised, we will take our daughter and go. (Gen 34:14–17)

On the basis of Exod 12:43–49, circumcision would allow the Shechemites to participate in the cult and so intermarry. The brothers cite Hamor's words about intermarriage and political relationships, adding, with irony, "and become one people." "'To become one people' is a blueprint for

---

41. Ibid., 235.
42. The LXX fills this gap by having the pair respond here: "And Symeon and Levi, the brothers of Dinah, said to them."
43. *Targum Onqelos* and *Targum Neofiti* have them answering Hamor "with wisdom."
44. The last time we met this phrase was in Gen 27:35—"your brother came here with guile and carried off your blessing." Jacob himself used the verbal root to complain to Laban, who switched Leah for Rachel on the bridal night: "why did you deceive me?" (ולמה רמיתני, Gen 29:25).

national suicide."[45] Assimilation would be the end of the divine experiment with Abraham and his seed.

> Their proposal pleased Hamor and his son Shechem. The young man lost no time in acting on the proposal, since he wanted Jacob's daughter. (Gen 34:18–19)

Biblical law on the violation of unbetrothed virgins conforms to Shechem's request. Deuteronomy 22:28–29 (see also Exod 22:15–16) says, "If a man comes upon a young woman, a virgin who is not betrothed, seizes her and lies with her, and they are discovered, the man who lay with her shall give the young woman's father fifty silver shekels and she will be his wife, because he has violated[46] her. He may not divorce her as long as he lives." Compensation and marriage (without possibility of divorcing the woman) would be enough.[47] The brothers, however, pitched the matter on the religious plane of circumcised versus uncircumcised, with the accompanying idea of defilement.

Hamor and his son fell for it. Shechem wasted no time in getting himself circumcised. He delighted that much in Jacob's daughter (כי חפץ בבת־יעקב), the narrator again tells us. Because Shechem was very highly regarded in the city, it was possible for him and his father to convince the men at the gate of the city: the men are friendly, we have ample room, let them settle with us and move about as they wish.

> We can take their daughters in marriage and give our daughters to them. But only on this condition will the men agree to live with us and form one people with us: that every male among us be circumcised as they themselves are. Would not their livestock, their property, and all their animals then be ours? Let us just agree with them, so that they will settle among us. (Gen 34:21b–23)

To sway the people, they presented the matter in a manner that would appeal to them. They lose nothing, they might even gain from the transaction! Persuasion consists in playing to the perspectives and interests of the audience. "They thought to despoil them and were themselves

---

45. Sternberg, "Biblical Poetics and Sexual Politics," 485. One finds an echo in Antiochus's decree in 1 Macc 1:42: "that all should be one people, and abandon their particular customs."
46. The verb in the phrase "because he has violated her" (ענה) is the same verb as in Gen 34:2.
47. Sternberg argues that this law obtains only between Israelite parties and that Deut 7:1–4 (Canaanites) and Deut 23:4 (Ammonites and Moabites) disqualify others. He hangs this argument on the phrase "in your midst" ("Biblical Poetics and Sexual Politics," 482).

despoiled," says *Gen. Rab.* 80:8. They agreed: "and all the males, all those who went out of the gate of the city, were circumcised" (Gen 34:24b). That this did not include the children, we learn from v. 29. "All who went out of the gate of the city" means either free citizens or perhaps men of military age who go out of the gates to war.[48] They were all willing to go through the pain and discomfort with Shechem.

> On the third day, while they were still in pain, two of Jacob's sons, Simeon and Levi, brothers of Dinah, each took his sword, advanced against the unsuspecting city and massacred all the males. After they killed Hamor and his son Shechem with the sword, they took Dinah from Shechem's house and left. (Gen 34:25–26)

The protagonists, Simeon and Levi, were full brothers of Dinah, but so were Reuben, Judah, Issachar, and Zebulon, all Leah's sons. Was the singling out of Simeon and Levi read back into the story from Jacob's reproof of them in Gen 49:5–7? The midrash answers that Dinah is called by their name because they risked their lives for her sake (*Gen. Rab.* 80:10).[49] The two brothers took Dinah and left. We learn incidentally that Dinah was in Shechem's house all along. This hostile confrontation with the surrounding peoples is out of character for the patriarchal stories, for the patriarchs were usually portrayed as living peacefully with their neighbors, even adopting their altars for the worship of Yhwh.

> Then the other sons of Jacob followed up the slaughter and sacked the city because their sister had been defiled. They took their sheep, cattle and donkeys, whatever was in the city and in the surrounding country. They carried off all their wealth, their children, and their women, and looted whatever was in the houses. (Gen 34:27–29)

The other sons of Jacob add looting to massacre. The narrator tells us why: "because *they defiled* their sister." This is collective punishment: the entire city becomes guilty for the crime of one person. There is irony here. Shechem "took" a daughter of Jacob; after massacring the men, the sons of Jacob "took" everything, including the women and children and all their wealth! "The brothers reject the alliance and see the threat to their uniqueness as a people as a declaration of war or as foreigners trying to turn them toward idol worship. As such, the brothers engage the rules of holy war in their vengeance."[50]

---

48. Sarna, *Genesis*, 234.
49. Just as Miriam was called sister of Aaron (Exod 15:20), who pleaded for her, though she was also the sister of Moses.
50. Joseph, "Is Dinah Raped?," 35. She posits two levels of redaction: an earlier

IV. Jacob and His Sons (34:30–31)

> Jacob said to Simeon and Levi: "You have brought trouble upon me by making me repugnant to the inhabitants of the land, the Canaanites and the Perizzites. I have so few men that, if these people unite against me and attack me, I and my household will be wiped out." But they retorted, "Should our sister be treated like a prostitute?" (Gen 34:30-31)

A prostitute offers her wares without discrimination to all who will pay. For the brothers, accepting any gifts for Dinah in the circumstances reduces her to the status of a prostitute. Why address Simeon and Levi when the other sons also did the massacre?[51] The brothers seem to censure the passivity of their father, perhaps because Dinah was not the daughter of his favorite wife. The threat to the family was real, and Jacob had the duty of protecting his family. In fact, were it not for the terror from God that fell upon the surrounding towns (Gen 35:5), what Jacob feared would have happened. The brothers acted without thinking through the likely consequences of their action.

Dinah entered the story as the daughter of Jacob and ended as the sister of Simeon and Levi. She disappears from the Bible, except for the oblique reference in the list of Jacob's children descending to Egypt: "these were the sons whom Leah bore to Jacob in Paddan-aram, along with his daughter Dinah—thirty-three persons in all, sons and daughters" (Gen 46:15), which seems to count Dinah (though it is unclear how the number there adds up to seventy). We never hear of any children of Dinah! Gunkel suggests that, at the origin of the story, "Dinah was an Israelite tribe related to Simeon and Levi, overpowered by Shechem and forced to join it, but avenged by the fraternal tribes."[52]

---

redaction focused on the shame that is brought to the house of Jacob, which marrying the victim as in Deut 22:28–29 could alleviate, and a postexilic redaction focused on defining the people's identity and consistent with values expressed in Ezra-Nehemiah. See also Gunkel, Westermann, and Frankel in n. 37 above.

51. Westermann suggests that, in the family narrative, Simeon and Levi killed Shechem to atone for the outrage to their sister. In fact, in *T. Levi* 6:4–5, Levi says he killed Shechem first and Simeon killed Hamor; only subsequently did the brothers come and smite the city with the edge of the sword. In the midrash, Dinah became the wife of Job (*Gen. Rab.* 57:4); a variant is that Simeon buried her in the land of Canaan (*Gen. Rab.* 80:11). Still another, *Jub.* 34:14, says that she expired from mourning over the news that a beast had devoured Joseph and was buried by the tomb of Rachel.

52. Gunkel, *Genesis*, 360.

■ V. Narrative Intention

Shechem was a city hallowed by the patriarchs and regarded as sacred even in Joshua and Judges. "Abraham passed through the land as far as the sacred place at Shechem, by the oak of Moreh . . . he built an altar there to the LORD who had appeared to him" (Gen 12:6, 7). At Shechem, Joshua gathered all the tribes of Israel and there they put away their foreign gods and swore: "We will serve the LORD, our God, and will listen to his voice" (Josh 24:24). Shechem did not become "unholy" until the Deuteronomistic movement condemned Jeroboam and his apostasy. Shechem in this story is unholy ground.

According to Noble,

> [Genesis 34] is a story about *issues*: through pondering, under the guidance of the narrator, upon the (largely unsatisfactory) ways in which the characters handle their situation, the reader's own moral sensibilities are sharpened. What one gains thereby is not, primarily, a straightforward set of rules, but a heightened awareness of the complexity of the situation, a deeper understanding of the terms in which such problems must be thought about ("crime," "punishment," "recompense," "just proportion," "lack of self-interest," "consequences"), and experience of thinking in such terms.[53]

Intentions seem to conflict with each other in this text. "The dilemma raised by th[is] story is so complex and each choice so problematic that [the narrator] cannot fully identify with any of the positions taken."[54] The narrator empathizes with Shechem (he indeed loved Dinah, spoke to her heart, was willing to do anything, even being circumcised). Yet he justifies the guile with which the brothers spoke and sides with them in defining the action as defilement. The laws of the Pentateuch envisage the solution of marriage without ability to divorce. Other parts of the same Pentateuch call for imposing the ban on peoples of the land. "Become one people" sounds like a declaration of war (assimilation would mean the end of Israel) and might have triggered the idea of the ban.

The narrator employs this story in the "construction of identity."[55] Hivites are one of the seven nations of Canaan. "In the background stands the command of Deut 7:1–5 which forbids intermarriage with the

---

53. Paul Noble, "A 'Balanced' Reading of the Rape of Dinah: Some Exegetical and Methodological Observations," *BibInt* 4 (1996) 173–204, here 195 (emphasis original).
54. Sternberg, "Delicate Balance in the Rape of Dinah," in *Poetics of Biblical Narrative*, 445–75, here 475.
55. Lopez, "Telling and Retelling the Story of Dinah," 275.

Canaanites and demands their extermination."[56] That "the prohibition of marriage with the inhabitants of the land applies even to those who are circumcised"[57] may contain a hidden polemic against Jewish priestly groups and elites (cf. Neh 13:8) who were vying with each other to marry women of the land. It is noteworthy that Ezra 9 transposed the extermination inward. Instead of Israel exterminating the other nations, Israel is to "exterminate" its own unfaithful members:

> Ezra 9:1–2 reinterpreted the law of extermination in terms of dispossession and exclusion from the community. . . . Ezra 9 updated the list of Canaanite nations in Deut 7:1–6 by adding Moabites, Ammonites, and Egyptians . . . adapting the law to the postexilic situation.[58]

Terence Fretheim believes that the final retort throws negative light on the brothers: "by leaving the reader with the sons' question, standing over against the word of the head of the family oriented toward life and promise, the narrator shows how narrow and self-serving their perspective and actions have been. The question also leaves the reader with an agenda to consider: How would they respond?"[59]

Alexander Rofé sees Genesis 34 as internally inconsistent;[60] similarly, Gunkel, Westermann, and Frankel.[61] A *documentary* solution sees the chapter composed of two separate stories that were blended together by a redactor; a *supplementary* hypothesis holds that the original story has been substantially modified by major additions from a later hand.[62] Historical critics speak of sources and redactions. A narrative reading notes the conflicting emotions raised by the reading and envisages a narrator highlighting some features of the story to convey certain messages to his audience. In line with an increasing body of scholars, the message can be read as addressed to the postexilic community.[63]

---

56. Westermann, *Genesis*, 2:537.

57. Yairah Amit, *Hidden Polemics in Biblical Narrative* (BibInt 25; Leiden: Brill, 2000) 195. The Holiness Code, having combined the Priestly laws with the separatist views of the Deuteronomistic Historian, would prohibit marriage with the circumcised foreign population.

58. James Okoye, "The Pontifical Biblical Commission, the Old Testament, and Christ as the Key to All Sacred Scripture," *CBQ* 80 (2018) 670–86, here 682.

59. Terence E. Fretheim, "The Book of Genesis," *NIB* 1:1–276, here 213.

60. Rofé, "Defilement of Virgins," 370. Whereas Rofé speaks of redactions, I view the story as being reread in a different context. Other biblical and extrabiblical rereadings move along the same trajectory.

61. See n. 37 above.

62. See Robin Parry, "Source Criticism and Genesis 34," *TynBul* 51 (2000) 121–38, here 122.

63. Joseph Blenkinsopp writes, "[T]here is less resistance today to reading J as later than the P narrative and perhaps composed as a kind of ongoing critical comment on it"

■ VI. Rereadings

The biblical and extrabiblical rereadings emphasize the narrator's message. In her prayer, Judith picks up the language of defilement and calls on the "Lord, God of my father Simeon, into whose hand you put a sword to take revenge upon the foreigners who had defiled a virgin by violating her.... [T]herefore you handed over their rulers to slaughter ... and all the spoils you divided among your favored children who burned with zeal for you and in their abhorrence of the defilement of their blood called on you for help" (Jdt 9:2–4).[64] God himself gave the swords to Simeon and Levi.

The *Aramaic Levi Document* is dated to the third century or early second century B.C.E.[65] After the massacre and after cleansing himself, Levi uttered a prayer that ended with, "And have mercy upon me, my Lord, and bring me forward, to be your servant and to minister well to you.... Hearken also to the prayer of your servant Levi to be close to you, And make (me) a participant in your words, to do true judgment for all time, me and my children for all the generations of the ages. And do not remove the son of your servant from your countenance all the days of the world" (3:10, 16–18). In a vision he is taken up to heaven and installed a high priest (chap. 4).

The extrabiblical Book of *Jubilees* was written around the mid-second century B.C.E. in the context of the struggle with the people of the land and of fear of assimilation. It draws on the *Aramaic Levi Document* for the story of Dinah.[66] Intermarriage with gentiles was viewed as defilement. "Dinah ... was snatched away to the house of Shechem ... and he lay

---

(*Creation, Un-Creation, Re-Creation: A Discursive Commentary on Genesis 1–11* [London: T&T Clark, 2011] 7). See also Blenkinsopp, "A Post-Exilic Lay Source in Genesis 1–11," in *Abschied vom Jahwisten: Die Komposition des Hexateuch in der jüngsten Diskussion* (ed. Jan Christian Gertz, Konrad Schmid, and Markus Witte; BZAW 315; Berlin: de Gruyter, 2002) 49–61; John Van Seters, *The Yahwist: A Historian of Israelite Origins* (Winona Lake, IN: Eisenbrauns, 2013).

64. The Book of Judith is dated to the late second century or early first century B.C.E.

65. Jonas C. Greenfield, Michael E. Stone, and Esther Eshel, *The Aramaic Levi Document: Edition, Translation, Commentary* (VTSup 19; Leiden: Brill, 2004) 19–22 (the translation is from Greenfield et al.).

66. See George W. E. Nickelsburg, *Jewish Literature between the Bible and the Mishnah: A Historical and Literary Introduction* (2nd ed.; Minneapolis: Fortress, 2005) 164–65.

with her and defiled her, but she was little, only twelve years old" (*Jub.* 30:2). The killing of the populace was done by Simeon and Levi (30:4–5): "The judgment was ordered in heaven against them that they might annihilate with a sword all of the men of Shechem because they caused a shame in Israel" (30:5). *Jubilees* 30:7–10 ends with an injunction:

> And let any man who causes defilement surely die, let him be stoned.... And there is no limit of days for this law. And there is no remission or forgiveness except that the man who caused defilement of his daughter will be rooted out from the midst of Israel because he has given some of his seed to Moloch and sinned so as to defile it. (vv. 8–10)[67]

Giving seed to Moloch refers to Lev 18:21, "you shall not offer any of your offspring for immolation to Molech, thus profaning the name of your God, I am the LORD." Molech was the god of the Phoenicians and Canaanites to whom people sacrificed their children. The text equates giving one's daughter to a gentile to sacrificing her to Molech. The violence "turns into the shining example of the purity of Levi and his total devotion to God."[68] Thereafter, "the seed of Levi was chosen for the priesthood and Levitical (orders)... because he was zealous to do righteousness and judgment and vengeance against all who rose up against Israel" (30:18).[69] Noteworthy is how the terms "defile" and "disgrace in Israel" are now applied inward to Israelites who dare to give or be given in intermarriage with gentiles. Kathryn M. Lopez suggests that the men of Shechem stand for the Zadokite priesthood of the time, circumcised men who are nonetheless impure representations of the deity.[70]

Josephus writes of Jacob: "but Jacob not knowing how to deny the desire of one of such great dignity, and yet not thinking it lawful to marry his daughter to a stranger, entreated him to give leave to have a consultation" (*Ant.* 1.21.1 §338; trans. Whiston).

■ VII. Ethical Implications

As shaped readers,

> We read this chapter in a world in which sexual violence is horribly present, on local streets, in homes, and in wars around the globe. Ethnic

---

67. Translations of *Jubilees* are from O. S. Wintermute, "Jubilees," *OTP* 2:112–13.
68. Lopez, "Telling and Re-telling the Story of Dinah," 276.
69. See Wintermute, "Jubilees," 30–31.
70. Lopez, "Telling and Re-telling the Story of Dinah," 281.

conflict seemingly is gaining force even as we become more globally interconnected. Gender conflict, to understate the matter, is not absent from our experience.[71]

Responsible exegesis must see to it that the word of God be not co-opted for violence of any type. It is heartening that this word does not give the brothers the last word. In Gen 49:5–7, Jacob roundly condemns the passion and trickery of Simeon and Levi and rejects community with them.[72] In view of this, Gen 48:22 is a puzzle. Jacob says to Joseph, "I give to you, as to the one above his brothers, Shechem, which I captured from the Amorites with my sword and bow."[73] Augustine was right to ask, "If now, rejoicing in that victory, he gives that land to his son Joseph, why then did the sons who did this act [Genesis 34] displease him?" (*Questions on Genesis* 167).[74] According to George W. E. Nickelsburg, the reference may be to the wars of the sons of Jacob known from some extrabiblical writings.[75]

One man's passion destroyed a whole city. The ethical repercussions could not be more severe. In an honor-and-shame culture, rape induces horror. Because the woman embodies the honor of the entire people, to rape her is to rape the entire community. This merits as much force as the community can prudently exert.

In the context of the story, it was the brothers' duty to avenge the crime inflicted on Dinah. In Gen 24:58, Rebekah had already been called and asked, "Will you go with this man?" From here Jewish practice developed that stipulates that a marriage without the (adult) girl's consent is not valid. Modern ethical sensitivity gives the woman the same rights of auto-determination as a man; Dinah needed to be given voice to express herself.

Hopelessly outnumbered, Levi and Simeon and the brothers used the ruse of circumcision, but this is problematic. A covenant offered and willingly accepted was unilaterally and deceitfully broken. The religious rite of circumcision, which incorporates adherents into Israel, became a ploy

---

71. Notes from seminar on April 17, 2006, led by Richard Nysse, "Genesis 34: Can this chapter be read as 'Scripture' in the contemporary church?"

72. Gunkel, *Genesis*, 362. Their later demise was viewed as just punishment.

73. The versions struggle: "and now, I assign to you one portion more than to your brothers, which I wrested from the Amorites with my sword and bow" (TNK; something similar in the NRSV).

74. Translation from sites.google.com/site/aquinasstudybible/home/genesis/augustine-questions-on-genesis.

75. Nickelsburg, *Jewish Literature between the Testaments*, 159; also 383 n. 225, which refers the reader to Greenfield et al., *Aramaic Levi Document* (see n. 65 above).

for the massacre of the very people who painfully submitted to circumcision. This became an embarrassment when Judaism opened itself to receiving God-fearers and gentile converts. Josephus removes the element of circumcision: "It being now the time of a festival, when the Shechemites were employed in ease and feasting, they fell upon the watch when they were asleep, and, coming into the city, slew all the males as also the king, and his son, with them" (*Ant.* 1.21.1 §340). There is a lack of proportionality here: the crime of one person is visited upon a whole city. It would have preserved a certain proportionality had the brothers killed only Shechem and perhaps his father.

Where is God in Genesis 34? God seems absent from this chapter. God's reaction is noted only in Gen 35:5:

> As they set out, a great terror fell upon the surrounding towns, so that no one pursued the sons of Jacob.

"Great terror" is literally "terror from God." God protected his protégé from an obliterating countermassacre that would have frustrated God's promise. Did God here condone the evil in order to save the Israelites, or did he save them despite the evil? Perhaps, as is clear in his dealings with Jacob, "God does not perfect people before deciding to work in and through them."[76]

If stories in Scripture have moral lessons, can we seek moral guidance from this story? Fretheim sees here

> another instance in which the community of faith fails to serve as a chance for the blessing of God to outsiders. Rather than treat the rape of Dinah according to the law, as Hamor's family was openly willing to do, Israel takes the way of anarchy and violence. Rather than honor a genuine change on the part of Dinah's victimizers, the brothers ignore it and take a sharply overdrawn retributive form of behavior that serves to alienate the outsider. . . . Israel loses the opportunity to bring good out of suffering, and Dinah becomes even more of a victim.[77]

■ VIII. Conclusion

John Sailhamer interprets Genesis 34 in this way: "God's purpose in setting apart the seed of Abraham comes into jeopardy with the proposal of

---

76. Terence Fretheim, "Which Blessing Does Isaac Give Jacob?," in *Jews, Christians, and the Theology of Hebrew Scriptures* (ed. Alice Ogden Bellis and Joel S. Kaminsky; SymS 8; Atlanta: Society of Biblical Literature, 2000) 289–91, here 284.
77. Fretheim, "Genesis," 214.

marriage between Dinah and Shechem."[78] The request to be "one people" threatens to reverse God's intention, which is separation from the rest of the nations. Jacob and family often attempted to carry out God's intentions by means of their own plans and schemes. The narrative shows the eventual success of God's intentions.[79]

Yet "separation from the rest of the nations" does not define the whole of God's plan for Israel. Judah married a Canaanite woman who became the ancestor of the Messiah. Joseph married the daughter of the high priest of On, and his children from her, Ephraim and Manasseh, became the dominant tribes in Israel. Israel is called to be "a kingdom of priests" (Exod 19:6), ministering to the nations. Israel is to be a "blessing for all families of the earth." The prophets entertain the hope of a pilgrimage of the nations to Zion (Isa 2:1–5; Mic 4:1–4), when "the LORD will be king over the whole earth; on that day, the LORD will be the only one, and the LORD's name the only one" (Zech 14:9).

---

78. John H. Sailhamer, *The Pentateuch as Narrative: A Biblical-Theological Commentary* (Grand Rapids: Zondervan, 1992) 200.

79. Ibid., 202.

Tamar and Judah (Genesis 38) in Early Jewish and Christian Traditions

JOHN R. BARKER, OFM

My first Bible course at Catholic Theological Union, Introduction to the Old Testament, was taught by Leslie Hoppe, OFM, and it was in this course that I discovered that the Old Testament was much richer and more rewarding spiritually and intellectually than I had ever imagined. Subsequent courses with Leslie and other members of the CTU faculty confirmed and deepened this insight and, consequently, my love for Sacred Scripture. Years later I had the great fortune to join the faculty of CTU and to have my former professor as my colleague. And he has been an excellent colleague: supportive, at times corrective, insightful, and always able to approach the absurd aspects of academic and institutional life with a warm humor. Over many years Leslie has offered generous service to CTU, the biblical guild, the Church, and our Franciscan Order. I am honored to offer this essay in gratitude to my brother and colleague on the occasion of his retirement, although I have a feeling he will remain almost as busy in the future as he has been all these years.

The story of Tamar and Judah in Genesis 38 presented interpretive challenges for ancient exegetes, both Jewish and Christian, confronted with the two main characters' morally problematic behavior. Judah's giving custom to what he believed to be a prostitute was no less troubling than Tamar's briefly playing the prostitute to deceive her father-in-law and conceive by him.[1] Aside from the fact that both Tamar and Judah

---

1. Scripture as well as the later Jewish and Christian ethical traditions look down on or condemn outright these behaviors. Being or frequenting a prostitute was unacceptable according to Lev 19:29; Deut 23:18; Prov 23:27; Sir 19:2. It must be said, though, that some of these texts may not condemn prostitution per se. Leviticus 19:29

were revered ancestors, the need to account satisfactorily for their behavior was made all the more urgent by the fact that the ultimate outcome of their liaison was King David and, later, the royal Messiah.[2] Yet it was precisely through this potentially troublesome association of the episode with David and the Messiah that the story would become transformed in both traditions from an embarrassing tale into one that played a crucial role in the salvific purposes of the God of Israel. In the process, the actions of Judah and Tamar would take on new color, and their disturbing behavior would be understood by many readers as meritorious rather than disgraceful.

■ I. Jewish Tradition

Some of the earliest attempts to grapple with the story of Tamar and Judah are found in retellings of Genesis 38 in *Jubilees* (41:1–24) and the *Testament of Judah* (10:1–12:17), both of which focus primarily on Judah. As neither of these sources deviates significantly from the biblical account, they will not be explored in detail here. I note only that these accounts contain a few additional details intended to exonerate both Judah and Tamar. In the case of the latter, the alterations have the added effect of making Tamar a completely passive character in a story that revolves entirely around her. The result is a portrait of a victim of circumstances beyond her control and therefore a much weaker character than in the biblical account. Although God figures in the accounts in a way not found in the biblical text, it is only to forgive Judah for his transgressions or to assure Judah that Tamar is telling the truth. There is no hint of any higher or larger purposes to which the event contributes.

---

addresses the particular situation of a father consigning his daughter to prostitution, and Deut 23:18 may have to do with a cultic functionary. Articulating biblical attitudes toward prostitution is also complicated by such texts as Joshua 2 and 1 Kgs 3:16–28, which do not betray a disapproval of prostitution. I am indebted to Jon D. Levenson for pointing out to me that, generally speaking, "the later you get (e.g., Sira), the greater the calumny the institution has relative to its status in hoary antiquity" (private communication).

2. Ruth 4:18–22; 1 Chr 2:3–15; Matt 1:3; Luke 3:33. Although the Christian tradition associated Jesus's messianic status with his Davidic lineage (particularly in Matthew's Gospel: 9:27; 12:23; 15:22; 21:15), Jewish tradition supported several different understandings of the Messiah(s), only some of which had anything to do with the House of David. See Jacob Neusner, William Scott Green, and Ernest Frerichs, eds., *Judaisms and Their Messiahs at the Turn of the Christian Era* (Cambridge: Cambridge University Press, 1987).

The targumim take a different approach. *Targum Neofiti* and *Targum Pseudo-Jonathan* present essentially the same story, which itself is very close to the biblical account, with some minor additions here and there, and a large addition at v. 25.[3] After Tamar's pregnancy is discovered, she searches for the three pledges given by Judah, praying for help and promising to raise up for God three holy men who will sanctify the divine name by going down into the furnace in the valley of Dura, namely, Hananiah, Azariah, and Mishael of the Book of Daniel (3:19–23). In response, God sends the angel Michael to open Tamar's eyes to find the pledges. After she presents them to the judges and explains their relevance, Judah stands up and announces that it is better for him to suffer punishment or shame in this world than in the next and declares that Tamar is "innocent." Immediately, a *bat qol* affirms that both of them are just, for the entire matter has come about "from before the LORD" (*Tg. Neof.* Gen 38:25; *Tg. Ps.-J.* Gen 38:25). The story then resumes according to the biblical account.

Rather than simply being excused for their behavior, Judah and Tamar are lauded. Judah's willingness to endure disgrace and even death rather than face his righteous ancestors and the Almighty as a guilty man makes him a model of the God-fearing Israelite. Tamar is portrayed not as a passive observer of her own life but, in accordance with the biblical text, as a woman who takes steps to rectify her situation. These steps are sanctioned by God, whose declaration of the innocence of both Judah and Tamar is accompanied by the surprising disclosure that the entire situation was divinely orchestrated: "Both of them are just; this matter has come from before the LORD" (*Tg. Neof.* Gen 38:25).[4]

This revelation has two immediate effects. The first is that a story that has heretofore possessed no real sense of divine purpose or providence is now strongly marked by it, altering significantly the terms by which readers may evaluate the actions of Judah and Tamar. Tamar's "playing the harlot," deceiving Judah and conceiving by him, and Judah's frequenting a prostitute have all been by the hand of God, or at least according to God's will, and are therefore, we are given to understand, justified.[5]

Later rabbinic literature, on the whole, also presents Judah and Tamar in a positive light and not only accepts the targumic notion that the entire affair was orchestrated by God but also deepens it. Whereas the

---

3. This insertion is lacking in *Targum Onqelos*.
4. *Tg. Ps.-J.* Gen 38:26 has merely, "The matter has come from before me."
5. As far as I can tell, neither the Jewish nor the Christian tradition seems to have questioned God's judgment in carrying out his purposes by means of an illicit sexual liaison.

targumim give no hint of God's motives, simply stating that the whole matter came "from before the LORD," the rabbis make explicit what may be implicit in the targumim by linking the affair with the Messiah, for whose sake Tamar conceives children by Judah. It is a straightforward interpretive move: Scripture states that David will be the descendant of Tamar and Judah, and later messianic traditions will expect a royal Messiah from this line (Ruth 4:18–22; 1 Chr 2:3–15). Thus, Tamar and Judah are the ancestors of the Messiah, and this fact is then read back into various features of the biblical story. For example, the three pledges given by Judah to Tamar are associated with a royal Messiah: the signet ring signifies dominion (Jer 22:24); the cord refers to the Sanhedrin (Num 15:38); and the staff refers to the royal Messiah himself (Ps 110:2) (*Gen. Rab.* 85:9).

More importantly, the behavior of Tamar and Judah is explicitly interpreted in light of the messianic outcome. Judah's role as the predestined progenitor of the Messiah is highlighted in *Aggadat Bereshit*, where God is disconcerted by Judah's marital selection: "When he took her, the Holy One said: The Messiah is destined to arise from Judah, and now he went and took a Canaanite wife? What will I do? I will arrange matters and I will let his son marry Tamar" (*Ag. Ber.* 64C).[6] Once the wife is dead, God reasons, Judah can impregnate the more suitable Tamar, and the line of the Messiah will be preserved. This, of course, requires Judah to have sex with his daughter-in-law, something he would presumably never consider. *Genesis Rabbah* suggests that when Judah saw Tamar on the side of the road, because he thought her a prostitute he intended to pass her by but instead was persuaded by an angel of lust sent by God to turn aside: "The angel said, 'Where are you going? From whence will kings arise, and from whence will redeemers arise?' He went over to her at the roadside against his will, not for his own desire at all" (*Gen. Rab.* 85:8).[7] In both traditions, Judah and his family are maneuvered by God to bring about the desired outcome. Judah's part in this divine plan is, it seems, entirely unwitting, but it exonerates him of wrongdoing nonetheless.

Tamar receives rabbinic praise, although there is no specific indication that her deception and subsequent pregnancy in any way contribute to a divine plan. She is praised for her modesty, and in fact this becomes a virtue that is ascribed to her more than anything else. While the biblical

---

6. Translation from *Aggadat Bereshit* (trans. Lieve M. Tuegels; Jewish and Christian Perspectives 4; Leiden: Brill, 2001) 194.

7. Translation from *Genesis Rabbah* (trans. Jacob Neusner; 3 vols.; BJS 106; Atlanta: Scholars Press, 1985) 3:212.

text says that Judah failed to recognize Tamar "because she had veiled her face" (Gen 38:16), the rabbis do not consider this a reference to her covering her face at that time, but rather to her habit of veiling her face in Judah's house. Such was her modesty that Judah never knew what she looked like (and so could not recognize her on the road), and it is this same modesty that gains her such revered descendants, for it is asserted that the fact that every bride who is modest in her father-in-law's house will be rewarded with kings and prophets as her descendants is proven by Tamar (*b. Meg.* 10b; *b. Soṭah* 10a).

This is the Jewish tradition concerning Judah and Tamar, as it is found in the early narratives and in the rabbinic literature. Overall, it is a positive tradition, which eventually seeks to understand the behavior of Judah and Tamar in light of the divine purposes, an interpretive move that we find also in the early Christian reflections on Genesis 38.

■ II. Christian Tradition

The story of Tamar and Judah is largely absent from the extant writings of the early church. Its apparent lack of theological import may account for this to some degree, although the primary reason for its neglect may be the moral difficulties the story presents. Like the Jewish tradition, the early church considered fornication to be an extremely serious sin, and as long as Tamar and Judah were understood to be engaging in it, the tale presented grave difficulties, particularly as there did not seem to be much point to it.[8]

Yet there were at least two reasons the early church could not ignore the story altogether. The first was its very presence in the Old Testament, which must be in accord with the divine will. If God had placed Genesis 38 in the Bible, it must have been for a good reason. The church was also impelled to comment on Tamar, in particular, because of her noteworthy appearance in Matthew's genealogy of Jesus: Ἰούδας δὲ ἐγέννησεν τὸν Φάρες

---

8. In the early church, impurity (i.e., adultery and fornication), idolatry, and murder were the three capital offenses. The biblical basis for this was Acts 15:20, 28–29, in which the apostles agree that abstention from these three is required for converts. Citing this passage, Tertullian (*Pud.* 12) as well as Pacian, bishop of Barcelona (*Paraenesis ad poenitentiam*), argued that these three sins were singled out by the Holy Spirit as being particularly grave (Oscar D. Watkins, *A History of Penance: Being a Study of the Authorities* [2 vols.; New York: Longmans, Green, 1920] 2:13–14).

καὶ τὸν Ζάρα ἐκ τῆς Θάμαρ (Matt 1:3).⁹ Indeed, the Gospel of Matthew might be considered the earliest Christian commentary on the actions of Tamar and Judah. It is difficult to know, however, what theological point the evangelist was trying to make by including Tamar (along with Rahab, Ruth, and "the wife of Uriah") in Jesus's genealogy.¹⁰ This question piqued the interest of early exegetes, as we will see, and it is while considering Tamar's presence in the genealogy that the writers offered commentary on Genesis 38. That Matt 1:3 should be explained in light of Genesis 38 is logical: the verse is referring directly to the story. That Genesis 38 would also be understood in light of Matt 1:3 is also logical, given the christological thrust of much patristic exegesis. This hermeneutical stance of reading the earlier text in light of later events mirrors that of the Jewish tradition's reading of David and the royal Messiah back into the actions of Judah and Tamar.

Patristic comments about Genesis 38 or Matt 1:3 tend to fall into two categories. The first is a typological reading of the two sons, Perez and Zerah, uniformly seen to represent in some way Israel and the church; these readings will not be examined here. The second is a specifically

---

9. Judah and Perez also appear in Luke's genealogy (3:33), but in such a thoroughly conventional manner that their presence does not appear to have occasioned any comment on Genesis 38.

10. Tryggve Kronholm suggests that the evangelist's decision to include Tamar (and the other women) in the genealogy was based on, suggested by, or allowed by current Jewish messianic interpretations of Genesis 38 ("Holy Adultery: The Interpretation of the Story of Judah and Tamar [Gen 38] in the Genuine Hymns of Ephraem Syrus [ca. 306–373]," *Orientalia Suecana* 40 [1991] 149–63). Contemporary feminist biblical scholars offer the following interpretations. Elaine M. Wainwright notes, "These women are not the traditional matriarchs of Israel, mothers of the famous sons; they are women who are anomalous or dangerous in relation to the traditional patriarchal family model where women are simply the vehicles for the bearing of significant sons and thus rendered invisible historically and narratively. Perhaps women were the makers as well as shapers of this alternative tradition, constructing a female genealogy for Mary in whom Israel's God was doing a new thing that could not be contained within the traditional cultural constructs" ("Tradition Makers/Tradition Shapers: Women of the Matthean Tradition," *Word & World* 18 [1998] 380–88). Amy-Jill Levine sees that each of the women is removed from traditional domestic arrangements and "each—from a relatively powerless position—seeks justice not through violence but through cleverness" ("Matthew," in *Women's Bible Commentary* [ed. Carol A. Newsom, Sharon H. Ringe, and Jacqueline E. Lapsley; 3rd ed.; Louisville: Westminster John Knox, 2012] 465–77, here 467). Beverly Roberts Gaventa observes that there is no single category that all four fit. Each threatens the status quo in some way and is threatened. Each is delivered and the line is preserved (*Mary: Glimpses of the Mother of Jesus* [Studies on Personalities of the New Testament; Columbia: University of South Carolina Press, 1995]).

moral assessment of the actions of Tamar and, to a much lesser extent, Judah.[11] Some of these assessments are very brief, being embedded in references to Tamar as part of larger arguments. For example, Tamar served for some as an object lesson in female comportment. Cyprian of Carthage (*Test.* 30) and Tertullian (*Cult. fem.* 2.2.12) warned their readers that Judah took Tamar for a prostitute because she had adorned herself, which was one very good reason why Christian women ought not to wear a lot of jewelry and cosmetics. Augustine, noting that Tamar deceived Judah not out of lust but out of a desire to bear a child, argued that, despite this, her deception should not be taken as scriptural permission to lie (*C. mend.* 14.30).

A more direct assessment of the moral character of Tamar is found in comments made on her presence in Matthew's genealogy. Some argued that she, along with Ruth, Rahab, and Bathsheba, represent sinful women whose presence in Christ's genealogy is to show that when he came into the world he took on our sinful flesh in order to redeem it.[12] Such a negative assessment of Tamar was not universally accepted, however, and those few commentators who devoted more than a line or two to her story usually viewed her more sympathetically.[13]

Eusebius of Caesarea (260–341)

In question 7 of his *Quaestiones evangelicae ad Stephanum*, Eusebius of Caesarea is asked by his interlocutor why Tamar was included in Matthew's genealogy instead of another woman more notable for her good actions. Eusebius protests that, although some consider Tamar to have been a woman of ill repute, she was in fact a righteous woman, as evidenced by

---

11. Unlike Jewish tradition, the early church tended to focus almost exclusively on Tamar. It is difficult to know exactly how to account for this, but it is highly probable that Tamar's unusual presence in the Matthean genealogy just naturally led some commentators to focus on her actions rather than on Judah's. One also suspects that the high position accorded to the Virgin Mary may also have inclined the Fathers to examine with particular care the actions of other women in "salvation history."

12. Origen, *Hom. Luc.* 27; Jerome, *Comm. Matt.* 1:15–20; Severus of Antioch, *Hom. cath.* 94.

13. Modern commentators on Matthew's genealogy have tended to see the inclusion of the four women as pointing toward or foreshadowing Mary, in which case identifying them as "sinful women" would not cohere with the evangelist's intentions. Daniel J. Harrington captures the general consensus among such commentators when he states, "It seems best to leave the idea expressed by the inclusion of the four women at the level of 'irregularity' or 'departure from the ordinary.' In their own distinctive ways they prepare for and foreshadow the irregular birth of Jesus" (*The Gospel of Matthew* [SacPag 1; Collegeville, MN: Liturgical Press, 1991] 32).

Judah's confession. Tamar was a woman of noble intention, who pursued Judah only for the sake of perpetuating the family (7.1; *PG* 22:905).

Tamar's virtue is exhibited also in how she chose to carry out her plan to conceive by Judah. Before doing anything, she prayed to be found worthy of the people "beloved by God," she being of a different people, and she waited until Judah's wife died rather than sleep with him while he was still married (Eusebius of Caesarea, *Quaest. evang. ad Steph.* 7.2; *PG* 22:908). The proof that she acted in accord with God's designs is the birth of the two children, whose symbolic significance demonstrates that everything happened according to God's mysterious designs (ibid.). For Eusebius, then, Tamar is a model of virtue and discretion, but what ultimately makes her behavior acceptable is the divine design behind it. Eusebius does not read this design back into the story by introducing nontextual details but rather discerns it by its outcome, not of the Messiah but of the symbolic twins. Nevertheless, this interpretation of the story as following divine purposes mirrors that of the Jewish tradition.

Ambrose of Milan (340–397)

Ambrose of Milan also insists that Tamar was a good woman who acted to secure children, the lack of which was thought shameful in her time and place (*Exp. Luc.* 3.17–18; *PL* 15:1595–96).[14] He goes on to present a sympathetic portrait of a woman cheated by her father-in-law, who nevertheless waited until his wife was dead to deceive him (as he had deceived her) to obtain the fruit promised her. He also offers an evaluation of Judah (who is typically ignored by Christian writers) by comparing him with Tamar. The result is not in Judah's favor, however, as he comes across as something of a cad who not only reneged on his duty to have his youngest son, Shelah, marry Tamar, but who, the moment his wife was dead, went in pursuit of a prostitute (3.18; *PL* 15:1596).[15] Tamar, on the other hand, was the very model of chaste restraint.

What is noteworthy about the approach Ambrose takes, and what distinguishes it most from Eusebius's presentation (as well as from most of the Jewish traditions), is that it is based *entirely* on a literal reading of the Genesis text, without any reference to the fact that Tamar is the ancestor of Christ, or to any higher purpose on the part of Tamar or of God that might excuse her behavior. For Ambrose, a providential reading

---

14. This was, Ambrose notes, before the coming of Christ, when the virtues of virginity and celibacy were acknowledged and embraced.

15. Ambrose does, however, excuse him in the end, given the ultimate outcome of his lustful behavior, that is, the Messiah (*Exp. Luc.* 3.19; *PL* 15:1596–97).

of the text is not necessary to exonerate Tamar. He takes it for granted that she was acting according to the values of her culture, and this is enough, as far as he is concerned, to excuse her. Given that his own culture considered fornication a grave sin, and whose frank anti-Judaism allowed for an easy dismissal of ancient Israel's benighted mores, such a sympathetic recognition by Ambrose of the societal and personal pressures that led Tamar to sleep with her father-in-law is remarkable.

Ephrem the Syrian (ca. 307–373)

Ephrem of Syria produced a large and complex body of exegetical works of various genres.[16] His hymns, in particular, have played an important role in Syriac Christianity, having been incorporated early into the liturgical tradition.[17] Tamar appears in four of these hymns, three on the Nativity and one on virginity, all of them presenting her positively. As might be expected, the Nativity hymns focus on her role as ancestor of Christ, and so her actions in Genesis are understood from that perspective. In the hymn on virginity, she is presented as a type of the Samaritan woman at the well in John 4 and is also viewed through a messianic lens (*Hymn. virg.* 22.19–21).[18]

It is well established that Ephrem drew heavily on Jewish tradition in his exegesis.[19] His treatment of Tamar reflects this particularly

---

16. Lucas Van Rompay, "The Christian Syriac Tradition of Interpretation," in *Hebrew Bible / Old Testament: The History of Its Interpretation*, vol. 1, *From the Beginnings to the Middle Ages (until 1300)*, pt. 1, *Antiquity* (ed. Magne Sæbø; Göttingen: Vandenhoeck & Ruprecht, 1996) 622–23.

17. Kathleen McVey, Introduction to *Ephrem the Syrian: Hymns* (Classics of Western Spirituality; Mahwah, NJ: Paulist, 1989) 3–4.

18. All references to, and citations of, Ephrem's hymns are from Ephrem the Syrian, *Hymns* (trans. McVey; see preceding note). Critical editions of the hymns in the original Syriac can be found in Ephrem the Syrian, *Hymni de nativitate* (ed. Edmund Beck; 2 vols.; CSCO 186–87; Scriptores Syri 82–83; Louvain: Secrétariat du CSCO, 1959); and *Das heiligen Ephraem des Syrers Hymnen de Virginitate* (ed. Edmund Beck; 2 vols.; CSCO 223–24; Scriptores Syri 94–95; Louvain: Secrétariat du CSCO, 1962).

19. See, e.g., Nicolas Séd, "Les hymnes sur le paradis de Saint Éphrem et les traditions juives," *Le Muséon* 81 (1968) 455–501; Sten Hidal, *Interpretatio syriaca: Die Kommentare des heiligen Ephräm des Syrers zu Genesis und Exodus mit besonderer Berücksichtigung ihrer auslegungsgeschichtlichen Stellung* (ConBOT 6; Lund: Gleerup, 1974); Antoine Guillaumont, "Un midrash d'Exode 4,24–26 dans Aphraate et Éphrem de Nisibe," in *A Tribute to Arthur Vööbus: Studies in Early Christian Literature and Its Environment, Primarily in the Syrian East* (ed. Robert H. Fischer; Chicago: Lutheran School of Theology at Chicago, 1977), 89–95; Sebastian Brock, "Jewish Traditions in Syriac Sources," *JJS* 30 (1979) 212–32; Paul Feghali, "Influence des targums sur la pensée exégétique d'Éphrem?," in *IV Symposium Syriacum 1984: Literary Genres in*

well.[20] Ephrem takes up the rabbinic notion that God orchestrated the encounter between Judah and Tamar to produce the Messiah, but he develops it by presenting Tamar as a knowing, active participant in God's plan. In the first hymn on the Nativity, Ephrem proclaims, "Since the King was hidden in Judah, Tamar stole him from his loins; today shone forth the splendor of the beauty whose hidden form she loved" (*Hymn. nat.* 1.12). In the manner of a prophet, Tamar has seen that the Messiah is meant to come from Judah and acts accordingly. Without Tamar's action, the king who lay hidden would have remained unborn, and so her "theft" is at the service of God's purposes for the world.[21] Ephrem acknowledges that this was a costly gambit on her part and for that reason, in the fifteenth hymn on the Nativity, praises her courage. Here Mary reflects on the fact that she is "slandered and oppressed" on account of her pregnancy, but she takes heart because she knows that God will vindicate her: "For if Tamar was acquitted by Judah, how much more will I be acquitted by You!" (*Hymn. nat.* 15.7, 8).

The most extensive treatment of Tamar is in the ninth hymn on the Nativity, which devotes seven of its sixteen stanzas to her. The focus of the hymn is on the mediators of the Messiah, primarily Tamar and Ruth, who are again seen to have acted to bring forth the Christ. Ephrem presents Tamar ardently pursuing a single goal:

> Tamar went out and in darkness
> she stole the light, and by filth
> she stole chastity, and by nakedness
> she entered furtively on You, the Honorable One,
> Who produces chaste [people] from the licentious.
> . . . . . .
> For the adultery of Tamar was chaste
> because of You. For You she thirsted,
> O Pure Fountain. Judah cheated her
> of drinking You. A thirsty fount

Syriac Literature, Groningen-Oosterhesselen 10–12 September (ed. H. J. W. Drijvers et al.; OrChrAn 229; Rome: Pontficium Institutum Studiorum Orientalium, 1987) 71–82.

20. Kronholm, "Holy Adultery," 149–63; Phil J. Botha, "Ephrem the Syrian's Treatment of Tamar in Comparison to that in Jewish Sources," *Acta Patristica et Byzantina* 6 (1995) 15–26; idem, "Tamar, Rahab, Ruth, and Mary—The Bold Women in Ephrem the Syrian's *De Nativitate 9*," *Acta Patristica et Byzantina* 17 (2006) 1–21.

21. In the next verse, he will say the same thing of Ruth. This same motif appears in *Hymn. virg.* 22.20, although here she is said to have stolen the "symbol" of the king who would arise from Judah. This most likely refers to the pledges and, if so, may reflect familiarity with the rabbinic association of the three pledges with the royal Messiah, discussed above.

stole Your drink from its source.
She was a widow for Your sake.
She desired You, pursued You, and even
became a harlot for Your sake.
For You she longed, You she kept [in memory], and she became
a chaste woman. She loved You. (*Hymn. nat.* 9.8, 10–11)

Once again, she is courageous in the face of possible death, refusing to be deflected from her purpose even by the devil himself:

Satan saw Him and was afraid and ran
as if to hinder [her]; He reminded [her] of judgment,
but she feared not, of stoning and the sword
but she was not afraid. The teacher of adultery
was hindering adultery to hinder You. (*Hymn. nat.* 9.9)[22]

The same image of Tamar as an active agent of a divine purpose is found in Ephrem's commentary on Genesis. A particular feature of this commentary, unusual and perhaps even unique among ancient Christian commentaries, is Ephrem's construction of speeches and para-narratives for biblical personalities, which has the effect of creating a biblical commentary that often resembles rabbinic haggadah.[23] In Ephrem's hands, Tamar manifests a deep sense of faith in the divine purpose and her part in it.

Ephrem begins by telling the biblical story, adding only that Judah believes that his first two sons have died because of Tamar's sins (*Comm. Gen.* 34.1).[24] When she learns that Shelah has been denied her, Tamar wonders how she might "make the Hebrews realize that it is not marriage for which I am hungering, but rather that I am yearning for the blessing that is hidden within them?" (34.2).[25] Having relations with Shelah might still be possible, but this is not what she wants, for she would not be able to make her "faith victorious" through Shelah. She knows that she ought

---

22. Of course, the biblical text speaks of burning, not of the sword or stoning.

23. Jeffrey Wickes, "Ephrem's Interpretation of Genesis," *SVTQ* 52 (2008) 45–65, here 48; Edward G. Mathews Jr. and J. P. Amar, introduction to St. Ephrem the Syrian, *Selected Prose Works* (ed. Kathleen McVey; trans. Edward G. Mathews and Joseph P. Amar; FC 91; Washington, DC: Catholic University of America Press, 1994) 63.

24. All references to, and citations of, Ephrem's Genesis commentary are based on Ephrem the Syrian, *Commentary on Genesis* in St. Ephrem the Syrian, *Selected Prose Works* (ed. McVey; trans. Mathews and Amar; see preceding note) 67–213. The critical edition of the commentary in the original Syriac can be found in Ephrem the Syrian, *In Genesim et in Exodum commentarii* (ed. R.-M. Tonneau; CSCO 152; Scriptores Syri 71; Louvain: L. Durbecq, 1955).

25. Ephrem does not specify what he means by this, but familiarity with his hymns allows us to understand that he is referring to Christ.

to conceive by Judah, not only obtaining a child by him but also making it clear to everyone that it is the child, not the man, that she desires (ibid.).

Before carrying out her plan, Tamar asks God for a sign that what she intends to do is pleasing, for God knows quite well that it is for "what is hidden in the Hebrews that I thirst," and not for anything else (34.3). She then suggests two signs: the first, that God will make her unrecognizable to Judah, and the second, that Judah will proposition her. If both of these things happen, Tamar will know that it is acceptable to God that "the treasure, which is hidden in the circumcised, may be transmitted even through the daughter of the uncircumcised" (ibid.).

While she is still making her prayer, Judah appears and, "contrary to his usual habit," he approaches her. Ephrem's paraphrase then continues very much according to the biblical account, with only a few additions, such as Judah's response to the three pledges by first marveling at Tamar's faith and only then announcing that she is more righteous than he, not only because he withheld his son from her but also because she was innocent of killing his first two sons through her sins. It is Tamar's faith that is the focus of Ephrem's attention and admiration more than anything else.

In both his hymns and his commentary, Ephrem presents a remarkably positive image of Tamar. He understands her behavior entirely from the perspective of its ultimate outcome, the Incarnation, and this alone is quite enough to justify it. As Phil Botha notes, the element of divine providence is much stronger in the rabbinic tradition than in Ephrem,[26] but the element of human agency is much stronger in Ephrem than in the rabbinic tradition. While Tamar clearly understands herself to be working in accordance with a divine plan (*she* must extract what lies hidden, presumably by God, in the Hebrews), nowhere is there any indication that God has actually asked her to do anything. On the contrary, in the commentary it is Tamar who comes to God with her plan, and it is God who acts according to *her* designs. The overall characterization of Tamar is thus consonant with the biblical account, which also presents us with a woman who knows her own mind, and yet at the same time this characterization is much more exalted. In Ephrem's version, Tamar is a woman of faith who acts as a "proactive" participant in God's redemptive plan. Judah, for his part, serves only as a relatively passive donor of the required genetic material.[27]

---

26. Botha, "Ephrem the Syrian's Treatment of Tamar," 21.

27. It is here that another parallel with Mary, perhaps not even consciously intended by Ephrem, comes into focus: Mary, too, actively participated with God in

John Chrysostom (ca. 347–407)

The sixty-seven extant exegetical homilies that John Chrysostom wrote on Genesis constitute a complete commentary on the book. As the homilies follow the order of the biblical book, his commentary on Genesis 38 is the first part of a larger homily on the Joseph story. Noting that this chapter interrupts that story, Chrysostom does not wish to pass the chapter over, but rather wants to explain it as best he can before resuming the main tale. His exposition follows the biblical account very closely, with few additions or imaginative flourishes. He offers some insight into Tamar's mind, however, by suggesting that her desire to have a child by Judah was prompted by a wish to avoid appearing "nameless" (ἀνώνυμος),[28] but, as a matter of fact, her purely human motivation was actually in the service of a divine design (οἰκονομία) (*Hom. Gen.* 62.1; *PG* 54:533). Chrysostom goes on to describe Tamar's deceit, stopping at the end to urge his audience not to condemn Tamar (or Judah), for neither did anything blameworthy: "For as I have already said, she was serving the divine plan [οἰκονομίᾳ ὑπηρετεῖτε]." He explains briefly that he is referring to the fact that Christ will trace his lineage from the fruit of this liaison (ibid).

Chrysostom then paraphrases the rest of the story until he arrives at Judah's confession. At this point, he decides to explain in some detail what Judah might mean by his statement that Tamar is more righteous than he. It means, of course, that he failed to do the right thing and give his son Shelah to her. But Chrysostom also suggests a deeper meaning to the words. Judah acted out of fear for his son Shelah, supposing that Tamar was responsible for the deaths of Er and Onan. Judah had not only refused Tamar children by his son, but he had also sullied her reputation. Perhaps, Chrysostom suggests, Judah had intercourse with his daughter-in-law, entirely unaware that he was doing so, only to learn through what ensued that it was because of his sons' wickedness, and not Tamar's, that they had died. Chrysostom's suggestion that this happened "in order that he might know" (ἵνα γνῷ) that Tamar was not responsible for their deaths, means that this vindication was also part of the divine plan (62.2; *PG* 54.534). Not only was it God's purpose to provide the Christ, but it was also God's purpose to repair Tamar's reputation. Chrysostom concludes

---

order to bring about a birth, with the role of Joseph (like that of Judah) being extremely minimal, except genealogically.

28. This is an interesting twist. Whereas the levirate custom and thus the biblical text are concerned that the dead husband not be "nameless," as it were, Chrysostom attributes the potential namelessness to Tamar.

with the suggestion that, by allowing him to explain the story according to its deeper meaning, his audience has gained valuable insight into and appreciation for a story that might otherwise have been dismissed as unworthy of consideration (62.2; PG 54:535).

Given the approach Chrysostom takes in his Genesis homily, it is interesting to note that in a homily on Matthew, he falls back on the standard trope that Tamar's presence there signifies that Christ was willing to take on human evils. Why, he asks, would the evangelist want his readers to recall such a sordid tale of "unlawful intercourse" (παράνομον μίξιν)? If one were telling the family history of any other man, he answers, one would naturally pass over such things in silence. But because we are speaking of the Incarnate God, we must not only refer to such things, but glory in them, for they proclaim God's mercy and power. It was to take away our disgraces, rather than to avoid them, that Christ came. Just as his death was ignominious, so was his birth, in which he accepted the evils of his ancestors as part of his heritage (*Hom. Matt.* 3.2; PG 57.33). God condescended, he says, to become espoused to a nature that played the harlot (πορνείαν) to teach us that Christ came to take away our ills (3.4; PG 57.35).

Unlike in the Genesis homily, nowhere in this homily does Chrysostom make any attempt to interpret the actions of Tamar and Judah from the perspective of providence, or to offer a sympathetic reading of the story. On the contrary, he goes out of his way to play up the sinfulness of the tale in order to bring out his key theological point. Yet the purpose is not to denigrate either Tamar or Judah but rather to magnify God, albeit at the expense of the reputations of the pair. His listeners here are not exhorted to come to a better understanding of Tamar and Judah. Rather, they are urged to recognize that in these characters Christ was willing to assume even the basest aspects of human nature in order to redeem it. It does not serve Chrysostom's purposes to rehabilitate Tamar and Judah in this homily in the way that it does in the Genesis homily. Such is the nature of preaching, that the same story can offer different, perhaps even contradictory, lessons depending on the circumstances and the theme of that day's homily.

■ III. Conclusion

The focus of this study has been on the portrayal of Judah and Tamar, both of whom found favor in the Jewish and Christian exegetical traditions. After what might in retrospect be considered something of a false start in *Jubilees* and the *Testament of Judah*, in which mere excuses were made for both of these figures, the potentially ignominious reputations of Judah and Tamar were eventually redeemed through association of their behavior with the redemptive purposes of God. By discerning divine providence at work in what at first glance is a purely human story, the traditions transformed the character and significance of their actions, and thus the significance of their characters. When God is seen to be at work, normal sexual mores become relativized and reconsidered, and the traditions' evaluation of the human protagonists must follow suit.

At the same time, both traditions were able to appreciate at least the actions of Tamar from a purely human perspective, understanding them to be motivated by the social situation in which she found herself. Thus, whether as a woman of virtue or a woman of faith, Tamar was exonerated of any wrongdoing and even vindicated by both Jews and Christians. Judah's fate was somewhat less uniform. In the rabbinic tradition, he is for the most part acquitted. The Christian tradition pays scant attention to him, and, when it does, it tends either to exculpate him along with Tamar (on her coattails, as it were) or to contrast him to her, in which case he does not come across particularly well.

The Jewish and Christian interpretations of Genesis 38 are instructive, for they demonstrate the ability of each tradition to draw on its scriptural, hermeneutical, and theological resources to transform a story that is at best meaningless or, at worst, scandalous, into an edifying and theologically significant tale. The process by which this was done is elegant in its religious logic: if the result of such apparently illicit behavior was (or will be) the Messiah, then God must have had a hand in it, and if that is the case, then the behavior must be understood accordingly. As far as early Jewish and Christian traditions are concerned, Tamar and Judah, far from needing excuses, deserve praise for the part they played in the mysterious workings of divine providence.

Tamar, Delilah, and a Nameless Timnite: Women as (De)constructions of Social Landscape

MAHRI LEONARD-FLECKMAN
College of the Holy Cross
Worchester, Massachusetts

I write this article with gratitude for Leslie Hoppe, for his mentorship and wisdom, his gentleness and generosity. In the poignant opening to his presidential address at the Catholic Biblical Association's Annual Meeting in 2016, Leslie recalled the names of his teachers and invited a moment of silence. It is true that we all stand on the shoulders of those who precede us. One of the many sets of shoulders that I stand on are Leslie's, and I count him among the cloud of witnesses that has trained and cultivated me into this community that we call biblical scholarship, and into Catholic biblical scholarship more particularly. Memory is a fraught term, but I am certain that I not only will remember Leslie, but will also "remember" him to others in the future. Given Leslie's interests in geography, history, and Deuteronomistic History, and his openness to new methodologies and their integration, I dedicate this article to him.

Located between the highlands of Judah and what we call Philistia on the coast, Israel's Shephelah is a complicated area to understand in terms of its identities throughout the Iron Age. Arguably, and from the outsider perspective, it was an entangled social landscape, meaning that social groups intermingled and people defied the available social and political categories that come to us through text (including "Philistine," "Canaanite," "Israelite," and "Judahite").[1] The region has largely become the domain

---

1. "Landscape" refers to place transformed by, and incorporated into, a broader world of human action and activity. See Adam T. Smith, *The Political Landscape:*

of archaeologists, who seem to have the most secure evidence for the period. Yet there is space for renewed textual evaluations of the region in dialogue with archaeology, evaluations that take seriously literary representations of the social landscape and their value for further contextualization of the region. Such evaluations recognize the power of these representations and their authors to construct or "language" particular ideas of ancient society over time as part of a broader social discourse,[2] and use them to probe historical questions. In the case of the Shephelah and its seeming entanglement from the archaeological perspective, what historical value might be found in the literary sources, specifically by exploring how scribes represented and thereby sought to remember people in this region?

With this question in mind, I will examine the Bible's portrayals of three women in the Shephelah: Delilah from the Wadi (נחל) Sorek in Judges 16, an unnamed woman from around Timnah in Judges 14–15, and Tamar on the road to Timnah in Genesis 38 (which is perhaps the Shephelah Timnah, though perhaps not). I propose that these women serve as the central representations of indefinable social space. Not subjects but objects, they become geographical markers and the place of

---

Constellations of Authority in Early Complex Polities (Berkeley: University of California Press, 2003) 10–11. "Identity," broadly defined, is that which is observable in the context of the social and political landscape (e.g., one's family or kinship group, tribe, relationship to a larger political group, one's gods, etc.). For a broader discussion of the terms "identity" and social or cultural identity, see Richard Jenkins, *Social Identity* (3rd ed; London: Routledge, 2008) 16–18. On the idea of "entanglement," see Louise A. Hitchcock and Aren M. Maeir, "Beyond Creolization and Hybridity: Entangled and Transcultural Identities in Philistia," in *Archaeology and Cultural Mixture* (ed. W. Paul van Pelt; *Archaeological Review from Cambridge* 28.1 [April 2013]; Cambridge: Cambridge University Press, 2013) 51–74.

2. The verb "to language" draws from the field of second-language acquisition; it refers to the dialogical process between speaker and listener through which language externalizes or articulates the inner world while internalizing or shaping ideas and perceptions, and vice versa. In the case of texts, this process takes place between scribes and the scribal process, on the one hand, and readers or interpreters on the other, to construct or "language" particular representations of ancient society through text. See Merrill Swain, "Languaging, Agency and Collaboration in Advanced Second Language Proficiency," in *Advanced Language Learning: The Contribution of Halliday and Vygotsky* (ed. Heidi Byrnes; London: Continuum, 2006) 95–108; Merrill Swain et al., "Languaging: University Students Learn the Grammatical Concept of Voice in French," *Modern Language Journal* 93 (2009) 5–29. Swain draws from psychologist Lev S. Vygotsky's earlier theories as articulated in, e.g., "Thought and Word," in Lev Vygotsky, *Thought and Language* (translation revised and edited by Alex Kozulin; Cambridge, MA: MIT Press, 1986) 210–56; also idem, *Mind in Society: The Development of Higher Psychological Processes* (ed. Michael Cole et al.; Cambridge, MA: Harvard University Press, 1978) 38–51.

convergence for intercultural contact, for the intermingling of vaguely defined people, and for strange, unusual (often sexual) activity. In essence, they represent the Shephelah. Such gendered literary depictions of the region become a provocative space for historical discussions, to which I will return at the end.

■ I. THE SAMSON MATERIAL

Samson is an elusive character in the Book of Judges. His story rests awkwardly toward the end of the book (Judges 13–16) between the savior figures of chaps. 3–12 and the final stories of chaps. 17–21. Unlike the major characters in chaps. 3–12, Samson resides south of Benjamin in the Shephelah. The Samson cycle also lacks the editorial framing that links the final chapters (17–21) with the expression "in those days there was no king in Israel." Samson is therefore something apart from the other Judges figures. Yet the Book of Judges devotes more space to Samson than to any other character.

From the perspective of the whole, interpretations of the Samson cycle, and of Samson's character in conjunction, vary widely. J. Cheryl Exum proposes that there are more distinct interpretations of Samson than perhaps of any other biblical figure; Samson can be anything from "heroic fool, foolish hero, trickster, tragic wild man, comic bandit, tragicomic-trickster-terrorist, foolish-freedom-fighter-type-of-Israel, fool-for-love-Nazirite-judge, negative example and hero of the faith."[3] In its current location toward the end of the book, some understand the Samson cycle to witness to the breakdown of society and the decline of the period of the judges.[4] Attempting to bind Samson to the preceding savior figures, others view the Samson cycle as a story about antagonistic relations between Israel and foreign enemies,[5] or as a warning of the danger

---

3. J. Cheryl Exum, "The Many Faces of Samson," in *Samson: Hero or Fool? The Many Faces of Samson* (ed. Erik Eynikel and Tobias Nicklas; Themes in Biblical Narratives: Jewish and Christian Traditions; Leiden: Brill, 2014) 13–32, here 30; also Mahri Leonard-Fleckman, "Samson and Our Reactions to the Strongman," *Word & World* 37.3 (2017) 217–25.

4. For example, K. Lawson Younger Jr. writes that the Samson cycle is part of the slow "unraveling" of the book that "helps communicate the moral deterioration" during the period of the judges (*Judges and Ruth* [NIV Application Commentary; Grand Rapids: Zondervan, 2002] 36).

5. According to Susan Niditch, "the tale of Samson is a powerful statement of hope and vindication as well as a visceral comment on problems inherent in relations with the non-Israelite world" ("Samson as Culture Hero, Trickster, and Bandit: The Empowerment of the Weak," *CBQ* 52 [1990] 608–24, here 624).

of crossing borders from Israel to Philistia.[6] An underlying assumption of these views is that Samson can be categorized clearly as Judahite or Israelite, in contrast to the Philistines, who roam the coastland and include the women with whom Samson consorts in Judges 14–16.

Such an array of interpretations reflects the cycle's literary-historical complexity, which allows the reader to view Samson as if choosing a particular angle or perspective through a kaleidoscope.[7] Further, while an in-depth discussion of the cycle's diachronic complexity is outside the bounds of this essay, I view the cycle's stages of growth (in broad strokes) as follows:[8] first, tales about Samson and the Timnite woman in Judges 14–15;[9] second, the incorporation of the Delilah story (Judges 16) and the possible continued development of Judges 14–16 together;[10] and, third, the

---

6. On border crossing, see Lawrence E. Stager, *Ashkelon Discovered: From Canaanites and Philistines to Romans and Moslems* (Washington, DC: Biblical Archaeology Society, 1991) 17–18; Steven Weitzman, "The Samson Story as Border Fiction," *BibInt* 10 (2002) 158–74; idem, "Crossing the Border with Samson: Beth-Shemesh and the Bible's Geographical Imagination," in *Tel Beth-Shemesh, A Border Community in Judah: Renewed Excavations 1990–2000; The Iron Age* (ed. Shlomo Bunimovitz and Zvi Lederman; 2 vols.; SMNIA 34; Winona Lake, IN: Eisenbrauns, 2016) 1:266–80; Philippe Guillaume, *Waiting for Josiah: The Judges* (JSOTSup 385; London: T&T Clark, 2004) 156–62; Gregory Mobley, *Samson and the Liminal Hero in the Ancient Near East* (LHBOTS 453; New York: T&T Clark, 2006) 30; and Walter Groß, *Richter* (HThKAT; Freiburg im Breisgau: Herder, 2009) 739–43. These scholars acknowledge that Samson eludes social categorization, yet they ultimately label him Israelite or Judahite. See the discussion in Mahri Leonard-Fleckman, "Binding Samson to Yhwh: From Disorder to Order in the Samson Cycle," in *God and Gods in the Deuteronomistic History* (ed. Corrine Carvalho and John McLaughlin; CBQI 2; Washington, DC: Catholic Biblical Association of America, 2021) 49–68.

7. Marc Zvi Brettler warns against trying to distill the complexity and diversity of the Samson material down to a single theme or purpose, which reflects the imposition of "our desire to find order and coherence" where there is none (*The Book of Judges* [Old Testament Readings; London: Routledge, 2002] 59–60).

8. For a more careful discussion of the cycle's literary history, see Leonard-Fleckman, "Binding Samson to Yhwh."

9. For discussions regarding earlier material in Judges 14–15, see Brettler, *Book of Judges*, 40–60; Reinhard G. Kratz, *The Composition of the Narrative Books of the Old Testament* (trans. John Bowden; London: T&T Clark, 2005) 205, 214–15; and Groß, *Richter*, 657. Kratz limits earlier written traditions about Samson to portions of 14:1–15:8, while Groß has a slightly more extended view that would include material in 14:1–15:17.

10. Some, including Brettler, argue that Judges 14–15 and 16 began as independently circulating stories; Brettler proposes that chap. 16 was eventually attached to chaps. 13–15 in connection with the repetition of the editorial line in 16:31 (= 15:20): "and he had judged Israel for twenty years" (*Book of Judges*, 54, 60). Similarly, Groß views chap. 16 as an independent tale that was edited and incorporated into the cycle by the same hand(s) who wrote chap. 13 as the cycle's introduction

inclusion or creation of the annunciation story in Judges 13 as the cycle's introduction, in conjunction with other editorial elements in Judges 13–16 that give Samson a clearly defined social location: he is an Israelite, from the tribe of Dan, who grows up between Zorah and Eshtaol, and who will deliver Israel from the Philistines (13:1, 2, 5, 25; 14:1-5; 15:20; 16:31).[11] Stripped of these editorial elements, however, Samson is a socially enigmatic, lone-ranging loose cannon in chaps. 14–16. He roams the Shephelah without a definitive geographical home, independent of any family, tribe, or fighting unit. His affiliation with Dan evaporates as we enter the stories of his exploits in chap. 14 and returns only in 16:31 to package the stories into the cycle and the Book of Judges as a whole. Without this packaging, Samson's adventures are fantastic, ridiculous stories of a strongman unleashed: he tears apart a full-grown lion with his bare hands (14:5-6); kills first thirty men (14:19), then one thousand men with an animal's jawbone (15:15); sets flame to foxes' tails and lets them loose to torch grain, vineyards, and olive trees (15:4-5); beats people up (15:8); and melts restraining ropes from his arms (15:14).

While Samson (understandably) stands at the center of myriad interpretations of the cycle, we often fail to notice how our perspectives on Samson—specifically how we define him socially and how he does or does not fit in the Shephelah's social landscape—are dependent on and shaped by his relationship with women. According to Susan Niditch, the

---

(adding in 16:17a and 31 to connect the folklore-ish tale of Samson's strength to his nazirite status) (*Richter*, 657–59). In contrast, James L. Crenshaw proposed that Judges 14–16 was a unified source and that the editorial repetition between 15:20 and 16:31 came from the later addition of the etiology in 15:18–19 (*Samson: A Secret Betrayed, a Vow Ignored* [Atlanta: John Knox, 1978] 40–41). For a reverse line of dependence, J. Cheryl Exum has argued that Samson's encounters with the woman from Timnah and with the Judahites in chaps. 14–15 were modeled after the Samson–Delilah episode. She rightly warns that we oversimplify the process by which the traditions about Samson developed when we conclude that chaps. 14–15 and 16 represent two originally separate cycles of tradition. Her study demonstrates how chaps. 14–15 correspond to chap. 16, while chap. 13 balances chap. 16 and chap. 14 parallels chap. 15; see "Literary Patterns in the Samson Saga: An Investigation of Rhetorical Style in Biblical Prose" (Ph.D. diss., Columbia University, 1976) 28, 197.

11. On Judges 13 as a later addition to the cycle, see J. Cheryl Exum, "The Theological Dimension of the Samson Saga," *VT* 33 (1983) 30–45; eadem, "Many Faces of Samson," 13–32; Mobley, *Samson and the Liminal Hero*, 33–34; Yairah Amit, "The Nazirism Motif and the Editorial Work," in eadem, *In Praise of Editing in the Hebrew Bible: Collected Essays in Retrospect* (HBM 39; Sheffield: Sheffield Phoenix, 2012) 131–46; Groß, *Richter*, 657–59; Leonard-Fleckman, "Samson and Our Reactions," 217–25. Alternatively, an earlier version of Judges 13 might have circulated independently and without awareness of chaps. 14–16; see Brettler, *Book of Judges*, 43.

women in Samson's adventures are the "mediating doorways linking or separating groups of men"; they are "sources of deception, betrayal, and destabilization rather than sources of stability and union."[12] My perspective is slightly different. In my view, women both "stabilize" or ground the cycle and simultaneously serve as tools within a broader construction of social ambiguity (which is not "destabilization," though this social ambiguity may destabilize the reader).

In relation to stability, it is the women who ground the cycle relationally and geographically. Without these women, Samson has no clear social or geographical affiliations. Samson's contact with other characters in his tales comes through the women as relational links. These are not women whom Samson admires from afar; rather, these are women with whom he has physical, intimate, likely sexual relations, most explicitly with the briefly mentioned prostitute from Gaza in 16:1–3. The longer, independent stories of Samson's two key female consorts, one named (Delilah in chap. 16), the other not (the woman from somewhere around Timnah in chaps. 14–15), connect in various ways; for example, the driving plot line involves both women "deceiving" (פתה, 14:15; 16:5) and "harassing" (צוק, 14:17; 16:16) Samson until he divulges the answers to riddles and secrets; and both extended stories involve Samson's capture and binding with "new ropes" (עבתים חדשים, 15:13; 16:11–12).[13]

Yet the primary connection between these two women, I propose, is the ambiguity of their identities, which is created first and foremost through geography. They, like Samson, reside in the Shephelah. One comes from Timnah, the other from somewhere unspecified in the Wadi Sorek. Descriptions of the characters' movement in and around the Shephelah are imprecisely defined throughout the cycle, marked only by travel "up" and "down" between the Coastal Plain and the hill country.[14] There is a lack of scribal interest in constructing clearly delineated boundaries or identities in the Shephelah, or perhaps the interest is the intentional blurring of such demarcations. This literary fuzziness contrasts with descriptions of the "Philistines" in the cycle as the categorical Other on the coast, and of the mass of "men of Judah" from the hill country, who appear briefly in chap. 15, as something apart from the other characters. Yet the

---

12. Niditch, *Judges*, 154.

13. The story of the Timnite woman ends in 15:6 after she is killed, yet the repercussions continue through chap. 15. Parallels and contrasts between the stories of the Timnite woman in 14:11–19 and Delilah in 16:4–22 likely indicate a complex process of growth in Judges 14–16. See Exum's "Literary Patterns in the Samson Saga."

14. On the cycle's interest in geography, see Weitzman, "Samson Story as Border Fiction," 163.

Shephelah is a hazy place, a permeable landscape. And it is the women, I argue, who become the primary representations of this space, the symbols of its social obscurity. They are therefore not the sources or sole characters who destabilize an otherwise stable landscape; rather, they highlight a social and geographical landscape that is, at its core, elusive. It is to these women I now turn, drawing them out from the shadows behind Samson into the spotlight where they belong.

■ II. That Woman from Timnah

The unnamed woman from Timnah first appears in the bridge text of Judg 14:1–4 that links Samson's birth narrative to his exploits in chaps. 14–15.[15] The story opens with Samson "going down" or "descending" (ירד) "toward Timnah" (תמנתה). Going to Timnah is not *arrival at* but rather *movement toward*, as depicted by the directional suffix *he*.[16] As he goes down, he sees אשה בתמנתה ("a woman from Timnah [or toward Timnah]"), מבנות פלשתים ("from the daughters of the Philistines," 14:1). He then goes back "up" (עלה) and declares to his parents that he saw this woman from around Timnah, from the daughters of the Philistines, and he wants her as his wife/woman (14:2). His parents (or perhaps just his father) protest: Isn't there some other woman he could take, either "from the daughters of your relatives or from all my people" (בבנות אחיך ובכל עמי) rather than "from the uncircumcised Philistines" (מפלשתים הערלים, 14:3)? According to these verses, the woman's identity is both specific—she is a daughter of those uncircumcised Philistines—and vague—she is from somewhere around Timnah. Samson and his parents (or his father) then "descend" back down "toward Timnah" and toward the woman (14:5, 7), after which the place-name drops entirely from the narrative.

In the beginning of the narrative of the marriage (or perhaps betrothal) feast in Judges 14, Samson's father "goes down to the woman" (14:10).[17]

---

15. Scholars have long treated the inclusion of the mother in vv. 1–4 (or 5) as secondary. See George Foot Moore, *A Critical and Exegetical Commentary on Judges* (ICC; New York: Scribner, 1895) 327; more recently, Brettler, *Book of Judges*, 43; and Groß, *Richter*, 657.

16. In biblical texts, Timnah takes the directional suffix *he* consistently (Gen 38:12–14; Josh 19:43; Judg 14:1–2, 5), with the exceptions of Josh 15:10, 57; and 2 Chr 28:18. It is likely that the suffix became a fixed part of the name, as we also see in the Greek translations (see also n. 27).

17. The repeated statements of movement "down toward" throughout vv. 1–7 and v. 10, the choppiness of the story line throughout vv. 1–7, and the sudden singularity of the father's involvement here, without Samson's mother, suggest that v. 10

From now until her death in 15:6, it is the woman herself, not the place Timnah, that is the locus of intercultural mingling and activity. Samson's father descends to her, not to Timnah. Around her, the story and its entangled interweaving of people revolves. No longer does the narrator distinguish clearly between Samson and those around him, despite the fact that they are identified in vv. 1–4 unambiguously as those "uncircumcised Philistines." Samson is a loner, without family or attendants to speak of (his father has disappeared), yet he is also someone apart from those who have gathered for the party, referred to only as "them" or "they." Thirty of "them" become his "companions" (מרעים) for the party's duration (14:11). The woman calls them "my people" (בני עמי, v. 16), yet they threaten to kill her and her father's household (בית אב) and imply that they had traveled to the town from elsewhere to be part of the festivities (v. 15).[18] There is no language barrier, as depicted through direct discourse and the first of the cycle's key riddles.[19] At the end of the tale, Samson disappears "down" to Ashkelon for the first of his revenge killings. Are these coastland dwellers, these poor victims from Ashkelon, part of the same cultural group as those farther "up" at the party, including the unnamed woman? It is puzzling—and makes little sense—that he would seek revenge in Ashkelon against the riddle-breaking men in the Shephelah unless they were all culturally affiliated. But the text does not read by our logic. Most importantly, Samson never kills anyone explicitly from the Shephelah, only those labeled "Philistines," the categorical Other. Those of the Shephelah, meanwhile, are left uncategorized.

After this chapter, the identity of the unnamed woman blurs further. She and her people become simply "other," separate from Samson and separate from the Philistines. Again, it is the woman herself who becomes the geographical or directional focus; to come to her is to arrive at the space for intercultural contact. Samson leaves her following the seven-day celebration in Judges 14 and she is given to another without his knowledge. Samson then expects easy access to her room when he comes to visit her in her father's house (15:1).[20] He learns that she no longer

---

begins an earlier, independent account of Samson's involvement with the woman, to which vv. 1–7 were tacked on.

18. The MT reads, הלירשנו קראתם לנו הלא ("Have you not invited us in order to impoverish us?") I translate הלא as הלם (as does the JPS) in line with Hebrew variants and the Targum: "Have you invited us here in order to impoverish us?"

19. On the importance of riddles and the wisdom influence in Judges 14–15 (including connections with Proverbs 1–9 and Job), see Brettler's careful discussion in *Book of Judges*, 52–54; also Crenshaw, *Samson: A Secret Betrayed*, 99–120.

20. Middle Assyrian Laws include scenarios in which a woman continues to reside in her father's house while married because of issues with the marriage. See

belongs to him and reacts by destroying Philistine crops in Timnah (15:4–5). Like his earlier act of aggression against the men of Ashkelon, this act of retaliation suggests that the Timnite family is Philistine, or that Samson associates them with the Philistines.

Yet this link is not quite so simple. In Judges 15, it is not the father of the woman who responds to Samson's destructive act but rather the Philistines, who "go up" to Timnah and burn the Timnite woman and her father (or perhaps her father's household, according to various manuscripts) to death in their own act of retaliation (15:4–6). Clearly labeled "Philistines," these do not appear to be the same men who threatened the woman in 14:15 and who arrived from elsewhere for the party. Yet, ironically, the woman ends up meeting the fate that she was trying to escape by pestering Samson for the answer to the riddle in chap. 14.[21] Here, the Philistines kill her not because of her actions but rather because of Samson's, associating her not with themselves but with Samson and viewing the family as responsible for their impoverished crops. These Philistines have power over the woman and her father, but this is no kinship-based or deeply allied relationship (unlike in chap. 14, there is no reference to the woman's "people"). Samson then disappears, descending to a cave in an uncertain location. The woman is dead, and so the geographical focus shifts.

■ III. Delilah

Despite being the only named woman in the Samson cycle, Delilah's identity in Judges 16 is even more ambiguous than the unnamed woman in chaps. 14–15. She may have a name, but she has no place or people. Like the unnamed woman, she becomes a place for intercultural contact between "the Philistines" and Samson, yet she does not quite belong (culturally speaking) to either. Instead, she is a narrative tool, a contact zone, a nucleus of activity set somewhere farther inland from the coast. Judges 16 distinguishes her only as a woman in the Wadi Sorek (16:4), to whom the "lords" (סרני) of the Philistines "come up" (עלה) from the coast and whom they convince to find the source of Samson's strength. They have

---

Laws 27, 32, 36, and 38 in Martha T. Roth, *Law Collections from Mesopotamia and Asia Minor* (2nd ed.; SBLWAW 6; Atlanta: Scholars Press, 1997) 163–67. In the case of Judges 15, the issue may be lack of commitment, which provides the grounds for dissolution of the marriage.

21. On this point, see Jeremy Schipper, "Narrative Obscurity of Samson's חידה in Judges 14.14 and 18," *JSOT* 27 (2003) 339–53, here 347.

to bribe her with a ridiculously large sum of money into tricking Samson, which implies that she, like the unnamed woman, is perhaps more akin to Samson than to the Philistines.[22]

Yes, perhaps Delilah *is* closely related to Samson and his cultural group, whatever that may be. He trusts her implicitly, and her name (דלילה), while etymologically enigmatic, is at least phonologically similar to "night" (לילה) in relation to the sun (שמש) for Samson. She and Samson therefore manifest as temporal opposites.[23] Yet she has no family to speak of, no clan, tribe, or visible connections other than Samson, who falls in love with her. Her affiliations are simply unimportant to the narrator. She is merely a pawn, an object that serves as the space in which the Philistines and Samson come together. As stated earlier, her story mirrors that of the unnamed woman, both of whom "deceive" (פתה, 14:15; 16:5) and "harass" (צוק, 14:17; 16:16) Samson until he divulges the answers to his riddles and secrets. Again, there is no language barrier. Scribal play sexualizes the encounter between Samson and Delilah as a subtle, narrative undercurrent, most obviously in their final scene together, when Delilah "lulls him to sleep on her knees" (16:19).[24] These sexual hints, coupled with Delilah's deception, have made her somewhat of an ugly fascination in the history of interpretation, especially in artistic renderings of the scene that exploit her sexually far beyond (and far more negatively than) the text's scribal suggestions.[25] Once she succeeds in her task

---

22. As Tammi J. Schneider writes, "The book of Judges never defines the precise borders of Philistia and thus neither Delilah's abode nor her name defines her ethnicity or occupation" (*Judges* [Berit Olam; Collegeville, MN: Liturgical Press, 2000] 220). Contra Brettler, who defines Delilah as Philistine (*Book of Judges*, 56; see also Royce M. Victor, "Delilah—A Forgotten Hero (Judges 16:4–21): A Cross-Cultural Narrative Reading," in *Joshua and Judges* [ed. Athalya Brenner and Gale A. Yee; Texts @ Contexts; Minneapolis: Fortress, 2013] 235–56). Victor proposes, creatively, that the story first circulated in Philistine circles as a story about Delilah as a hero and was eventually adopted and altered for Israelite purposes (see esp. 249).

23. Though the name is unlikely to be etymologically related to "night," the allusion nonetheless works on the phonological level. See also the discussion in Schneider, *Judges*, 219. Some interpreters have rendered her name as etymologically related to "flirt" (see, e.g., Robert Boling, *Judges: Introduction, Translation, and Commentary* [AB 6A; Garden City, NY: Doubleday, 1975] 248), or "hair" (see דלת ראשך in Song 7:6, "locks of your head"; personal communication from Marc Brettler), which perhaps tells us more about interpreters' perspectives of Delilah than the actual etymology of the name.

24. Mieke Bal views this image as maternal rather than sexual, based on her proposal that the Hebrew על ("upon") allows for the translation "between her knees," as if Delilah were giving birth to Samson (*Death & Dissymmetry: The Politics of Coherence in the Book of Judges* [CSHJ; Chicago: University of Chicago Press, 1988] 225).

25. See, e.g., Solomon Joseph Solomon's *Samson* (1887) (Walker Art Gallery,

of tricking him (which does not take much), the Philistine lords promptly depart from the Wadi Sorek "down" to Gaza on the coast with Samson as their hostage (16:21), and Delilah disappears from the narrative. Her work is done, the Shephelah encounter with Samson is over, and Samson disappears down to the clearly delineated enemy on the coast.

Throughout Judges 14–16, scribal constructions—or deconstructions—of social landscape begin with these two women. Their identities are ambiguous. They reside somewhere in the Shephelah—one in or around Timnah, the other close by, somewhere around the Wadi Sorek. Narrative details separate them implicitly from the Philistines and from Samson, the latter of whom is also difficult to define socially, and whose ambiguity is underscored by that of his female companions. Both the unnamed woman and Delilah become the space for cultural entanglement, for the coming together and meeting of these different people and groups. In this way, they embody the Shephelah and become its primary narrative representations, caught somewhere in the middle, neither Philistine nor Canaanite, Israelite or Judahite.

■ IV. Tamar

Shifting from Judges 14–16 to Genesis 38, we enter a similar, socially entangled landscape. There, Judah mistakes his daughter-in-law Tamar for a prostitute and sleeps with her somewhere on the road to Timnah. In the story, Canaanites mingle with Judahites, eventually leading to the continuation of Judah's line without narrative concern for intermarriage or Tamar's potentially non-Judahite status (though the text never directly states that she is Canaanite).[26] Geographical references are imprecise and, as in the Samson cycle, associated with movement "up" and "down." The story begins with Judah "going down" (ירד) to "camp" (נטה) near a certain Adullamite man (v. 1); later he "goes up" (עלה) toward Timnah (תמנתה) to

---

Liverpool); Avi Katz's *Samson and Delilah* in the Alien Corn Series (late twentieth century) (http://www.avikatz.net/sf/aliencorn/alienframe.htm); also J. Cheryl Exum's discussion in "Why, Why, Why, Delilah?," in eadem, *Plotted, Shot, and Painted, Cultural Representations of Biblical Women* (JSOTSup 25; Sheffield: Sheffield Academic Press, 1996) 175–237; and eadem, "Aspects of Symmetry and Balance in the Samson Saga," *JSOT* 19 (1981) 3–29.

26. On Tamar's identity, see Tamara Cohn Eskenazi and Andrea L. Wiess, eds., *The Torah: A Women's Commentary* (Women of Reform Judaism; New York: WRJ Press, 2008) 216.

his sheepshearers (v. 12).[27] Given the pastoral-nomadic context of the passage, it is not entirely clear whether he settles in Adullam itself—a town south of Beth-Shemesh overlooking the Elah Valley (cf. Josh 15:35)—or simply near a man who originally came from Adullam. Regardless, we might infer that the location is somewhere in the environs of Adullam, given the subsequent reference to "Chezib" in v. 5 (= Achzib), southwest of Adullam (cf. Josh 15:44; Mic 1:14).[28] Whatever the place may be, it is considered Judahite territory in v. 22, when Judah "returns to Judah" (וישב אל־יהודה).

The only other locations mentioned in the text are Timnah (vv. 12, 14) and the unlocatable "Enaim" (עינים) in vv. 14 and 21 (perhaps connected to the word "river/brook," עין) which is somewhere "on the road toward Timnah" (על־דרך תמנתה, v. 14) or simply "by the road" (בדרך, v. 21). The location of Timnah is also unclear; perhaps it is the Shephelah location, though based on the concentration on Judah in the story and geographical references to Adullam and Achzib, it may make more sense to connect this Timnah with the Timnah listed in Josh 15:57, in the area southwest of Hebron, near Adullam.[29]

Understandably, scholars have found the Tamar–Judah story thoroughly perplexing.[30] Often, discussions of the narrative focus on its literary placement within the Jacob and Joseph stories, or on its links with the David material, most notably the Tamar story of 2 Samuel 13.[31] Most

---

27. Interestingly, the LXX preserves the directional *he* as part of the place-name in the Samson cycle, but not in Genesis 38.

28. On the link between the otherwise-unattested Chezib and the biblical Achzib, see, e.g., Gerhard von Rad, *Genesis* (trans. John Marks; rev. ed.; OTL; Philadelphia: Westminster, 1973) 353; and Nahum M. Sarna, *Genesis* בראשית: *The Traditional Hebrew Text with the New JPS Translation* (JPS Torah Commentary; Philadelphia: Jewish Publication Society, 1989) 265.

29. A number of studies conflate these two Timnahs, the distinct locations of which we see in Josh 15:10 (the Shephelah Timnah) and Josh 15:57 (Judahite Timnah). Most notably, see the excavation reports on Tel Batash/Timnah, in which both George L. Kelm and Amihai Mazar state that the basis for linking biblical Timnah with the contemporary site Tel-Batash is the perceived connection between Timnah in Josh 15:10 and Genesis 38 (*Timnah: A Biblical City in the Sorek Valley* [Winona Lake, IN: Eisenbrauns, 1995] 4–5; Amihai Mazar, *Timnah [Tel Batash]: Final Reports*, vol. 1.1, *Stratigraphy and Architecture, Text* [Qedem 37; Jerusalem: Institute of Archaeology, Hebrew University of Jerusalem, 1997] 3–4).

30. For example, Walter Brueggemann comments, "This peculiar chapter stands alone, without connection to its context. It is isolated in every way and is most enigmatic" (*Genesis* [IBC; Atlanta: John Knox, 1982] 307).

31. Regarding the placement of Genesis 38 within the broader Joseph and Jacob story in chaps. 37–50, the common view is that chap. 38 was originally independent of the surrounding narrative; see, e.g., von Rad, *Genesis*, 351–52; Martin Noth, *A History*

scholars view Judah as the primary character; a minority focus (aside from self-described feminist interpretations) has been Tamar. Yet it is she who lies at the epicenter of the plot, she who underscores the story's geographical and social ambiguity. The text never tells us to which social group she belongs, though her name תמר designates and plays on the role of the date palm in Hebrew.[32] She becomes the place for intercultural (sexual) activity throughout the narrative, beginning with Judah's sons and ending with Judah. When she takes her place "at the entrance to Enaim, which is on the road toward Timnah" (בפתח עינים אשר על־דרך תמנתה), she becomes the focal point for the story's climax.

In the stories of both Samson and Tamar, questionable sexual or cross-cultural activity takes place in Timnah or somewhere toward Timnah, activity outside the appropriate contours and structures of society. Perhaps the name Timnah is akin to what Michel Foucault would describe as a heterotopia, an alternative construction of space incompatible with real society that inverts the known world as if looking through a mirror, a place reserved for moments of crisis or for deviant characters.[33] What remains unclear is whether the orientation toward Timnah in both Genesis 38 and the Samson cycle could reflect intentional scribal communication or textual dependence. Based on the vague descriptions, it is also impossible to know for certain which Timnah is the directional focus of Genesis 38.[34] In the Samson cycle, this heterotopia of chaps. 14–15 is

---

of Pentateuchal Traditions (trans. Bernhard W. Anderson; 1972; repr., Chico, CA: Scholars Press, 1981) 42; and David M. Carr, *Reading the Fractures of Genesis: Historical and Literary Approaches* (Louisville: Westminster John Knox, 1996) 249–53. More recent literary studies, however, have argued that Genesis 38 belongs within the surrounding narrative and is indispensable to it, most notably Robert Alter in his seminal study, *The Art of Biblical Narrative* (rev. and updated ed.; New York: Basic Books, 2011) 1–24. For a recent advocate of Alter's view and a discussion of the history of scholarship, see Richard J. Clifford, "Genesis 38: Its Contribution to the Jacob Story," *CBQ* 66 (2004) 519–32. See also the scholarly genealogy in Mark Leuchter, "Genesis 38 in Social and Historical Perspective," *JBL* 132 (2013) 209–27.

32. The date palm reproduces in a manner similar to humans. It is dioecious, meaning that individual plants have either female or male reproductive organs. The female must be pollinated by the male to be reproductive, and the male date palm is of value only as a pollinator. Similarly, the perpetuation of Judah's family line owes itself to Tamar's ingenuity and action, and her value relative to Judah therefore echoes the higher value of the female plant.

33. Michel Foucault, "Des espaces autres," Conférence au Cercle d'études architecturales, 14 mars 1967, published in *Architecture, Mouvement, Continuité* 5 (1984) 46–49.

34. If Judah "goes up" from somewhere around Adullam, a place between the plains and the hill country, could it make sense geographically for that direction to be toward the Shephelah?

reframed and given a new sense of order and literary coherence by labeling Timnah and the unnamed woman "Philistine," and by turning Samson into Israel's savior. Genesis 38 becomes rooted in David's genealogy in its final verses, and the chapter also provides the Genesis narrative with a southern perspective that is otherwise missing in the ending of the book.

■ V. The Archaeological Discussion (in Brief)

Curiously, archaeological data (or at least, debates of the data) are not discordant with the literary portrait we have seen, specifically in the Shephelah. The evidence arguably reveals the Shephelah to have been a perplexing, indefinable social area for much of the Iron Age. During the tenth to late eighth centuries, up to the destruction of the area during Sennacherib's campaign (ca. 701 B.C.E.), people whom the Bible labels simply as Philistine, Canaanite, Judahite and/or Israelite appear to have interacted and coexisted, and identities were more fluid than we might imagine. There is no clear consensus on the relationship between the archaeological evidence and cultural reality, specifically how to reconstruct or label people in this region from the evidence—largely pottery and faunal remains—and the evidence varies depending on the time and the site.[35]

For example, places like Beth-Shemesh and Lachish appear to have thrived as Judah's western border towns from the tenth through mid-eighth

---

35. For a sampling of the debates, see the articles in Oded Lipschits and Aren M. Maeir, eds., *The Shephelah during the Iron Age: Recent Archaeological Studies* (Winona Lake, IN: Eisenbrauns, 2017); also Avraham Faust, "Pigs in Space (and Time): Pork Consumption and Identity Negotiations in the Late Bronze and Iron Ages of Ancient Israel," *NEA* 81 (2018) 276–99; Lidar Sapir-Hen, "Pigs as Ethnic Markers? You Are What You Eat," *BARev* 42 (2016) 41–43, 70; eadem, "Food, Pork Consumption, and Identity in Ancient Israel," *NEA* 82 (2019) 52–59; Susan Sherratt, "'Sea Peoples' and the Economic Structure of the Late Second Millennium in the Eastern Mediterranean," in *Mediterranean Peoples in Transition: Thirteenth to Early Tenth Century BCE* (ed. Seymour Gitin, Amihai Mazar, and Ephraim Stern; Jerusalem: Israel Exploration Society, 1998) 292–313; eadem, "'Ethnicities,' 'Ethnonyms,' and Archaeological Labels: Whose Ideologies and Whose Identities?," in *Archaeological Perspectives on the Transmission and Transformation of Culture in the Eastern Mediterranean* (ed. Joanne Clarke; Levant Supplementary Series 2; Oxbow: Council for British Research in the Levant, 2005) 25–38; and Ron E. Tappy, "Tel Zayit and the Tel Zayit Abecedary in Their Regional Context," in *Literate Culture and Tenth-Century Canaan: The Tel Zayit Abecedary in Context* (ed. Ron E. Tappy and P. Kyle McCarter; Winona Lake, IN: Eisenbrauns, 2008) 1–44. See also Daniel Pioske, *Memory in a Time of Prose: Studies in Epistemology, Hebrew Scribalism, and the Biblical Past* (New York: Oxford University Press, 2018).

centuries B.C.E. But evidence from sites slightly farther west and running along the base of the hills during the same period is much more debatable, including places like Tel Zayit and Timnah. Conflating political dependency with cultural composition and often incorporating facile interpretations of the Bible into archaeological interpretations, some would argue that these sites seesaw over time: first Philistine, then Judahite, and so on. Regarding Tel Batash (the site largely accepted as ancient Timnah in the 1960s), site director Amihai Mazar's once clear-cut proposals for the site's shifting direction of political dependency have, notably, softened over time. Based on his earliest reports, he still proposes that the pottery and other artifacts from the late twelfth and eleventh centuries B.C.E. (Stratum V) point to "Philistine dominance" that reflects the "geopolitical reality" of the Samson material. Yet he has also admitted that the question of the extent to which the town was inhabited by "Philistines" is "hard to answer."[36] He and others are similarly conflicted about the material evidence from the short-lived tenth-century town (Stratum IV) and the last stratum prior to Sennacherib's campaign (Stratum III, eighth century), which reveals a combination of coastal and inland elements.[37] Even after the area's reconfiguration toward the coast in 701 B.C.E., Mazar has stated that the question of Timnah's political alliance (let alone its social makeup) cannot be answered definitively.[38]

---

36. Amihai Mazar, "Concluding Remarks," in *Timnah (Tel Batash): Final Reports*, vol. 3, *The Finds from the Second Millennium BCE* (ed. Amihai Mazar and Nava Panitz-Cohen; Qedem 45; Jerusalem: Institute of Archaeology, Hebrew University of Jerusalem, 2006) 323–30.

37. Amihai Mazar has proposed that the tenth-century occupation was "Israelite" and that of the eighth century, "Judahite"; see Mazar, *Timnah (Tel Batash)*, 1.1: 249–63. See the arguments against Mazar's interpretations in Shlomo Bunimovitz and Zvi Lederman, "The Early Israelite Monarchy in the Sorek Valley: Tel Beth-Shemesh and Tel Batash (Timnah) in the 10th and 9th Centuries BCE," in *"I Will Speak the Riddles of Ancient Times": Archaeological and Historical Studies in Honor of Amihai Mazar on the Occasion of His Sixtieth Birthday* (ed. Aren M. Maeir and Pierre de Miroschedji; Winona Lake, IN: Eisenbrauns, 2006) 407–27. See also the discussion of the area in a broader sense in Aren M. Maeir and Louise A. Hitchcock, "The Appearance, Formation and Transformation of Philistine Culture: New Perspective and New Finds," in *Sea Peoples Up-to-Date: New Research on Transformations in the Eastern Mediterranean in the 13th–11th Centuries BCE; Proceedings of the ESF-Workshop Held at the Austrian Academy of Sciences, Vienna, 3–4 November 2014* (ed. Peter M. Fischer and Teresa Bürge; Denkschrift der Gesamtakademie 81; Contributions to the Chronology of the Eastern Mediterranean 35; Vienna: Austrian Academy of Sciences, 2017) 149–62.

38. Amihai Mazar and Nava Panitz-Cohen, *Timnah (Tel Batash): Final Reports*, vol. 2, *The Finds from the First Millennium BCE* (Qedem 42; Jerusalem: Institute of Archaeology, Hebrew University of Jerusalem, 2001) 282.

▪ VI. HISTORICAL CONFLATIONS

It would be methodologically problematic to think that we could take such a complex literary masterpiece as Judges 14–16, dig down through and date its various textual layers, and reach some unadulterated early "core" or objective notion of historical reality mirrored in the text as if it were a pot discovered in situ. Yet texts are not temporally dislocated; someone (or more than one) constructed such representations of social landscape for particular purposes, within and for particular historical context(s). These representations of the past then changed and evolved over time and throughout the scribal process. Moreover, not only was this process shaped by its context but it could, in turn, shape culture, ideology, and perspectives. So, while texts may not reflect historical reality, they are historically valuable.

In dating the central Samson material, or seeking to explain the motivations behind its vague landscape, some would argue that the stories "mirror" the cultural ambiguity of the archaeological evidence prior to Sennacherib's destruction and realignment of the area in 701 B.C.E., perhaps prior to the mid-800s and as early as the Iron IIA.[39] Others would say that the stories promote to a Judahite audience or to a later audience "border maintenance" and a warning on the dangers of *political* border crossing between Philistia and Judah.[40] This may be true of the editorial schemes, yet the exploits with the unnamed woman and Delilah reflect little interest in clear border construction as we see in, say, Joshua or Numbers (which consistently use the word גבול, "border/territory," a term that is unattested in Judges 14–16). Rather, the lack of intentional scribal interest in border construction is demonstrated by the social ambiguity of the characters and the region.

We see a similar ambiguity in the Tamar–Judah story. A long-standing view is that Genesis 38 had a prehistory in legends related to the settlement of Israel's ancestors.[41] But it could also recall a later Judahite

---

39. See, e.g., Lawrence Stager, "Forging and Identity: The Emergence of Ancient Israel," in *The Oxford History of the Biblical World* (ed. Michael D. Coogan; New York: Oxford University Press, 1998) 123–75; Peter Machinist, "Biblical Traditions: The Philistines and Israelite History," in *The Sea Peoples and Their World: A Reassessment* (ed. Eliezer D. Oren; University Museum Monograph 108; Philadelphia: University Museum, University of Pennsylvania, 2000) 53–83; Niditch, *Judges*, 144–45, 154–55.

40. See, e.g., Weitzman, "Samson Story as Border Fiction" and "Crossing the Border with Samson"; also Guillaume, *Waiting for Josiah*, 156–62; Groß, *Richter*, 739–43.

41. See the discussion in Carr, *Reading the Fractures of Genesis*, 250.

perspective.⁴² In the text, Judah's identity and social location are clear. Tamar's are not. Arguably, there is no narrative judgment against her as a foreigner (or against the clearly identified Canaanite Shua). Tamar and the road toward Timnah bear striking resemblance to the women and the geography of the Samson cycle.

All of these stories speak into different Iron Age realities and, in my view, reflect a conflation of times remembered or constructed from the area's long and socially complicated Iron Age past.⁴³ At the earliest stages of composition, they all indicate preexilic writing, likely prior to the end of the eighth century B.C.E. In the case of Tamar, the story represents an era during which those outside of urban settlements were more culturally diverse than we might assume. As for Judges 14–16, these highly literary tales set within an obscure Shephelah landscape resemble the complexity of the archaeological portrait throughout the Iron Age, and especially prior to the Neo-Assyrian reorganization of the area ca. 701 B.C.E. Only later does the editorial framework offer clearer categories and boundaries for the Samson cycle, as part of the process of drawing the stories together and shaping them into the literary arc of Judges within the Deuteronomistic History.

In all of these texts, female characters are the primary representations of obscure social landscapes. They become the texts' geographical markers, the space for intercultural contact and entanglements, and for unusual activity. They therefore serve a rhetorical function as symbols of the region and creations of the outsider's gaze. The name "Shephelah" itself, from the root שפל ("to become low or abased"), betrays this outside, highland perspective, the view of someone looking down upon the region and seeking to describe it from elsewhere. To pay attention to these women—the woman from Timnah, Delilah, and Tamar—is to view the texts from a fresh angle, and to provoke new questions about the relationship between literary representations of social landscape and historical questions of identity in ancient Israel.

---

42. For example, Mark Leuchter argues that Genesis 38 reflects a Judahite agrarian lifestyle during Hezekiah's urbanization project of 705–701 B.C.E., when rural Judahites were uprooted from their land. He proposes that the text could not date much beyond this period for various linguistic reasons, and for the author's/authors' ability to "recall" with "authentic detail" earlier Judahite agrarian practices and customs that fit well with the archaeological evidence from pre-701 B.C.E. The linguistic reasons include connections with 2 Samuel 13, as well as textual features that lack a conceptual orientation toward writing and a higher level of literacy ("Genesis 38 in Social and Historical Perspective," 214–18, 223).

43. Mark S. Smith refers to this as the process of "shifting recollection" ("Remembering God: Collective Memory in Israelite Religion," *CBQ* 64 [2002] 631–51, here 633).

Historiography across the Book of Judges

MARK S. SMITH
Princeton Theological Seminary
Princeton, New Jersey

Leslie Hoppe has dedicated his life to Scripture and the Church, in his teaching and preaching, scholarly research and institutional service. I am honored to join in this celebration of Leslie's many contributions. Among his wide-ranging areas of professional expertise, Leslie has taken a major interest in the Deuteronomistic History. For this part of the Bible, historiography has been a long-standing concern,[1] and the Book of Judges is no exception.[2] This essay focuses on historiography across the Book of

---

1. John Van Seters, *In Search of History: Historiography in the Ancient World and the Origins of Biblical History* (New Haven: Yale University Press, 1983).

2. Baruch Halpern, *The First Historians: The Hebrew Bible and History* (San Francisco: Harper & Row, 1988); Marc Zvi Brettler, *The Creation of History in Ancient Israel* (London: Routledge, 1995); idem, *The Book of Judges* (Old Testament Readings; London: Routledge, 2002); and Susan Niditch, "Historiography, 'Hazards,' and the Study of Ancient Israel," *Int* 57 (2003) 138–50. The most extensive work on historiography in Judges has been conducted on the Gideon cycle by Pierre Gibert, *De l'élaboration historiographique: Le cas du cycle de Gédéon (Livre des Juges 6–8)* (2 vols.; Ph.D. thesis, Université de Paris – Sorbonne IV, 1988); and idem, *Vérité historique et esprit historien: L'historien biblique de Gédéon face à Hérodote; Essai sur le principe historiographique* (Initiations; Paris: Cerf, 1990). See also Nadav Na'aman, *Yeriot: The Past That Shapes the Present; The Creation of Biblical Historiography in the Late First Temple Period and after the Downfall* (Hebrew; Jerusalem: Orna Hess, 2002) 104–6 (brought to my attention by Amihai Mazar and provided by Tallay Ornan). Some articles have appeared as well: K. Lawson Younger Jr., "Judges 1 in Its Near Eastern Literary Context," in *Faith, Tradition, and History: Old Testament Historiography in Its Near Eastern Context* (ed. Alan R. Millard, James K. Hoffmeier, and David W. Baker; Winona Lake, IN: Eisenbrauns, 1994) 207–27; Koert van Bekkum, "De historiografie van Israëls vestiging in Kanaän aan de hand van Richteren 1:1–2:5," *NTT* 54 (2000) 295–309; Sandra Scham, "The Days of the Judges: When Men and Women Were Animals and Trees Were Kings," *JSOT* 97 (2002) 37–64; Mark J. Boda, "Recycling Heaven's Words:

Judges and not within the individual units, which bear very different historiographical perspectives.

The forms that the representations of the past take in a historiographical work such as Judges have come under scrutiny in recent decades.[3] Among historians, it is Hayden White (1928–2018) who most famously noted that historiography often bears tropes found in other genres of literature, such as fiction.[4] In response to this approach, Arnaldo Momigliano warned about the "dissolution of history into the history of historiography," the very field that he himself founded.[5] This broader debate about history and historiography has influenced Judges research, illustrated by Baruch Halpern's effort at historical reconstructions of Israel's "ancient historians" and the responses to this project by Marc Zvi Brettler, who has taken Hayden White's fundamental observation to heart.[6]

A major difficulty with the historiography of Judges lies in its complex development, which nonetheless yielded a larger historiographical picture. In Luis Alonso Schökel's terms, the successive stages of Judges represent different instances of "secondary unity" relative to what preceded: "A later writer could take already completed pieces and bring them together skillfully to form a new and complex unity."[7] This observation applies to the book's historiographical construction. While the individual stories do not express an overarching vision of the book, their secondary arrangement does. With these issues in mind, the basic claim informing the observations that follow is that the process of collecting the various accounts in the Book of Judges issued in a larger historiographical vision, one particularly framed in terms of geography and chronology. These twin axes are what the historian Anthony Grafton calls

---

Receiving and Retrieving Divine Revelation in the Historiography of Judges," in *Prophets, Prophecy, and Ancient Israelite Historiography* (ed. Mark J. Boda and Lissa M. Wray Beal; Winona Lake, IN: Eisenbrauns, 2013) 43–67; and Moshe Sokolow, "The Book of Judges in Medieval Muslim and Jewish Historiography," *JANES* 11 (1979) 113–30.

3. See the works cited in the preceding note.

4. Hayden White, *Tropics of Discourse: Essays in Cultural Criticism* (Baltimore: Johns Hopkins University Press, 1978).

5. Arnaldo Momigliano, *Essays on Ancient and Modern Judaism* (ed. Silvia Berti; trans. Maura Masella-Gayley; Chicago: University of Chicago Press, 1987) 5–7; and Carlo Ginzburg, *Threads and Traces: True, False, Fictive* (trans. Anne C. Tedeschi and John Tedeschi; Berkeley: University of California Press, 2012) 69.

6. Halpern, *First Historians*; Brettler, *Creation of History*, 5, 11–12, and 18 with 159–60 n. 124.

7. Luis Alonso Schökel, *A Manual of Hebrew Poetics* (SubBib 11; Rome: Pontificio Istituto Biblico, 1988) 189.

"the two eyes of history."[8] I begin with these two aspects of Judges, more specifically the geographical order of tribes and then the chronological order of the book, and then offer some historiographical observations based on the patterning in its representation of men and women. As the following discussion illustrates, further chronological notices indicate that the point of these historiographical constructions was the audience's own time.

The highest-order structure within the book involves its sequence of twelve leaders: (1) Othniel (3:9–11); (2) Ehud (3:12–30); (3) Shamgar (3:31); (4) Deborah (chaps. 4–5); (5) Gideon, identified also as Jerubbaal (chaps. 6–9); (6) Tola (10:1); (7) Jair (10:3–5); (8) Jephthah (11:1–12:6); (9) Ibzan (12:8–10); (10) Elon (12:11); (11) Abdon (12:13–15); and (12) Samson (chaps. 13–16). Notably, the number of leaders in Judges tallies to the famous number of the twelve tribes. At the same time, the twelve tribes are not neatly matched to these twelve figures. Several otherwise standard tribes, including Reuben, Simeon, Naphtali, Asher, and Gad, are absent from Judges; perhaps not unexpectedly, Levi also goes unrepresented (cf. 5:14–18). Gilead, rather uncommon in tribal listings (cf. 5:17), seems to stand in for the Transjordanian tribes of Reuben and Gad.

Each leader in Judges is representative of a tribe and region, as shown by the geographical order of the "judges" stories:

Judah:	Othniel (3:7–11a)
Benjamin:	Ehud (3:11b–30)
?:	Shamgar (3:31; see 5:6)
Ephraim:	Deborah (chaps. 4–5)
Manasseh:	Gideon/Jerubbaal (chaps. 6–9)
Issachar/Ephraim:	Tola of Issachar lived in the hill country of Ephraim (10:1–3)
Zebulun:	Ibzan (12:8–10) and Elon (12:11–12)
Gilead:	Jair (10:3–5) and Jephthah (10:7–12:7)
Ephraim:	Abdon (12:13–15)
Dan, with reference to Judah:	Samson (chaps. 13–16)

It has often been remarked that the order moves, relatively speaking, from south to north and then circles back south.[9] The geography of

---

8. Anthony Grafton, *What Was History? The Art of History in Early Modern Europe* (Cambridge: Cambridge University Press, 2007) 8.
9. The classic statement on this point is Abraham Malamat, "Charismatic Leadership in the Book of Judges," in *Magnalia Dei, the Mighty Acts of God: Essays on*

Judges shows a massive core of northern stories (chaps. 4–12), bookended by a series of southern additions (chaps. 3 and 13–16). More specifically, the book's geographical order shows a doubly circular route. It begins in Judah (Othniel in 3:7–11a), moves northward to Benjamin (Ehud in 3:11b–30), and then continues north to Ephraim (Deborah in chaps. 4–5, with Shamgar in 3:31 and 5:6). Then the stories turn farther north to Manasseh (Gideon/Jerubbaal in chaps. 6–9), combined with Issachar (Tola in 10:1–3, possibly buried in Manasseh) and then Zebulun (Ibzan in 12:8–10 and Elon in 12:11–12). The order then turns eastward into Transjordanian Gilead (Jair in 10:3–5 and Jephthah in 10:7–12:7), without mention of Transjordanian Manasseh or the more southerly Gad or Reuben. The book comes full circle, first by returning to Ephraim (Abdon in 12:13–15) and then farther back to the region of Judah in the Samson cycle (see 13:24 and 16:31, with 18:11–12; 15:9–13; 16:3). The tribal units that bookend the collection are Judah (Othniel and Samson) and Ephraim (Deborah in chaps. 4–5, with Shamgar in 3:31 and 5:6; Abdon in 12:13–15), with some attention paid also to Gilead (Jair in 10:3–5 and Jephthah in 10:7–12:7). The doubly circular route beginning and ending with Judah and Ephraim may signal a historiographical statement about these two historical giants (cf. the divine rejection of Shiloh and Ephraim in favor of Jerusalem and Judah in Psalm 78; cf. Shiloh and Jerusalem in the Epilogue).

The book's general south–north geographical progression is developed in the Prologue and Epilogue. The Prologue in 1:1–36 broadly recapitulates the book's overarching south–north order. Verses 1–21 focus on Judah, while vv. 22–36 concentrate on the northern tribes, beginning with Bethel (in Benjamin) in vv. 22–26 and moving through Manasseh in vv. 27–29, followed in quick succession by Zebulun, Asher, Naphtali in vv. 30–33 before returning south to Dan in vv. 34–36. The Epilogue also shows a south–north progression. It connects to Judah broadly (17:7–9; 18:12; 19:1–2, 18; 20:18) before recounting Dan's migration from the south (cf. "camp of Dan" in the south, in 18:12)[10] to the north (chap. 18). The Epilogue further provides representation for the tribe of Levi (17:7–13; 18:3, 15; 19:1; 20:4). The Prologue and Epilogue also reflect a royal perspective in the book's frame, with its references to national centers,

---

the Bible and Archaeology in Memory of G. Ernest Wright (ed. Frank Moore Cross, Werner E. Lemke, and Patrick D. Miller Jr.; Garden City, NY: Doubleday, 1976) 153–55.

10. See also the reference to "the camp of Dan" in 13:25.

whether Jerusalem in the south (1:7–8, 21; 19:10), or Bethel in the north (1:22–23; 20:18, 26, 31; 21:2, 19; cf. 4:5) or Dan (20:1; cf. 8:29).[11]

In addition to these representations of geography, the book shows a concern for chronology. While the Epilogue and Prologue lack notices for years, the accounts for the major judges in 2:11–16:31 alternate years of service to other foreign leaders with years of the land's quiet or of the judge's leadership. The brief notices for the minor judges provide only their number of years of service without reference to enemies:

Othniel:	8 years of Israelite service (3:8) and 40 years of quiet (3:11) [50 LXX A]
Ehud:	18 years of Israelite service (3:14) and 80 years of quiet (3:30)
Deborah/Barak:	20 years of Israelite service (4:3) and 40 years of quiet (5:31)
Gideon:	7 years of Israelite service (6:1) and 40 years of quiet (8:28)
Abimelech:	3 years of rule (9:22)
Tola:	23 years of leadership (10:2)
Jair:	22 years of leadership (10:3)
Jephthah:	18 years of Israelite service (10:8) and 6 years of leadership (12:7) [60 LXX B]
Ibzan:	7 years of leadership (12:9)
Elon:	10 years of leadership (12:11)
Abdon:	8 years of leadership (12:14)
Samson:	40 years of Israelite service (13:1) and 20 years of leadership (15:20), and 20 years of leadership (16:31)
TOTAL (MT):	430 years[12]

The periods of 40 years (with Deborah/Barak, Gideon, Samson; 20 plus 20 with Samson) evoke the passing of a generation. The years for the so-called minor judges are likewise irregular, yet they add up to 70,

---

11. See also the references to the Danites in 1:34; 5:17; 18:2, 16, 22–23, 25–26, and 30 (see below for the "camp of Dan" in Judah). Interestingly, Shiloh, too, is relegated to the Epilogue (18:31; 21:12, 19, 21).

12. Several commentators give a count of 410 years for the Book of Judges, but their listings of years omit the second notice of 20 years for Samson. See the survey of views in Trent C. Butler, *Judges* (WBC 8; Nashville: Nelson, 2009) 488; cf. Jack M. Sasson, *Judges 1–12: A New Translation with Introduction and Commentary* (AYB 6D; New Haven: Yale University Press, 2014) 8–14.

suggestive of a prior (archival?) source, perhaps with its own historiographical goal.

A number of modern commentators apply the years listed in Judges toward the 480 years given as the time from the exodus to the construction of the Jerusalem temple in 1 Kgs 6:1.[13] This verse has further inspired attempts at a historical chronology beginning from the exodus allegedly in the late fifteenth century.[14] However, these efforts omit some numbers from their counts. The period from Judges 1 to the building of the temple comes to 532 years, and the wilderness years would add another forty years,[15] bringing the total to 572 years. As another approach to Judges' chronology, some interpreters take the large numbers in this range as part of a larger chronological project (e.g., 400 years in Egypt according to Gen 15:13). For example, Joseph Blenkinsopp proposes that 480 years separate the exodus, the temple of Solomon, and the temple built in the Persian period.[16]

These approaches have overshadowed a potentially significant point about the chronology in Judges: the exact numbers of years in the MT Book of Judges is 430 years. While caution is warranted given variations in the LXX, the MT's number of years sounds suspiciously like the 430 years calculated for the time in Egypt according to Exod 12:40–41 (echoed in Gal 3:17), and the 430 years of exile that Ezekiel was commanded to symbolize by lying on his two sides for 430 days, 390 on one side and then 40 on the other[17] (Ezek 4:5–6; cf. the LXX numbers of 150 and 40 days, respectively).[18] In view of these two passages, the period of the Judges

---

13. For example, Ernst Bertheau, *Das Buch der Richter und Ruth erklärt* (2nd ed.; KHAT 6; Leipzig: Hirzel, 1883), xiii.

14. For example, A. E. Steinman, "The Mysterious Numbers of the Book of Judges," *JETS* 48 (2005) 491–500.

15. See Num 32:13; Deut 1:3; Josh 5:6; cf. 45 years according to Josh 14:10.

16. Joseph Blenkinsopp, *The Pentateuch: An Introduction to the First Five Books of the Bible* (ABRL; New York: Doubleday, 1992) 47–50.

17. For Exod 12:40 and Ezek 4:5–6, see Siegfried Kreuzer, "430 Jahre, 400 Jahre oder 4 Generationen: Zu den Zeitangaben über den Ägyptenaufenthalt, der 'Israeliten,'" *ZAW* 98 (1986) 199–210, here 208–9; see also idem, "Zur Priorität und Auslegungsgeschichte von Exodus 12,40 MT: Die chronologische Interpretation des Ägyptenaufenthalts in der judäischen, samaritanischen und alexandrinischen Exegese," *ZAW* 103 (1991) 252–58. Blenkinsopp suggests that Ezek 4:5–6 symbolizes the period of sojourning in Egypt following Exod 12:40 (*Pentateuch*, 49–50).

18. For the numbers in the LXX as a reflection of Babylonian divinatory practice, see Abraham Winitzer, "Assyriology and Jewish Studies in Tel Aviv: Ezekiel among the Babylonian *literati*," in *Encounters by the Rivers of Babylon: Scholarly Conversations between Jews, Iranians, and Babylonians in Antiquity* (ed. Uri Gabbay and Shai Secunda; TSAJ 160; Tübingen: Mohr Siebeck, 2014) 170–75.

gives the appearance of an era of Israelite suffering, analogous to the times of the Israelites in Egypt and in exile. In all three periods, the Israelites are subject to the oppression of foreign powers. Thus, the 430 years in MT Judges may bear particularly powerful symbolic freight.

This negative sense of the book's chronology also fits with its cyclical view of the past, perhaps the most famous aspect of its historiography in later literature (e.g., Ps 106:34-46; Neh 9:27-31; *1 En.* 89:41). The book gives the impression of the past as a repeating cycle involving individual leaders, thanks primarily to the introductions to major sections (2:11-23; 6:1-6; 10:6-16), also the borrowing of idioms in Deuteronomy and thus called "Deuteronomistic."[19] The following idioms in 2:11-19 are illustrative of the basic, repeating historiographical cycle in the panels: Israelite sin ("the Israelites acted wickedly in Yhwh's eyes. . . . They abandoned Yhwh. . . . They followed other gods"); divine anger ("Yhwh became angry at Israel"); punishment ("he gave them over into the power of" an enemy); the distress of the Israelites ("they were in dire straits"); and divinely designated judges (or better, "leaders") for military deliverance ("Yhwh raised up leaders and they saved them").[20] Then the cycle would begin once more ("the leader died, and they would revert to sinning"). This cyclical structure is reinforced by expressions linking episodes (see 3:8, 12; 4:2; 13:1). This historiography is sermonic in force, reinforced by the speeches added in 2:1-5 and 6:7-10. At the same time, it is also not entirely without parallel.[21]

The three Deuteronomistic introductions in 2:11-23; 6:1-6; and 10:6-16 shifted the stories' perspective to a primarily religious vision focusing on Israelite sin and divine help. The Deuteronomistic idiom informing the three introductions may be illustrated by a summary comparison of Deut 29:19-27 with Judg 2:12-15, part of the first introduction in 2:11-23.[22]

---

19. For Deuteronomic idioms in Judges, see Moshe Weinfeld, *Deuteronomy and the Deuteronomistic School* (Oxford: Clarendon, 1972; repr., Winona Lake, IN: Eisenbrauns, 1992) 320-59; and Corinne Lanoir, *Femmes fatales, filles rebelles: Figures féminines dans le livre des Juges* (Sciences bibliques: Actes et recherches; Geneva: Labor et Fides, 2005) 73-87. Cf. Frederick E. Greenspahn, "The Theology of the Framework of Judges," *VT* 36 (1986) 385-96.

20. For some caveats, see Greenspahn, "Theology of the Framework," 385-96.

21. K. Lawson Younger Jr. compares the pattern of disobedience and devastation followed by divine reconciliation and reconstruction in Esarhaddon's Babylonian inscriptions, which were used to explain the destruction of Babylon ("Judges 1 in Its Near Eastern Literary Context," in Millard, Hoffmeier, and Baker, *Faith, Tradition, and History*, 207-28, here 223, citing John A. Brinkman, "Through a Glass Darkly: Esarhaddon's Retrospects on the Downfall of Babylon," *JAOS* 103 (1983) 35-42.

22. Walter Groß similarly compares 2:11-12, 14-16, and 18-19 with Deut

Deuteronomy 29:19–27 promises divine anger for the worship of "other gods" in the land. It also offers an indictment of Israel in language echoed in Judg 2:12–15: "they abandoned the covenant of Yhwh the god of their fathers" (Deut 29:24; cf. Judg 2:12a); "when he brought them out of the land of Egypt" (Deut 29:24; cf. Judg 2:12a); "they went and served other gods and worshiped them" (Deut 29:24; cf. Judg 2:12a); "Yhwh was angry" (Deut 29:26 [see also v. 19]; cf. Judg 2:14a); "Yhwh will separate it out for evil" (Deut 29:20; cf. Judg 2:15a).[23] Notably, Deut 29:12 refers to the covenant and its terms, "just as he said to you and just as he swore to your fathers." This clause may be echoed in Judg 2:15: "just as Yhwh had said and just as Yhwh had sworn." The combination of these two verbs preceded by "just as" (כאשר) occurs only in these two verses. Deuteronomy 29:13 offers a further feature that the composer of Judg 2:15 might have found particularly suitable. In Deut 29:13, God is quoted saying that the covenant applies to "those who are standing here with us this day," and also to "those who are not with us this day." Judges 2:15 may be referring back to Deut 29:12.

While the ultimate inspiration for its idioms as described in the three introductions is the Book of Deuteronomy, the cyclical view of the past in Judges does not appear in Deuteronomy.[24] This cycle is an additional construction in terms of historiographical representation, and this order of features appears in varying attestations in other passages (e.g., Josh 23:14–24; 2 Kgs 13:3–6; Ps 106:34–46). Thus, this rather malleable template is not unique to Judges. Its origins remain unclear, although it might have been inspired by the succession of kings mostly doing "evil in the eyes of Yhwh." Two of the introductions detailing this cycle add deities identified as "the Baal/the baals and the astartes/asherahs" (Judg 2:11, 13; 10:6, 10; see also 1 Sam 7:4; 12:10; 1 Kgs 18:18), a feature also not in the Book of Deuteronomy.

Each of the three introductions (2:11–23; 6:1–6; 10:6–16) illustrates a repeating cycle, yet taken together they further represent a situation spiraling out of control.[25] The point may be illustrated by a summary comparison of the introductions in 2:11–23 and 6:1–6 with the introduction

---

31:16–29 ("Der Gottesbund im Richterbuch – eine Problemanzeige," in *Für immer verbündet: Studien zur Bundestheologie der Bibel* (ed. Christoph Dohmen and Christian Frevel; SBS 211; Stuttgart: Katholisches Bibelwerk, 2007) 102.

23. Note also "gods whom they did not know" in Deut 29:25 and Judg 2:10.

24. So Greenspahn, "Theology of the Framework," 389–90.

25. The view is common; see, e.g., Tammi J. Schneider, *Judges* (Berit Olam; Collegeville, MN: Liturgical Press, 2000) xii.

in 10:6–16. The first two introductions note Israelite idolatry, but the third introduction goes further, enumerating the various peoples' gods by whom the Israelites betray their own god (10:6). The first two introductions show no admission of Israelite guilt, while the third shows a double confession (10:10 and 15), even to the point of the Israelites trying to remedy the situation (10:16a). The first introduction shows the deity's compassion, for example, "Yhwh would feel compassion at their groaning because of their crushing oppressors" (2:18). By contrast, the third marks the severity of the situation: "I will not again save you" (10:13). Moreover, unlike the first introduction's show of divine pity (2:18), the third does not mention any divine compassion. Instead, the corresponding affective statement made about the deity in the third introduction states that the deity "grieved over the misery of Israel" (NABRE), more literally, the deity's נפש (life-force) was cut short (קצר) because of the trouble of Israel" (10:16b). The verbal idiom קצר נפש signals either divine impatience or weariness or perhaps both.[26] For the three introductions to the book's stories, this dire statement marks the book's downward trend. Indeed, Jephthah, the next "judge," is not divinely selected or divinely marked in any manner. He is a purely human choice (10:17–11:11), and his circumstances are reminiscent of Abimelech's more than the circumstances of any other preceding leader. An additional marker of the downward trend is the distribution of the phrase "the land was tranquil for X years" (3:11, 30; 5:31; 8:28). Notably, this phrase ends with the figure of Gideon, suggesting a less tranquil time beginning with Abimelech. Taken together, the three introductions reflect not only a cycle but also a downward spiral for the period that they purport to represent.

While the book's Deuteronomistic structure governing Judg 2:11–16:31 appears imposed on the "judges" stories, the arrangement of the stories adds to the effect, representing the period of Judges not only as a repeating cycle but also as a downward spiral. Exploring "the possibilities and failings of leadership,"[27] the "major judges" move generally from better to worse: the relatively positive figures of Othniel, Ehud, Deborah and

---

26. The Biblical Hebrew idiom קצר נפש may denote impatience (Zech 11:8) and weariness (Judg 16:16). See Robert D. Haak, "A Study and New Interpretation of QṢR NPŠ," *JBL* 101 (1982) 161–67, including Ugaritic attestations to both meanings. Haak also favors seeing a double entendre. For the idiom, see also Shalom M. Paul, "Samson on the Brink of Death," *VT* 60 (2010) 664–65.

27. Diana V. Edelman, "Remembering Samson in a Hellenized Jewish Context (Judges 13–16)," in *Leadership, Social Memory, and Judean Discourse in Fifth–Second Centuries BCE* (ed. Diana V. Edelman and Ehud Ben Zvi; Worlds of the Ancient Near East and Mediterranean; Sheffield: Equinox, 2016) 231–47, here 232.

Barak;[28] the ambiguous figure of Gideon/Jerubbaal and his unambiguously murderous son, Abimelech; Jephthah, whose vow incurs the death of his own daughter; and, finally, Samson, entertaining yet tragic in his death, regarded as a leader who in the end never leads.[29] The book's women, so clearly central to its purpose,[30] offer a progression parallel to that of the men, largely in how they fare at the hands of men.[31] Initially, the book shows heroic women often working against their circumstances: the war trophy yet assertive Achsah, who petitions her father for a better bride gift and thus emerges as the hero for her family and its future; the heroic Deborah, working in conjunction with the somewhat limited Barak; and the no less heroic Jael, who kills Sisera. In the stories of Gideon and Jephthah, the women are anonymous. Gideon has an unnamed concubine who is mother to Abimelech, himself avenged by an unnamed woman. Jephthah has a prostitute concubine as well as the daughter whom he stupidly condemns to death. Perhaps echoing Achsah as a "trophy wife" given to Othniel for his victory, Jephthah's daughter is her victor-father's war victim. The Samson cycle is particularly rich with women: Samson's sage mother, who implements the "nazirite" terms imposed by the angel on her pregnancy and understands the divine visitation, unlike her husband; the unnamed women with whom Samson is entangled; and the

---

28. Daniel I. Block suggests that the judges even at the outset are negative figures ("The Period of the Judges: Religious Disintegration under Tribal Rule," in *Israel's Apostasy and Restoration: Essays in Honor of Roland K. Harrison* [ed. Avraham Gileadi; Grand Rapids: Baker, 1988] 39–57).

29. See Eliyahu Assis, *Self-Interest or Communal Interest: An Ideology of Leadership in the Gideon, Abimelech, and Jephthah Narratives (Judg. 6–12)* (VTSup 106; Leiden: Brill, 2005) 127–30.

30. See Mieke Bal, *Death & Dissymmetry: The Politics of Coherence in the Book of Judges* (CSHJ; Chicago: University of Chicago Press, 1988); Lanoir, *Femmes fatales, filles rebelles*, 107–10, 145–46; and Christina García-Alfonso, "Judges: Subaltern Women," in *Postcolonial Commentary and the Old Testament* (ed. Hemchand Gossai; London: Bloomsbury, 2019) 106–21.

31. See Bal, *Death & Dissymmetry*, 1; Lanoir, *Femmes fatales, filles rebelles*, 107–10; Jo Ann Hackett, "Violence and Women's Lives in the Book of Judges," *Int* 58 (2004) 356–64; Yairah Amit, "Women Frame the Book of Judges – How and Why?," in *Joshua and Judges* (ed. Athalya Brenner and Gale A. Yee; Texts @ Contexts; Minneapolis: Fortress, 2013) 125–38; André Wénin, "Le récit et le lecteur," *Greg* 94 (2013) 503–23, here 519; and Mercedes L. Garcia Bachmann, *Judges* (WCS 7; Collegeville, MN: Liturgical Press, 2018) xlv–xlvi, 245–48. See also Vanessa Lovelace, "Intersections of Ethnicity, Gender, Sexuality, and Nation," in *The Hebrew Bible: Feminist and Intersectional Perspectives* (ed. Gale A. Yee; Minneapolis: Fortress, 2018) 88–93. Note further Natashia C. van der Merwe and Johan H. Coetzee, "An Alternative Ideology Relating to Difference as Hidden Polemic in the Book of Judges: Judges 4–5 as an Illustration," *OTE* 22 (2009) 677–94.

infamous Delilah, who betrays him under terrible duress from the Philistines.

The Epilogue further accelerates the negative trend in how women fare at the hands of men,[32] also showing the terrible fallout among the tribes at the book's end. The tribes, apart from Judah, are engaged in idolatry (chap. 17) and illicit priesthood (chap. 18), followed by the torturous, terrible rape of a vulnerable woman abetted by her husband (chap. 19) and a resulting civil war (chap. 20), itself issuing in the wholesale slaughter of one town's people except for the women forcibly seized (chap. 21).[33] The Epilogue also names a historiographical *telos* for this terrible situation, namely, the monarchy; "in those days there was no king in Israel; each man did what was good in his own eyes" (17:6; 21:25; see also 18:1; 19:1).[34] These are, by implication, conditions for misconduct (cf. Deut 12:8: "You shall not do . . . , each man doing what is right in his eyes"). While this expression may denote "each person" (as opposed to "each man"), the expression may very well denote "each man" as a final comment on Judges' many stories about how women fare poorly at the hands of men. As noted by many commentators (such as Baruch Spinoza),[35] this expression also gestures toward the monarchy, itself the time frame for the construction of the historical sequence of "judges and kings" (2 Kgs 23:22; cf. 2 Sam 7:11 = 1 Chr 17:10). In sum, these interactions between men and women[36] represent a downward spiral, particularly in the postwar treatment of women. While the introductions frame the issue in terms of apostasy,[37] the stories rarely do (see 8:27b). The religious perspective is at best symptomatic of Israel's broader situation:

---

32. See Lanoir, *Femmes fatales, filles rebelles*, 171–241.

33. See Will Briggs, "'A Man's Gotta Do What a Man's Gotta Do?' The Criticism of Hegemonic Masculinity in Judges 19,1–20,7," *JSOT* 42 (2017) 51–71.

34. For this idiom, see also Exod 15:26; 1 Kgs 11:33, 38; 14:8; 2 Kgs 10:30; Jer 34:15; 40:4–5. For its context in the Epilogue, see Weinfeld, *Deuteronomy*, 170; and Gregory T. K. Wong, *Compositional Strategy of the Book of Judges: An Inductive, Rhetorical Study* (VTSup 111; Leiden: Brill, 2006) 191–223.

35. Baruch Spinoza, *Tractatus Theologico-Politicus* (Gebhardt edition, 1925) (trans. Samuel Shirley; 2nd ed.; Leiden: Brill, 1991; orig., 1670) 168.

36. The point applies more generally to the families in Judges according to Nathan Hays, "Family Disintegration in Judges 17–18," *CBQ* 80 (2018) 373–92; see also M. J. Smith, "The Failure of the Family in Judges," *BSac* 162 (2005) 282–97 and 424–36. The judges also represent, with two exceptions (Othniel and Achsah, Manoah and his unnamed wife), departures from the social norms of marriage relationships, according to Thomas Hanks, cited in Garcia Bachmann, *Judges*, 12–15.

37. Block, "Period of the Judges," 39–57. See above for a critique of Block's overreading of the stories with this religious perspective reinscribed from the introductions.

"Entrapment is symptomatic of a malaise in Judges, in which the same 'road' is habitually taken with worsening results."[38]

Key to the overarching negative structure and message of Judges are its temporal conventions relating to times of its imagined audiences. The initial impression given by the book is a lengthy narrative set in the distant past between the conquest and the period leading up to the monarchy. At the same time, the book refers to later times in many ways. First, place-names are given different names in the past (לפנים) relative to the implied narrator's present (e.g., 1:10, 11, 23; cf. Josh 14:15; 15:15; 1 Sam 9:9).[39] These geographical notices ground the landscape as known to the author and audiences in the deep past.[40] The past and present are the two lenses of the narrative. Second and related, Judges refers eight times to "to this day" (1:21, 26; 6:24; 10:4; 15:19; 18:1, 12; 19:30),[41] a time represented as later than the events as narrated in the book. In Burke Long's words, "the phrase 'until this day' reaches far into the future into the time of the implied reader."[42] These etiological notices represent realities as rooted in the past and current in the time of authors and their audiences. Several texts explain the geography of different groups (1:21; 10:4; 15:19; 18:12). Thus, they provide a landscape of the authors' present, perceived to be rooted in the past. Third, the past is distinguished from the present by the expressions "at that time" (Judg 3:29; 4:4; 12:6; 14:4; 21:14) and "in those days," a particular feature of Judges in chaps. 17–21 (17:6; 18:1; 19:1; 20:27–28; 21:25; cf. 1 Sam 3:1). The expression "in those days" is sometimes combined in the Epilogue with reference to the lack of kingship (17:6; 18:1; 19:1; 21:25). Fourth, ritual practice in the narrator's present is given a basis in the past. An explanation of an otherwise obscure

---

38. Eric S. Christianson, "The Big Sleep: Strategic Ambiguity in Judges 4–5 and in Classic Film Noir," *BibInt* 15 (2007) 519–48, here 539.

39. See Erhard Blum, "Die Stimme des Autors in den Geschichtsüberlieferungen des Alten Testament," in *Historiographie in der Antike* (ed. Klaus-Peter Adam; BZAW 373; Berlin: de Gruyter, 2008) 113–14. Cf. Uriah Y. Kim, "Where Is the Home for the Man of Luz?," *Int* 65 (2011) 250–62, here 254.

40. As a related matter, explanations are provided for various proper names: the town Hormah (1:17); the town Bochim, 2:1–5; Gideon's name of Jerubbaal (6:32); the Rock of Oreb and Winepress of Zeeb as locales where Ephraimites killed the Midianite generals Oreb and Zeeb (7:25); the town Lehi/Ramat-Lehi (15:9, 16–17); cf. Danites maintaining Micah's sculptured image "throughout the time that the House of God stood at Shiloh" (18:31). These expressions, while not marking the past in the same manner, disclose the narrator's sense of past times and the understanding of the past through the lens of the present.

41. See Blum, "Die Stimme des Autors," 111.

42. Burke O. Long, "Framing Repetitions in Biblical Historiography," *JBL* 106 (1987) 385–99, here 389.

ritual practice is rooted in a story in the past (11:34–40). Another ritual situation is said to persist from the time of Moses "until the time the land went into captivity" (18:30), which looks like a reference to the fall of the northern kingdom (cf. Jer 7:12; Ps 78:60). Here the narrative refers to the monarchic period. The other notices likewise allude to the time of the monarchy or later. These sorts of "past–present" notices, what Adele Berlin calls "time-bridges,"[43] were a norm in Genesis–Kings, suggesting that, for a good deal of biblical historiography, the endpoint was the point.[44] The historiographical features surveyed above point to an effort or a series of efforts to render a larger picture of the past, one devoted as much to prescription as description. In short, the Book of Judges as a whole issued in a religious vision of the past cast in highly sermonic terms for the present.

43. Adele Berlin, *Poetics and Interpretation of Biblical Narrative* (Bible and Literature; Sheffield: Almond, 1983) 107–10. See further Susan Zeelander, *Closure in Biblical Narrative* (BibInt 111; Leiden: Brill, 2012) 47–48.

44. In her discussion of identity-building structures, Ulrika Wolfs-Knuts comments insightfully, "Regardless of whether informants regard time as linear or cyclic, they place themselves in the middle of it. They and their experiences are the hub and yardstick" ("Contrasts as a Narrative Technique in Emigrant Accounts," *Folklore* 114 [2003] 91–105, here 100).

The Exact Same Thing Only Different: "Hebrews" and "Israelites" in 1 Samuel

JOHN L. MCLAUGHLIN
University of St. Michael's College
Toronto, Ontario, Canada

I am pleased to offer this study in honor of Leslie Hoppe. I hope my effort to engage in detailed attention to the biblical text combined with archaeological evidence is a fitting tribute to Leslie's years of careful scholarship in both fields that I have come to count on as fellow members of the Old Testament Colloquium and during his two terms as General Editor of the *Catholic Biblical Quarterly*.

■ I. INTRODUCTION

The term "Hebrew" (עברי) occurs thirty-four times in the First Testament, compared with nearly twenty-five hundred references to "Israelite" (e.g., בן/בני ישראל, etc.).[1] This striking disparity suggests that the two are not synonymous and interchangeable, but that "Hebrew" conveys something "Israelite" does not, justifying its use in a limited number of contexts. "Hebrew" has traditionally been understood as differentiating between Israelites and other ethnic groups. The entry in BDB (720a) is typical: "**adj. et n. gent. Hebrew**, either **a.** put into the mouth of foreigners (Egypt. and Philist.), or **b.** used to distinguish Isr. from foreigners" (see also GKC §2b). This view is still found in modern lexica and dictio-

---

1. For ease of expression, I use "Israelite" to encompass all references to members of the sociopolitical entity "Israel," regardless of the exact phrase or grammatical construction used in each instance.

naries, monographs and commentaries, the latter as recently as 2011.[2] However, it is usually simply asserted without the kind of close analysis of texts supplemented with archaeological evidence that I offer below in the hope of providing a firmer footing for adjudicating the matter.

Most instances of "Hebrew" do occur during interactions between Israelites and non-Israelites, clustered in three main settings: the Joseph story (Gen 39:14, 17; 40:15; 41:12; 43:32), the exodus event (Exod 1:15, 16, 19, 22; 2:6, 7, 11, 13; 3:18; 5:3; 7:16; 9:1, 13; 10:3), and 1 Samuel (1 Sam 4:6, 9; 13:3, 7, 19; 14:11, 21; 29:3).[3] But the meaning of "Hebrew" must be determined from its contextual usage, and I have chosen the 1 Samuel texts as a test case to that end, for two reasons. First, usage can change over time, but, with the most recent historical setting, 1 Samuel has greater probability in general of reflecting the actual historical usage. Second, since Israel's independence is seriously threatened in the narratives in 1 Samuel, one expects a heightened sense of Israelite distinctiveness vis-à-vis the encroaching Philistines.[4]

In what follows I present a close reading of the Israelite and Philistine use of "Hebrew" in 1 Samuel, contrasted with the use of "Israel" by Canaanites. I will then consider an analogy between "Hebrews" and the ancient ʿapiru, followed by observations on the historicity of the 1 Samuel texts.

■ II. ISRAELITE USE OF "HEBREW"

The term "Hebrew" is used by an Israelite individual (Saul) in 1 Sam 13:3 and by the biblical (Israelite) narrator in 1 Sam 13:7 and 14:21. Careful

---

2. See under עברי or "Hebrew" in *TWOT* (1980), *TWAT* (1985) and its English translation *TDOT* (1999), *ABD* (1992), *HALOT* (1995), *NIDB* (2007), *DCH* (2007) and *EBR* (2015). Cf. also Graham Harvey, *The True Israel: Uses of the Names Jew, Hebrew, and Israel in Ancient Jewish and Early Christian Literature* (AGAJU 35; Leiden: Brill, 1996) 106; Kenton L. Sparks, *Ethnicity and Identity in Ancient Israel: Prolegomena to the Study of Ethnic Sentiments and Their Expression in the Hebrew Bible* (Winona Lake, IN: Eisenbrauns, 1998) 246, 248; David Toshio Tsumura, *The First Book of Samuel* (NICOT; Grand Rapids: Eerdmans, 2007) 193, 352, 361, 663; A. Graeme Auld, *I & II Samuel: A Commentary* (OTL; Louisville: Westminster John Knox, 2011) 66.

3. References to Abraham (Gen 14:13) and Jonah (Jonah 1:9) as "Hebrews" fit the lexical definition, but such isolated texts cannot establish consistent contextual usage. The "Hebrew" slave texts (Exod 21:2; Deut 15:12; cf. Jer 34:9, 14) are also widely dispersed, but, more importantly, they do not occur in the context of Israelite interaction with foreigners. They therefore militate against the traditional dictionary definition.

4. See Avraham Faust, *Israel's Ethnogenesis: Settlement, Interaction, Expansion and Resistance* (Approaches to Anthropological Archaeology; London: Equinox, 2006) 138.

attention to the content of these verses in their narrative contexts demonstrates that the term in these verses does not refer to Israelites.

a. "Saul blew the trumpet throughout all the land, saying, 'Let the Hebrews hear!'" (1 Sam 13:3)

In this verse Saul proclaims Jonathan's victory at Geba by calling out to "the Hebrews." The LXX avoids having an Israelite address supposed Israelites as "Hebrews" by rendering Saul's words as λέγων ἠθετήκασιν οἱ δοῦλοι ("saying, 'the slaves have revolted'"). The LXX's *Vorlage* might have contained עבדים ("slaves") rather than עברים ("Hebrews") (*resh* and *daleth* are often confused), but this is more likely the translator's intentional change of a presumed scribal error. This is exemplified by the fact that, in four of the five instances when Philistines use "Hebrew," the LXX has a transliterated form of "Hebrew" (1 Sam 4:6, 9; 13:19; 14:11; the exception [1 Sam 29:3] is discussed in detail in section III below), but every time an Israelite character or the narrator distinguishes between Hebrews and Israelites, the LXX has something other than "Hebrew": "slaves" is used here and in 1 Sam 14:21 while עברים is read as the plural participle of עבר ("cross over") in 1 Sam 13:7 and 29:3. The Greek translator consistently changed any distinction between Israelites and Hebrews, and the simplest explanation is that he considered them to be the same. Therefore, the MT should be followed in each instance.[5] Thus, even though most commentators adopt the LXX's verb ("revolted") they retain "Hebrews" in 1 Sam 13:3 but transpose the phrase before Saul's trumpet blast ("the Philistines were told, 'The Hebrews have revolted'").[6] This assumes, how-

---

5. Even if the LXX's Hebrew *Vorlage* contained עבדים in 1 Sam 13:3 and 14:21, a divergence between it and the MT at precisely those two crucial places would have to be purposeful. But a change from עבדים to עברים serves no purpose in the MT but rather introduces what was a problem for later versions and commentators, whereas a change in the opposite direction removes it. Thus, as the more difficult reading, the MT is to be preferred, and any variation in a purported Hebrew *Vorlage* for the LXX should be attributed to the qualms of a Hebrew scribe similar to those proposed for the Greek translator. However, the lack of Hebrew manuscript support plus the LXX's reading of עברים as a participle in the other two problematic places make it more likely that the alteration stems from the translator rather than from his text.

6. E.g., Hans Wilhelm Hertzberg, *Die Samuelbücher* (4th ed.; ATD 10; Göttingen: Vandenhoeck & Ruprecht, 1968) 79 n. 4; Peter R. Ackroyd, *The First Book of Samuel* (CBC; Cambridge: Cambridge University Press, 1971) 105; John Mauchline, *1 and 2 Samuel* (NCB; Grand Rapids: Eerdmans, 1971) 112; P. Kyle McCarter Jr., *I Samuel: A New Translation with Introduction, Notes, and Commentary* (AB 8; Garden City, NY: Doubleday, 1980) 225; Tsumura, *First Book of Samuel*, 336; see also Moshe Greenberg,

ever, that Saul would not address his countrymen as "Hebrews," which is precisely the point of contention.

b. *"Some Hebrews crossed the Jordan to the land of Gad and Gilead."* (1 Sam 13:7)

The use of "Hebrews" in subsequent narrative texts reinforces that Saul is not addressing Israelites in 1 Sam 13:3, and therefore that those Hebrews are a different group. In 1 Sam 13:6 the Israelites fled the Philistines at Michmash and "hid themselves in caves and in holes and in rocks and in tombs and in cisterns." Verse 7 then states that some "Hebrews" moved across the Jordan River. If "Hebrews" is used in v. 7 because Philistines were present, then it should have been used instead of "Israelites" in v. 6 as well; instead, the presence of both terms in successive verses indicates a distinction between the two groups. The LXX's καὶ οἱ διαβαίνοντες διέβησαν ("those who go over went over," reading ועברים עברו in v. 7a) eliminates the "Hebrews," and this, minus the awkward participial subject, is the basis for many modern translations,[7] although some avoid the problem by rearranging ועברים as ועם רב ("many people").[8] Both approaches presuppose that the Hebrews of v. 7 are a subset of the Israelites in v. 6, but that the former term should not have been used in the absence of foreigners. S. R. Driver justifies his change by claiming that "v. 7 carries on the thought of v. 6," but a ו plus a non-verb signals a disjunctive clause

---

The Ḥab/piru (AOS 39; New Haven: American Oriental Society, 1955) 92; NEB; NJB. Auld has Saul say, "The slaves have revolted" (*I & II Samuel*, 137). In contrast, Martin Rehm (*Die Bücher Samuel* [Echter Bibel; Würzburg: Echter, 1949] 31; Ralph W. Klein (*1 Samuel* [2nd ed.; WBC 10; Nashville: Thomas Nelson, 2008] 121, 122, 125–26), NABRE, and NRSV all follow the MT.

7. E.g., NJB, NEB, RSV (*contra* the NRSV), McCarter, *I Samuel*, 226. Going further, Auld adopts the LXX's subject as well (*I & II Samuel*, 138). An unpointed Hebrew text could lead to either the vocalized MT or the LXX, but in light of the translator's practice elsewhere (see the preceding paragraph), the MT is preferred. Contra McCarter, who reads ויעברו מעברות הירדן ("and crossed the fords of the Jordan"), the Greek does not support his emendation of the MT. Οἱ διαβαίνοντες is in the nominative case and therefore the subject; the accusative would be required if it were the object.

8. Henry Preserved Smith, *A Critical and Exegetical Commentary on the Books of Samuel* (ICC; Edinburgh: T&T Clark, 1899) 96; Rehm, *Die Bücher Samuel*, 31; Samuel Rolles Driver, *Notes on the Hebrew Text and the Topography of the Books of Samuel* (2nd rev. and enlarged ed.; Oxford: Clarendon, 1960) 99; Hertzberg, *Die Samuelbücher*, 79 n. 11. Smith traces the proposal to August Klostermann, *Die Bücher Samuelis und der Könige* (Kurzgefasster Kommentar zu den heiligen Schriften Alten und Neuen Testamentes 3; Nördlingen; C. H. Beck, 1887).

in Biblical Hebrew.⁹ This syntax at the beginning of v. 7 introduces a new subject distinct from the Israelites of v. 6, followed by another disjunctive clause (ו + Saul's name: ושאול) in v. 7b, creating a parenthetical reference to Hebrews as distinct from Israelites.¹⁰

> c. *"Now the Hebrews who previously had been with the Philistines and had gone up with them into the camp turned and joined the Israelites who were with Saul and Jonathan." (1 Sam 14:21)*

Once again, the fact that "Hebrews" and "Israelites" occur in the same verse points to a narrative distinction between them. Moreover, v. 22 adds, "when all the Israelites who had gone into hiding in the hill country of Ephraim heard that the Philistines were fleeing, they too followed closely after them in the battle" (alluding to 1 Sam 13:6). The phrase "they too" (גם־המה) clearly distinguishes the Israelites in this verse from the Hebrews in v. 21, similar to Israelites who hid themselves plus a separate group called Hebrews encountered earlier in 1 Sam 13:6–7. But the Hebrews in 1 Sam 13:7 and 14:21 are not the same group: the former fled because of the Philistine army's size (see 1 Sam 13:5), while the latter were with the Philistine forces. There are two groups of non-Israelite "Hebrews" in 1 Samuel 13–14, one that withdraws to the Transjordan in the face of the Philistine army while the other goes into battle with the Philistines but deserts to the Israelites when the latter gain the ascendancy.

The preceding reinforces that in 1 Sam 13:3 "Hebrews" does not refer to Israelites. Since the Israelite narrator used "Hebrew" in 1 Sam 13:7 and 14:21 to distinguish between Israelites and another group, it is unlikely that he would have Saul identify Israelites and Hebrews in 1 Sam 13:3. Rather, Saul's call for the "Hebrews" to hear was addressed not to Israelites but to either or both groups of Hebrews identified in 1 Sam 13:7 and 14:21.¹¹ Thus, Israelites are not distinguishing themselves from foreigners, so "Hebrew" must have some other nuance for them.

---

9. Contrast Driver (*Notes*, 99) and Bruce K. Waltke and Michael O'Connor, *An Introduction to Biblical Hebrew Syntax* (Winona Lake, IN: Eisenbrauns, 1990) §39.2.3. Driver's acceptance of the emendation ועם רב does not avoid this fact.

10. The fact that the LXX did not read "Hebrews" here supports this understanding of the verse. The translator recognized that a different subject is introduced in v. 7, and since he equated Israelites and Hebrews he read the word as a participle rather than as "Hebrews."

11. Cf. Norman K. Gottwald, *The Tribes of Yahweh: A Sociology of the Religion of Liberated Israel, 1250–1050 B.C.E.* (Maryknoll, NY: Orbis Books, 1979) 423.

III. Philistine Use of "Hebrew"

Philistines use "Hebrew" five times in 1 Samuel, and four times they clearly mean Israelites. Those four instances, therefore, can be treated together and briefly:

   a. "What does this great shouting in the camp of the Hebrews mean?" (*1 Sam 4:6*)
   b. "Take courage, and be men, O Philistines, in order not to become slaves to the Hebrews as they have been to you; be men and fight." (*1 Sam 4:9*)
   c. "The Hebrews must not make swords or spears for themselves." (*1 Sam 13:19*)
   d. "Look, Hebrews are coming out of the holes where they have hidden themselves." (*1 Sam 14:11*)

The Philistines' question in 1 Sam 4:6 is in response to the Israelites celebrating the arrival of "the ark of the covenant of Yhwh" in their camp, and so in 1 Sam 4:9 the Philistines warn themselves of their fate if they are defeated. In 1 Sam 13:19 the Philistines justify their metallurgical monopoly, and the reference to "all the Israelites" in v. 20 shows they meant Israelites. In 1 Sam 14:11, as Jonathan and his armor bearer approach the Philistine garrison at Michmash, the Philistines' comment alludes to the earlier actions of the Israelites in 1 Sam 13:6. By themselves these verses shed little light on Philistine usage of "Hebrews."

   e. "What/who (are) these Hebrews?" (*1 Sam 29:3*)

The final instance of Philistine usage of "Hebrew" is different from the preceding four and, in fact, undermines the traditional understanding of it as a contrastive ethnic term. In 1 Sam 29:3, the Philistine military commanders (שרי פלשתים) see David's men and ask, מה העברים האלה? (1 Sam 29:3). This is usually translated as, "What are those Hebrews doing here?" and is considered a clear example of foreigners using "Hebrews" to refer to Israelites.[12] But "doing here" is not in the Hebrew; the MT merely asks "What/who (are) these Hebrews?," a straightforward request for information that conveys neither surprise nor opposition. If "Hebrew" here is the Philistines' term for an Israelite, then David and his men must have

---

12. E.g., by the standard English versions plus McCarter, *I Samuel*, 424; and Tsumura, *First Book of Samuel*, 633.

been clearly identifiable as Israelites, but that is not the case. Wilhelm Hertzberg claimed that David's men had distinctive weapons and racial characteristics.[13] However, distinctive "Hebrew" weaponry is inconsistent with the larger context. Granted, the Philistine's control of metalworking in 1 Sam 13:19–23 meant that only Saul and Jonathan possessed swords or spears (v. 22), but the notion that David's band was identified as Israelites because they were armed with plowshares, mattocks, axes and sickles (cf. 1 Sam 13:20) is suspect. It stretches the imagination that they previously defeated the Philistines (1 Sam 18:27; 19:8) or enjoyed a lengthy raiding career armed only with agricultural implements. Even more unlikely is that, immediately after their dismissal here, a mere two hundred of them, so equipped, could defeat a band of Amalekites large enough that *just the survivors* of the rout numbered four hundred Amalekites (1 Sam 30:17). In fact, they did possess swords (1 Sam 25:13), but it is unlikely the Philistine monopoly on metalworking would have been breached at the zenith of their military success (the Philistine's victory over the Israelites and Saul's death are narrated in 1 Samuel 31). Since previously "there was no smith to be found throughout all the land of Israel" (1 Sam 13:19), it is improbable that the skill could have been mastered and a distinctive "Israelite" style developed so quickly, to say nothing of it being recognized as such. The more likely scenario within the narrative's worldview is that any weapons possessed by an Israelite would have been acquired by trade or capture from either Philistines or Canaanites and would not be distinctively "Israelite."[14]

More importantly, while some physiological characteristics may have distinguished Semitic Israelites from the Philistines,[15] this assumes that David's men were the only Semites present. But the social and political structure within Philistine territory indicates otherwise. The Philistines settled in the area as mercenaries protecting Egyptian interests, and when Egyptian power waned they assumed more direct and self-interested control of the territory.[16] But rather than eradicating the indigenous popula-

---

13. Hertzberg, *Die Samuelbücher*, 181; see also Smith, *Books of Samuel*, 244. Cf. the assertion in *HALOT* that "Hebrew" is commonly used "to indicate the distinctive racial features of Israel and its ancestors" (s.v. עברי).

14. Gottwald, *Tribes of Yahweh*, 655; David O'Brien, "David the Hebrew," *JETS* 23 (1980) 193–206, here 201.

15. On the Philistine's Aegean or western Anatolian origins, see, e.g., Othniel Margalith, *The Sea Peoples in the Bible* (trans. Othniel Margalith and S. Margalith; Weisbaden: Harrassowitz, 1994); Ed Noort, *Die Seevölker in Pälastina* (PA 8; Kampen: Kok Pharos, 1994).

16. See initially Albrecht Alt, "Ägyptische Tempel in Pälastina und die Landnahme der Philister," in *Kleine Schriften zur Geschichte des Volkes Israel* (3 vols.; Munich: C. H.

tion, they imposed their military and economic rule, with minimal evidence of destruction at Canaanite sites.[17] The Philistine metal monopoly fits this view, as do the material remains. The earliest level of Philistine occupation at Ashdod yielded locally produced Philistine I (= Mycenean IIIC:1b) monochrome pottery (characteristic of the Philistines) together with Canaanite pottery in the same stratum, and preliminary reports from Gath (Tell eṣ-Ṣafi) indicate a similar mixture during Iron Age I.[18] At Tel Qasile, a city founded by the Philistines, only 20 percent of pottery

---

Beck, 1953–64) 1:216–30, here 228–30. In addition to the references in the preceding note, for more recent discussions see the following scholars, who argue for an initial period of overlapping Philistine and Egyptian presence followed by increasing independence for the former: Manfred Bietak, "The Sea Peoples and the End of the Egyptian Administration of Canaan," in *Biblical Archaeology Today 1990: Proceedings of the Second International Congress on Biblical Archaeology, Jerusalem, June–July 1990* (ed. Avraham Biran and Joseph Aviram; Jerusalem: Israel Exploration Society, 1993) 292–306; Itamar Singer, "Egyptians, Canaanites, and Philistines in the Period of the Emergence of Israel," in *From Nomadism to Monarchy: Archaeological and Historical Aspects of Early Israel* (ed. Israel Finkelstein and Nadav Na'aman; Jerusalem: Israel Exploration Society; Washington: Biblical Archaeology Society, 1994) 282–338; and Łukasz Niesiołowski-Spanò, *Goliath's Legacy: Philistines and Hebrews in Biblical Times* (trans. Maria Kantor; Philippika: Altertumswissenschaftliche Abhandlungen / Contributions to the Study of Ancient World Cultures 83; Wiesbaden: Harrassowitz, 2016) 36–37. This model has been challenged by some; see the review by Assaf Yasur-Landau, *The Philistines and Aegean Migration at the End of the Late Bronze Age* (Cambridge: Cambridge University Press, 2010) 320–23.

17. See the discussions of Hanna E. Kassis, "Gath and the Structure of the 'Philistine' Society," *JBL* 84 (1965) 259–71; Gottwald, *Tribes of Yahweh*, 410–14; Ann E. Killebrew, *Biblical Peoples and Ethnicity: An Archaeological Study of Egyptians, Canaanites, Philistines, and Early Israel 1300–1100 B.C.E.* (ABS 9; Atlanta: Society of Biblical Literature, 2005) 200–201, 208; and the related yet wider-ranging comments of George E. Mendenhall, *The Tenth Generation: The Origins of the Biblical Tradition* (Baltimore: Johns Hopkins University Press, 1973) 146–53. On the general lack of destruction, see Yasur-Landau, *Philistines and Aegean Migration*, 288, 340.

18. On Ashdod, see Trude Dothan, *The Philistines and Their Material Culture* (New Haven: Yale University Press; Jerusalem: Israel Exploration Society, 1982; orig., 1967) 37; Amihai Mazar, *Archaeology of the Land of the Bible: 10,000—586 B.C.E.* (ABRL; New York: Doubleday, 1992) 308. For Gath, see preliminarily Alexander Zukerman, "Iron Age I and Early Iron Age IIA Pottery," in *Tell es-Safi/Gath*, vol. 1, *The 1996–2005 Seasons*, part 1, *Text* (ed. Aren M. Maeir; ÄAT 69; Wiesbaden: Harrassowitz, 2012) 265–312. On the correlation of both imported and locally produced Philistine pottery with Canaanite pottery in general, see John F. Brug, *A Literary and Archaeological Study of the Philistines* (BAR International Series 265; Oxford: B.A.R, 1985) 53–144; Carl S. Ehrlich, *The Philistines in Transition: A History from ca. 1000–730 B.C.E.* (SHCANE 10; Leiden: Brill, 1996) 11; Killebrew, *Biblical Peoples and Ethnicity*, 208, 233; Penelope A. Mountjoy, "A Note on the Mixed Origin of Some Philistine Pottery," *BASOR* 359 (2010) 1–12; contrast Faust, *Israel's Ethnogenesis*, 211–13.

remains reflect Philistine influence.[19] In fact, some of the monochrome (Philistine) and Canaanite pottery at Tel Qasile appears to come from the same workshop.[20] Estimates place the amount of Philistine pottery in the Pentapolis higher at 30–50 percent,[21] but that is an aggregate average for the entire Pentapolis, and the percentage could be lower in some of those cities. At the same time, some portion of "Philistine" pottery could be the result of its adoption by the native population.[22] In any case, Canaanite pottery continued to exist alongside the Philistine remains. Moreover, Philistine presence is even less significant farther inland. For instance, Philistine rule by "garrisons" in the hill country (1 Sam 10:5; 13:3, 23; etc.) is consistent with the archaeological evidence from Gezer, where the small amount of distinctively Philistine pottery from this period suggests that their control of the city was indirect.[23]

In sum, the ceramic remains point to the Philistines as a minority presence in the land, with "a symbiosis between the new Philistine population and the local Canaanite population. We may assume that the Philistines became overlords in an area which remained to a large extent populated by Canaanites."[24] Some of those Canaanites would have been

---

19. Dothan, *Material Culture*, 37; Mazar, *Archaeology of the Land*, 308.

20. Amihai Mazar, "The Iron Age I," in *The Archaeology of Ancient Israel* (ed. Amnon Ben-Tor; trans. R Greenberg; New Haven: Yale University Press; Tel Aviv: Open University of Israel, 1992) 258–301, here 271; Mazar, *Archaeology of the Land*, 317. He suggests that the potters were Canaanites who added Philistine-style items to their wares.

21. Lawrence E. Stager, "The Impact of the Sea Peoples in Southern Canaan (1175–1000 B.C.E.)," in *The Archaeology of Society in the Holy Land* (ed. Thomas E. Levy; New York: Facts on File, 1995) 333–48, followed by Bryan Jack Stone, "The Philistines and Acculturation: Culture Change and Ethnic Continuity in the Iron Age," *BASOR* 298 (1995) 7–32, here 18. Stone acknowledges that Canaanite pottery continued alongside the Philistine examples.

22. Robert Drews, "Canaanites and Philistines," *JSOT* 81 (1998) 39–61, here 45.

23. See *Gezer IV: The 1967–71 Seasons in Field VI, "The Acropolis"* (ed. William G. Dever; 2 vols.; Annual of the Nelson Glueck School of Biblical Archaeology 4; Jerusalem: Nelson Glueck School of Biblical Archaeology, 1986) 1:60–116; William G. Dever, "Archaeology, Ideology, and the Quest for an 'Ancient' or 'Biblical' Israel," *NEA* 61 (1998) 39–52, here 47; Nadav Na'aman, "The Contribution of Trojan Grey Ware from Lachish and Tel Miqne-Ekron to the Chronology of the Philistine Monochrome Pottery," *BASOR* 317 (2000) 1–7, here 2–3.

24. Amihai Mazar, "The Emergence of the Philistine Material Culture," *IEJ* 35 (1985) 95–107, here 106. See also Brug, *Literary and Archaeology Study*, 201–5; Mazar, *Archaeology of the Land*, 313, 327; Ehrlich, *Philistines in Transition*, 12–13, 20. Yasur-Landau suggests that at their height Philistines constituted only 50 percent of the population in Philistia (*Philistines and Aegean Migration*, 342). For the biblical "Philistines" themselves as a mixture of foreign and indigenous (Canaanite) elements, see

present for this battle. In particular, David is in the service of Achish, and there is some evidence that the latter was not a Philistine. Elsewhere he is called "the king" (המלך) of Gath (1 Sam 21:11, 13 [Eng. 10, 12]; 27:2; 1 Kgs 2:39), the common designation for Semitic rulers in and around Canaan, whereas סרן ("lord") is used in the First Testament exclusively for the Philistine overlords.[25] Achish's different title correlates with the differentiation between him and two classes of Philistines.[26] First of all, he is positioned in the rear of the army, away from the "lords."[27] Granted, leaders may direct battles from the rear lines (or an even greater distance),[28] but Achish is being reviewed by the Philistine lords (they are "passing on"; v. 2), and he appears to subordinate himself to them in vv. 6–7.[29] Moreover, Achish is challenged by the Philistine military commanders (v. 3), indicating not only that he is not a "lord" but also that he has an even lower status than the commanders.[30] Finally, Achish responds to the Philistine reference to "Hebrews" in his retinue by referring to Saul as the king of "Israel" (v. 3), echoing his identification of David's people as "Israel" in 1 Sam 27:12 (see further below concerning

---

Noort, *Die Seevölker in Pälastina*, 179, 183; Helga Weippert, *Palästina in vorhellenistischer Zeit* (HdA, Vorderasien 2.1; Munich: C. H. Beck, 1988) 392; Niesiołowski-Spanò, *Goliath's Legacy*, 40–52.

25. The only person explicitly called both a Philistine and a king is Abimelech (Gen 26:1, 8), but the time presupposed by the patriarchal narratives predates the Philistine arrival by centuries.

26. The differentiating significance of Achish's title is noted by Peter Machinist, "Biblical Traditions: The Philistines and Israelite History," in *The Sea Peoples and Their World: A Reassessment* (ed. Eliezer D. Oren; University Museum Monograph 108; Philadelphia: University Museum, University of Pennsylvania, 2001) 53–83, here 58. See also Niesiołowski-Spanò, *Goliath's Legacy*, 183.

27. Kassis, "'Philistine' Society," 267; G. E. Wright, "Fresh Evidence for the Philistine Story," *BA* 29 (1966) 70–86, here 81; Machinist, "Biblical Traditions," 58.

28. Israelite leaders absent from the vanguard include Moses on a hill above the battle (Exod 17:8–12) and David remaining in Jerusalem at his soldiers' insistence (2 Sam 18:3; he also stays away on his own initiative in 1 Sam 10:7; 11:1); cf. Ahab disguising himself in battle (1 Kgs 22:30). The possibility that Achish's position indicates a superior status was suggested to me by Greg Doudna (private communication), but the biblical text indicates otherwise.

29. Achish's reference to them as "the lords of the Philistines" in v. 7 after just "the lords" in the previous verses further distinguishes him from them in particular and the Philistines in general. Cf. below concerning 1 Sam 5:8, 11; 6:4.

30. See also Machinist, "Biblical Traditions," 71 n. 27 (he refers to "1 Sam 9; cf. 3:4" rather than 1 Sam 29:3–4). For the subordinate connotations of שר, see BDB, 978. The NEB and the JPSV translate the final clause in 1 Sam 29:6 as, "The other princes are not willing to accept you," making Achish one of them (see also Tsumura, *First Book of Samuel*, 635), but the MT reads simply הסרנים, "the lords/princes."

Canaanite vs. Philistine practice). The cumulative force of the preceding supports Achish's being a Canaanite vassal to the Philistines.[31] But even if this proposal is rejected, David's men would not have stood out from the Semitic Canaanites among Achish's own forces as well as those from other Canaanite towns under Philistine control.[32]

Another argument against taking 1 Sam 29:3 as a challenge to the inclusion of "Hebrews" among the Philistine forces is their prior presence there: in 1 Sam 14:21, Hebrews who were among the Philistines abandoned them to join the Israelites, and the Hebrews that Saul called to in 1 Sam 13:3 may also have been in the Philistine camp.[33] Some suggest that the Philistine commanders object because "Hebrews" is a synonym for "Israelites" and they cannot be trusted in battle against their kin.[34] But in 1 Sam 14:21 (and perhaps 13:3), Hebrews were present with the Philistines when they were battling the Israelites, so that cannot be the reason. Smith suggested that the commanders objected precisely because the Hebrews defected in 1 Sam 14:21;[35] but since those "Hebrews" were clearly distinguished from the Israelites, the commanders' objection here cannot be to including Israelites in the Philistine retinue. Moreover, the way that the commanders' objection develops argues against Smith's proposal. First, if "Hebrews" in 1 Sam 29:3 refers to Israelites, then Achish's

---

31. See further Kassis, "'Philistine' Society"; Wright, "Fresh Evidence," 81. This would facilitate Achish's transition to an apparent Israelite vassal in 1 Kgs 2:39–40; cf. 1 Chr 18:1. Achish's non-Semitic name does not make him a Philistine; history is replete with subject peoples taking names from their overlords' language as a means of accommodation and/or ingratiation. Biblical examples include the Yahwistic name of Uriah the Hittite under David, the Babylonian names of Sheshbazzar and Zerubbabel during the return from exile, and the Hellenistic names of Jason and Menelaus, high priests under the Seleucid King Antiochus IV. In this regard, Abimelech (LXX: Achimelech) in Ps 34:1 may preserve Achish's original Semitic name, subsequently altered to the non-Semitic "Achish" to emphasize his "otherness" (Cynthia Edenburg, "Notes on the Origin of the Biblical Tradition Regarding Achish King of Gath," *VT* 61 [2011] 34–38, here 36–37). Certainly his father's name (Maacah; 2 Kgs 2:39) was common to Semites of both genders: it was shared by Absalom's mother and daughter (2 Sam 3:3; 1 Kgs 15:2), Abraham's nephew (Gen 22:24), and the father(s?) of two members of David's bureaucracy (1 Chr 11:43; 27:16).

32. O'Brien, "David the Hebrew," 201. For a combination of Philistines and Canaanites in Iron I Gath, see William M. Schniedewind, "The Geopolitical History of Philistine Gath," *BASOR* 309 (1998) 69–77, here 73; Daniel Pioske, "Material Culture and Making Visible: On the Portrayal of Philistine Gath in the Book of Samuel," *JSOT* 43 (2018) 3–27, here 9–13.

33. Gottwald, *Tribes of Yahweh*, 423, followed by Tsumura, *First Book of Samuel*, 337.

34. E.g., Hertzberg, *Die Samuelbücher*, 181; Mauchline, *1 and 2 Samuel*, 184.

35. Smith, *Books of Samuel*, 244.

reference to David's former association with Israel through Saul is superfluous. His identification of David as an Israelite conveys information the commanders did not already have, which means they did not use "Hebrew" as a substitute for "Israelite." Second, the Philistine commanders demand the Hebrews' removal from the assembled forces *only after* they learn that David leads them, and not just because he is an Israelite but precisely because he is David, who in the past had "slain . . . his ten thousands" of Philistines (1 Sam 29:4–5). Third, if Achish's statement, "Since he deserted to me I have found no fault in him to this day" (1 Sam 29:3b), was meant as a defense of David's presence, it would serve this function much better *after* the commanders questioned his reliability. Coming *before* their objection, the emphasis is not on David as a traitor to Saul but on the quality of "Hebrew" service David has rendered to Achish since defecting.

In sum, "Hebrews" does not denote Israelites in 1 Sam 29:3. The question מה העברים האלה is a request for more information about a subgroup of the assembled "Hebrews" (as distinguished from the Philistine military), not a statement of opposition to including them in the impending battle. The sense of the phrase is, "What kind of Hebrews are these?" to which Achish replies, in effect, "Good ones, tested and true."[36] "Hebrew" here has a nuance comparable to "mercenary." This echoes the term's use in 1 Sam 14:21 and reflects the activity of David's band under Achish (see 1 Samuel 28). Thus, "Hebrew" in 1 Sam 29:3 does not have an ethnic denotation, because the Philistine commanders did not initially realize that they were speaking about an Israelite.

This in turn calls into question whether the Philistines use the term in 1 Sam 4:6, 9; 13:19; and 14:11 as a synonym for Israelite. Since Israelites never use "Hebrew" to distinguish themselves from foreigners in 1 Samuel (section II above), neither contemporaneous Israelites nor the author/editor of 1 Samuel is a likely source for a different Philistine practice. Rather, since Israelites did not use "Hebrew" as a contrastive term for Israelites in 1 Samuel, the Philistines probably did not either. Here too the word must have another nuance, and the use of "Israel" by non-Israelites in the same context as the Philistines' use of "Hebrews" is relevant for determining that nuance.

---

36. Ibid. 244; O'Brien, "David the Hebrew," 201. That Achish's evaluation is wrong (see 1 Sam 27:8–12) is beside the point. BDB (553a, s.v. מה) cites this verse as an example of מה with the meaning, "of what kind?" Although the LXX has apparently read עברים ("passing") from v. 2 at this point as well, the Greek still reflects this sense: τινές οἱ διαπορευόμενοι οὗτοι ("What kind are these who are passing by?"; τινές has a similar nuance in LXX Exod 3:11; Jdt 12:14).

■ IV. Canaanite Use of "Israel"

The Canaanites' use of "Israel" in the same context as their Philistine overlords using "Hebrew" is clearly relevant to this issue. Specifically, the fact that they diverge from the Philistine usage has significant implications for the nuance of "Hebrew." Philistines use "Hebrew" in 1 Sam 13:19 and 14:11, but, with no indication that Canaanites were present, those chapters do not figure in the following discussion. This leaves 1 Sam 4:6, 9 plus 1 Sam 29:3. Achish's reference to "Israel" after the Philistines used "Hebrews" in 1 Sam 29:3 was considered above, so the following focuses on the distinctive Canaanite and Philistine usage in the larger context of 1 Sam 4:6, 9.

a. "The ark of the God of Israel" (1 Sam 5:7, 8 [2x], 10, 11; 6:3)
b. "Give glory to the God of Israel." (1 Sam 6:5)

The Philistine's use of "Hebrews" in 1 Sam 4:6, 9 is part of the "Ark Narrative" (1 Samuel 4–6), during which the ark is moved to three different "Philistine" cities, where "the men of Ashdod," "the men of Gath," and "the Ekronites" refer to the sacred object as "the ark of the God of Israel" (ארון אלהי ישראל, 1 Sam 5:7, 8 [2x], 10, 11). Two elements suggest that these are not Philistines. First, the Philistines use the phrase "the ark of Yhwh" instead (1 Sam 6:2; see further below). Second, "the men of Ashdod" and "the Ekronites" are explicitly distinguished from their Philistine rulers by the repeated phrase, "So they sent and gathered together all the lords of the Philistines" (1 Sam 5:8, 11; see further below concerning 1 Sam 6:4b). A majority Canaanite presence in Ashdod and Ekron is consistent with the Philistine hegemony outlined earlier, in which case Canaanite use of "the ark of the God of Israel" stands out compared to the use of "Hebrews" by their Philistine rulers in 1 Samuel 4.

Elsewhere in the Ark Narrative, priests and diviners summoned by the Philistines use "Israel" in 1 Sam 6:3 and 5. The former verse repeats "the ark of the God of Israel," while the latter calls for an offering to appease "the God of Israel." In light of the Philistine adoption of the indigenous religion, these cultic functionaries would most likely have been Canaanites rather than Philistines.[37] This is supported by 1 Sam

---

37. Philistine adoption of Canaanite religion is exemplified in their worship of the Semitic deities Dagon, Astarte, and Ba'al-zebub (probably a polemical corruption by the biblical writers of Ba'al-zebul ["Prince Ba'al"]). On the archaeological evidence for Philistine religion, including their rapid movement away from Mycenaean to

6:4b, where they tell the Philistines that "the same plague was upon all of you and all of your lords." This is the only place where סרן occurs with a suffix (i.e., סרניכם, "your lords"), and, coming directly after the priests and diviners refer to "the lords of the Philistines" it distances and distinguishes the priests and diviners from both the Philistine populace and their leaders.[38] Furthermore, the Philistines' question what to do about "the ark of Yhwh" in 1 Sam 6:2 supports a distinction between them and the priests and diviners. Their use of the divine name by non-Israelites is suspect, and the same phrase in the preceding (narrative) verse suggests Israelite editorial influence here. In contrast, the cultic officials do not repeat "the ark of Yhwh" in v. 3 but instead substitute "the ark of the God of Israel." Their failure to use the phrase with which they were addressed is striking, especially coming immediately afterwards. They do echo the Philistines' phrase in v. 8, but only after another reference to "the God of Israel" in v. 5. Since the editorial hand evident in the Philistines' use of Yhwh in v. 2 could have redacted vv. 3 and 5 in the same way, the failure to do so is significant.[39] Having the priests and diviners associate the ark with Israel rather than the direct reference to Yhwh that they have just heard highlights and emphasizes the Philistine use of the divine name. Looked at from the other side, if the cultic functionaries could refer to "the God of Israel" in v. 3, why did the Philistines not do so in v. 2? The Philistines have an aversion to the terms "Israel" and "Israelite," which needs to be factored into understanding both their use of "Hebrew" and its overall meaning in the book.

Canaanite cult objects, see Dothan, *Material Culture*, 219–51; see also Neal Bierling, *Giving Goliath His Due: New Archaeological Light on the Philistines*, foreword by Paul L. Maier (Grand Rapids: Baker, 1992) 128; Ehrlich, *Philistines in Transition*, 14. The NJB, McCarter (*I Samuel*, 127), and Auld (*I & II Samuel*, 71) translate v. 2 as "their priests and diviners" (see also Rehm, *Die Bücher Samuel*, 18: "ihre Priester und Wahrsager"), and they are called "Philistine priests and diviners" by Patrick D. Miller Jr. and J. J. M. Roberts, *The Hand of the Lord: A Reassessment of the "Ark Narrative" of 1 Samuel* (JHNES; Baltimore: Johns Hopkins University Press, 1977; repr., Atlanta: Society of Biblical Literature, 2008) 72; however, the possessive pronoun is absent from the MT and present only in the LXX's additional phrase, "and their magicians" (καὶ τοὺς ἐπαοιδοὺς αὐτῶν).

38. Antony F. Campbell, *The Ark Narrative [1 Sam 4–6; 2 Sam 6]: A Form-Critical and Traditio-Historical Study* (SBLDS 16; Missoula, MT: Scholars Press, 1975) 108.

39. Even if this stems from the union of disparate sources (Smith, *Books of Samuel*, 42; Campbell, *Ark Narrative*, 113) the heuristic value of retaining different terms of reference stands. Against Smith and Campbell, however, see the discussion of Miller and Roberts, *Hand of the Lord*, 69–74.

▪ V. ʿAPIRU IN 1 SAMUEL?

The results of the previous three sections require that the following elements be included in any comprehensive definition of the word "Hebrew" as used in 1 Samuel:

1. It does *not* contrast Israelites with non-Israelites.
2. Philistines do not use it solely as an alternative to "Israelite."
3. It can denote Israelites and non-Israelites alike.
4. It refers to groups that might (but need not) function as mercenaries.
5. It has a more acceptable connotation for Philistines than the word "Israelite."

In light of this, the ʿapiru, known from Egyptian, Ugaritic, Hittite, and Mesopotamian sources, are sometimes proposed as an appropriate analogy for, if not an exact equivalent of, the "Hebrews" as outlined above. Yet, as with the traditional understanding of "Hebrew," the analogy is usually asserted rather than argued.[40] The scholarly consensus concerning the ʿapiru is stated by Marvin Chaney: "ʿapiru is not primarily or originally an ethnic designation. Instead, it refers basically to various elements in the population who were declassed, fugitive, uprooted, or who otherwise stood outside the acknowledged social system."[41] As the marginalized of ancient Near Eastern society, they often survived by hiring themselves

---

40. E.g., André Caquot and Philippe de Robert, *Les livres de Samuel* (CAT 6; Geneva: Labor et Fides, 1994) 78, 162; David Jobling, *1 Samuel* (Berit Olam; Collegeville, MN: Liturgical Press, 1998) 215; Tony W. Cartledge, *1 & 2 Samuel* (SHBC; Macon, GA: Smyth & Helwys, 2001) 330. Cf. Walter Brueggemann, *First and Second Samuel* (IBC; Louisville: John Knox Press, 1990) 104, 197.

41. Marvin L. Chaney, "Ancient Palestinian Peasant Movements and the Formation of Premonarchic Israel," in *Palestine in Transition: The Emergence of Ancient Israel* (ed. David Noel Freedman and David Frank Graf; SWBA 2; Sheffield: Almond, 1983) 39–90, here 53. This quotation constitutes the second and third of his five-point presentation of the "consensus"; see also his own seven conclusions on p. 57. Treatments of the ʿapiru include Jean Bottéro, *Le problème des Ḫabiru à la 4e Rencontre assyriologique internationale* (Cahiers de la Société Asiatique 12; Paris: Imprimerie Nationale, 1954); Greenberg, *Ḫab/piru*; Manfred Weippert, *The Settlement of the Israelite Tribes in Palestine: A Critical Survey of Recent Scholarly Debate* (SBT 2/21; London: SCM, 1971) 63–102; Mendenhall, *Tenth Generation*, 122–41; Oswald Loretz, *Habiru-Hebräer: Eine sozio-linguistische Studie über die Herkunft des Gentiliziums ʿibrî vom Appellativum ḫabiru* (BZAW 160; Berlin: de Gruyter, 1984). For a fuller bibliography, see Loretz, *Habiru-Hebräer*, 276–99.

out to whoever could provide them with a degree of social and economic security, sometimes as laborers and sometimes as mercenaries.

However, not all accept the appeal to the ʿapiru in this context. Significantly, none of the book-length treatments of the ʿapiru make the connection.[42] In particular, some scholars object to using "Hebrew" (עברי) or ʿapiru to illuminate each other because of the different vowels and middle consonants in the two terms, plus the fact that עברי reflects the gentilic form.[43] Manfred Weippert, however, has conclusively demonstrated a shift in both directions between the labials b and p in Semitic languages, while M. B. Rowton presents evidence for the development of a social term into an ethnic one in both the ancient and the modern world.[44] Social appellations with gentilic endings in the First Testament include "foreigner" (נכרי)[45] and "free man" (חפשי).[46] Another objection is the chronological distance between the second-millennium texts concerning the ʿapiru and the biblical texts.[47] However, the description of David's band in 1 Sam 22:2 is comparable to the social status of the ʿapiru: "Everyone who was in distress, and everyone who was in debt, and everyone who was discontented gathered to him; and he became captain over them."[48] Moreover, Nadav Na'aman has identified eight other examples of such groups in the Deuteronomistic History, parallel to what he calls "ḫabiru-like bands" mentioned in eighth- to seventh-century B.C.E. Assyrian royal inscriptions.[49] In other words, marginal groups comparable to

---

42. Apart from the review of scholarship, any link between the ʿapiru and Hebrews is simply not addressed in Bottéro, *Le problème des Ḫabiru*. In contrast, Greenberg (*Ḫab/piru*, 91–96) and Loretz (*Habiru-Hebräer*, passim [on 1 Samuel in particular, 101–22]) explicitly reject any connection.

43. E.g., McCarter, *I Samuel*, 240–41.

44. Manfred Weippert, *Settlement of the Israelite Tribes*, 74–82; M. B. Rowton, "Dimorphic Structure and the Problem of the ʿapiru-ʿibrîm," *JNES* 35 (1975) 13–20, here 15–16.

45. See Julius Lewy, "Ḫābirū and Hebrews," *HUCA* 14 (1939) 587–623.

46. Manfred Weippert, *Settlement of the Israelite Tribes*, 82; Loretz highlights the same shift with respect to the final vowel from Akkadian ḫupšu as from ʿapiru to עברי. (*Habiru-Hebräer*, 252–63).

47. Greenberg, *Ḫab/piru*, 93–96.

48. Recent correlations of David with the ʿapiru include Nadav Na'aman, "David's Sojourn in Keilah in Light of the Amarna Letters," *VT* 60 (2010) 87–97; and Daniel Bodi, "David as an 'Apiru in I Samuel 25 and the Pattern of Seizing Power in the Ancient Near East," in *Abigail, Wife of David, and Other Ancient Oriental Women* (ed. Daniel Bodi; HBM 60; Sheffield: Sheffield Phoenix, 2013) 24–59.

49. Nadav Na'aman, "Ḫabiru-like Bands in the Assyrian Empire and Bands in Biblical Historiography," *JAOS* 120 (2000) 621–24. Brian R. Doak ("'Some Worthless and Reckless Fellows': Landlessness and Parasocial Leadership in Judges," *JHebS* 11

the ʿapiru existed long after the El Amarna texts, regardless of what they were called. In any case, the following does not depend on a direct relationship between the "Hebrews" and the ʿapiru. I am not suggesting an *equation* between the two but rather that both words are social terms that meet the criteria listed above.

In that respect, when Saul and the Israelite narrator use "Hebrews" (1 Sam 13:3, 7; 14:21), it is analogous to the ʿapiru as a group without solid roots in society who serve whoever best suits their needs. Similarly, the Philistines apply the term to David in 29:3 with the nuance of "mercenary." Not only is this in keeping with David's actual activity at that time (cf. 1 Samuel 28), but, as noted above, the summary in 1 Sam 22:2 of his band's establishment is a classic description of the formation of ʿapiru groups from the marginalized and disenfranchised segments of society.[50] Moreover, the nuances associated with the ʿapiru in the El Amarna letters provide an explanation for the Philistine preference for "Hebrew" over "Israelite" used by their subjects. In the El Amarna documents, ʿapiru had an intrinsically negative connotation, as seen in its application by Canaanite rulers to anyone, including other kings, who had moved outside of or even simply resisted the established political structure. When the first four Philistine uses of "Hebrew" are read in light of this, it is easy to see just such a nuance in 1 Sam 4:6, 9; 13:19; and 14:11.[51] Indeed, 1 Sam 4:9 indicates that the Philistines considered the Israelites' proper status to be as their slaves.[52]

This explains why the Philistines referred to "the ark of Yhwh" in 1 Sam 6:2 even though their Canaanite subjects use the phrase "the ark of the God of Israel." The latter implies acknowledgment of Israelite independence, so in order to avoid imparting any legitimacy to Israelite social and political aspirations the Philistines use a phrase that would be more

---

[2011] article 2) discusses Abimelech, Jephthah, and the Danites (Judges 9, 11, and 18), all mentioned by Na'aman, in greater detail in terms of the ʿapiru.

50. Cf. Mendenhall, *Tenth Generation*, 135–36. On this phenomenon in the ancient Near East, see M. B. Rowton, "Dimorphic Structure and the Parasocial Element," *JNES* 36 (1977) 181–98.

51. On the negative connotations of the Philistine usage, see Julius Lewy, "Origin and Signification of the Biblical Term 'Hebrew,'" *HUCA* 28 (1957) 1–13, here 6; Mary P. Gray, "The Ḫâbirū-Hebrew Problem in the Light of the Source Material Available at Present," *HUCA* 29 (1958) 135–202, here 180; Tsumura, *First Book of Samuel*, 367–68; Klein, *1 Samuel*, 43, 127, 136, 277.

52. Thus J. P. Oberholzer, "The ʿibrîm in I Samuel," *Studies in the Book of Samuel: Papers Read at 3d Meeting Held at Stellenbosch, 26–28 January 1960* (Pretoria: OTWSA, 1960) 54; Manfred Weippert, *Settlement of the Israelite Tribes*, 87–88; Gottwald, *Tribes of Yahweh*, 421; Niels Peter Lemche, "Hebrew as a National Name for Israel," *ST* 33 (1979) 1–23, here 22.

at home in the Israelite national cult than in the mouth of a Philistine. Although this use of "Yhwh" is probably an editorial construct, it is a purposeful one that points to divergent attitudes by Philistines and Canaanites toward Israel. Narrative and Israelite usage throughout the ark narrative supports this interpretation. Various formulae appear in these contexts to refer to the ark, including "the ark of the covenant of Yhwh" (1 Sam 4:3, 4a, 5), "the ark of the covenant of God" (1 Sam 4:4b), "the ark of Yhwh" (1 Sam 4:6; 5:3, 4; 6:11, 15, 17), and "the ark of God" (1 Sam 4:11, 13, 17, 18, 21, 22; 5:1, 2, 10), but only once do Israelites associate it with "Israel": "the ark of the God of Israel" (1 Sam 5:9). The references to Yhwh and "God" (used absolutely) by an Israelite narrator or speaker obviate the need to identify the sacred object explicitly with Israel. An Israelite narrator, speaker, or reader knew that Yhwh was the God of Israel and, therefore, that the ark was associated with Israel, and all three individuals would also have accepted the nation's validity as a social and political organization differentiated from the Philistine system. As this reality was a "given," it was not necessary to have it repeatedly affirmed by Israelites in the story. On the other hand, the use of "Israel" by the Philistines' Canaanite subjects constitutes a rejection of their masters' political worldview. Their indirect affirmation of Israel's legitimacy is both emphasized and reinforced by the absence of "Israel" from Israelite lips throughout the Ark Narrative.

■ VI. THE DATE AND HISTORICITY OF THE TEXTS

Even if one accepts this interpretation of the "Hebrew" texts in 1 Samuel, the term's nuances could simply be the invention of the book's writer and/or editor. It is necessary, therefore, to address the historicity of the texts in question, which is itself linked to their date of composition.

The scholarly consensus holds that 1 Samuel reached its final form as part of the Deuteronomistic History during or after the Babylonian exile, but many scholars also acknowledge that some passages were composed earlier and incorporated later. For instance, Patrick D. Miller Jr. and J. J. M. Roberts argue that the Ark Narrative (1 Samuel 4–6) presupposes a time of composition close to the events it relates. Its purpose is to affirm Yhwh's superiority despite the Philistines' defeat of the Israelites and their capture of the ark.[53] Since the need for such reassurance

---

53. Miller and Roberts, *Hand of the Lord*, 88–91. Ancient Near Eastern comparative material where the capture and subsequent return of divine images serve the

presupposes a situation before the reversal of fortunes described in 2 Sam 5:17–25, they claim that the most likely date for its composition is between the Israelite defeat at Ebenezer and David's victory at Ba'al-Perazim.[54] On the other hand, Oswald Loretz dates all biblical texts referring to "Hebrews" to the postexilic period.[55] Kenton L. Sparks goes even further, arguing that the word itself derives from sixth- and fifth-century B.C.E. Egyptian texts that use it to refer to the land of Israel.[56]

In adjudicating these divergent views, the texts' content helps determine a relative date of composition. If "Hebrew" in 1 Samuel has a non-ethnic—that is, a social—meaning, this cannot derive from the exilic or postexilic periods, since that contradicts the understanding of the term in texts from those eras. For instance, Deut 15:12 calls Hebrew slaves "your brother" (אָחִיךָ), indicating an ethnic understanding of "Hebrew," in contrast to the law's earlier version in Exod 21:2, which lacks any kinship language. In Jer 34:9, King Zedekiah proclaims, "Everyone must free his Hebrew slaves, male and female, so that no one should enslave a Judahite, his brother [אָחִיהוּ]." If this verse is a case of Deuteronomistic editing,[57] then the identification of "Hebrew slaves" with a Judahite "brother" confirms that the Deuteronomists understood "Hebrew" as an ethnic designation. On the other hand, if Jer 34:9 is not Deuteronomistic, it and Deut 15:12 still show that the social nuances identified above were secondary, if not nonexistent, shortly before the Babylonian exile. In either case, one would have to explain why the Deuteronomists would introduce a social nuance into 1 Samuel contrary to their own understanding of "Hebrew" as an ethnic term. Moreover, since this ethnic understanding endured throughout the postexilic period and into the Christian era, as indicated by the self-designations of Jonah and Paul as a "Hebrew" and the LXX's attempts to obscure those instances in 1 Samuel that do not fit an ethnic denotation, the social meaning cannot result from an even later redactor

---

same purpose is presented in Campbell, *Ark Narrative*, 179–91; Miller and Roberts, *Hand of the Lord*, 12–26.

54. Miller and Roberts, *Hand of the Lord*, 91–94.

55. Loretz, *Habiru-Hebräer*, 181–82.

56. Sparks, *Ethnicity and Identity*, 247–48. See earlier Donald B. Redford, "The 'Land of the Hebrews' in Gen XL. 15," *VT* 15 (1965) 529–32, here 531–32.

57. Thus, e.g., Wilhelm Rudolph, *Jeremia* (3rd ed.; HAT 12; Tübingen: Mohr Siebeck, 1968) 222–23; Helga Weippert, *Die Prosareden des Jeremiabuches* (BZAW 132; Berlin: de Gruyter, 1973) 86–106; Robert P. Carroll, *Jeremiah: A Commentary* (OTL; Philadelphia: Westminster, 1986) 646–50; William L. Holladay, *Jeremiah 2: A Commentary on the Book of the Prophet Jeremiah, Chapters 26–52* (Hermeneia; Philadelphia: Fortress, 1989) 238.

either.[58] Therefore, the social nuances of "Hebrew" must predate the editors of the Deuteronomistic History, increasing the possibility that the texts in 1 Samuel were composed earlier. A precise date of composition cannot be established, but two considerations suggest an approximate period of time. First, there must be a sufficient interval prior to Jeremiah and/or the Deuteronomists for the memory of the original social connotations of "Hebrew" to fade. Second, the rise of a monarchy, with its emphasis on homogeneity and unity, is a likely one in which the distinction between "Hebrews" and "Israelites" would begin to be blurred. 1 Samuel 13–14 and 29 do not allow a more precise dating, but sometime before the early tenth century B.C.E. would be consistent with Miller's and Roberts's proposed date for the Ark Narrative.[59]

An early date for the texts has implications for their historicity. Chronological proximity to the time they describe results in a greater probability of historical accuracy than if they were much later compositions. Granted, antiquity and historicity do not always coincide. Earlier writers are just as capable of error as those further removed in time. However, the attention to details such as the distinction between the Philistines and their subjects in the Ark Narrative and the relative status of Achish in the Philistine army indicates that this author had a great concern for accuracy in reporting historical events.[60] While I make no claim concerning every detail in the "Hebrew" texts in 1 Samuel, this evidence does suggest that the texts preserve a historically based memory of Philistine and Canaanite usage, with their attendant sociopolitical ramifications.[61]

---

58. See Jonah 1:9; Phil 3:5. For the early postexilic dating of Jonah, see Jack M. Sasson, *Jonah: A New Translation, with Introduction, Commentary, and Interpretation* (AB 24B; New York: Doubleday, 1989) 20–28, here 27. On the LXX, see especially the beginning of section I and nn. 5 and 10 above.

59. See Miller and Roberts, *Hand of the Lord*, 91–94.

60. For a similar argument with respect to other sections of the Deuteronomistic History, see Baruch Halpern, *The First Historians: The Hebrew Bible and History* (San Francisco: Harper & Row, 1988). In contrast, the Book of Daniel, written ca. 170 B.C.E. but set during the Babylonian exile, is full of historical and chronological errors.

61. Ithamar Singer also asserts a core historical memory for the biblical Philistine narratives ("The Philistines in the Bible: A Short Rejoinder to a New Perspective," in *The Philistines and Other "Sea Peoples" in Text and Archaeology* [ed. Ann E. Killebrew and Gunnar Lehmann; ABS 15; Atlanta: Society of Biblical Literature, 2013] 19–27, here 25–27).

VII. Conclusion

In 1 Samuel, Israelites and Hebrews were "the exact same thing, only different," depending on one's perspective. The Philistines saw little difference between the Israelites who were resisting their control and other marginalized ʿapiru-like groups, so they called them "Hebrews." On the other hand, Israelites differentiated themselves from such "Hebrew" groups by using the term for others but never of themselves in 1 Samuel. Since the social nuance for the "Hebrew" texts in 1 Samuel stems from an early period, the events described should be taken into account in reconstructing the history of early Israel, especially the presence of ʿapiru-like groups in the region during this period, at least some of which affiliated themselves with the emerging Israelite state. Whether similar claims can be made for the use of "Hebrews" elsewhere in the First Testament awaits further investigation.

The End of Humiliation in LXX Isaiah 40

ANDREW R. DAVIS
Boston College School of Theology and Ministry
Boston, Massachusetts

■ INTRODUCTION

In his commentary on the Book of Isaiah, Leslie J. Hoppe, OFM, invites readers into "creative interaction with the [biblical] text" and recommends "a sustained reading [that] will evoke from the reader a variety of responses."[1] These lines from the commentary's introduction express well the kind of reading modeled by Hoppe himself in the Isaiah commentary, in which he provides insights on history, archaeology, poetry, theology, and so on, all while maintaining focus on the book's central themes, namely, Yhwh's holiness and Zion. I am honored to offer this essay in appreciation of Leslie, a colleague and friend whose work has facilitated creative interaction with the biblical text for me and his other readers.

Hoppe's emphasis on creative interaction and a variety of responses could serve as an apt description of LXX Isaiah, which is the focus of this essay. The Greek version of Isaiah is widely recognized as a mixed bag that is difficult to characterize.[2] The differences between the Old Greek

---

1. Leslie J. Hoppe, *Isaiah* (New Collegeville Bible Commentary 13; Collegeville, MN: Liturgical Press, 2012) 8–9.
    2. See Moisés Silva, "Esaias," in *A New English Translation of the Septuagint and Other Greek Translations Traditionally Included under That Title* (ed. Albert Pietersma and Benjamin G. Wright; New York: Oxford University Press, 2007) 823–24 (hereafter *NETS*).

of Isaiah (as reconstructed by Joseph Ziegler[3]) and the Masoretic Text (as well as 1QIsa[a]) are well known and include additions, omissions, misunderstandings of the Hebrew text, and other sorts of variants.[4] The question is how much weight to give these differences in our overall assessment of LXX Isaiah and its translator.[5] On the one hand, some scholars find the divergences substantial enough in number and kind to describe the Greek version as "a very free translation, verging on paraphrase."[6] According to Joseph Blenkinsopp, LXX Isaiah is the product of "a conscious process of contemporizing and actualizing by the translator."[7] On the other hand, there are scholars who think that the freeness of LXX Isaiah has been overstated and highlight instead the translator's fidelity to his Hebrew *Vorlage*.[8] This was the position of early scholars of LXX Isaiah, such as

---

3. Joseph Ziegler, *Isaias* (Septuaginta: Vetus Testamentum Graecum Auctoritate Academiae Scientiarum Gottingensis editum 14; 3rd ed.; Göttingen: Vandenhoeck & Ruprecht, 1983).

4. See first and still foremost the compilation and discussion of the variants by Joseph Ziegler, *Untersuchungen zur Septuaginta des Buches Isaias* [Alttestamentliche Anhandlungen 12; Münster: Aschendorff, 1934]). For lists of selected examples, see R. R. Ottley, *The Book of Isaiah according to the Septuagint* (*Codex Alexandrinus*) (2 vols.; London: Cambridge University Press, 1904, 1906) 52-53; Eugene Ulrich, "Light from 1QIsa[a] on the Translation Technique of the Old Greek Translator of Isaiah," in *Scripture in Transition: Essays on Septuagint, Hebrew Bible, and Dead Sea Scrolls in Honour of Raija Sollamo* (ed. Anssi Voitila and Jutta Jokiranta; JSJSup 126; Leiden: Brill, 2008) 193-204, here 200-204; Shalom M. Paul, *Isaiah 40-66: Translation and Commentary* (ECC; Grand Rapids: Eerdmans, 2012) 66-68.

5. On the probability of a single translator, despite LXX Isaiah's inconsistencies (and notwithstanding chaps. 3-39), see Isac Leo Seeligmann, *The Septuagint Version of Isaiah and Cognate Studies* (ed. Robert Hanhart and Hermann Spieckermann; FAT 40; Tübingen: Mohr Siebeck, 2004 [orig., 1948]) 179-83; and Marshall S. Hurwitz, "The Septuagint of Isaiah 36-39 in Relation to That of 1-35, 40-66," *HUCA* 28 (1957) 75-83.

6. P. Kyle McCarter, *Textual Criticism: Recovering the Text of the Hebrew Bible* (Guides to Biblical Scholarship; Philadelphia: Fortress, 1986) 90.

7. Joseph Blenkinsopp, *Isaiah 1-39: A New Translation with Introduction and Commentary* (AB 19; New York: Doubleday, 2000) 77.

8. We should note that some of the divergences found in the Old Greek may already have been present in the Hebrew *Vorlage*. For examples, see Alfred Zillessen, "Bemerkungen zur alexandrinischen Übersetzung des Jesaja (c. 40-66)," *ZAW* 22 (1902) 238-63, here 242, 253; see also Ziegler, *Untersuchungen zur Septuaginta des Buches Isaias*, 77-78, 109-10, 153, 165, 168; and Ronald L. Troxel, *LXX-Isaiah as Translation and Interpretation: The Strategies of the Translator of the Septuagint of Isaiah* (JSJSup 124; Leiden: Brill, 2008) 73-77. See also, however, Jean Koenig's critique of such proposals as too speculative (*L'herméneutique analogique de Judaïsme antique d'après les témoins textuels d'Isaïe* [VTSup 33; Leiden: Brill, 1982] 10-12).

Anton Scholz,[9] and has been championed more recently by scholars like Timothy Law, who insists that "the translator [of Isaiah] follows very faithfully his Hebrew source, rendering the sense as he understands it and often producing a highly styled Greek."[10]

A central issue is the question of actualization in LXX Isaiah. Already in the early twentieth century scholars recognized that the Greek translation of Isaiah had been influenced by other chapters of Isaiah and other books of the Bible.[11] Moving beyond such intra- and intertextual influences, Isac Leo Seeligmann argued that LXX Isaiah was also influenced by the translator's own religious and cultural context. Seeligmann points out numerous instances where the translator has opted for Hellenistic verbal constructions rather than Hebraic ones and argues that "not only these isolated, direct renderings, but also the entire tone of the translation breathes the spirit of the Jewish-Hellenistic milieu in which it came into being."[12] For him this milieu is apparent in the grammar and terminology of LXX Isaiah as well as in "allusions to events happening in the more or less immediate neighbourhood of the translator's place of residence [i.e., second-century B.C.E. Alexandria]."[13] Seeligmann saw the translation as a work that "contemporized" its Hebrew *Vorlage* and could be used as a source for shedding light on the Jewish-Hellenistic community of Alexandria.

The influence of Seeligmann's analysis has been considerable and is apparent in the number of studies that expand on his theory. In his view, the allusions to events in the translator's time and place were to be found only in Isaiah 8–23,[14] but subsequent scholars have argued for allusions outside of these chapters.[15] Especially noteworthy in this regard is the

---

9. See Anton Scholz, *Die alexandrinische Übersetzung des Buches Jesaias* (Würzburg: L. Woerl, 1880).

10. Timothy Law, *When God Spoke Greek: The Septuagint and the Making of the Christian Bible* (New York: Oxford University Press, 2013) 51–52.

11. Zillessen, "Bemerkungen zur alexandrinischen Übersetzung des Jesaja," 238–63; Ottley, *Book of Isaiah according to the Septuagint*, 1:47. Here again Ziegler's work is foundational; see his *Untersuchungen zur Septuaginta*, 103–34 ("die Beziehungen der Js-LXX zu anderen Schriften des AT") and 134–75 ("gegenseitige Beeinflussung sindverwandter Stellen in der Js-LXX").

12. Seeligmann, *Septuagint Version of Isaiah*, 186. See, once again, Ziegler, whose last chapter is dedicated to "der alexandrinisch-ägyptische Hintergrund der Js-LXX" (*Untersuchungen zur Septuaginta*, 175–212).

13. Seeligmann, *Septuagint Version of Isaiah*, 128.

14. Ibid., 180.

15. E.g., J. C. M. das Neves, *A teologia da tradução grega dos Setenta no livro de Isaías (Cap. 24 de Isaías)* (Lisbon: Universidade Católica Portuguesa, 1973); Koenig, *L'herméneutique analogique*; Robert Hanhart, "Die Septuaginta als Interpretation und

work of Arie van der Kooij. Like Seeligmann, he recognizes instances of contemporization, interpretation, and fulfillment, but he goes further to argue that fulfillment is not confined to individual instances. Rather *Erfüllungsinterpretation* represents the basic mode of interpretation of the LXX translator and the very genre of LXX Isaiah.[16] According to van der Kooij, the translation of Isaiah was not just a linguistic or philological undertaking but also the updating of "a text which was understood as making sense as 'prophecy' at the time of the translator."[17]

Other scholars, most notably Ronald Troxel and J. Ross Wagner, have been less sanguine about the approach of Seeligmann and van der Kooij. Troxel acknowledges isolated instances where the translator has provided additional nuance to a verse or resolved a difficult textual issue by using alternative wording, and he recognizes the influence of Alexandrian textual scholarship on the translator. He insists, however, that the source of additions and substitutions is the biblical text itself rather than the translator's external context. According to Troxel, the LXX translator is above all "concerned to bring an *understanding* of Isaiah to his Greek readers";[18]

Aktualisierung: Jesaja 9:1(8:23)–7(6)," in *Isac Leo Seeligmann Volume: Essays on the Bible and the Ancient World* (ed. Alexander Rofé and Yair Zakovitch; 3 vols.; Jerusalem: Rubinstein, 1983) 3:331–46; Stanley E. Porter and Brook W. R. Pearson, "Isaiah through Greek Eyes: The Septuagint of Isaiah," in *Writing and Reading the Scroll of Isaiah: Studies of an Interpretive Tradition* (ed. Craig C. Broyles and Craig A. Evans; 2 vols.; VTSup 70; Leiden: Brill, 1997) 2:531–46; Florian Wilk, "Vision wider Judäa und wider Jerusalem (Jes 1 LXX): Zur Eigenart der Septuaginta-Version des Jesajabuches," in *Frühjudentum und Neues Testament im Horizont Biblischer Theologie* (ed. Wolfgang Kraus and Karl-Wilhelm Niebuhr; WUNT 162; Tübingen: Mohr Siebeck, 2003) 15–35; David A. Baer, "It's All about Us! Nationalistic Exegesis in Greek Isaiah (Chapter 1–12)," in *"As Those Who Are Taught": The Interpretation of Isaiah from the LXX to the SBL* (ed. Claire Mathews McGinnis and Patricia K. Tull; SymS 27; Atlanta: Society of Biblical Literature, 2006) 29–47.

16. The first mention of *Erfüllungsinterpretation* occurs in van der Kooij, *Die alten Textzeugen des Jesajabuches: Ein Beitrag zur Textgeschichte des Alten Testaments* (OBO 35; Freiburg, Switzerland: Universitätsverlag; Göttingen: Vandenhoeck & Ruprecht, 1981) 33. Further discussion of the term occurs in the following works by van der Kooij: "Accident or Method? On 'Analogical' Interpretation in the Old Greek of Isa and in 1QIsa," review of *L'herméneutique analogique du Judaïsme antique d'après les témoins textuels d'Isaïe*, by Jean Koenig, BO 43 (1986) 366–76, here 368–70; *The Oracle of Tyre: The Septuagint of Isaiah 23 as Version and Vision* (VTSup 71; Leiden: Brill, 1998) 5–19.

17. Arie van der Kooij, "Isaiah in the Septuagint," in Broyles and Evans, *Writing and Reading the Scroll of Isaiah*, 2:513–29, here 516. Elsewhere, he argues comparable actualization in the targum and Vulgate ("Interpretation of the Book of Isaiah in the Septuagint and in Other Ancient Versions," in McGinnis and Tull, *"As Those Who Are Taught"*, 49–68).

18. Troxel, *LXX-Isaiah as Translation and Interpretation*, 288 (italics original).

any glosses, changes, or additions he introduces to the text are meant to facilitate this understanding rather than show the fulfillment of Isaiah's prophecy in the translator's own time. Such changes are not "'manipulations' or an 'exegetical method.' Rather, they are products of the translator using the state of knowledge of Hebrew of his time and place to provide a clear representation of the message of Isaiah in Greek."[19]

Wagner's monograph likewise concludes that there is no evidence that the LXX translator of Isaiah actualized the book for his Jewish Hellenistic audience in Alexandria. He acknowledges the "cultural encyclopedia" (i.e., linguistic, textual, and literary norms) that informed the translator's work but is wary of making historical events part of this encyclopedia, not least because the details of the time and place of translation remain uncertain.[20] Wagner focuses instead on the Greek Pentateuch, which for him serves as the centerpiece of the translator's encyclopedia. It was the authoritative textual tradition to which all subsequent translations of the Bible would be expected to adhere. Like Troxel, Wagner emphasizes the translator's fidelity to his Hebrew source text. The changes he makes to his *Vorlage* are a matter not of actualizing ancient prophecies but of elucidating and accenting themes already present in the Book of Isaiah and the Pentateuch.[21]

Against this backdrop of scholarly debate over translation technique, I will examine an instance of creative interaction in LXX Isaiah that has received almost no attention to this point, even though its divergence from the Hebrew text is considerable and its interpretive character seems apparent. The verse is Isa 40:2, and the word in question is Hebrew צבא ("term [of service]"), which is translated in the LXX as ταπείνωσις ("humiliation"). I will show how this rendering exemplifies the method of translation behind LXX Isaiah by examining three levels of influence: first, the use of ταπείνωσις in the Greek Pentateuch; second, the use of ταπείνωσις elsewhere in LXX Isaiah, especially 53:8; and, third, the use of the word and related forms in other Jewish Hellenistic literature. I will show that, of these three, the first two are the most relevant for interpreting ταπείνωσις in LXX Isaiah 40:2. Together they show a deliberate effort by the translator to connect two moments of exile in Israel's history: the slavery in Egypt and the Babylonian exile.

---

19. Ibid., 288–89. Likewise, Ulrich writes that even the substitution of contemporary place-names does not affect the meaning of the text: "there is no sign of 'actualizing exegesis'" ("Light from 1QIsa[a]," 202).

20. J. Ross Wagner, *Reading the Sealed Book: Old Greek Isaiah and the Problem of Septuagint Hermeneutics* (Waco, TX: Baylor University Press, 2013) 56–63.

21. Ibid., 235–37.

■ Ταπείνωσις in LXX Isaiah 40:2 and the Greek Pentateuch

Some of the most famous lines in the Book of Isaiah, perhaps in the entire Hebrew Bible, come at the beginning of chap. 40, where Yhwh orders his divine council to bring comfort to his people exiled in Babylon:

Isaiah 40:1–2 (MT)	
Comfort, O comfort, my people, says your God. Speak to the heart of Jerusalem, And proclaim to her that her term is complete, That her guilt has been expiated, That she received from Yhwh's hand double for all her sins.	נחמו נחמו עמי יאמר אלהיכם: דברו על־לב ירושלם וקראו אליה כי מלאה צבאה כי נרצה עונה כי לקחה מיד יהוה כפלים בכל־חטאתיה:

The word that is the focus in this essay is צבאה, which is here translated as "term." Before I examine its translation in LXX Isaiah, I should note that Hebrew צבא is itself a curious word. The root meaning of the word has to do with service, sometimes cultic (Exod 38:8; 1 Sam 2:22) but most often military.[22] The latter informs the most common meaning of the noun צבא as "army" or "military division," which is the basis for the principal epithet of the God of Israel: יהוה צבאות, "Yhwh of Hosts." This meaning is found throughout Second Isaiah, most often in the aforementioned divine name and epithet (44:6; 45:13; 47:4; 48:2; 51:15; 54:5), but also in 40:26 and 45:12, where it refers to the divine army.[23] As this brief survey of צבא shows, its use in 40:2 to denote "term of service" is unique in Second Isaiah, indeed in the entire Book of Isaiah, where the word uniformly means "army," including once in the same chapter (40:26).

If we look outside the Book of Isaiah, we find some comparable examples that shed light on צבא in 40:2. The Book of Job is especially helpful in this regard. In 7:1, for example, Job draws a parallel between humans' צבא on the earth and the workday of a hireling, and in 14:14 he longs for release from "all his days of צבא."[24] Another significant verse is Sir 7:15, which advises the audience not to rush through a toilsome work assignment (צבא מלאכת עבדה) from God. In all these examples צבא is associated with a fixed amount of time, and it is implied that this term of

---

22. See *HALOT*, 994–97; *DCH*, 7:64–69.

23. The meaning "army" also accounts for all sixty-five instances of the root in First Isaiah, including fifty-eight occurrences of the divine name יהוה צבאות ("Yhwh of Hosts"). The root is altogether absent in Third Isaiah.

24. A third example may be Job 10:17, which, like 14:14, combines צבא and חליפה ("release").

service is a burden and a hardship. For many commentators on Isaiah, these comparative examples of צבא inform the meaning of the word in 40:2, which they take to mean a "term set by God for the people's exile."[25] Thus, the use of צבא in 40:2 is unusual but readily explained with comparative examples from the books of Job and Sirach.

Our main interest in צבא, however, is not the meaning of the Hebrew word in Isa 40:2, but its translation in the LXX. In the Old Greek we do not find the word for "army" or any word related to the military or service.[26] Instead we find the word ταπείνωσις, meaning "humiliation, abasement."

Isaiah 40:2 (OG)	
ἱερεῖς λαλήσατε εἰς τὴν καρδίαν Ἰερουσαλημ παρακαλέσατε αὐτήν ὅτι ἐπλήσθη ἡ ταπείνωσις αὐτῆς λέλυται αὐτῆς ἡ ἁμαρτία ὅτι ἐδέξατο ἐκ χειρὸς κυρίου διπλᾶ τὰ ἁμαρτήματα αὐτῆς	O priests,[27] speak to the heart of Ierousalem; comfort her, because her humiliation has been fulfilled, her sin has been done away with, because she has received from the Lord's hand double that of her sins.[28]

The root meaning of this Greek word has to do with lowliness.[29] Its adjectival form, ταπεινός, refers to the low status of a person or place, and its verbal form, ταπεινόω, means "to belittle, humiliate," or even "to oppress." This last meaning accounts for most uses of ταπείνωσις in the LXX, where it occurs most often as a translation of Hebrew עני ("suffering, affliction"). The combination of עני and ταπείνωσις is used to denote the suffering endured by Hagar (Gen 16:11), Joseph (Gen 41:52), the Israelite slaves in Egypt (Deut 26:7), Hannah (1 Sam 1:11), or a distressed pray-er of the psalms (Pss 9:14; 25 [24]:18; 31 [30]:8; 119 [118]:50, 92, 152). Isaiah 40:2 contains the only instance in the Greek Bible of this word as a translation of צבא.[30] The predominance of עני behind instances of ταπείνωσις

---

25. See Claus Westermann, *Isaiah 40–66: A Commentary* (trans. D. Stalker; OTL; Philadelphia: Westminster, 1969) 35; Paul, *Isaiah 40–66*, 129.
26. Cf. στρατεία in Aquila and δύναμις in Symmachus and Theodotion, both meaning "army." The Vulgate translates צבא as *malitia* ("malice"), but Ottley suggests that this word may be a mistake for *militia* ("military service") (*Book of Isaiah according to the Septuagint*, 2:297).
27. On this insertion, see Ziegler, *Untersuchungen zur Septuaginta*, 71.
28. Translation from Silva, "Esaias," *NETS*, 853.
29. See Walter Grundmann, "ταπεινός, ταπεινόω, ταπείνωσις, ταπεινόφρων, ταπεινοφροσύνη," *TDNT* 8 (1972) 1–26.
30. Notably, ταπείνωσις occurs in none of the instances of צבא that establish its meaning as "term of service." Instead we find πειρατήριον ("trial") in Job 7:1 and 10:17, ἐπίπονον ("labor") in Sir 7:15, and no translation in Job 14:14.

in the LXX led Ziegler to propose that the Greek translator had עֲנִי in mind when rendering Isa 40:2 and that the word might have even been written as a marginal gloss in the *Vorlage*.³¹ Furthermore, he cites the use of עֳנִי/ταπείνωσις in Gen 16:11 and 29:32 as examples of the meaning that influenced the translation.

Setting aside Ziegler's speculation about a marginal gloss, I agree that Hebrew עֳנִי has informed the translator's use of ταπείνωσις as a rendering of צָבָא and that comparative verses from the Pentateuch can illuminate the translation in Isa 40:2. I disagree, however, that Gen 16:11 and 29:32, which feature instances of personal affliction, are the most instructive examples. More relevant, in my opinion, are verses in which ταπείνωσις is used to denote national calamity. This is how the term is used in Isa 40:2, so my search for intertextual comparisons will focus on examples with this corporate meaning. In particular, Deut 26:6–7 provides an important parallel for Isa 40:2, as do Gen 15:13 and Exod 1:12. Although the latter two verses feature the verb ταπεινόω rather than the noun ταπείνωσις, they nonetheless offer insight into the use of this Greek root to denote a national experience of exile, which was brought to an end by Yhwh's divine intervention.

Deuteronomy 26:5–9 gives instructions to the Israelites on the recitation of history that should accompany their offering of firstfruits. Part of this recitation is the remembrance that

> the Egyptians did ill to us and humbled [ἐταπείνωσαν] us and imposed hard work on us, and we cried to the Lord, the God of our fathers, and the Lord listened to our voice and saw our humiliation [ταπείνωσιν] and our toil and our oppression. And the Lord brought us out of Egypt with great strength [ἰσχύι] and with a strong hand [χειρί] and a high arm [βραχίονι] and with great spectacles and with signs and with wonders. (LXX Deut 26:6–8)³²

In this recitation, ταπείνωσις encapsulates the oppression endured by the Israelites in Egypt, and it is also significant that the modes of divine deliverance—Yhwh's strength (ἰσχύι), hand (χειρί), and arm (βραχίονι)—all find echoes in LXX Isaiah 40. The opening pericope that begins with ταπείνωσις ends with the announcement that "the Lord comes with strength (ἰσχύος), and his arm (βραχίων) with authority" (v. 10).³³

---

31. Ziegler, *Untersuchungen zur Septuaginta*, 123.
32. Translation of Melvin K. H. Peters, "Deuteronomion," *NETS*, 165.
33. Greek χειρός ("hand") also occurs in LXX Isaiah 40 but as an instrument of divine punishment rather than deliverance (v. 2).

The same meaning is found in Gen 15:13–16 and Exod 1:12, which use the verb ταπεινόω to describe Israel's oppression in Egypt. The former is part of the prediction at the end of Abram's covenant ceremony, warning of the hardship that awaits his descendants:

> Knowledgeably you shall know that your offspring shall be alien in a land not its own, and they shall enslave them and maltreat them and humble [ταπεινώσουσιν] them for four hundred years. But I will judge the nation that they are subject to; then afterward they shall come out here with much baggage. Now as for yourself, you shall depart to your fathers in peace, buried in a good old age. Then in the fourth generation they shall be brought back here, for the sins of the Amorites are not yet, to the present, filled up [ἀναπεπλήρωνται]. (LXX Gen 15:13–16)[34]

Like ταπεινόω and ταπείνωσις in Deut 26:6–7, the verb ταπεινόω is used here to describe the oppression suffered by the Israelites in Egypt.

Exodus 1:12 occurs in the actual exodus narrative rather than in a historical summary. As in Gen 15:13, we find the verb ταπεινόω rather than the root's nominal form, but the verse is still useful for establishing the meaning of ταπείνωσις in the Septuagint. Here we read that "as much as [the Egyptians] were humbling [ἐταπείνουν] [the Israelites], by so much the more they kept becoming more numerous and stronger" (LXX Exod 1:12).[35]

■ Ταπείνωσις IN LXX ISAIAH 53:8

The Greek Pentateuch is not the only biblical material that sheds light on ταπείνωσις in LXX Isa 40:2. Much closer to home, we find an instance of the Greek noun later in Second Isaiah itself, namely, in the fourth Servant Poem, where it occurs as the translation of Hebrew מעצר at the beginning of 53:8:

Isaiah 53:8 (MT)	
By oppressive judgment he was taken away, Who could describe his abode? For he was cut off from the land of the living Through the sin of my people, who deserved the punishment.	מעצר וממשפט לקח ואת־דורו מי ישוחח כי נגזר מארץ חיים מפשע עמי נגע למו:

---

34. Translation of Robert J. V. Hiebert, "Genesis," NETS, 14.
35. Translation of Larry J. Perkins, "Exodus," NETS, 52.

Isaiah 53:8 (OG)	
ἐν τῇ ταπεινώσει ἡ κρίσις αὐτοῦ ἤρθη	In his humiliation his judgment was taken away.
τὴν γενεὰν αὐτοῦ τίς διηγήσεται	Who will describe his generation?
ὅτι αἴρεται ἀπὸ τῆς γῆς ἡ ζωὴ αὐτοῦ	Because his life is being taken from the earth,
ἀπὸ τῶν ἀνομιῶν τοῦ λαοῦ μου ἤχθη εἰς θάνατον	he was led to death on account of the acts of lawlessness of my people.[36]

In some ways, this instance of ταπείνωσις complicates as much as it elucidates. The difficulties we encountered with צבא/ταπείνωσις in 40:2 recur, as we find ταπείνωσις again used to translate a Hebrew word other than the usual עני. Like 40:2, the Hebrew text of 53:8 is obscure and departs from the Greek translation. The Hebrew root עצר, meaning "to constrain," occurs only here and in Prov 30:16 and Ps 107:39, and although its basic meaning "to constrain" seems clear enough, it is less clear how it should be read together with ממשפט. The Greek text reads משפט without the preposition מן and understands it, not the servant, as the subject of לקח.[37] As in the case of ταπείνωσις in 40:2 for צבא, this verse is the only time it occurs in the LXX as a translation of עצר.

Little attention has been paid to this odd translation and its connection to ταπείνωσις in LXX Isa 40:2. One exception is Eugene Robert Ekblad's monograph on the LXX version of the so-called Servant Songs in Isaiah.[38] In addition to noting the issues mentioned in the previous paragraph, Ekblad considers why the LXX translator would have chosen ταπείνωσις as a translation of Hebrew מעצר, citing occurrences of the word in the Greek Pentateuch (Gen 16:11; 29:32; 31:42; 41:52; Deut 26:6-8) as well as in LXX Isa 40:2.[39] His focus, however, is on the intertextual influence of Isaian verses other than 40:2. Although he does mention briefly that "the servant's experience of a lack of justice could be interpreted as embodying and accomplishing Jerusalem's humiliation (40:1–2),"[40] he does not expand on this possibility, which, in my opinion, is crucial to understanding the method of the LXX translator.

---

36. Translation of Silva, "Esaias," NETS, 866. On the quotation of this verse in Acts 8:33, see Paul B. Decock, "The Understanding of Isaiah 53:7–8 in Acts 8:32–33," Neot 14 (1980) 111–33.

37. See Pierre Grelot, Les poèmes du Serviteur: De la lecture critique à l'herméneutique (Lectio Divina 103; Paris: Cerf, 1981) 106.

38. Eugene Robert Ekblad, Isaiah's Servant Poems according to the Septuagint: An Exegetical and Theological Study (CBET 23; Leuven: Peeters, 1999).

39. Ibid., 231.

40. Ibid., 232.

Ekblad's analysis is helpful as far as it goes, but it stops short of exploring the full significance of ταπείνωσις in LXX Isa 40:2 and 53:8. The most important result of the repetition is the homology it establishes between exiled Israel and the servant. Of course, the identity of the servant is a well-known question in the history of interpretation of Second Isaiah; I myself side with those who see the servant as a prophetic minority in exile.[41] This interpretation accounts for the mixed imagery associated with the servant, who is sometimes identified as a group ("Israel/Jacob") and other times described as an individual (especially in 50:4–9).[42] This mixture makes sense for a prophetic group, whose leader and members share the role of servant; what is said of the leader applies to the group and vice versa. Moreover, this prophetic group serves a purpose on behalf of the larger exilic community. Their suffering has been redemptive for the rest of the exiles and has made it possible for this larger Jacob to return to Zion (49:5–6).

This last part of the servant's mission is highlighted by the repetition of ταπείνωσις in 40:2 and 53:8. It makes more explicit a connection that is already apparent in the Hebrew text, namely, that the humiliation suffered by the servant is the same as the humiliation of the people; the former has brought the latter to an end and made restoration and return possible for Israel in exile. This connection is most apparent in the repetition of Hebrew עון in Isa 40:2 and 53:5, 6, and 11. Isaiah 40:2 declares that the iniquity of Jerusalem (here representing the people of Israel; cf. 52:9) has been expiated, but we do not learn until 53:5, 6, and 11 the servant's role in the expiation. The servant (a prophetic minority in exile) has borne the iniquities of the larger exilic community and thus made possible the restoration announced in 40:1–2. Against this backdrop, the LXX translator's use of ταπείνωσις in 40:2 and 53:8 may be seen as the addition of another link in this chain connecting the fate of the servant and the restoration of Israel. The translations of צבא and ערץ with this Greek word are indeed free and interpretive but nonetheless consistent with the overall meaning and style of Second Isaiah.

---

41. See Richard J. Clifford, *Fair Spoken and Persuading: An Interpretation of Second Isaiah* (Theological Inquiries; New York: Paulist, 1984) 56–58, 152–53. Alternatively, Shalom Paul sees the servant as a righteous minority within the exilic majority but not necessarily a prophetic group (*Isaiah 40–66*, 398).

42. For a good presentation of the mixed imagery, see Peter Wilcox and David Paton-Williams, "The Servant Songs in Deutero-Isaiah," *JSOT* 42 (1988) 79–102, though I disagree with them that the identity of the servant changes from chaps. 40–48 to chaps. 49–55.

When we look outside LXX Isaiah and the Greek Pentateuch, the occurrences of ταπείνωσις (and the related verb ταπεινόω) are not as illuminating. According to Seeligmann and van der Kooij, an important criterion for identifying an instance of contemporization or *Erfüllungsinterpretation* is any sign of influence from the translator's own context. Evidence of such influence may be an allusion to a historical event or a distinctly Hellenistic perspective on exile. Unlike earlier biblical traditions, which saw exile as the just punishment of sin, this later view saw diaspora as an injustice inflicted on Israel by foreign oppressors.[43] Certainly, the former perspective is expressed in LXX Isa 40:2, but this is also the case for examples of ταπείνωσις in other Jewish Hellenistic texts. In texts from the Book of Judith (6:19; 7:32; 13:20), for example, the word is used to describe the subjugation of the people at the hands of a foreign enemy, but unlike in LXX Isaiah, where the word conveys the humiliation of forced exile, these occurrences describe oppression taking place in the land (cf. 4:3).[44] Similarly, in 1 Macc 3:51 ταπείνωσις denotes humiliation that takes place within the land of Israel, in particular, the abasement of the priests at the Jerusalem temple. Even in 3 Maccabees, which was written in Alexandria and set in the third century B.C.E. (though probably written in the first century B.C.E.), ταπείνωσις refers to past humiliation suffered in the land (2:12) rather than expulsion from it. This brief survey of ταπείνωσις in deuterocanonical texts from the Hellenistic and Roman periods shows that the use of the word is quite different from what we find in LXX Isa 40:2. Unlike the occurrence there and in the Greek Pentateuch, which used the word to depict Israel's forced exile, these texts do not associate ταπείνωσις with diaspora. Instead it refers to humiliation within the land of Israel.

■ CONCLUSION

I began this essay with a discussion of how different scholars of LXX Isaiah have viewed the book as a work of translation. On the one hand are those, like Seeligmann and van der Kooij, who have argued that it should be read as an *Erfüllungsinterpretation* and actualization of its Hebrew *Vorlage* reflecting the translation's Jewish Hellenistic milieu. On the other hand are those like Troxel and Wagner, who acknowledge instances of

---

43. Seeligmann, *Septuagint Version of Isaiah*, 279–84.
44. A possible exception to this point is the lone instance in Judith of the verb ταπεινόω, which in 5:11 refers to the abasement of the Israelites by Pharaoh in Egypt.

updating and interpretation in the translation but argue that the overriding concern of the translator is to convey the meaning of the Hebrew original.

By way of conclusion, I reflect on how this test case can be instructive for our own creative interaction with the Hebrew Bible. Focusing, in particular, on contemporary Catholic approaches to Scripture, we should note that "actualization" is a method of reading that is highly endorsed by the Pontifical Biblical Commission in its 1993 document *The Interpretation of the Bible in the Church*. The document defines actualization as the process of "reread[ing] in the light of new circumstances and applied to the contemporary situation of the People of God."[45] Such reading engages the richness of Scripture and its capacity to speak to people and situations beyond its first authors and audiences. Through this actualization communities of faith place themselves "in explicit continuity with the communities which gave rise to Scripture and which preserved and handed it on."[46]

The document is quick, however, to caution readers against the misuse of this approach. It cannot be a means to project onto Scripture one's personal opinions, to remake it in our image. The commission recommends several safeguards against such manipulation. One is proper exegesis. By using critical methodologies to gain insight into what a biblical text meant to its author and first audiences, we can establish parameters for its meaning today. Another is to situate the biblical text within the rest of the Scripture, especially if it is reinterpreted by a later text in the Hebrew Bible or New Testament. The actualization that takes place within the Bible itself can be instructive for how we actualize the biblical text today.

The Commission advises readers to take cues from the actualization found in traditional Jewish and Christian sources and even cites specific examples, such as the targums, midrashim, and patristic authors—but not the Septuagint. This omission is unfortunate because the translation technique behind the LXX exemplifies the kind of actualization the document recommends. This essay has focused on just one instance of that technique at work in LXX Isaiah, but that instance is emblematic of the larger lesson that can be drawn from the Septuagint as a model of actualization. My analysis of ταπείνωσις in LXX Isa 40:2 has shown that, although the word differs from its Hebrew *Vorlage*, its departure should

---

45. Pontifical Biblical Commission, *The Interpretation of the Bible in the Church* (Boston: Pauline Books & Media, 1993) 117.
46. Ibid., 118.

be seen as an effort to convey more clearly the meaning of the Book of Isaiah as a whole and its connection to the Greek Pentateuch. The translation updated the Hebrew text of Isaiah by employing a Greek word that resonated with Isa 53:8 and with occurrences of ταπείνωσις in the Greek Pentateuch. In this way, this translation, like most of the Septuagint, strikes a balance between adapting the verse for a new audience and remaining faithful to the unity of its source text. It is balance achieved often by Leslie Hoppe in his writing and preaching and one to which we all should aspire.

My, What a Big Ship You Have! Ezekiel's Jealousy of the Favored Minority

CORRINE CARVALHO
University of St. Thomas
Saint Paul, Minnesota

I humbly offer this study to my admired colleague, Fr. Leslie Hoppe, whose body of work serves as a model for the interconnected spheres of ancient literature and archaeological discovery.

The poetic oracles directed at Tyre in the Book of Ezekiel preserve the social memory of the historical context of Tyre during the eighth to sixth centuries from the perspective of the Judean former elites. Archaeological studies in the past two decades have greatly enhanced our understanding of Tyre's unique place in and beyond the Levant, and these studies in turn bring new perspectives to the literature. Using an economic analysis of the material reveals the complexity and variety of colonization during this period not only within the Levant but across the Mediterranean world as well. The texts in Ezekiel 26–28 display ambivalence toward Tyre and reflect the variety of colonial strategies in the Assyrian and Babylonian periods.

The oracles in Ezekiel characterize Tyre as materially and economically advantaged. From the elaborate description of a merchant ship in Ezekiel 27 to its bedazzled prince in a luxurious garden in chap. 28, Tyre represents the center for trade in luxury goods of the ancient world. This characterization preserves memories of the city's great trade network, which affected its fate under the Assyrians. But, while geography and natural resources played some part in the city's trade, Tyre's own interaction with the indigenous settlements among whom they resided belie a distinct attitude toward the Other in the context of ancient colonization.

■ ECONOMIC COLONIZATION BY TYRE

While economic analyses of ancient Israelite society have been appearing for years,[1] this subject has received renewed interest with Roland Boer's book *The Sacred Economy of Ancient Israel*, published in 2015.[2] Widely praised,[3] it provides a macro-structure and shared vocabulary for analyzing the complexities of ancient Near Eastern economies. Boer uses Marxist theory to examine production, exchange, and social formation, dividing the ancient economy into three general spheres: subsistence economy, kinship/household-based economy, and plunder economy, each one overlaid with systems of allocation and extraction.[4] While Boer utilizes texts like Ezekiel's oracles against Tyre to flesh out his ideas, more work can be done on the application of the economic theory to biblical passages.

The economic setting of the texts collected in the Book of Ezekiel is clearly that of imperial imposition and extraction. The removal of workforces to Babylon constitutes a major source of this extraction,[5] but the book also attests to accompanying economic devastation. While both

---

1. See the discussion in Roland Boer and Christina Petterson, *Idols of Nations: Biblical Myth at the Origins of Capitalism* (Minneapolis: Fortress, 2014). See also Morris Silver, *Prophets and Markets: The Political Economy of Ancient Israel* (Social Dimensions of Economics; Boston: Kluwer-Nijhoff, 1983); M. A. Dandamaev, "Neo-Babylonian Society and Economy," in *Cambridge Ancient History*, vol. 3, part 2: *The Assyrian and Babylonian Empires and Other States of the Near East, from the Eighth to the Sixth Centuries BC* (2nd ed.; ed. John Boardman, I. E. S. Edwards, E. Sollberger, and N. G. L. Hammond; Cambridge: Cambridge University Press, 1992) 252–75; Christine Roy Yoder, "The Woman of Substance (אשת־חיל): A Socioeconomic Reading of Proverbs 31:10–31," *JBL* 122 (2003) 427–47; Matthew J. M. Coomber, *Re-Reading the Prophets through Corporate Globalization: A Cultural-Evolutionary Approach to Economic Injustice in the Hebrew Bible* (Biblical Intersections 4; Piscataway, NJ: Gorgias, 2010); Philippe Guillaume, *Land, Credit and Crisis: Agrarian Finance in the Hebrew Bible* (BibleWorld; Sheffield: Equinox, 2012); Roger S. Nam, *Portrayals of Economic Exchange in the Book of Kings* (BibInt 112; Leiden: Brill, 2012).
2. Roland Boer, *The Sacred Economy of Ancient Israel* (LAI; Louisville: Westminster John Knox, 2015).
3. See the responses to Boer's book in *HBT* 38 (2016).
4. This is similar to the schema provided by Elman R. Service, *Primitive Social Organization: An Evolutionary Perspective* (2nd ed.; Studies in Anthropology; New York: Random House, 1971).
5. Gershon Galil, *The Lower Stratum Families in the Neo-Assyrian Period* (CHANE 27; Leiden: Brill, 2007). On the effect of increased labor in the Neo-Assyrian period as well, see Peter R. Bedford, "The Persian Near East," in *The Cambridge Economic History of the Greco-Roman World* (ed. Walter Scheidel, Ian Morris, and Richard Saller; Cambridge: Cambridge University Press, 2008) 302–29.

Jeremiah and Ezekiel depict post-Babylonian Jerusalem as an economic wasteland, biblical scholars have shown that this depiction does not account for the complexity of the archaeological evidence.[6] While Jerusalem fell, many other parts of Judah have little evidence of total collapse. The increasing availability of economic texts from Mesopotamia and the application of more sophisticated economic models demonstrate the interdependence of local and imperial economies.[7]

The prophetic texts themselves mix the hyperbolic portrayal of devastation with the reality of ongoing populations, trade, commerce, and local economic structures. It is not possible to engage the economics of exile without also addressing the broader context of colonization and the clash of values it involves. Colonization takes many forms—not just military conquest and plunder but also cultural, ideological, and theological changes that threaten group identity, whether deliberately imposed or organically developed. The material in Ezekiel's oracles against the nations is preserved because it speaks to the cultural memory of these events, which shaped the identity of later generations. The texts I will address are cast in "poetic" or highly formalized language, deploying increased use of metaphor, evocative images, and hyperbolic descriptions.

Extraction via tribute and taxation coexisted with trade. Exports depended on a sustainable local economy, and temple–state international relations functioned side by side with internal client–patron systems, as well as patrilocal micro-economies. Traditionally, the focus on the differences between the Neo-Assyrian policies and the Neo-Babylonians has been on workforce and deportation strategies.[8] Clearly both monarchies needed to replace their own domestic workforces with cheap labor to sustain the expense of a large military. Assyrian hegemony lasted longer, was more organized, and therefore left more evidence than the relatively short-lived supremacy of Babylon. There is some evidence, however, especially in

---

6. Most notable here are scholars associated with the theory of the Myth of the Empty Land. The archaeological record clearly shows far less destruction in Benjamin than is described in the biblical texts. I do not find it at all surprising that some locations would suffer huge amounts of damage, while others would be relatively unscathed.

On Phoenicia in the post-Babylonian period, see Vadim S. Jigoulov, *The Social History of Achaemenid Phoenicia: Being a Phoenician, Negotiating Empires* (BibleWorld; London: Equinox, 2010).

7. See also discussions in Guillaume, *Land, Credit and Crisis*; and Boer, *Sacred Economy*.

8. On Assyrian deportations, see Yifat Thareani, "From Expelled Refugee to Imperial Envoy: Assyria's Deportation Policy in Light of the Archaeological Evidence from Tel Dan," *Journal of Anthropological Archaeology* 54 (2019) 218–34.

Babylon, of the concomitant need for a more international, educated workforce, although the exact labor of this workforce is not always known. Israelite collective memory of colonization and exile blends these two entities, as Margaret S. Odell's presentation of Ezekiel has clearly shown.[9]

Tribute is not the only explanation for the economic growth of empires. The cost of military expansion was offset by the economic benefits of new trade routes, secure travel, new technologies, and increased opportunities for expanding resources. In addition, a secure empire meant fewer expenses for conquest and increased production in both urban and rural centers no longer interrupted by war.[10] Decrease in siege and war stresses could lead to an increase of child and infant survival rates and less risk of the virulent spread of communal diseases. These changes would increase the development of the workforce and lead to higher production. While there is some evidence that Assyria reaped a few of these benefits,[11] Babylon became markedly more prosperous. Some scholars estimate that the Babylonian economy grew by about 50 percent over the course of the sixth to fourth centuries.[12]

Increased trade in the Assyrian and Babylonian periods is another indication of stability and growth. There are a variety of ways this economic boom can be traced, including a rise in luxury items, across Mesopotamia and the Levant. These items included exotic animals and skins,

---

9. Margaret S. Odell, *Ezekiel* (SHBC; Macon, GA: Smyth & Helwys, 2005) 335–70.

10. These assertions are based on the descriptions of losses caused by siege warfare. See, e.g., Brad E. Kelle, "Dealing with the Trauma of Defeat: The Rhetoric of the Devastation and Rejuvenation of Nature in Ezekiel," *JBL* 128 (2009) 469–90.

11. See, e.g., Moshe Elat, "The Economic Relations of the Neo-Assyrian Empire with Egypt," *JAOS* 98 (1978) 20–34.

12. Martha Roth, "The Material Composition of the Neo-Babylonian Dowry," *AfO* 36–37 (1989–90) 1–55, here 3; T. M. Lemos, *Marriage Gifts and Social Change in Ancient Palestine, 1200 BCE to 200 CE* (Cambridge: Cambridge University Press, 2010); Cornelia Wunsch, "Neo-Babylonian Entrepreneurs," in *The Invention of Enterprise: Entrepreneurship from Ancient Mesopotamia to Modern Times* (ed. David S. Landes, Joel Mokyr, and William J. Baumol; Kauffman Foundation Series on Innovation and Entrepreneurship; Princeton, NJ: Princeton University Press, 2010) 40–61; Michael Jursa, *Aspects of the Economic History of Babylonia in the First Millennium BC: Economic Geography, Economic Mentalities, Agriculture, the Use of Money and the Problem of Economic Growth* (AOAT 377; Münster: Ugarit-Verlag, 2010); and idem, "Babylonia in the First Millennium BCE: Economic Growth in Times of Empire," in *The Cambridge History of Capitalism*, vol. 1: *The Rise of Capitalism: From Ancient Origins to 1848* (ed. Larry Neal and Jeffrey G. Williamson; Cambridge: Cambridge University Press, 2014) 24–42.

ivories, silver, spices, and food items. These luxury items show up in both material and textual remains, including Neo-Babylonian dowries.[13] There has been a growing interest in the development of "collecting" as a mark of elite status arising in the Neo-Assyrian period, another indication of stability and economic growth.[14]

Recent excavations in the Levant have revealed large facilities constructed for the purpose of increasing production of trade items. The Neo-Assyrian remains at Ekron reveal a vibrant business in olive oil, beyond what would have been needed for local use.[15] Finds at Ashkelon show that Ekron's industry was not an isolated phenomenon.[16] Grain storage capacities in the Levant also increased beyond local need. According to Matthew J. M. Coomber, there is also evidence that Judah profited from Assyrian imperial stability, as inferred from the increased trade in spices from Arabia, the presence of more luxury items in Jerusalem, and increased urbanization with more centralized infrastructure.[17]

Further evidence of increased Levantine trade comes from Phoenicia.[18] There is a marked increase in the number of Phoenician remains in southern Europe during the Neo-Assyrian period. While it is not clear whether this was due to explicit Assyrian direction or was simply a way for Tyre and other cities to counteract the effects of Assyrian expansion remains unclear. What is clear is that both Ekron and Tyre found ways to profit from the Assyrian expansion, through economic adaptation and cooperation.[19]

---

13. Roth, "Material Composition of the Neo-Babylonian Dowry," 1–55; Bedford, "Persian Near East," 308–10.

14. Allison Karmel Thomason, *Luxury and Legitimation: Royal Collecting in Ancient Mesopotamia* (Perspectives on Collecting; Aldershot: Ashgate, 2005) 119–214; Jaqueline S. du Toit, *Textual Memory: Ancient Archives, Libraries, and the Hebrew Bible* (SWBA 2/6; Sheffield: Sheffield Phoenix, 2011).

15. On this and other Levantine trade, see Bedford, "Persian Near East," 308–9.

16. See the discussion of both Ekron and Ashkelon in Coomber, *Re-Reading the Prophets*, 77–134.

17. Ibid.

18. I use the word "Phoenicia" in this essay to designate a group of cities that modern scholarship groups together, including Tyre, Sidon, and Byblos. I recognize that this is not a designation used by these cities during the periods under study. See Josette Elayi, *The History of Phoenicia* (trans. Andrew Plummer; Atlanta: Lockwood, 2018), 4–7; Josephine Crawley Quinn, *In Search of the Phoenicians* (Miriam S. Balmuth Lectures in Ancient History and Archaeology; Princeton, NJ: Princeton University Press, 2018) 3–24; and Hélène Sader, *The History and Archaeology of Phoenicia* (ABS; Atlanta: SBL Press, 2019) 1–32.

19. Coomber, *Re-Reading the Prophets*, 77–134.

Although there is a general rise of economic increase throughout western Asia in the Assyrian period, it is also clear that Philistia and Phoenicia thrived in ways that other groups did not. In fact, the devastation suffered by Lachish and Samaria contrast with the growth of Ekron and Tyre. What economic and cultural factors contributed to this contrast? While part of the answer lies in different geographical locations,[20] the Judean texts address the cultural differences that the economic fates reflect.[21]

Phoenicia serves as an interesting test case for this intersection. Not only did Tyre avoid destruction at the hand of the Assyrians, but it also avoided a successful siege by Babylon. That alone, however, did not make Tyre unique. It also spearheaded its own colonizing effort along the Mediterranean rim, projects that changed the shape of North African history into the Roman period. Yet biblical scholars rarely depict Tyre as a colonizer. Recent archaeological investigations in southern France and Spain have enhanced our knowledge of Phoenician expansion.[22] New excavations in Portugal are beginning to reveal that this expansion did not stop at Gibralter but continued into the Atlantic.[23] In North Africa, except for Carthage, which is a planned large-scale settlement,[24] many of the Tyrian outposts were small trading centers often located on islands. Trade

---

20. For Mesopotamia, see Guillermo Algaze, *Ancient Mesopotamia at the Dawn of Civilization: The Evolution of an Urban Landscape* (Chicago: University of Chicago Press, 2008) 15–20.

21. On Philistia's cultural assimilation, see Seymour Gitin, "The Philistines: Neighbors of the Canaanites, Phoenicians and Israelites," in *One Hundred Years of American Archaeology in the Middle East: Proceedings of the American Schools of Oriental Research Centennial Celebration, Washington DC, April 2000* (ed. Douglas R. Clark and Victor H. Matthews; Boston: ASOR, 2003) 57–85.

22. Timothy Champion, Clive Gamble, and Stephen Sheenan examine the influence of both Greek and Phoenician trade after the eighth century in sub-Alpine Europe (*Prehistoric Europe* [1984; repr., London: Routledge, 2016], 244–54).

23. Ann Neville, *Mountains of Silver and Rivers of Gold: The Phoenicians in Iberia* (University of British Columbia Studies in the Ancient World 1; Oxford: Oxbow, 2007).

24. Carthage is a unique case in the African settlement. It was founded anew in the Iron Age and, from its beginnings, was a large settlement supported by local grain production and a large harbor. Although the Phoenicians played a role in founding the city, a fact preserved within Carthage's own cultural memory, we do not know the role local peoples played in its founding. We do know, however, that by the Neo-Babylonian period Carthage acted as an independent city-state allied with Tyre. Neville suggests that it gained its ascendancy in the period during which the Babylonians besieged Tyre (*Mountains of Silver*, 163–64).

with North African settlements provided access to ivory and exotic animals, such as those recorded in lists of Phoenician tribute to Assyria.[25]

In the western Mediterranean, while there are some trading posts, there are far more pure Tyrian settlements. In southern France and the Iberian Peninsula, the Phoenicians first established trading posts on islands near harbors. In the most advantageous spots, they then built settlements on the mainland near where rivers emptied into a navigable harbor. These settlements could be quite large, replicating planned Phoenician cities. Material remains at indigenous settlements upstream include Tyrian products gained through trade and not conquest. In addition, agricultural growth supported these new sites, indicating general cooperation between the Phoenicians and the indigenous populations.[26]

Tyre settled in these areas in order to have access to mineral deposits, especially silver, which became more valuable with the rise of protocoinage in the Assyrian Empire. Tyre traded grain to these areas, as well as some luxury goods, such as the purple dye for which they were so famous.[27] They also traded Levantine wine, olive oil, and some timber, as well as Arabic spices. In addition, they brought with them goods from other trading partners in the Greek isles, Cyprus and Crete, civilizations that also benefited from Iberian metals.

Scholars differ on whether Tyre's economic spread constituted an expanded trade network solely for their own benefit or whether it was necessitated by demands from the Assyrians.[28] Either way, did Tyre's expanded presence in the Mediterranean make them a colonial power? What makes trade, which extracts goods from one place for the benefit of another, different from economic colonization? And is there enough separation of commerce and political power in the ancient world to even try to distinguish between economic and political colonization?

While we do not have the voices of the indigenous Iberian or North African groups to give us their experience of the Phoenician "trade," we do have a growing picture from archaeological excavations of the method of expansion preferred by the Tyrians, and it is quite different from that

---

25. Elat notes the presence of African animals in lists of Phoenician tribute to Assyria ("Economic Relations," 22 n. 14).
26. Neville, *Mountains of Silver*, 105–34.
27. For a good discussion of the dye, see Odell, *Ezekiel*, 351.
28. See Marilyn J. Bierling and Seymour Gitin, eds., *The Phoenicians in Spain: An Archaeological Review of the Eighth–Sixth Centuries B.C.E.; A Collection of Articles Translated from Spanish* (Winona Lake, IN: Eisenbrauns, 2002); Neville, *Mountains of Silver*, 159–70.

of Assyria or Babylon.[29] When Phoenicians did settle in an area, they created their own settlements near their trading partners rather than take over already settled areas. Even the name "Carthage" means literally a "new city." The larger settlements of one thousand to fifteen hundred inhabitants were designed to house settled families. In a variety of ways, Phoenicians avoided overt cultural colonization. Their diet differed from that of the local community,[30] and they maintained their own religious and burial practices as a distinct marker of identity.[31] Although Phoenician wares were found at inland indigenous sites, the Phoenicians lived separately, which allowed each group to maintain its own markers of identity.

This picture changes dramatically in the Neo-Babylonian period. The archaeological record presents stark evidence of the collapse of Tyrian presence in the northwest Mediterranean coinciding with the gradual collapse of Assyrian hegemony in the Levant and the rise of Babylonian power. This political change within the Tyrian homeland must have affected Tyre's economic efforts. With the withdrawal of Tyre from Iberia and southern France, the resulting power vacuum in southern Europe was filled in by North African colonization stemming from the Phoenician hybrid city of Carthage. In contrast to Tyre, this new encroachment did include military incursions and imposition of religious beliefs. So, although Carthage was an example of a Phoenician settlement, its hybrid identity differed from that of its Tyrian origins. Carthage's assimilation to colonial practices, which turns those they interact with into foreign threats, a practice called "othering," puts into even more stark relief the uniqueness of Tyre's interactions in the Mediterranean.

The evidence of a uniquely Tyrian approach to the Other is found in various aspects of Tyre's cultural history. Scholars have always viewed the Phoenicians themselves as a culturally hybrid group. In fact, identifying Phoenician presence in material remains has always been complicated by their use of Egyptian and Hellenistic motifs. I find this fact interesting because it suggests that their own cultural attitude is that of seeing connections between themselves and other people. Their identity did not depend on being different from others, but rather on their ability to adapt,

---

29. Information in this paragraph depends on Neville, *Mountains of Silver*, 105–34.

30. Hans Georg Niemeyer, "The Phoenician Settlement at Toscanos: Urbanization and Function," in Bierling and Gittin, *Phoenicians in Spain*, 31–48.

31. On Phoenician religion, see Sader, *History and Archaeology of Phoenicia*, 181–48; and Brian R. Doak, *Phoenician Aniconism in Its Mediterranean and Ancient Near Eastern Contexts* (ABS 21; Atlanta: SBL Press, 2015).

blend, and appreciate. Inculturation was more than an economic ploy to drum up business in another land, since these same "foreign" motifs are found in native Phoenician lands.

Maria Eugenia Aubet attributes the interruption in the Tyrian presence in the Mediterranean to the collapse of Assyria, the major consumer of silver.[32] Vadim S. Jigoulov asserts that Neo-Babylonian presence in the Levant was "relaxed," with little cultural imposition, but we also know that some kind of crisis occurred that dramatically affected Tyrian presence in the west.[33] We know that Tyre experienced a very long Babylonian siege, which they eventually withstood. Scholars have often noted that their survival probably was a factor of geography, which both protected Tyre from the landed siege-works normally employed and allowed for sea trade that kept the citizens fed. That trade, however, was no longer with the Iberian markets. We also know that Levantine allies, like the Philistines, suffered deportation under the Babylonians; so, while Babylonian colonization may not have involved cultural imposition or the establishment of permanent settlements, it did include forced migration and significant extraction of at least human resources from select communities.

Why was the fate of Phoenicia different under the Assyrians than under the Babylonians? Was it because the Babylonians were not interested in economic partner ventures? Or was it increased resistance on the part of Phoenicia to cooperate or adapt? If the Tyrians had started to insist more on their own unique identity, it might have made their interaction with Babylon more like that of Judah, which also sought to retain distinct markers of identity throughout its history.[34]

---

32. Maria Eugenia Aubet, *The Phoenicians and the West: Politics, Colonies and Trade* (2nd ed.; trans. Mary Turton; New York: Cambridge University Press, 2001) 273–76.

33. Jigoulov, *Social History of Achaemenid Phoenicia*, 21–25.

34. David Aberbach, *Imperialism and Biblical Prophecy 750–500 BCE* (London: Routledge, 1993); Elizabeth Bloch-Smith, "Israelite Ethnicity in Iron I: Archaeology Preserves What Is Remembered and What Is Forgotten in Israel's History," *JBL* 122 (2003) 401–25; Avraham Faust, "Trade, Ideology, and Boundary Maintenance in Iron Age Israelite Society," in *A Holy People: Jewish and Christian Perspectives on Religious Communal Identity* (ed. Marcel Poorthuis and Joshua J. Schwartz; Jewish and Christian Perspectives 12; Leiden: Brill, 2006) 17–35. For a discussion of the Philistine as Other in 1 Samuel, see Robert Polzin, *Samuel and the Deuteronomist: 1 Samuel* (Literary Study of the Deuteronomic History 2; San Francisco: Harper & Row, 1989) 58–70; Susan Niditch, "Samson as Culture Hero, Trickster, and Bandit: The Empowerment of the Weak," *CBQ* 52 (1990) 608–24; David Jobling *1 Samuel* (Berit Olam; Collegeville, MN: Liturgical Press, 1998) 214–32; Tammi J. Schneider, *Judges* (Berit Olam; Collegeville,

■ Ezekiel's Oracles against Tyre

It is appropriate to turn back to the biblical texts at this juncture. Ezekiel's oracles against the nations focus on the larger world stage. This rhetorical strategy supports the book's agenda of minimizing Judean claims of unfairness on the part of God. In light of the international scope of conquest, Jerusalemites have no right to say they have been treated unfairly.[35] Ezekiel's oracles, while predicting failure for nations such as Tyre and Egypt, do so with grudging praise of their wealth and prosperity.

The rhetoric of these oracles combines judgment and admiration in stark contrast to Jeremiah's rhetorical strategies, for example, especially in the oracles against Babylon, which Amy Kalmanofsky characterizes as "revenge fantasy."[36] This contrast between Ezekiel and Jeremiah illustrates the variation of colonized responses following on Babylonian military aggression. While Ezekiel's oracles against foreign nations focus on two groups that Judeans did not consider "kin" to them, this section in Jeremiah starts by condemning Judah's neighbors in the southern Levant: Philistia, Ammon, Edom, and Moab. While Ezekiel's oracles build up to the sevenfold condemnation of Egypt (with no mention of Babylon), Jeremiah's culminate in vitriol toward Babylon, to whom serpentine language is applied (51:36–44).

While the oracles in Jeremiah depict the foreigners as evil "others," the oracles against foreign nations in Ezekiel draw intricate parallels between the nations it condemns and the Judean elite, and it does so by focusing on those most often othered in biblical texts: Egypt, the quintessential evil foreigner, and Tyre, a city-state that was closely tied to the Philistines during the Neo-Assyrian period. Yet the poet does not play with the expected tropes of evil in these texts. In the oracles against Egypt, for example, there is no allusion to the exodus narratives; these are poems wholly reflecting the contemporaneous Egypt. The poems use Egyptian images known to the Judean audience and pick images that

---

MN: Liturgical Press, 2000) 204–25; Steve Weitzman, "The Samson Story as Border Fiction," *BibInt* 10 (2002) 158–74.

35. See a similar conclusion in Lydia Lee, *Mapping Judah's Fate in Ezekiel's Oracles against the Nations* (ANEM 15; Atlanta: SBL Press, 2016) 79–122.

36. Amy Kalmanofsky, "'As She Did, Do to Her!': Jeremiah's OAN as Revenge Fantasies," in *Concerning the Nations: Essays on the Oracles against the Nations in Isaiah, Jeremiah and Ezekiel* (ed. Else K. Holt, Hyun Chul Paul Kim, and Andrew Mein; LHBOTS 612; London: Bloomsbury, 2015) 109–27.

reflect Egyptian cross-cultural influence in the Levant and Mesopotamia, images such as the Pharaoh as sea monster, and Egypt as the cosmic tree.[37]

The placement of the oracles against Egypt, which quickly follow the oracles against Tyre, further contrasts the rhetorical aims of each group of texts. In Ezekiel 29–32, Egypt is described in monstrous fashion: a serpentine creature wallowing in the muddy Nile, a leader with a broken arm, ending with the assembly of the impure dead. The cumulative images in the oracles against Egypt then function to maintain the villainization of Egypt even while using images familiar to the audience. Taken together, the collection of the oracles against the nations in Ezekiel places more blame for Judah's fate on Egypt than on Tyre, not just militarily but also economically.

In contrast, the oracles against Tyre begin with a more conventional approach in chap. 26. The poems that open the condemnations against Tyre castigate it for its plan to loot Jerusalem after the latter's fall to Babylon (26:2) and predict Jerusalem's utter ruin at the hands of Nebuchadnezzar (26:7–14), a prediction that never materialized. The poems in chap. 26 follow the more normal pattern of revenge fantasy—appropriately, since the "sin" of Tyre (the looting of Jerusalem) was so personal. The poet imagines a future when the Wall Street of the ancient Levant would be transformed into nothing more than a rocky seabird haven.

The details in chap. 26 provide a specific historical backdrop for this material. The oracles against Tyre open with a date formula that places the material in the year that Jerusalem fell.[38] The naming of Nebuchadnezzar in v. 7 reinforces this date. This setting has two implications. First, the movement of the poems against Tyre parallels those against Egypt in that both move from poems that are more historically grounded to those that are more mythic, thereby expanding the import of the events of the Babylonian invasion onto a cosmic plane.[39] Second, the oracle against Tyre explicitly contrasts the already accomplished destruction of Jerusalem, the focus of Ezekiel 24, with the hope of a similar fate for Tyre.[40] In other words, the narrative places the poems in the mouth of those who

---

37. Corrine L. Carvalho, "A Serpent in the Nile: Egypt in the Book of Ezekiel," in Holt, Kim, and Mein, *Concerning the Nations*, 195–220.

38. On structural elements in the oracles against Tyre, see Markus Saur, *Der Tyroszyklus des Ezechielbuches* (BZAW 386; Berlin: de Gruyter, 2008); Greg Schmidt Goering, "Proleptic Fulfillment of the Prophetic Word: Ezekiel's Dirges over Tyre and Its Rulers," *JSOT* 36 (2012) 483–505.

39. Carvalho, "Serpent in the Nile," 216–19.

40. See a similar argument in John T. Strong, "Tyre's Isolationist Policies in the Early Sixth Century BCE: Evidence from the Prophets," *VT* 47 (1997) 207–19, here 215–17.

are defeated looking at a Levantine neighbor who survives. This chronological setting previews the jealousy that comes to the fore in chaps. 27 and 28.

By contrast, the latent admiration of Tyre's maritime trade in chap. 27 and the Jerusalemite parallels in the description of the Tyre's leader in chap. 28 result in a depiction of Tyre as less foreign, more connected to the Judeans than to other groups.[41] Tyre is depicted as the proximate Other. In fact, the poems seem to have a hard time separating this "foreign" power from Judah's own traditional tropes. The prince is not just a primal figure; he is *Israel's* primal figure. Tyre is not just a paradise, it is *Judah's* paradise. These elements are deliberate choices made by the poet to draw a close connection between Judah and a foreign neighbor from which it wants to distinguish itself.

Scholars have wavered as to whether Ezekiel's oracles against Tyre were based more on the charge of hubris (seen especially in chap. 28) or on their economic prowess (seen especially in chap. 27).[42] These interpretations, of course, are not mutually exclusive, but, as Ian Wilson points out, the descriptions of both the ship of Tyre and the primal prince exhibit a certain level of admiration for the seaside city.[43] The extended metaphor of the ship demonstrates Judah's awareness of the kind of trade Tyre engaged in. The ship, built from wood gained via trade, carries a combination of mundane and luxury items, and the sailors have international origins. This author depicts Tyre as a people rushing out to interact with other nations.

Although hubris does seem to be an element in chap. 27, the material attests to the intercultural slant of Tyre's interactions with the world. The poet does not depict these goods as plunder or the result of violent extraction. The ship is itself a visual icon for the multicultural world of the ancient Mediterranean. The place-names explicitly represent lands near, far, and mythic.[44] While Noah's ark in Genesis becomes a visual

---

41. On connections between the Tyre oracles and Zion theology, see John T. Strong, "The God That Ezekiel Inherited," in *The God Ezekiel Creates* (ed. Paul M. Joyce and Dalit Rom-Shiloni; LHBOTS 607; London: Bloomsbury, 2015) 24–54, here 45–52.

42. I follow Madhavi Nevader in seeing the charge as a generic one leveled against evil rulers "YHWH and the Kings of Middle Earth: Royal Polemic in Ezekiel's Oracles against the Nations," in Holt, Kim, and Mein, *Concerning the Nations*, 161–78, here 163 n. 9.

43. Ian Douglas Wilson, "Tyre, a Ship: The Metaphorical World of Ezekiel 27 in Ancient Judah," *ZAW* 125 (2013) 249–62.

44. J. B. Geyer, "Ezekiel 27 and the Cosmic Ship," in *Among the Prophets: Language, Image, and Structure in the Prophetic Writings* (ed. Philip R. Davies and David J. A Clines; JSOTSup 144; Sheffield: JSOT Press, 1993) 105–26.

icon for global species, Tyre's ship represents global economies. Aubet points out that the goods it contains reflect an earlier stage of Tyrian trade, and some scholars therefore view this text as a reuse of an earlier poem.[45] But this misses the artistic choices the poet makes.[46] This poem is not a description of trade but a representation of Tyre as economic colonizer par excellence, and a colonizer from whom the Judean elite benefited. The connection to colonization is made more explicit by the words used to describe the goods, many of which are borrowed from Akkadian and Aramaic, as Daniel Bodi has demonstrated.[47]

The predicted destruction of Tyre in Ezek 27:26–36 extends the metaphor of the heavily laden ship. The ship sinks into the sea during a storm, literally taken down by its economic strength. Through the extended metaphor, the poet captures two important elements of Tyre's experiences during the Neo-Babylonian period. First, Tyre's "destruction" is economic collapse on the "sea," that is, the destruction of its Mediterranean trade. Second, this cessation of Tyrian trade affects and is witnessed by the various nations along "the coastland" (27:35), resulting in a new economic world order as North African Phoenician settlements benefit from the vacuum left by Levantine Tyrian sea trade.

The description of the primal prince in Ezekiel 28 even more explicitly utilizes motifs seen in Israelite texts. The primal אדם itself is perhaps the most obvious, but recently Madhavi Nevader has explored the use of royal motifs in the poem as well.[48] Although some scholars have noted the parallels with temple imagery in this chapter and have subsequently associated the passage with Hiram of Tyre's supposed involvement in the

---

45. See, e.g., Aubet, *Phoenicians and the West*, 123–25, although note the continuation of Tyrian trade in the Persian period, as argued by Benjamin J. Noonan, "Did Nehemiah Own Tyrian Goods? Trade between Judea and Phoenicia during the Achaemenid Period," *JBL* 130 (2011) 281–98. See also the essays by Markus Saur ("Tyros im Spiegel des Ezechielbuches") and Karin Schöpflin ("Die Tyrosworte im Kontext des Ezechielbuchs") in *Israeliten und Phönizier: Ihre Beziehungen im Spiegel der Archäologie und der Literatur des Alten Testaments und seiner Umwelt* (ed. Markus Witte and Johannes Friedrich Diehl; OBO 235; Fribourg: Academic Press; Göttingen: Vandenhoeck & Ruprecht, 2008) 165–89 and 191–213, respectively.
46. M. Liverani, "The Trade Network of Tyre according to Ezekiel 27," in *Ah, Assyria . . . ! Studies in Assyrian History and Ancient Near Eastern Historiography Presented to Hayim Tadmor* (ed. Mordechai Cogan and Israel Eph'al; ScrHier 33; Jerusalem: Magnes, 1991) 65–79.
47. Daniel Bodi, "Les denrées du commerce Phénicien à partir de quelques *hapax* de l'oracle contre Tyr en Ez 27," in *Phéniciens d'Orient et d'Occident: Mélanges Josette Elayi* (ed. André Lemaire; Cahiers de l'Institut du Proche-Orient ancien du Collège de France 2; Paris: Maisonneuve, 2014) 97–112.
48. Nevader, "YHWH and the Kings of Middle Earth," 163–68.

building of the temple of Solomon,[49] such a view has fallen out of favor. The historicity of that account is too complex to address here, except to say that the Deuteronomistic Historian wanted to depict the first temple as stemming from Phoenician sources. The temple imagery in Ezekiel 28 is of a different order. This poem draws on the trope of primordial space as sacred, which underlies the architectonic elements of temple building and not the other way around.[50]

Perhaps the most striking feature of the poems concerning the Tyrian leader in chap. 28 is the praise heaped onto this figure. The poet acknowledges his mental acumen, his successful trade ventures, his wealth, and his divine favor.[51] In the history of the interpretation of the passage, the prince's divine status and the identity of the cherub have become focal points. The ancient versions evidence very early variations on scribal traditions around these elements.[52] Does the prince claim to be "a god" or simply "God"? Is the prince the cherub, or is he accompanied by a cherub? While I suspect an early tradition declaring the prince divine became the catalyst for the variations, all of the versions attest to significant exaltation of this human leader.[53] In addition, this exaltation is based on Israelite acknowledgment of his qualifications for kingship (wisdom, prosperity, and divine favor, most prominently).[54] As the poem continues, it froths with envy of Tyre's favored fate, predicting doom where none is immedi-

---

49. See, e.g., Pierre-Maurice Bogaert, "Montagne sainte, jardin d'Éden et sanctuaire (Hiérosolymitain) dans un oracle d'Ézéchiel contre le prince de Tyr (Éz 28, 11–19)," in *Le mythe, son langage et son message: Actes du colloque de Liège et Louvain-la-Neuve 1981* (ed. H. Limet and J. Ries; Homo Religiosus 9; Louvain-la Neuve: Centre d'Histoire des Religions, 1983) 131–53.

50. See Silviu N. Bunta, "Yhwh's Cult Statue after 597/586 B.C.E.: A Linguistic and Theological Reinterpretation of Ezekiel 28:12," *CBQ* 69 (2007) 222–41; and Stefan Gathmann, *Im Fall gespiegelt: Der Abschluss der Tyrus-Sprüche in Ez 28,1–19* (ATSAT 86; St. Ottilien: Eos, 2008) 461–565.

51. John T. Willis, "National 'Beauty' and Yahweh's 'Glory' as a dialectical Key to Ezekielian Theology," *HBT* 34 (2010) 1–18.

52. Bunta, "Yhwh's Cult Statue," 222–41; and Hector M. Patmore, "Did the Masoretes Get It Wrong? The Vocalization and Accentuation of Ezekiel xxviii 12–19," *VT* 58 (2008) 245–57.

53. Bogaert, "Montagne sainte, jardin d'Éden et sanctuaire (Hiérosolymitain)," 131–53. See also Matthieu Richelle, "Le portrait changeant du roi de Tyr (Ezéchiel 28,11–18) dans les traditions textuelles anciennes," in Lemaire, *Phéniciens d'Orient et d'Occident*, 113–25.

54. See Dexter E. Callender Jr., "The Primal Human in Ezekiel and the Image of God," in *The Book of Ezekiel: Theological and Anthropological Perspectives* (ed. Margaret S. Odell and John T. Strong; SymS 9; Atlanta: Society of Biblical Literature, 2000) 175–94; and Patmore's discussion of the luxuriousness of Ezekiel's Eden in "Did the Masoretes Get It Wrong?"

ately apparent. When the condemnations come, they are leveled for weak reasons: pride in his supposed invulnerability (vv. 5–6) and "violence" in v. 16. Neither of these charges contains the vitriol leveled in other exilic literature against military enemies. This rhetoric of backhanded praise mirrors the jealousy that permeates the description of the metaphoric merchant ship in chap. 27. With very few changes, parts of the poems in both chap. 27 and chap. 28 could be odes to Tyre's economic prowess and political stability.

The variations in the poems reflect the complex colonial status of Tyre in the Neo-Assyrian and Neo-Babylonian periods. When chap. 26 depicts Tyre as complicit in the violent colonizing activities of Nebuchadnezzar, the collective memory doles out a violent utopia that scrubs its presence off the face of the earth. When chap. 27 reflects on the economic global colonization that allowed Tyre to thrive for a time, the poem contains measured admiration for a Levantine neighbor who escaped the worst that the Assyrian military machine had to offer. And as chap. 28 personifies that activity in the figure of the Tyrian leader, the poems cannot help but note that Israel's God had a part to play in their favored status, stressing the point by condemning their neighbor for thinking they had succeeded by their own cleverness and planning. All three poems capture the varying reactions to a favored neighbor in the mass colonization stemming from Mesopotamia.

■ Conclusion

This examination of references to Tyre in Ezekiel's oracles against the nations through an economic lens reveals the literary function of this material. The prophet's engagement with the economic status of Tyre serves larger rhetorical purposes in the book. The Book of Ezekiel depicts Tyre as an ally who failed Judah and, therefore, whose survival of the Babylonian encroachment is depicted as being only temporary. The Book of Ezekiel demonstrates the variety of economic options that different nations had available during the Assyrian and Babylonian advance. The author's jealousy of Tyre's booming trade reflects the archaeological record from the Assyrian period. Although Ezekiel 26–28 predicts the collapse of the city, the reality is that the city's trade ventures abruptly ceased, perhaps due to Babylonian encroachment, but the city remained intact. The jealousy of Jerusalem's elite of Tyre's less disastrous fate is preserved in the social memory of these poems.

Ezekiel 17: Zedekiah's Idolatrous Invocation of the Divine Name as a Capital Crime

DALE LAUNDERVILLE, OSB
Saint John's University School of Theology and Seminary
Collegeville, Minnesota

With the deportation of the Davidide king Jehoiachin to Babylonia in 597 B.C.E., his uncle Mattaniah was selected by Nebuchadnezzar to serve as a vassal king in Judah and Jerusalem and was renamed Zedekiah (2 Kgs 24:17). In the installation of Zedekiah in this position within the imperial system of Babylon, Nebuchadnezzar "made a covenant [ברית]" with Zedekiah "and brought him under an oath [אלה]" (Ezek 17:13). Because such an oath was made according to the protocol of overlord–vassal relationships in the empires of the ancient Near East, the depth of Zedekiah's personal commitment to Nebuchadnezzar would probably have been lacking.[1] This point is particularly evident when Ezekiel 17 is read as a sequel to Ezekiel 16 in the final form of the Book of Ezekiel. Zedekiah as a royal symbol for the Judean community is to be seen as an instantiation of those treaty-making forces within the Judean community as metaphorically embodied in wife Jerusalem (Ezek 16:15–43). Wife Jerusalem's practice of making multiple treaties with other lands was the polar opposite of an exclusive relationship of a vassal to an overlord. This practice of opportunistically seeking out treaty partners would have been in place in the late seventh- to early sixth-century

---

I dedicate this article to Leslie Hoppe, whose careful scholarship on Deuteronomy and the prophets has challenged his colleagues to a higher standard.

1. Moshe Weinfeld, "The Loyalty Oath in the Ancient Near East," *UF* 8 (1976) 378–414, here 378–82.

Davidic monarchy in Jerusalem.[2] Just as wife Jerusalem was charged with idolatry when she became enamored of her own beauty and sought out multiple "lovers" or treaty partners, so also Zedekiah can be charged with idolatrous self-securing by seeking support from the Egyptian Pharaoh after having called upon Yhwh to guarantee his loyalty to Nebuchadnezzar. Zedekiah's rebellion against Nebuchadnezzar in Ezek 17:15–21 is equated with a rebellion against Yhwh and thus manifests a drive for autonomy that is idolatrous (cf. 16:15–29).

To substantiate this claim that the practice of pronouncing the Name of Yhwh without appropriately honoring the divine presence called forth reveals the idol of autonomous power governing Zedekiah and the people of Judah, I will examine the following five points: (1) How the genre and literary context of Ezek 17:1–21 show that this riddling allegory invites the reader to reflect on the ways that Zedekiah's treaty-making and treaty-breaking behavior mirrors that of wife Jerusalem in Ezek 16:15–43. (2) How pronouncing one's name on someone or a symbolic object in the Book of Ezekiel is an act establishing a relationship with that person or object and is not simply a reference to the one who claims to possess a people, an object, or a place. This solemnly pronounced relationship is a dynamic reality that requires ongoing attention in order to function rightly. (3) How the vassal treaty operative in the seventh and sixth centuries in Judah illustrates the pattern of the loyalty oath common to Neo-Assyrian imperial politics and how the swearing of the curses at the conclusion of the treaty calls upon Yhwh to be a witness and guarantor of the oath. The breaking of the vassal treaty provides an immediate reason for Yhwh's support of Nebuchadnezzar's execution of Zedekiah and his destruction of Jerusalem, but at a deeper level this punishment of Zedekiah and the Judeans is a calling to account of their efforts to govern their own affairs without accountability to an earthly or a heavenly sovereign, a further illustration of the practices condemned in Ezek 16:15–43. (4) How this oath swearing of exclusive loyalty to the earthly sovereign Nebuchadnezzar stands in tension with the love command in Deut 6:4 and its call for an exclusive relationship with Yhwh. Yhwh's identification of Nebuchadnezzar's loyalty oath as his own oath indicates that divine sovereignty is fundamental to earthly political power and suffuses legitimate forms of such power. Finally, (5) how trust in Yhwh as the promise keeper sustains the covenant relationship for the long term. Yhwh's keeping the promise

---

2. Daniel I. Block, *The Book of Ezekiel* (2 vols.; NICOT; Grand Rapids: Eerdmans, 1997–98) 1:494–98.

sworn in his name by Zedekiah is consistent with his promise of an everlasting covenant with the Israelites/Judeans (Ezek 16:60).

■ Zedekiah's Treaty Making and Treaty Breaking as an Instantiation of Wife Jerusalem's Idolatrous Practices

In Ezek 17:1–2, Yhwh gives Ezekiel the following command: "Son of man, pose a riddle and craft a comparison for the house of Israel." This riddling allegory will invite the audience to reflect on the justice of Yhwh's punishment of Zedekiah and the Judeans in 588–586 B.C.E. Ezekiel recognizes in the fable of "the cedar, vine, and eagles" in 17:3–8 as applied to international relations that the temptation to break loose from the overlord–vassal relationship would have been strong for any vassal king. But in Ezekiel, this fable in vv. 3–8 constitutes the opening accusation section within a bipartite judgment oracle.[3] The subsequent judgment oracle in vv. 9–10 decrees that no human power can save the rebellious vine, for the "east wind" will make it wither. The allegorical interpretation of this fable and judgment oracle in 17:11–21 identifies the two eagles as Nebuchadnezzar and the Egyptian pharaoh, respectively, and the vine as Zedekiah. The "east wind" is identified as Yhwh's instrument for judging the rebellious vassal Zedekiah; the identification is made clear when Yhwh declares, "As I live, the one who has despised my oath and broken my covenant, I shall surely hold him accountable" (v. 19). Thus, the siege of Jerusalem in 587 B.C.E. and the capture of the fleeing Zedekiah, from the perspective of the cosmic or heavenly level, are identified here as decreed by Yhwh (vv. 12–18; see also 12:12–15). The reason given in vv. 19–20 is that the vassal oath imposed by Nebuchadnezzar was in effect Yhwh's oath since the name of Yhwh had been invoked to call upon Yhwh to be the guarantor of Zedekiah's promised obedience. Even though vv. 12–14 acknowledge that, on the earthly plane, Zedekiah was pressured into swearing an oath of loyalty as part of his covenant with Nebuchadnezzar, vv. 19–21 on the heavenly plane understand this loyalty oath to require Zedekiah to take a subordinate, lowly position in relation to Nebuchadnezzar. Zedekiah's solemn pronouncement of Yhwh's name in the standard oath-taking, covenant-making ritual of a vassal to an over-

---

3. Walther Zimmerli, *Ezekiel: A Commentary on the Book of the Prophet Ezekiel* (trans. Ronald E. Clements; 2 vols.; Hermeneia; Minneapolis: Fortress, 1979–83) 1:359; Leslie Allen, *Ezekiel 1–19* (WBC 28; Nashville: Thomas Nelson, 1994) 254.

lord was world-making, performative speech that carried severe consequences for noncompliance from the divine perspective.

Zedekiah's rebellion is a poignant example of the rebelliousness of wife Jerusalem condemned in Ezekiel 16. The phrase "you have despised my oath and violated my covenant" in 16:59b makes clear this connection between the rebellious treaty making of wife Jerusalem and that of Zedekiah. Wife Jerusalem's entering into multiple treaty arrangements is seen as a consequence of her forgetting her covenant with Yhwh and his claim on her exclusive devotion for the course of her life (16:22, 43). Zedekiah's oath of loyalty to Nebuchadnezzar was a commitment that Zedekiah did not honor since he was plotting a rebellion about four years later (ca. 594 B.C.E.; Jer 27:2–15). Zedekiah is condemned in Ezek 17:15–18 for stepping back from this commitment to Nebuchadnezzar when a more promising option was presented by the appearance of the Egyptian pharaoh as the second eagle in 17:7. The consequence of Zedekiah's not taking this oath seriously is his execution as well as the exile of Judeans and the destruction of Jerusalem (17:15–21). In vv. 15–17, Yhwh decrees a death sentence for Zedekiah for despising this oath and breaking his covenant.[4]

Zedekiah's invocation of the name of Yhwh in this oath making is judged in 17:20 to be an act of deception (מַעַל) against Yhwh. Invoking the name of Yhwh with less than a wholehearted commitment is part and parcel of the rebellious act that results in the death sentence for Zedekiah. Zedekiah's treating lightly the name of Yhwh in his "despising, flouting [בזה]" an oath is at a comparable level of seriousness to the half-Israelite who was given the death sentence for pronouncing or "piercing [נקב] the name [שם] and belittling [קלל] it" in the heat of a quarrel (Lev 24:11).[5] Pronouncing the name of Yhwh calls forth the real, yet invisible presence of Yhwh that is to be honored. According to the oracular story in Lev 24:10–23, the consequences for not honoring the divine name are lethal.[6]

Ongoing attention to the justice of Yhwh's intervention in human affairs invites reflection on the mystery of the divine being. The exchange between the views of the scribes formulating Ezek 17:1–24 and Lev

---

4. M. Görg, "בָּזָה bāzāh," *TDOT* 2:60–63, here 62.
5. Cf. S. Tamar Kamionkowski, "Leviticus 24, 10–23 in Light of H's Concept of Holiness," in *The Strata of the Priestly Writings: Contemporary Debate and Future Directions* (ed. Sarah Shectman and Joel S. Baden; ATANT 95; Zurich: Theologischer Verlag Zürich, 2009) 73–86, here 79–80.
6. Simeon Chavel, "Numbers 15,32–36: A Microcosm of the Living Priesthood and Its Literary Production," in Shectman and Baden, *Strata of the Priestly Writings*, 45–55, here 47.

26:40–45 generated a fruitful dialogue in the sixth–fifth centuries B.C.E. on the nature of the covenantal relationship.[7]

■ PRONOUNCING THE NAME: CLAIMING POSSESSION OR PRESENCE? OR BOTH

Sandra Richter's 2002 study of "name theology" argued for a more contextually close reading of שכן ("to dwell") in the phrase "to cause his name to dwell there [לשכן שמו שם]."[8] Rudolph Smend's thesis of the dwelling of Yhwh's name in a place as a cultic presence that could be invoked has been widely embraced.[9] In other words, the name of a person participates in and makes present that person. However, Richter contends that this phrase in Deut 11:29–32; 12:1–4; and 27:1–8 refers to an installed inscription in a place and does not refer to an indwelling presence. It is a phrase that recognizes Yhwh's taking possession of a place.[10] But in Ezek 20:9, 14, 21, Yhwh says that he refrained from severely punishing the Israelites who rebelled against him and rejected his statutes and ordinances "for the sake of his name." By Yhwh's entering into covenant with the Israelites, they have become his people and reflect his capacity to guide and protect them. The seriousness of this connection of the well-being of the people with the essence of Yhwh is revealed in Ezek 20:33 in which Yhwh swears to be king over the Israelites so that they might not desecrate his name (20:39). Here the covenant relationship connects the holiness of Yhwh with the holiness of the people.[11] The invoking of the name of

---

7. Richard J. Bautch, *Glory and Power, Ritual and Relationship: The Sinai Covenant in the Postexilic Period* (LHBOTS 471; New York: T&T Clark, 2009) 32–36.

8. Sandra L. Richter, *The Deuteronomistic History and the Name Theology: lešakkēn šemô šām in the Bible and the Ancient Near East* (BZAW 318; Berlin: de Gruyter, 2002) 11–25.

9. Rudolph Smend, *Lehrbuch der altestamentlichen Religionsgeschichte* (2nd ed.; Sammlung theologischer Lehrbücher; Freiburg: J. C. B. Mohr, 1899) 277 n. 1.

10. Sandra Richter, "Placing the Name, Pushing the Paradigm: A Decade with the Deuteronomistic Name Formula," in *Deuteronomy in the Pentateuch, Hexateuch, and the Deuteronomistic History* (ed. Konrad Schmid and Raymond F. Person Jr.; FAT 2/56; Tübingen: Mohr Siebeck, 2012) 64–78, here 70–71.

11. S. Tamar Kamionkowski, "Did the Priests Have a 'Name' Theology?," in *Iggud: Selected Essays in Jewish Studies*, vol. 1: *The Bible and Its World, Rabbinic Literature and Jewish Law, and Jewish Thought* (ed. Baruch J. Schwartz, Abraham Melamed, and Aharon Shemesh; Jerusalem: World Union of Jewish Studies, 2008) 21–38, here 27–29; Dexter Callender Jr., "The Recognition Formula and Ezekiel's Conception of God," in *The God Ezekiel Creates* (ed. Paul M. Joyce and Dalit Rom-Shiloni; LHBOTS 607; London: Bloomsbury, 2015) 71–86, here 75–79; Jan Joosten, *People and Land in*

Yhwh in a curse sealing an oath has an impact on the essence of Yhwh and thus must be practiced with care and caution (Exod 20:7; Deut 5:11; 6:13).

▪ ZEDEKIAH'S MAKING AND BREAKING OF HIS LOYALTY OATH: A BLASPHEMOUS MANIPULATION OF THE DIVINE NAME

Loyalty oaths, which aimed to promote a long-term commitment to a king and his dynasty, are attested throughout the ancient Near East from the fourteenth through the seventh century B.C.E.[12] Common elements in these treaties are the obligation of those swearing the oath to act against rebels and to recite curses that will be activated against treaty breakers. The political loyalty expected of the treaty partners goes so far as the vassal's fighting for the overlord to the point of death (EST 46–54).[13] The overlord's enemies are to be the enemies of the vassal, and the friends of the overlord are to be the friends of the vassal (EST 167–72). The vassal is not to swear a loyalty oath to any other king or lord (EST 129). If someone speaks of insurrection against the overlord, one should, if possible, seize and slay that rebel (EST 130–61). If any treasonous word is heard from an enemy, an ally, a member of the king's family, a prophet, or anyone at all, it is to be reported to the overlord (EST 106–22). One should not even hold a negative thought about the overlord, much less an idea of revolting against him (EST 180–87). The longevity of this oath or treaty was promoted by extending the treaty promises to future offspring of the king (EST 283–301).[14] The oath was not to be undone (EST 377–84). Neither was the oath to be recited mechanically or less than wholeheartedly (EST 377–96). The fact that the loyalty oath makes clear and often repeats the ways in which vassals can revolt against their overlord indicates that breaking such loyalty oaths was probably not uncommon.[15]

The Book of Deuteronomy has been the focus for identifying parallels with Hittite and Neo-Assyrian loyalty oaths. Joshua Berman argues that Deuteronomy 13 draws on material from CTH 133, a treaty between

---

the Holiness Code: An Exegetical Study of the Ideational Framework of the Law in Leviticus 17–26 (VTSup 67; Leiden: Brill, 1996) 123.

12. Weinfeld, "Loyalty Oath," 380–82.

13. Simo Parpola and Kazuko Watanabe, Neo-Assyrian Treaties and Loyalty Oaths (1988; SAA 2; repr., Winona Lake, IN: Eisenbrauns, 2014) 28–58.

14. Weinfeld, "Loyalty Oath," 384–91.

15. Joshua Berman, Inconsistency in the Torah: Ancient Literary Convention and the Limits of Source Criticism (New York: Oxford University Press, 2017) 69.

Arnuwanda I of Hatti and the men of Išmerika in the fourteenth century B.C.E. and that Deuteronomy 28 draws on a group of curse formulations reaching back to the second millennium B.C.E.[16] But Bernard M. Levinson and Jeffrey Stackert strongly criticize Berman for not establishing a convincing argument for the transmission of a Hittite text from the fourteenth century to an Israelite or Judean audience in the seventh century.[17] Instead, they point out how Deuteronomy 13 mirrors themes from EST 101–46 that call for putting to death or reporting members of one's own family, a close friend, or inhabitants of a city who try to stir up revolt against the overlord. They argue that EST, drawn up in 672 B.C.E. and typically written as a display inscription to be placed in sanctuaries of the vassal kingdoms (e.g., the one recovered from Tel Ta'yinat in Syria), would have been known in Judah in the seventh century B.C.E.[18] They go on to point out that Deuteronomy 28 makes an even stronger case for literary borrowing from EST by word-for-word correspondences in a number of the curses. In accord with Eckart Otto's identification of close parallels of Deuteronomy 13 and 28 with EST, Levinson and Stackert argue that preexilic Deuteronomy drew on EST to subvert its main objective: to love the Assyrian overlord wholeheartedly (EST 266).[19] Instead the Shema in Deut 6:4–5 commands Israel "to love Yhwh, your God, with your whole heart, and with your whole being, and with your whole strength." Thus, they contend that these materials from EST provide a platform for the Deuteronomic scribes to promote the universal sovereignty of Yhwh in place of the Assyrian imperial system.[20] Preexilic Deuteronomy takes written form not only as a revision of the Code of the Covenant (Exod 20:22–23:33) from the eighth century B.C.E. but also as a replacement for the loyalty oath to a Neo-Assyrian overlord. Thus, Deuteronomy uses sections of EST in order to subvert the oaths made by Ahaz, Hezekiah, and Manasseh with Neo-Assyrian kings and to champion the view that the Judeans owed exclusive loyalty to Yhwh by their Sinaitic covenant with him.

---

16. Joshua Berman, "CTH 133 and the Hittite Provenance of Deuteronomy 13," *JBL* 130 (2011) 25–44, here 29–35.

17. Bernard M. Levinson and Jeffrey Stackert, "Between the Covenant Code and Esarhaddon's Succession Treaty: Deuteronomy 13 and the Composition of Deuteronomy," *JAJ* 3 (2012) 123–40, here 134–35.

18. Ibid., 130.

19. Eckart Otto, "Political Theology in Judah and Assyria: The Beginning of the Hebrew Bible as Literature," *SEÅ* 65 (2000) 59–76, here 61–62.

20. Levinson and Stackert, "Between the Covenant Code and Esarhaddon's Succession Treaty," 137–39; Otto, "Political Theology in Judah and Assyria," 62–64.

Ezekiel 17:18–19 does not state that Israel's covenant with Yhwh prohibits Zedekiah from making a covenant with Nebuchadnezzar. Instead, this passage lifts up the fact that Zedekiah swore an oath in Yhwh's name, an action that initially seems to obey the directive in Deut 6:17: "The LORD, your God, you shall fear; him you shall serve, and by his name you shall swear." Zedekiah's action of swearing by Yhwh's name suddenly transforms this loyalty oath to the Babylonian king into one that belongs to Yhwh. Because Zedekiah invoked Yhwh to punish any rebellion of the Judean vassal against the Babylonian overlord, this loyalty oath or covenant now depends on Yhwh's carrying out the words of the curse that sealed the loyalty oath. Yhwh punishes Zedekiah and the Judeans by letting the consequences of their wayward actions double back on their own heads.

The power granted to human speech in Zedekiah's invoking the divine name in a solemn pronouncement of a loyalty oath is striking. The reason for the commandment "you shall not lift up the name of the LORD, your God, for false concerns" (Exod 20:7; Deut 5:11) becomes all the more apparent. The sanction for breaking a solemnly sworn oath is not stated in the apodictic formulation of the "Ten Commandments" (Exod 20:1–17; Deut 5:6–21). However, Lev 24:15–16 gives the following ruling on a man who, in the midst of a fight, used the name of Yhwh in a curse (נקב, "pierce") and thus "blasphemed" (קלל, piel). He was stoned (רגם) by the whole community (כל־עדה). It seems then that using Yhwh's name in a curse "pierces" or impinges upon Yhwh's essence.[21] If the oath of loyalty followed the pattern of EST, blessings would have been omitted and only curses would have concluded the oath. The curse required by Nebuchadnezzar in Ezek 17:13, "he brought him under oath/curse [אלה]," is then identified as one to which Zedekiah "gave his hand" (17:18).

■ An Exclusive Relationship with the Sovereign Deity as Promoted by the Loyalty Oath

Origen claimed that Zedekiah should never have entered into a covenant relationship with Nebuchadnezzar in the first place.[22] However,

---

21. Kamionkowski, "Leviticus 24, 10–23 in Light of H's Concept of Holiness," 79–80; Mark Leuchter, "The Ambiguous Details in the Blasphemer Narrative: Sources and Redaction in Leviticus 24:10–23," *JBL* 130 (2011) 431–50.

22. Roger Pearse, ed., *Origen of Alexandria: Exegetical Works on Ezekiel* (trans. Mischa Hooker; Ipswich: Chieftain, 2014) 340–49.

Ezekiel 17 condemns Zedekiah not for taking the oath of loyalty to Nebuchadnezzar but rather for breaking it. Instead, Ezekiel 17 transforms the covenant made with Nebuchadnezzar into one belonging to Yhwh. The allegorical section of this chapter (vv. 12–21) builds on the fable of the cedar, the vine, and the eagles (vv. 3–8) and the judgment oracle attached to it (vv. 9–10). The first eagle plants the native seed in fertile soil near abundant waters so that it might grow as a low-lying vine. This humble status of being subservient to the first eagle is not one with which the vine is content and so turns toward a second eagle that tempted the vine to turn its roots toward it. This desire to move beyond its lowly yet secure state by turning toward another powerful figure echoes the behavior pattern of wife Jerusalem in Ezekiel 16. She trusted in the many possessions with which she had been gifted by Yhwh, who had entered into covenant with her (16:8–14). She forgot Yhwh and his care for her and sought to be more autonomous. But to secure herself in such an exposed condition apart from her covenantal relationship with Yhwh, she was driven to enter into alliances with many other nations (16:23–29). This violation of her marriage relationship with Yhwh led to promiscuous behavior in which she went so far as to sacrifice Yhwh's children to gain the favor of these so-called treaty partners (16:21). As the personification of collective Jerusalem and Judah, wife Jerusalem parallels the vine in Ezekiel 17, although the vine brings forward the element of royal leadership more than does wife Jerusalem. A significant point in this sequence is that the rebelliousness of Zedekiah is one more illustration of the collective waywardness of Jerusalem and Judah narrated in Ezekiel 16. Zedekiah's paying lip service to the oath he made with Nebuchadnezzar is of a piece with the lack of attention of wife Jerusalem to the covenant she entered into with Yhwh.

The king of Israel is mentioned in only one passage in Deuteronomy (Deut 17:14–20), in which he was summoned to shape his outlook and way of governing according to the Deuteronomic law. The call to exclusive fidelity to Yhwh in Deuteronomy is addressed to the individual members of the community (second person singular pronominal suffixes and verbs in Deut 6:10–19) rather than to the king as their representative. The call to individual responsibility sounded by Ezekiel in 18:20 has a forerunner in Deut 24:16 as part of the preexilic Book of Deuteronomy as mapped out by Otto.[23] This preexilic Book of Deuteronomy articulates

---

23. Deut 6:4; 12:13–27; 13:2–12; 14:22–15:23; 16:1–17; 16:18–18:5; 19:2–13; 19:15–21:23; 22:1–12, 13–29; 23:16–26; 24:1–4; 24:6–25:4; 25:5–10, 11–12; 26:2–13, 20–44. See Eckart Otto, "The History of the Legal-Religious Hermeneutics of the Book of Deuteronomy from the Assyrian to the Hellenistic Period," in *Law and Religion in the*

how Israel is to maintain its distinctive identity in the face of pressures toward syncretism and assimilation.[24]

If Zedekiah had followed the directions of Deut 17:14–20 through daily meditation on the laws of Deuteronomy, he would have understood that departure from exclusive fidelity to Yhwh would spell disaster. Otto argues that this passage was added to preexilic Deuteronomy by scribes in the first generation of the exile in a layer of Deuteronomic texts that he labels the Horeb redaction.[25] It seems, then, that Ezekiel and his scribal followers could have influenced the Deuteronomistic scribes who were reshaping preexilic Deuteronomy in light of the catastrophe of 586. Otto then argues that the second generation of Deuteronomistic scribes in the exile added Deuteronomy 1–3, 29–30 to generate hope that the exiles could return to the land of Israel, which Otto labels the Moab redaction.[26] This hope resonates with that which Ezek 20:32–44 aimed to generate.

▪ YHWH'S EVERLASTING COVENANT: A PROMISE REQUIRING DEEP TRUST IN DARK TIMES

In Ezekiel 16, Yhwh did not abandon his covenant relationship with wife Jerusalem. Instead he decreed that he would inflict on her "the sentence of adultery [נאפות] and murder [שפכת דם]" (16:38). This punishment took the form of her "lovers" (מאהבים, v. 37) leading an "assembly" (קהל) to "stone" (רגם) her. The punishment of stoning was typically reserved for the following capital offenses that violated the sphere of the holy: blasphemy (Lev 24:14, 16, 23), violation of the sabbath (Num 15:35–36), child sacrifice to Moloch (Lev 20:2), soothsaying (Lev 20:27), and defiance of one's parents (Deut 21:21).[27] The figure of wife Jerusalem attributes agency and intentionality to the collective actions of the Judean people in covenant with Yhwh. At the conclusion of this judgment narrative against wife Jerusalem, Yhwh states that he will hold her accountable and says, "You despised an oath [אלה] by breaking a covenant [ברית]" (16:59). The repeated adulteries of wife Jerusalem reveal the serious deficits of the Judean community, which values narcissistic autonomy over a committed relationship to Yhwh. This characterization of the Judean community

---

Eastern Mediterranean: From Antiquity to Early Islam (ed. Anselm C. Hagedorn and Reinhard G. Kratz; Oxford: Oxford University Press, 2013) 211–50, here 213.
   24. Otto, "History of the Legal-Religious Hermeneutics," 227.
   25. Ibid, 228.
   26. Ibid, 231.
   27. K.-D. Schunck, "רגם," *TDOT* 13:324–26, here 325.

shows that Zedekiah's oath breaking was not that much different from alliance-making practices of the Judean community. The startling revelation at the end of the narrative in Ezekiel 16 is that Yhwh "will establish [קום, *hiphil*] an everlasting covenant [ברית עולם]" with wife Jerusalem (v. 60). This covenant is the same covenant as that made at the outset of Yhwh's relationship with Jerusalem (v. 8). The action of Yhwh is to lift up or activate a covenant that has been neglected by the human partner but not abandoned by Yhwh.[28]

The addition of Ezek 16:59–63 to the story of the repeated infidelities of wife Jerusalem brings a hopeful message through the term ברית עולם. This term first appears in the Pentateuch in Gen 17:7 and is the priestly covenant that has shaped the Israelite identity as one founded on genealogy rather than on obedience to an oath.[29] If the Priestly Writing is dated as early as the late eighth century,[30] then this covenant would have shaped the outlook of the Zadokite priest-prophet Ezekiel. But the date of the Priestly document has been argued by many scholars since Wellhausen to be in the exilic period and its various redactional additions in postexilic times.[31] Ezekiel's vision of the כבוד יהוה ("the glory of Yhwh") departing from the Jerusalem temple in Ezek 10:3–4, 18–19; 11:22–23 and his vision of the return of the כבוד יהוה to the new temple in Ezek 43:4–5 confirms that he envisions the covenant relationship as surviving the destruction of the temple in 586. Furthermore, the Ezekielian oracle in 11:16 claims that Yhwh has remained present with the exiles as a "little sanctuary [מקדש מעט]." According to Christophe Nihan, the purpose of the basic Priestly document (Pg) in Gen 1:1–Lev 16:34 was to describe how Israel could serve Yhwh so that he might remain in their midst. Nihan dates Pg to the early Persian period. He argues that the continuity of the covenant from the preexilic to postexilic times "developed *simultaneously* and *in parallel* among the tradents of P and of restoration prophecy."[32] He affirms with earlier scholars that the unconditional character

---

28. Joosten, *People and Land in the Holiness* Code, 116; Bautch, *Glory and Power, Ritual and Relationship*, 35.

29. Christophe Nihan, "The Priestly Covenant, Its Reinterpretations, and the Composition of 'P,'" in Shectman and Baden, *Strata of the Priestly Writings*, 87–134, here 99, 103.

30. Jacob Milgrom, *Leviticus 1–16: A New Translation with Introduction and Commentary* (AB 3; New York: Doubleday, 1991) 34.

31. Douglas Knight, "Wellhausen and the Interpretation of Israel's Literature," *Semeia* 25 (1982) 21–36, here 26.

32. Nihan, "Priestly Covenant," 99–100; idem, *From Priestly Torah to Pentateuch:*

of the P covenant is probably based on the Davidic covenant, which extended to the people as a whole during the exile.[33]

In Lev 26:40–45, Yhwh predicts that the Israelites will "acknowledge publicly" (ידה, hithpael, v. 40) their sins, and, in their humbled state in exile, they will make amends (v. 41). Then Yhwh will remember (זכר) his covenant with the patriarchs (v. 42). The covenant relationship might have appeared to be absent in the exile, but it was lying dormant waiting to be revived when the people acknowledge their sins and repent.[34] Nihan contends that Ezek 16:59–63 and Lev 26:40–45 are roughly from the same time (cf. Isa 54:7–10).[35] As the conclusion to the Holiness Code (Leviticus 17–26), this text shows how H integrated the Sinai covenant from non-P texts with the P covenant. Otto and Nihan regard H not only as the author of Leviticus 17–26 but also as the redactor of the Pentateuch; in this role, H aimed to fold the non-P covenants into the P covenant so that only one covenant is in place in the Pentateuch.[36]

The scribes at work on the Pentateuch from the eighth to the fourth century B.C.E. and on the prophecy of Ezekiel from the sixth to the second century B.C.E. in Jerusalem, Babylonia, or Yehud would have been in communication with one another. Particular scribes identified with particular "streams of tradition" or prophetic figures, but yet there was communication or cross-fertilization between these groups.[37] The relative dating of these texts leaves much room for deciding which text borrowed from the other; in some cases the exchange between the authors of the texts might have been simultaneous and mutual (e.g., Lev 26:40–45 and Ezek 16:59–63).[38]

A Study in the Composition of the Book of Leviticus (FAT 2/25; Tübingen: Mohr Siebeck, 2007) 383–94.

33. Nihan, "Priestly Covenant," 101.
34. Bautch, *Glory and Power, Ritual and Relationship*, 72.
35. Nihan, "Priestly Covenant," 111.
36. Ibid., 109–12.
37. Konrad Schmid, "The Deuteronomistic Image of History as Interpretive Device in the Second Temple Period: Towards a Long-Term Interpretation of 'Deuteronomism,'" *Congress Volume: Helsinki 2010* (ed. Martti Nissinen; VTSup 148; Leiden: Brill, 2012) 369–88, here 380–81.
38. David M. Carr, "Scribal Processes of Coordination/Harmonization and the Formation of the First Hexateuch(s)," in *The Pentateuch: International Perspectives on Current Research* (ed. Thomas Dozeman, Konrad Schmid, and Baruch Schwartz; FAT 78; Tübingen: Mohr Siebeck, 2011) 63–84, here 73.

■ CONCLUSION

Yhwh's condemnation of Zedekiah for rebelling against Nebuchadnezzar and thereby breaking an oath sworn in Yhwh's name may seem extreme at first reading. However, the invocation of Yhwh's name in a solemn pronouncement in a mechanical fashion within a loyalty oath to an earthly overlord was an action in which Yhwh was treated as a mere tool at one's disposal in political negotiations. If the dialogical character of Judah's covenant with Yhwh devolves into a static arrangement regulating personal interactions, then the invocation of the divine name for a more immediate pragmatic role, relegates the divine presence to an afterthought, an act that verges on blasphemy. According to the H author in Lev 24:11, 13–16, the Israelite's "piercing" of the divine name, in which Yhwh himself was manipulated for the advantage of the human speaker, was a capital transgression punishable by stoning.

The riddling allegory of Ezek 17:1–24 invites the reader to reflect on the justice of Yhwh's punishment of the transgression of Zedekiah. Was a king expected to be so pious that he would not try to free himself from imperial overlordship if the opportunity presented itself? For Yhwh, a member of the covenant community who makes a solemn pronouncement in Yhwh's name in an oath or covenant, transfers the ownership of the covenant from the human partner to the divine one. The covenant imposed by Nebuchadnezzar on Zedekiah in Ezek 17:13 becomes a responsibility of Yhwh as guarantor of the oath if Zedekiah should renege. If such oath taking was not taken seriously by Zedekiah at the outset as an unbreakable covenant, then he was not thinking along the same lines as Yhwh about the seriousness of such oath taking (Ezek 17:15–21). The reality of shifting and changing political treaties in the ancient Near East seems to support Zedekiah's pragmatic approach to participating in a vassal treaty. But Yhwh's carrying out of the curse on Zedekiah shows that Yhwh takes seriously the pronouncing of his divine name in an oath.

The Diaspora as a Word and Concept in Early Judaism

MALKA ZEIGER SIMKOVICH
Catholic Theological Union
Chicago, Illinois

The divine promise that the Israelites will establish themselves in the land promised to the Abrahamic family is perhaps the foremost unifying theme of the Hebrew Bible. Its countertheme, the possibility that the Israelites might be displaced from this land, undergirds much of the Hebrew Bible as well, and the threat of exile looms large in the Deuteronomistic History and prophetic literature.[1] Peaceful settlement in the promised land was viewed as an indicator of God's satisfaction with Israel, while displacement signified just, divine punishment for Israel's sins.[2] The biblical prophets exploited the Israelites' fear of displacement by warning them of potential exile should they not repent of their sins. These warnings were realized with the Babylonian exile, an event that the Hebrew Bible refers to as the גולה (*gôlâ*), a term that appears forty times in the Hebrew Bible.[3] It is unclear whether the postexilic biblical authors viewed

---

1. Robert Carroll, "Deportation and Diasporic Discourses in the Prophetic Literature," in *Exile: Old Testament, Jewish, and Christian Conceptions* (ed. James M. Scott; JSJSup 56; Leiden: Brill, 1997) 63–88.

2. On the theology of the exile, see A. Thomas Kraabel, "Unity and Diversity among Diaspora Synagogues," in *The Synagogue in Late Antiquity* (ed. Lee I. Levine; Philadelphia: American Schools of Oriental Research, 1987) 49–60, here 49.

3. 2 Kgs 24:14–16; Jer 28:6 (LXX 35:6); 29:1 (LXX 36:1); 29:4 (LXX 36:4); 29:16, 20, 31 (LXX 36:31); 46:19 (LXX 26:19); 48:7 (LXX 31:7), 11 (LXX 31:33); 49:3 (LXX 30:19); Ezek 1:1; 3:11, 15; 11:24–25; 12:3–4, 7, 11; 25:3; Amos 1:15; Zech 6:10; 14:2; Ezra 1:11; 2:1; 4:1; 6:19–21; 8:35; 9:4; 10:6–8, 16; Neh 7:6. גולה also appears in six Qumran fragments (1QM 1.2, 3; 4QpNah [4Q169] 3–4 iv 1; 4QapocrJerC[a] [4Q385] 17a–e ii 7; 4Qpap psEzek[e] [4Q391] 77.2; 6Qpap apocrSam–Kgs [6Q9] 1.2).

the Babylonian exile as having come to a close following Cyrus's edict permitting the exiled Judeans to return to Yehud, since most Judeans did not return at that time. By the late Second Temple period, most Jews lived outside of Judea.

Scholars disagree as to whether Jews living in the Greek and Roman diaspora viewed the concept of diaspora, and their lives in the diaspora, as an extension of the biblical curse of גלות ("exile"). A. Thomas Kraabel has argued that diasporan Jews living in the Greco-Roman world did not view their lives as fulfillments of the biblical גלות, but viewed the two categories as being entirely distinct.[4] W. C. van Unnik, however, has posited that diasporan Jews viewed their lives as embodied fulfillments of scriptural promises to punish Israel with exile.[5] Both positions lack the nuance that is required to assess the attitudes of a diverse Jewish population spread across a massive region over the course of six centuries.[6]

While current scholarship tends to follow Kraabel's positive view of the diaspora, studies of the Jewish diaspora in antiquity generally neglect a thorough examination of the use of the word διασπορά in Second Temple literature. It is van Unnik who argues for a negative diasporan self-understanding. He analyzes the word διασπορά as it appears in Greek and Roman sources, concluding that the Septuagint's authors adopted the term διασπορά from these sources, which use the word in the context of colonization. According to van Unnik, Jewish authors borrowed the term and reframed it as a referent to the divine punishment of Israel. As later scholars have shown, however, van Unnik's research contains significant errors.[7] Most problematically, van Unnik presumes that the

---

4. Kraabel's claim that, at this early stage, "Diaspora was not Exile; in some sense it became a Holy Land, too," is an unverifiable overstatement (A. Thomas Kraabel, "The Roman Diaspora: Six Questionable Assumptions," *JJS* 33.1–2 [1982] 445–64, here 452).

5. W. C. van Unnik, *Das Selbstverständnis der jüdischen Diaspora in der hellenistisch-römischen Zeit* (ed. Pieter Willem van der Horst; AGAJU 17; Leiden: Brill, 1993) 95–101.

6. James M. Scott takes a middle ground by asserting that scholars must "reckon with the probability that Jews living in foreign lands represented a whole spectrum of different perspectives on their Diasporic situation, depending in part on time, place, and circumstances" ("Exile and the Self-Understanding of Diaspora Jews in the Greco-Roman Period," in Scott, *Exile: Old Testament, Jewish, and Christian Conceptions*, 173–218, here 182.

7. While van Unnik notes that διασπορά appears in the writings of Thucydides (*Peloponnesian War* 2.27), for example, the word used there is in fact σπείρω, which is related but not identical to the verb διασπείρω. The verb διασπείρω appears as early as the fifth century B.C.E., but the noun first appears only in the Septuagint. Stéphane Dufoix points out that, despite van Unnik's claims that διασπορά appears in Greek

literary function of a word correlates with a lived reality, which leads to his claim that, because διασπορά was used negatively, diasporan Jews must have perceived their lives negatively.[8]

Stéphane Dufoix has recently complicated this presumption in his study of how early Jewish writers deployed the word διασπορά. He argues that διασπορά is a neologism in the Septuagint and does not appear in earlier extant sources. Moreover, the Septuagint does not use διασπορά to translate the Hebrew words for banishment and exile (גלות and גולה), and גלות and διασπορά cannot, therefore, be equated. Instead, the authors of the Septuagint use διασπορά in the context of a divine punishment that transcends a particular past event, and, with the exception of one appearance in the Book of Judith, the term refers to a potential future event.[9] The correlative relationship between how διασπορά appears in the Septuagint and how Jews living outside of Judea assessed their diasporan lives is thus more complex than most scholars have assumed.

In this essay, I will suggest that the debate over whether diasporan Jews viewed the diaspora positively or negatively can be mapped onto negative literary usages of διασπορά and positive lived *realities* of the diaspora. In other words, texts that use διασπορά speak of it negatively, but texts about the diaspora that do not use the word speak positively about the diaspora as a place where Jews can thrive as practitioners of their ancestral customs. Instead of concluding that the negative uses of διασπορά in the Septuagint indicate a negative attitude toward diasporan Jews' lived reality, I will suggest that there was a dissonance between the negative connotation of the word διασπορά in the Septuagint and the positive lived reality within the diaspora, which caused later Jewish authors writing about the diaspora in the late Second Temple period to avoid using the term.[10]

---

literature in reference to displacement and colonization, "of all the occurrences of diaspora in the *Thesaurus Linguae Graecae* (TLG) . . . none refer to colonisation" (*The Dispersion: A History of the Word* diaspora [Brill's Specials in Modern History 1; Leiden: Brill, 2017] 29). Dufoix suggests that the identification of διασπορά as an originally non-Jewish Greek term "lies in a desire to constitute a concept applicable to several populations—this is particularly so in the contemporary context in which the term has assumed positive connotations" (30–34, here 34).

8. Dufoix, *Dispersion*, 30–37; Scott, "Self-Understanding of Diaspora Jews," 183–84.

9. Dufoix, *Dispersion*, 47; Stéphane Dufoix, "Diaspora before It Became a Concept," in *Routledge Handbook of Diaspora Studies* (ed. Robin Cohen and Carolin Fischer; New York: Routledge, 2019) 13–21; Stéphane Dufoix, *Diasporas* (trans. William Rodamor; Berkeley: University of California Press, 2008).

10. I refer to the Septuagint as a collection of texts produced over the last three

■ CAPTIVITY AND DISPLACEMENT: αἰχμαλωσία AND ἀποικία

The Septuagint's authors use three words to refer to Israel's experience of exile, each of which refers to a separate stage of its experience: αἰχμαλωσία ("captivity"), ἀποικία ("displacement"), and διασπορά ("dispersion"). Of these, the Greek word for captivity, αἰχμαλωσία, which also denotes spoils of war, is the most common, appearing 124 times in the Septuagint. Later Jewish authors made regular use of αἰχμαλωσία as well. Josephus uses the word twenty-nine times, but Philo uses it just once (*Leg.* 2.35), in a citation of the Septuagint's rendering of Num 31:25–26, verses that concern the laws of taking spoils in war. Αἰχμαλωσία also appears twenty-two times in other Jewish texts, including the *Testaments of the Twelve Patriarchs*, a collection that recounts the final words of Jacob's twelve sons on their deathbeds and uses the word fifteen times.[11] The *Testaments* inter-

---

centuries of the Second Temple period that was read by most Greek-speaking Jews as authoritative Scripture. While distinctions between scriptural and nonscriptural documents were fluid and varied from community to community (and also generation to generation), I will speak of the Septuagint as a family of texts that can be read in conversation with Hellenistic Jewish texts composed in the diaspora that were not, as far as I know, candidates for scriptural status, and do not use the word *diaspora* (but could easily have done so based on their subject matter). Such texts include Alexandrian documents like the *Letter of Aristeas* and *Joseph and Aseneth*, as well as the writings of Philo of Alexandria, who uses the word twice, but not in reference to contemporary Jewish life outside the Land of Israel. Though a detailed examination of these documents lies beyond the scope of this essay, it is sufficient for our purposes to note that the positive attitude toward diasporan Jewish life expressed in these writings, along with their thorough knowledge of the Septuagint, suggests a desire to dissociate from scriptural curses envisioning a diaspora. On the notion of canonicity in this period, see Timothy H. Lim, "A Theory of the Majority Canon," *ExpTim* 124.8 (2013) 365–73; idem, ed., *When Texts Are Canonized* (BJS 359; Providence, RI: Brown Judaic Studies, 2017).

11. The *Testaments of the Twelve Patriarchs* depicts the captivity of Jacob's family in Egypt as a divine punishment for the family's sins that seems to correlate with the suffering of Judean Jews in the first and second centuries. Despite its Jewish origins, the *Testaments* probably came to their final form in at least the second century at the hands of Christian redactors, and therefore αἰχμαλωσία, as an overarching theme in the collection, may represent the work of an early Christian editor. See Marinus de Jonge, *The Testaments of the Twelve Patriarchs: A Study of Their Text, Composition, and Origin* (Assen: Van Gorcum, 1975) 128; Elias J. Bickerman, "The Date of the Testaments of the Twelve Patriarchs," *JBL* 69 (1950) 245–60, here 260. Since there is no mention of the Roman Empire in the list of rulers in the *Testament of Naphtali* (5:8), the earliest stage of composition likely predates 63 B.C.E. The text's reliance on the Septuagint indicates a *terminus post quem* of 250 B.C.E., while references to the *Testa-*

pret the impending slavery of Jacob's descendants in Egypt and the Babylonian expulsion of Judeans many centuries later as predictable outcomes of Israel's failure to comply with the covenantal agreement between the elected people and God.[12] The *Psalms of Solomon*, a collection dated to the late first century B.C.E., also mentions αἰχμαλωσία in the context of Jewish captivity, as do other texts that were likely written shortly after the fall of the Jerusalem temple: 3 Baruch, 4 Baruch, 4 Ezra, and a fragment in Clement of Alexandria that is attributed to a Jew named Demetrius.[13]

While αἰχμαλωσία is the most common term for exile in Hellenistic Jewish literature, ἀποικία is more rare, appearing just twenty-eight times in the Septuagint, all in Ezra-Nehemiah, Jeremiah, 3 Maccabees, the Wisdom of Solomon, and Baruch, which use the term in reference to the recent past or to the people's contemporary displacement as a result of the exile.[14] Some references to ἀποικία in these texts are translations of the Hebrew גולה.[15] Ἀποικία also appears forty-four times in the writings of Philo, who uses it in reference to the two-phased experience of departing from one's ancestral homeland and colonizing another land, mostly in passages regarding the biblical patriarchs.[16] Philo views displacement and colonization positively, perhaps because he was influenced by the Egyptian tradition that communities throughout the world derived from

---

ment of Reuben in Origen's homilies and references to the *Testament of Naphtali* by Jerome suggest a *terminus ad quem* of the third century C.E.

12. See, e.g., *T. Naph.* 5:8. In certain passages of the *Testaments of the Twelve Patriarchs*, the word means "spoils of war" (*T. Jud.* 4:3; 5:6; 6:3; 7:8; 23:5). Though the term is used occasionally to specify incidents of captivity in the lives of the patriarchs (*T. Jos.* 1:5), most use αἰχμαλωσία to refer to the Israelites' slavery in Egypt in ways that potentially allude to later exiles as well (*T. Benj.* 7:2; *T. Dan* 5:11; *T. Naph.* 4:2, as well as *T. Dan* 5:7–8; *T. Levi* 13:6–7; and *T. Naph.* 5:8).

13. *Pss. Sol.* 2:6; 4 Esdr 14:21–22; 3 *Apoc. Bar.* 0:2–3; *4 Bar.* 6:19; 4 Ezra 5:16–18; Demetrius frag. 6:1, preserved in Clement of Alexandria, *Strom.* 1.141ff. Αἰχμαλωσία also appears in the *Lives of the Prophets* 12:1–2 and 20:1, but the provenance of this text is contested and may originate from a later Christian source.

14. Ezra 1:11; 2:1; 4:1; 9:4; 10:6, 16; Neh 7:6; 3 Macc 6:10; Wis 12:7; Jer 13:9; 30:19; 31:7; 35:4, 6; 36:1, 4, 22, 31; 37:3; 39:44; 40:7, 11; 47:11; Bar 3:7–8.

15. 2 Kgs 24:14–16; Jer 28:6 (LXX 35:6); 29:1 (LXX 36:1); 29:4 (LXX 36:4); 29:16, 20, 31 (LXX 36:31); 46:19 (LXX 26:19); 48:7 (LXX 31:7), 11 (LXX 31:33); 49:3 (LXX 30:19); Ezra 1:11; 4:1; 6:19–21; 9:4; 10:6–8, 16; Neh 7:6. The Septuagint also occasionally renders גולה as αἰχμαλωσία: 2 Kgs 24:14; Ezek 1:1; 3:11, 15; 11:24–25; 12:3–4, 7, 11; 25:3; Amos 1:15; Zech 6:10; 14:2; Ezra 2:1; 8:35; Neh 7:6.

16. Philo, *Opif.* 135; *Conf.* 77–78; *Migr.* 176; *Her.* 98; *Congr.* 84; *Fug.* 36, 95; *Abr.* 66, 68, 72, 77, 85; *Mos.* 1.71, 103, 163, 170, 195, 222, 233, 236, 239, 254–55; 2.232, 246, 288; *Spec.* 2.25, 146, 150, 158; 3.111; 4.178; *Virt.* 77, 102, 219; *Praem.* 16, 80; *Contempl.* 22; *Flacc.* 46; *Legat.* 281; *Q.G.* 1.27.

Egypt.[17] Josephus likewise uses ἀποικία to refer to colonization, using the word eight times.[18]

Of the three words used in the Septuagint to denote captivity, διασπορά is by far the most rare, appearing just twelve times. Though captivity and displacement are conceptual precursors to the diaspora, the Septuagint authors use διασπορά as an umbrella term that includes the experiences of captivity and displacement.[19]

▪ THE SCATTERING: διασπορά

The word διασπορά derives from the Greek prefix δια-, which indicates a motion of moving through or over a particular space, and here likely refers to separation or division, and σπείρω, which means "to sow." The word would have conveyed an image of seeds being scattered upon foreign lands. Besides its twelve appearances in the Septuagint, διασπορά appears twice in the writings of Philo of Alexandria: in a citation of the Septuagint (*Conf.* 197) and in a metaphorical comment about how vice leads to the dispersion of the soul (*Praem.* 115). Philo does not show awareness of διασπορά as a reference to Jewish populations outside of Judea. Nor does the word appear in the writings of Josephus. Διασπορά does, however, appear in three collections that date to the first century B.C.E. or the first century C.E.: the *Pss. Sol.* 8:28; 9:2; *T. Asher* 7:2; and the New Testament.

▪ Διασπορά IN THE SEPTUAGINT

The authors of works preserved in the Septuagint do not use διασπορά to translate any particular word of the Hebrew Bible. In three instances, the word is used to translate נדחים ("scattered ones"), which indicates that διασπορά was understood to be a population instead of (or in addition to) a designated space.[20] More often, however, the Septuagint translators

---

17. On this tradition in Egypt, see Diodorus Siculus, 1.28.1–3. See Scott, "Exile and Self-Understanding," 183; idem, "Philo and the Restoration of Israel," in *SBL 1995 Seminar Papers* (ed. Eugene H. Lovering Jr.; Atlanta: Scholars Press, 1995) 553–75; Erich S. Gruen, *Diaspora: Jews amidst Greeks and Romans* (Cambridge, MA: Harvard University Press, 2012) 242. Philo, *Conf.* 17.77–78; cf. *Flacc.* 7.46–47.

18. Josephus uses the word in *Ant.* 1.110–12, 120, 216, 255; 10.223, and in *Ap.* 2.38.

19. Karl Ludwig Schmidt, "διασπορά," *TDNT* 2:98–104.

20. Deut 30:4; Neh 1:9; Ps 147:2.

employ διασπορά to interpret an unrelated word in the context of divine punishment, or as an editorial insertion.

Διασπορά first appears in the Septuagint in Deut 28:25, in a passage that lists a series of curses that God will exact upon the Israelites should they violate the covenantal laws.[21] The Masoretic version of this passage first refers to Israelites being subject to foreign colonization in Deut 28:36, which declares that "the LORD will bring you, and the king whom you set over you, to a nation that neither you nor your ancestors have known."[22] The Septuagint translator transfers this punishment to the opening pericope by rendering Deut 28:25's "You shall become an object of horror [והיית לזעוה] to all the kingdoms of the earth," as "You shall be in dispersion [ἐν διασπορᾷ] in all the kingdoms of the earth." In defining זעוה as διασπορά, the translator clarifies that Israel's dispersion will be a source of horror to others, intended to publicly expose Israel's broken covenantal relationship to the nations, who will take note of Israel's fate and be reminded of God's fearsome power.

While the Septuagint's earliest reference to διασπορά links Israel's expulsion with public shame, its second reference to διασπορά appears shortly afterward in the context of restoration. In the Masoretic version, Deut 30:4-5 reads, "Even if your spread-out ones [נדחך] are at the edge of the heavens, from there the LORD your God will gather you, and from there he will bring you back. The LORD your God will bring you into the land that your ancestors possessed, and you will possess it; he will make you more prosperous and numerous than your ancestors."[23] By rendering נדחך as διασπορά, the translator implies that the shameful status of the dispersed people envisioned in the earlier pericope is temporary.[24] The juxtaposition of these two references to διασπορά points to the word's dual aspect: the diaspora will exacerbate the deteriorating relationship between God and Israel but will also be a harbinger of their future reconciliation.

The Septuagint renders זעוה as διασπορά in one other biblical verse, Jer 34:17 (LXX 41:17), which warns that, just as the people have not granted financial releases to their neighbors, God will not release the people from punishment. Instead, they will become a source of horror to

---

21. διασπείρω ("scatter") appears sixty-six times in the Septuagint and is most often used to translate נפץ ("shatter").

22. All English translations of the Hebrew Bible are from the NRSV unless specified otherwise. English translations of the Septuagint are from *NETS*.

23. In Deut 30:4-5 I have replaced the NRSV's translation "Even if you are exiled to the ends of the world," with my own more literal translation.

24. "If your dispersion [ἐὰν ᾖ ἡ διασπορά σου] be from an end of the sky to an end of the sky, from there the Lord your God will gather you, and from there he will take you" (Deut 30:4).

other nations.²⁵ The Septuagint translator clarifies that this horror will be experienced through the diaspora:

> Therefore, thus did the Lord say: You have not obeyed me by calling for a release each pertaining to his fellow. Behold, I am calling for a release for you to the dagger and to death and to the famine, and I will give you as a dispersion [εἰς διασποράν] to all the kingdoms of the earth.²⁶ (Jer 41:17 LXX)

The translator builds on the Hebrew version's reference to דרור, a term that elsewhere in the Hebrew Bible refers to the nullification of land contracts in the Jubilee year, to clarify the quid-pro-quo nature of the people's punishment: because they refused to grant such releases, the people will lose their own land (Lev 25:10).²⁷ Clarifying God's punishment as dispersion resolves another difficulty concerning the Hebrew verse: How can the people be a horror to all the kingdoms, when they reside in Judea? The answer is that they will not reside in Judea: they will be dispersed throughout the world, and this very dispersion will constitute the source of their humiliation.

Besides Deut 30:4, the Septuagint translates נדחים as διασπορά in two other passages: Neh 1:9 and Psalm 147.²⁸ The author of Nehemiah alludes to Deuteronomy 30 in Nehemiah's prayer, which asks God to remember the promise to gather the outcasts of Israel from exile.²⁹ Like its transla-

---

25. Jer 34:17 MT: "Therefore, thus says the LORD: You have not obeyed me by granting a release [דרור] to your neighbors and friends; I am going to grant a release [דרור] to you, says the Lord—a release to the sword, to pestilence, and to famine. I will make you a horror [לזעוה] to all the kingdoms of the earth."

26. Besides Deut 28:25, זעוה appears in Jer 15:4; 24:9; 29:18; 34:17; Ezek 23:46; and 2 Chr 29:8. All but Ezek 23:46 refer to the forced displacement of the people as being a product of God's anger. זעוה is not translated as διασπορά in the Septuagint in these verses (Jer 29:18 may be an exception, but no Septuagint translation of this passage survives). In some of these verses, translating זעוה as διασπορά would make some sense in context, such as in Jer 15:4: "I will make them a horror [ונתתים לזעוה] to all the kingdoms of the earth because of what King Manasseh son of Hezekiah of Judah did in Jerusalem." זעוה appears again in Jer 24:9, which likewise speaks of the upcoming exile, but the Septuagint uses διασκορπισμόν ("scattering") to translate זעוה. The fact that the Septuagint authors did not render זעוה as διασπορά in all verses that use זעוה in the context of exile suggests an unsystematic approach toward זעוה as a categorical experience.

27. The word also appears in conjunction with the release of captives (Isa 61:1; Jer 34:8, 15; Ezek 46:17). It occasionally means "sparrow" (Ps 84:4; Prov 26:2).

28. Of the twelve references to διασπορά in the Septuagint, six have no Hebrew equivalent, and six are translations of a Hebrew word.

29. Neh 1:8–9: "Remember the word that you commanded your servant Moses, 'If you are unfaithful, I will scatter you among the peoples; but if you return to me and

tion of נדחך in Deut 30:4 as διασπορά, the Septuagint translates Nehemiah's נדחכם as διασπορά, suggesting that the author of Nehemiah LXX noted the link between the two passages and viewed the returnees to Yehud as the diasporan Israelites alluded to in Deuteronomy 30.[30] The Septuagint also renders נדחי ישראל as τὰς διασπορὰς in its translation of Ps 147:2, which imagines God gathering the outcasts of Israel back to Jerusalem.[31] Given the association of נדחים and διασπορά, it is probable that, just as נדחים is associated in the Hebrew Bible with a group that experiences reconciliation following divine punishment, the translators associate διασπορά with punishment and reconciliation. When it comes to Psalm 147, therefore, the Septuagint translator might have intentionally translated נדחים as διασπορά in a verse that emphasizes divine compassion in the form of restorative ingathering.

The Septuagint authors' attitude toward διασπορά comes into full focus in their clarification of difficult Hebrew phrases. In Isa 49:6, God is cited as declaring that "it is too light a thing [נקל] that you should be my servant to raise up the tribes of Jacob and to restore the survivors of Israel [ונצורי ישראל]; I will give you as a light to the nations, that my salvation may reach to the end of the earth."[32] This verse presents a number of difficulties. The phrase "it is too light a thing that you should be my servant" implies that the prophet's burden should be even more difficult than it currently is. The particular identity of the "survivors of Israel" whom the prophet is meant to restore is also obscure. Finally, the verse's reference to the tribes of Jacob and the survivors of Israel seems repetitive. The Septuagint translator resolves all of these difficulties with the following rendering:

---

keep my commandments and do them, though your outcasts [נדחכם] are under the farthest skies, I will gather them from there and bring them to the place at which I have chosen to establish my name.'" Nehemiah paraphrases the curses of Deut 30:4, changing נדחך to נדחכם, conveying a second-person plural audience.

30. 2 Esdr 11:8–9: "Remember now the word that you commanded your servant Moyses, saying, 'You, if you are faithless, I will scatter you among my peoples, and if you return to me and keep my commandments and do them, if your dispersion [ἡ διασπορὰ ὑμῶν] is to the farthest skies, from there I will gather them and lead them to the place where I have chosen my name to encamp there.'" 2 Esdras 11 LXX corresponds to Nehemiah 1 MT.

31. Compare the Hebrew MT Ps 147:2: "The LORD builds up Jerusalem; he gathers the outcasts of Israel [נדחי ישראל]" with the Septuagint Ps 146:2: "The Lord builds up Jerusalem; he gathers the outcasts [τὰς διασπορὰς] of Israel."

32. This verse appears in the second of four Servant Songs in Second Isaiah (Isa 42:1–4; 49:1–6; 50:4–9; 52:13–53:12).

And he said to me, "it is a great thing [Μέγα σοί ἐστιν] for you to be called my servant so that you may set up the tribes of Iakob and turn back the dispersion of Israel [καὶ τὴν διασπορὰν τοῦ Ισραηλ ἐπιστρέψαι]. See, I have made you a light of nations, that you may be for salvation to the end of the earth."

The translator renders the Hebrew phrase "it is too light a thing" as "it is a great thing," clarifying that the servant's stewardship of Israel is a crucial role. Next, he interprets ונצורי ("survivors") as διασπορά, resolving the problems of repetition and the question of the survivors' identities. These changes clarify that the servant's job is to gather those who are scattered in the diaspora, and that the diaspora is a temporary state that culminates in divine restoration.

The Septuagint also uses διασπορά as a clarifying word in Jer 15:7, in which the prophet cites God as declaring, "I have winnowed them with a winnowing fork in the gates of the land."[33] The Septuagint translator interprets the verse's winnowing imagery as a divine scattering of Israel into διασπορά:

> And I will disperse them in a dispersion [καὶ διασπερῶ αὐτοὺς ἐν διασπορᾷ] in the gates of my people. I was made childless; I destroyed my people because of their evils. (Jer 15:7 LXX)

The translator replaces מזרה ("winnowing fork") with διασπορά, which denotes the dispersion of seeds. Besides the obvious agricultural connection, the passage's broader context offers insight as to why the translator renders "winnow" as διασπορά. Jeremiah 15:1–4 reads:

> Then the LORD said to me: "Though Moses and Samuel stood before me, yet my heart would not turn toward this people. Send them out of my sight, and let them go! And when they say to you, 'Where shall we go?' you shall say to them: 'Thus says the LORD: Those destined for pestilence, to pestilence, and those destined for the sword, to the sword; those destined for famine, to famine, and those destined for captivity, to captivity [לשבי לשבי]. . . . I will make them a horror to all the kingdoms of the earth because of what King Manasseh son of Hezekiah of Judah did in Jerusalem.'"

The translator extends the prediction of expulsion in Jer 15:2 by clarifying that the winnowing image in Jer 15:7 refers to the scattering of Israel. In doing so, the translator expands on the Hebrew's agricultural imagery

---

33. Jeremiah 15:7 reads, "I have winnowed them with a winnowing fork [ואזרם במזרה] in the gates of the land. I have bereaved them, I have destroyed my people; they did not turn from their ways."

while modifying the meaning of the verse. Whereas in the MT, God's winnowing the people is a punishment that takes place in the land, the translator envisions God scattering the people outside the land. This difference correlates with the rendering of the phrase "gates of the land" as "gates of my people," which allegorizes the image into one that alludes to the scattered community.³⁴ The Septuagint translator thus transforms this verse into a prediction of divine punishment through forced dispersion.

Other interpretive applications of διασπορά in the Septuagint build on its first appearance in Deuteronomy 28 by suggesting a connection between dispersion and collective shame. One such example occurs in the rendering of Dan 12:2. The MT reads,

> Many of those who sleep in the dust of the earth shall awake, some to everlasting life, and some to shame and everlasting contempt [לחרפות לדראון עולם].

This verse appears in a passage that fuses eschatological themes found in earlier prophetic texts concerning divine judgment in the end-time with the notion that the dead will be revived, envisioning a scenario in which the dead awaken to wonderful reward or terrible punishment.³⁵ The Septuagint translator situates this punishment within the experience of the diaspora:³⁶

> And many of those who sleep in the flat of the earth will arise, some to everlasting life but others to shame and others to dispersion and contempt everlasting [οἱ δὲ εἰς διασπορὰν καὶ αἰσχύνην αἰώνιον]. (Dan 12:2 LXX)

The translator adjusts the repetitive לחרפות לדראון עולם by interpreting דראון as διασπορὰν, thereby envisioning two distinct punishments. According to this version of this verse, only some people will be doomed to dispersion. Perhaps the translator viewed dispersion as an extreme form of punishment meant to shame only the worst sinners.

---

34. Cf. Isa 41:16 LXX, which renders the Hebrew's image of winnowing (תזרם ורוח תשאם וסערה תפיץ אותם, "you shall winnow them and a wind shall take them, and a tempest shall scatter them") as one of scattering by using the term διασπείρω (καὶ λικμήσεις, καὶ ἄνεμος λήμψεται αὐτούς, καὶ καταιγὶς διασπερεῖ αὐτούς).

35. John J. Collins, *Daniel: A Commentary on the Book of Daniel* (Hermeneia; Minneapolis: Fortress, 1993). Cf. Ezekiel's vision of the valley of the dry bones in Ezek 37:1–14.

36. Interestingly, the second-century Jewish Hellenistic scholar Theodotion removes reference to the dispersion in his Greek rendering of Daniel, closing Dan 12:2 with, "And many of those who sleep in a mound of earth will be awakened, these to everlasting life and those to shame and everlasting contempt."

Other late Second Temple texts use διασπορά in the context of salvation rather than punishment. In a letter appended to manuscripts of 2 Maccabees that was likely composed in the latter half of the second century B.C.E., representatives of the Jewish community in Jerusalem ask an Alexandrian Jewish priest named Aristobulus to ensure that he and his community observe the Purification holiday and "the festival of the fire" (2 Macc 1:10–2:18). The writers explain that this festival was instituted during the time of Nehemiah, after Judeans discovered a viscous liquid that had derived from the temple fire during the time of the First Temple and had been hidden by priests prior to their exile. When Nehemiah and other returnees from exile recovered the liquid and poured it onto an altar, it miraculously ignited, leading these Judeans to celebrate this event as a sign of God's divine favor. The letter recalls that a priest named Jonathan then offered a prayer that God

> gather together our scattered people [ἐπισυνάγαγε τὴν διασπορὰν ἡμῶν], set free those who are slaves among the Gentiles, look on those who are rejected and despised, and let the Gentiles know that you are our God. (2 Macc 1:27)

Jonathan's prayer links the experiences of Judean returnees from Babylonia with the authors' contemporary diaspora, suggesting that the authors expect Alexandrian Jews to hope for their own ingathering. Their reference to "our scattered ones" (τὴν διασπορὰν ἡμῶν) alludes not only to earlier scriptural references to the diaspora but also to the promised restoration that will follow.

Almost every reference to διασπορά in the Septuagint imagines a future scattering that will take place following Israel's abandonment of the covenantal laws. The sole exception appears in the Book of Judith, which treats the diaspora as a space occupied by Israel in the past. One of the book's central characters is an Ammonite named Achior, who, during a siege on the fictional Judean town of Bethulia, informs the enemy general Holofernes that the Israelites can be defeated only when they are disobedient to their God. In the past, Achior explains, God punished Israel for such disobedience with dispersion, but in recent times the Israelites have "come back from the places where they were scattered [ἐκ τῆς διασπορᾶς, οὗ διεσπάρησαν ἐκεῖ]" (Jdt 5:19). Besides its reference to a past diaspora, Judith is also unusual in its usage of διασπορά as a plural noun.[37] Perhaps the author, who likely lived in Judea under Hasmonean rule, was optimistic that Hasmonean autonomy would continue indefinitely, and

---

37. The only other appearance of a plural form of διασπορά appears in Ps 146:2.

he viewed the diaspora as a set of disparate spaces where the Jews once lived in a state of punishment.

While the authors of the Septuagint viewed the Hebrew Bible's predictions of divine curses as firmly situated within the experience of the diaspora, the word διασπορά rarely appears in other Jewish literature written under Greek and Roman rule.

■ Διασπορά in Late Second Temple Literature

Outside of the Septuagint, διασπορά appears in only a few documents: once in the *Testaments of the Twelve Patriarchs*, a text generally dated to the first century C.E. and likely edited in Syria;[38] twice in the *Psalms of Solomon*, a collection dated to the years following the Roman invasion of Jerusalem in 63 B.C.E.,[39] and three times in the New Testament.

In its edited form, the *Testaments of the Twelve Patriarchs* underscores the themes of Israelite captivity and exile. Nevertheless, διασπορά appears just once, when Jacob's son Asher predicts Israel's future captivity and dispersion:

> For I know that ye shall sin, and be delivered into the hands of your enemies; and your land shall be made desolate, and your holy places, and ye shall be scattered [διασκορπισθήσθε] unto the four corners of the earth; in the dispersion [ἐν διασπορᾷ] you shall be regarded as worthless, like useless water, until such time as the Most High visits the earth.[40]
> (*T. Asher* 7:2–3)

---

38. The collection as a whole derives from older Hebrew and Aramaic texts written in Judea; see n. 14 above.

39. Benedikt Eckhardt, "The Psalms of Solomon as a Historical Source for the Late Hasmonean Period," in *The Psalms of Solomon: Language, History, Theology* (ed. Eberhard Bons and Patrick Pouchelle; EJL 40; Atlanta: SBL Press, 2015) 7–30. Unlike Dufoix, I treat the *Psalms of Solomon* as lying outside the Septuagint collective, since the *Psalms* only appear in the fifth-century C.E. Codex Alexandrinus manuscript of the Septuagint, and not in the early fourth-century C.E. Codex Vaticanus or Codex Sinaiticus. See Greg Goswell, "The Order of the Books in the Greek Old Testament," *JETS* 52 (2009) 449–66, here 466.

40. The passage continues, "He shall come as a man eating and drinking with human beings, crushing the dragon's head in the water. He will save Israel and all the nations, God speaking like a man" (*T. Asher* 7:3). The text "He shall come as a man ... he will save Israel" suggests that at least part of this passage represents a later Christian interpolation, a suggestion made in H. C. Kee, "The Testaments of the Twelve Patriarchs," *OTP* 1:775–828, here 818. Either the entire passage was composed by an early Christian who viewed the fall of the temple and the consequent dispersion as a consequence of Israel's sins that was part of the divine plan from the early patriarchal

Given that this passage is set in the patriarchal period, one would expect Asher to predict the Israelites' upcoming slavery in Egypt. Instead, Asher envisions a series of dispersions in the distant future, implying that, for the author, biblical exile and contemporary diaspora are one and the same, and that scattering marks an ongoing and ever-present divine response to the sins of Israel.

It is possible that the *Testaments'* reference to διασπορά and its broader emphasis on exile and captivity as divine punishments for Israel's sins derive from the work of an early Christian editor who viewed the dispersion as a signifier of God's rejection that was predicted in the patriarchal period. Yet many Jews who lived well before Jesus's time espoused the notion that dispersion is a sign of divine punishment. The *Psalms of Solomon*, for instance, depicts the διασπορά as a punishment, albeit a temporary one that will soon be resolved on account of God's mercy. Its two references to διασπορά read:

> Gather together the dispersed [τὴν διασποράν] of Israel, with mercy and goodness. (*Pss. Sol.* 8:28 [8:34 in *OTP*])

> The dispersion of Israel [ἡ διασπορά τοῦ Ισραηλ] (was) among every nation, according to the saying of God; that your righteousness might be proven right, O God, in our lawless actions. For you are a righteous judge over all the peoples of the earth. (*Pss. Sol.* 9:2)

The *Psalms of Solomon* may mark the only Second Temple source outside of the Septuagint and the New Testament to use the word διασπορά. The term would not come to designate a contemporary global community of believers until the late first century, when early Christians began to use the term subversively.

▪ Diaspora in the New Testament

The early followers of Jesus were the first to employ διασπορά as a designation for a community in which members were bound to one another in faith rather than in attachment to Judea as a homeland (John 7:35; Jas 1:1; 1 Pet 1:1).[41] The earliest of the three New Testament documents to use

---

period, or *T. Asher* 7:4 represents an addition made by an early Jesus follower who qualified the preceding verses by overlayering them with a christology that presumes that Israel can be redeemed only through Christ.

41. See Shively T. J. Smith, *Strangers to Family: Diaspora and 1 Peter's Invention of God's Household* (Waco, TX: Baylor University Press, 2016) 23–24. The verb διασπείρω appears just three times in the New Testament as well, with all verbal forms appearing

the word is the Letter of James, which uses διασπορά in its opening greeting:

> James, a servant of God and of the Lord Jesus Christ, To the twelve tribes in the Dispersion [ἐν τῇ διασπορᾷ]: Greetings. (Jas 1:1)

References in James's letter to the synagogue, monotheistic ideas, divine law, and Old Testament imagery suggest that the author is addressing Jewish followers of Jesus who live in the diaspora.[42] By referring to these followers as "the twelve tribes in the Dispersion," James roots the apostles' mission in a biblical tradition, implying that the apostles are actualizing the scriptural prediction that the exiled tribes of Israel would one day gather and galvanize the messianic age. Referencing the followers of Jesus as tribes also suggests that Jews who reject Jesus as the Messiah are outsiders to the people of Israel and doomed to remain in exile.[43] Only followers of Jesus will be beneficiaries of the promises of restoration given to the Israelites.

Like James, 1 Peter addresses a community outside of Judea and weaves the nascent community of Jesus followers into the fabric of scriptural history by addressing the "exiles of the dispersion,"[44] a phrase similar to James's "twelve tribes in the Dispersion." Rather than expressing a yearning to return to a physical homeland, 1 Peter imagines the diaspora as a scattered population that will assemble together in a heavenly home following a temporary sojourn on earth.[45] Upon their arrival in heaven, the

---

in the Acts of the Apostles: 8:1, 4; 11:19. Narry F. Santos observes that these verses refer to Jewish followers of Jesus who served to expand their faith communities in areas of a non-Jewish majority ("*Diaspora* in the New Testament and Its Impact on Christian Mission," *Torch Trinity Journal* 13 [2010] 3–18, here 6). I question Santos's conclusion that "the *diaspeirō* and *diaspora* passages in the New Testament show how God used suffering, persecution, and dispersion as the context for expanding his kingdom [and] used the Jewish diaspora to expand the missionary work to the Jews, Samaritans, and Gentiles. . . . [T]he Jewish diaspora and the diaspora during the New Testament period prepared the way for Christian mission" (17–18). The argument that Jews function primarily as enablers of a Christian mission does not have a place in academic discourse.

42. See Jas 1:21, 24–25; 2:2, 8–13, 19; 4:4, 11–12 (Santos, "*Diaspora* in the New Testament," 4–5).

43. Herbert Basser, "The Letter of James," in *The Jewish Annotated New Testament* (2nd ed.; ed. Amy-Jill Levine and Marc Zvi Brettler; Oxford: Oxford University Press, 2017) 490.

44. 1 Pet 1:1: "Peter, an apostle of Jesus Christ, To the exiles of the Dispersion [διασπορᾶς] in Pontus, Galatia, Cappadocia, Asia, and Bithynia."

45. Peter H. Davids, *The First Epistle of Peter* (NICNT; Grand Rapids: Eerdmans, 1990) 46. On Peter's Jewish Christian and gentile audience, see Santos, "*Diaspora* in the New Testament," 5.

lives of those faithful to Jesus will truly begin and their spiritual diaspora will come to a close.

The Gospel of John references the diaspora in a more concrete and spatial manner. When the Pharisees attempt to have Jesus arrested at the temple during the Tabernacles holiday, Jesus predicts that he will soon depart and no one will find him. John describes the Jews' bewildered response to this prediction: "Where does this man intend to go that we will not find him? Does he intend to go to the Dispersion among the Greeks [εἰς τὴν διασπορὰν τῶν Ἑλλήνων] and teach the Greeks?" (John 7:35)

In John, the Jews become unknowing prophets of Jesus's teachings and the apostolic mission, which will spread word of Jesus's teachings to those outside Judea. Without understanding who Jesus truly is, the Jews foreshadow what Jesus will accomplish.[46] The Jews also do not comprehend that the diaspora will take on a new character once the mission arrives. No longer will this diaspora comprise Ἰουδαῖοι. Instead, it will comprise a new community of people, newly faithful to Jesus and his teachings.[47]

The New Testament authors redefine διασπορά in ways that depict Jesus's followers outside Judea as participating in the scriptural promises of a divine plan that will end in reward and restoration. The diaspora was thus transformed into a literal map by which Jesus's followers could place themselves into the story of God's covenantal engagement, which entailed both dispersion and restoration.

---

46. Understanding how to translate Ἰουδαῖος can help one discern what the author means by διασπορά. In most English translations of John, οἱ Ἰουδαῖοι is translated as "the Jews," and in our verse, the phrase contrasts with Hellenists (τῶν Ἑλλήνων . . . τοὺς Ἕλληνας). The Jews thus comprise an entity that lies outside of Greek society, and they view Greeks as living outside of Judea, in the dispersion. The question of whether to translate Ἰουδαῖοι as "Jews" or "Judeans" determines the extent to which John views the Jews as collectively responsible for the passion and crucifixion of Jesus. Most English translations render οἱ Ἰουδαῖοι as "Jews" because it parallels the reference to Greeks in the same verse, but I read the phrase as referencing Judean Jews who view the dispersion as a space outside of their immediate society. Some scholars who address the question of whether John intends to denote Jews or Judeans when referencing οἱ Ἰουδαῖοι miss the point that, by this period, the word almost certainly meant both things, and Jewish readers (not to mention the author of the Gospel himself) would have been sensitive to the word's ambiguity. See Steve Mason, "Jews, Judaeans, Judaizing, Judaism: Problems of Categorization in Ancient History," *JSJ* 38 (2007) 457–512; and Daniel Boyarin, *Judaism: The Genealogy of a Modern Notion* (Key Words in Jewish Studies 9; New Brunswick, NJ: Rutgers University Press, 2019).

47. On the Jews as portenders of Jesus's mission, see Adele Reinhartz, "Judaism in the Gospel of John," *Int* 63 (2009) 382–93; Johannes Beutler, *Judaism and the Jews in the Gospel of John* (SubBib 30; Rome: Pontificio Istituto Biblico, 2006).

■ Conclusion

The negative use of the word διασπορά in the Septuagint complicates the overly positive view among scholars that Jews in the Greco-Roman diaspora viewed their lives as a source of pride rather than shame.[48] With just one exception, διασπορά appears in the Septuagint in the context of a divine punishment that would mark God's response to Israel's abandonment of the covenantal relationship. It is not surprising that, as a word that was linked to divine rejection, horror, and shame, διασπορά barely appears in Jewish literature outside of the Septuagint, even in texts that take place within the diaspora. The Jews who authored Greek texts that depicted the diaspora as a thriving place where Jews could piously practice their ancestral laws avoided using the word, likely because they knew that it was associated with the divine rejection of Israel in the Septuagint. The literary use of the word διασπορά and its negative connotations are therefore in *tension* with the lived reality of a diaspora where Jews thrived.

Space restrictions prevent me from putting the Septuagint's negative applications of the word διασπορά into direct conversation with diasporan sources that interpret the diaspora in positive ways. These sources, which include passages from the *Letter of Aristeas*, the writings of Philo of Alexandria, and 3 Maccabees, have already been mined for clues regarding diasporan self-understanding by scholars such as John Barclay, Isaiah Gafni, and Erich Gruen.[49] My contribution here aims to set the stage for a future conversation that compares all of these sources alongside surviving personal letters from Judeans to Jews in the diaspora found at the beginning of 2 Maccabees, in Elephantine documents, and elsewhere, which instruct diasporan Jews on matters of ancestral practice and which pray for their permanent return to Judea. Taken together, all of these sources suggest that the diaspora was not a self-evident reality but a construction enforced by those who lived outside it. The authors of the Septuagint thus represent a particular viewpoint, explicit in Judean letters to Egyptian Jews, which

---

48. Kraabel, "Unity and Diversity," 49–60; idem, "The Roman Diaspora: Six Questionable Assumptions," *JJS* 33.1–2 (1982) 445–64; Isaiah M. Gafni, *Land, Center, and Diaspora: Jewish Constructs in Late Antiquity* (JSPSup 21; Sheffield: Sheffield Academic Press, 1997); Gruen, *Diaspora*.

49. John M. G. Barclay, *Jews in the Mediterranean Diaspora: From Alexander to Trajan (323 BCE–117 CE)* (Berkeley: University of California Press, 1996). Barclay later edited the volume *Negotiating Diaspora: Jewish Strategies in the Roman Empire* (Library of Second Temple Studies 45; London: T&T Clark, 2004); Gafni, *Land, Center, and Diaspora*; Erich S. Gruen, "Diaspora and Homeland," in *Diasporas and Exiles: Varieties of Jewish Identity* (ed. Howard Wettstein; Berkeley: University of California Press, 2002) 18–46; idem, *Diaspora*.

linked the diaspora to sin and exile. Future analyses of Jewish attitudes toward the diaspora in the Hellenistic period must take into account the Septuagint writers' references to diaspora and exile as discursive efforts to participate in an ongoing debate regarding whether the establishment of Jewish communities outside Judea was theologically meaningful.

It would be only in the first century, as early followers of Jesus began to use διασπορά in ways that presented themselves as the dispersed faithful who would become the beneficiaries of God's biblical promises of restoration, that diasporan Jews began to regularly speak of their contemporary dispersion as the fulfillment of scriptural curses. This shift, most explicit in the rabbinic use of the Hebrew word גלות, would reimagine dispersion as a punishment presently endured by all Jews, even by those living in Judea. The earlier dissonance between the negative use of διασπορά and widespread positive attitudes toward the diaspora would dissolve into a cohesive view that allegorized the dispersion into a temporal rather than a spatial state of being that pushed a messianic restoration into the distant future.[50]

Some scholars today treat the Jewish diaspora as a terrible but just predicament while others depict the diaspora as a glorified space of powerlessness that imbues the Jewish people with integrity and resilience. The former view can serve to buttress the notion that Jews are a people rejected by God, and the latter view can serve to delegitimize aspirations for self-governance in a Jewish homeland. Given how widespread these presumptions are, it is a particular privilege to honor a colleague whose work makes no such assumptions, whose scholarship is guided by meticulous analysis and uncompromising integrity, and who is considered by junior and senior scholars alike to be a friend and role model. Leslie Hoppe's scholarship is sure to impact generations to come, and it is my wish for him that, like the biblical Abraham at the age of seventy-five, Leslie is granted a bounty of divine blessings.

---

50. An extreme version of this view is articulated in the Tosefta: "R. Simeon ben Eleazar says, Israel(ites) in the diaspora are worshippers of idolatry" (*t. Abod. Zar.* 4:6). On rabbinic attitudes toward גלות, see Chaim Milikowsky, "Notions of Exile, Subjugation, and Return in Rabbinic Literature," in Scott, *Exile*, 265–96; Barbara Kirshenblatt-Gimblett, "Spaces of Dispersal," *Cultural Anthropology* 9.3 (1994) 338–44. Older treatments of the topic appear in the classic work Yitzhak Baer, *Galut* (New York: Schocken, 1947), and Gerald Serotta, *Galut in Rabbinic Literature* (Cincinnati, OH: Hebrew Union College-Jewish Institute of Religion, 1974).

"An Evangelizing Church": The Ecclesiology of Matthew's Gospel

DONALD SENIOR, C.P.
Catholic Theological Union (emeritus)
Chicago, Illinois

In his study of New Testament ecclesiologies, *The Churches the Apostles Left Behind*,[1] Raymond E. Brown defined what he called the "subapostolic era" of the early church. This period took place roughly during the last third of the first century, after the death of the first-generation apostles. It was during this crucial period that the early church, under the guidance of the Spirit, developed much of its key structures, practices, and theology—elements that were in continuity with the spirit and fundamental direction of Jesus and the first generation of his followers but, at the same time, incorporated new directions in order to sustain the Christian community as it moved out into the wider Greco-Roman world and forward into history.[2]

Among the seven examples of emerging ecclesiologies he studies, Brown considers Matthew's ecclesiology to be the most "successful": "Of all the gospels it was best suited to the manifold needs of the later church, the most cited by the church fathers, the most used in the liturgy, and the most serviceable for catechetical purposes."[3] This essay, honoring my longtime friend and colleague Leslie Hoppe on his seventy-fifth birthday,

---

Unless otherwise indicated biblical quotations are from the NABRE.

1. Raymond E. Brown, *The Churches the Apostles Left Behind* (New York: Paulist, 1984). Brown considered this his favorite among his prolific writings. See Donald Senior, *Raymond E. Brown and the Catholic Biblical Renewal* (New York: Paulist, 2018) 176.
2. See Brown's discussion in *Churches the Apostles Left Behind*, 13–30.
3. Ibid., 124.

focuses on Matthew's vision of the church and confirms Brown's estimate of its continuing relevance for ecclesiology today.[4]

■ I. Christology as Matthew's Guiding Star

There is a strong consensus in contemporary biblical scholarship about the context from which Matthew's Gospel emerged.[5] Written probably around 80 or 90 C.E. by a Jewish-Christian author, it was situated in the "sub-apostolic era" described by Brown, perhaps in a mixed gentile and Jewish community such as that at Antioch. A major concern of Matthew's Gospel was how to keep faith with the originating Jewish matrix out of which Jesus himself and his earliest followers emerged and yet make room for the gentiles, who were entering the church in increasing numbers. As John Meier has noted, the fundamental theme of Matthew's Gospel is "continuity within discontinuity"—a task even more challenging in the wake of the Jewish revolt against Rome (66–73 C.E.) and the consequent calamity caused by the destruction of Jerusalem and its temple.[6]

For Matthew, the guiding star for navigating this challenge was the authority of Jesus and the spirit of his mission as portrayed in the Gospel. Jesus emerged from Israel and embodied its sacred history (Matt 1:1–18). Even at his conception and birth Jesus experiences the travails of Israel—threatened by a pharaoh-like Herod, protected by another Joseph who is a dreamer, forced into exile, returning with his family but having to take refuge in Nazareth. But the future role of the gentiles also emerges during Jesus's infancy; astrologers from the east come to pay homage to Jesus, yet they must consult the Scriptures of Israel to consummate their journey.

What is anticipated about Jesus in the infancy narrative breaks into full bloom in the body of Matthew's Gospel. On the one hand, Jesus is the true Israelite, the Christ, and the beloved Son of God, who comes not to destroy the Law and the Prophets but to "fulfill" them (5:17). Beginning with the opening verse of the Gospel (1:1) and continuing throughout his

---

4. Although most of Leslie Hoppe's contributions have been studies of the Old Testament, I am happy to note he has published a book on Matthew's Gospel: Leslie Hoppe, *A Retreat with Matthew the Evangelist: Going beyond the Law* (Cincinnati, OH: St. Anthony Messenger Press, 2000).

5. See Donald Senior, "Matthew at the Crossroads of Early Christianity: An Introductory Assessment," in *The Gospel of Matthew at the Crossroads of Early Christianity* (ed. Donald Senior; BETL 243; Leuven: Peeters, 2011) 3–24.

6. See John P. Meier, *The Vision of Matthew: Christ, Church and Morality in the First Gospel* (Theological Inquiries; New York: Paulist, 1978) 28–29.

narrative, Matthew applies abundant titles to Jesus that confirm his unique identity: Christ, Son of David, Son of Abraham, Savior ("Jesus"), Emmanuel, Son of God, Lord, Lord of the Sabbath, the coming Son of Man.

In addition, throughout his narrative, Matthew anticipates the gentile mission alluded to with the coming of the Magi. At the moment of Jesus's entry into Galilee and the beginning of his mission there, Matthew adds a citation of Isa 8:22–9:1, "Land of Zebulun and land of Naphtali, the way to the sea, beyond the Jordan, Galilee of the Gentiles, the people who sit in darkness have seen a great light, on those dwelling in a land overshadowed by death light has arisen" (4:12–17). Similarly, in describing the healing mission of Jesus, Matthew employs a citation from Isa 42:1–4 that ends, "And in his name the Gentiles will hope" (12:21 NRSV). There are also two dramatic encounters in Matthew's narrative where gentiles seek Jesus for healing, the centurion in 8:5–13 and the Canaanite woman in 15:21–28. In both instances the faith of these gentiles amazes Jesus.

At the same time, Matthew retains an emphasis on the primacy of Israel in the unfolding plan of salvation; thus, the mission of the disciples, like that of Jesus himself, is confined to Israel during the earthly mission of Jesus (see 10:5; 15:24). But after the advent of the new age, with the death and resurrection of Jesus, the mission now extends to "all nations." As Matthias Konradt has demonstrated, for Matthew the mission to the gentiles is not based on the failure of the mission to Israel nor is it a rejection of the Jews. Rather, the extension of the mission to the gentiles is the fulfillment of Israel's own destiny, with God's salvific embrace of all nations through Jesus now actualized.[7]

■ II. "My Church"—Qualities of the *Ekklēsia* Formed in Jesus's Name

If, for Matthew, the expansion of the Christian mission is based on the unique identity and authority of Jesus, the glorified and risen Christ, the

---

7. Matthias Konradt concludes, "The interpretation of Jesus' death [as the turning point in salvation history] further illuminates the conceptual connection between the ministry to the Gentiles and the fulfillment of the promises given to Israel. With his salvific death, Jesus at the same time completes his Israel-oriented task to save his people from sin (1.21). That is, with the fulfillment of the promises of salvation to *Israel*, the foundation for the ministry of salvation to the *Gentiles* is simultaneously laid" (*Israel, Church, and the Gentiles in the Gospel of Matthew* [Baylor-Mohr Siebeck Studies in Early Christianity; Waco, TX: Baylor University Press, 2014] 375; italics original).

same is true for the defining characteristics of the community founded in Jesus's name. Matthew's ecclesiology is rooted in the Gospel's christology.[8]

As Brown and many commentators have noted, assuming the Two-Source Hypothesis, Matthew has given a more structured order to the portrayal of Jesus's public mission compared to that of Mark. The heart of that portrayal is found from the end of chap. 4 to the conclusion of the mission discourse in chap. 11. Faced with the crowds of the sick who seek him for healing, Jesus ascends the mount and begins the first and most fundamental discourse of the Gospel, the Sermon on Mount (chaps. 5–7). Here Matthew lays out Jesus's teaching concerning the "fulfillment" of the law as interpreted by Jesus, with the love command at its core (see 5:43–48; 22:34–40). This discourse is followed by a series of healings in chaps. 8 and 9, prompted by the plight of the same crowd that triggered Jesus's discourse (see 4:23–25 and 8:1).

This portrayal of Jesus as teacher and healer sets the pattern for the mission of the community, which follows immediately. The sight of the crowds again prompts Jesus's compassion (see the repeated summary of 4:23–5:1 and 9:35–36), and he now instructs his disciples to become laborers in the harvest, as elaborated in the mission discourse of 10:1–11:1. What Jesus has done, his disciples are to do. As already narrated in the call of the first disciples, Jesus invites them "to follow me" and to become like "fishers of people" (4:18–22). Faithful discipleship, illustrated by authentic teaching and compassionate healing as Jesus does, is the first characteristic of the ἐκκλησία, or assembly, of those who gather in his name.

There are two key passages in Matthew's Gospel where the term "church" (ἐκκλησία) is used, and each of these is important for understanding Matthew's vision of this missionary church.

The Authority of Peter

Although Peter's "confession" of Jesus's identity at Caesarea Philippi is found already in Mark's Gospel, Matthew significantly expands the passage (see 16:13–20; compare Mark 8:31–33). The emphasis of Matthew's text

---

8. In a recent work, *Matthew within Sectarian Judaism* (AYBRL; New Haven: Yale University Press, 2019), John Kampen correctly situates Matthew's Gospel in the context of Judaism but proposes that Matthew's primary purpose was polemical, that is, to defend the authentic Jewish identity of his community over against Pharisaic Judaism. While there is no doubt that Matthew defends the legitimacy of his community and its Jewish identity, to make that polemic the primary purpose of Matthew's narrative is a bridge too far. Proclamation of the gospel and its thoroughly christological foundation remains the primary purpose of Matthew's work.

falls on Peter and the role of authority given to him by Jesus. Peter's confession of Jesus as "the Messiah, the Son of the Living God" (the latter title not found in Mark's passage) triggers Jesus's acclamation: "Blessed are you, Simon son of Jonah. For flesh and blood has not revealed this to you, but my heavenly Father" (16:16–17). Peter is then designated as "the rock" upon which Jesus will build "my church" (ἐκκλησία), against which the "gates of the netherworld" will not prevail (16:18). And Peter is given "the keys to the kingdom of heaven" and the power of "binding and loosing," with his decision being ratified "in heaven" (16:19).

Most commentators find in this commissioning of Peter an allusion to Isa 22:15–25, where Eliakim succeeds the unfaithful Shebna as master of David's palace and is given the "key of the house of David" and the authority to open or shut the gates (Isa 22:22). Yet there is substantial debate about the interpretation of this Matthean passage. Most agree that it underscores Peter's role within Matthew's narrative as the first called to be a disciple (4:18) and his subsequent role as spokesperson for the disciples (see, e.g., 15:15; 16:16; 17:4; 17:24–27; 18:21). Most, too, see resonance with Peter's significant role in early Christianity, as among the first to encounter the risen Christ (see 1 Cor 15:5; in Luke and John, Peter is also among the first disciples to witness the empty tomb after the report of the women. See Luke 24:12; John 20:1–10; Peter is also singled out in Mark 16:7), and his role in fostering the gentile mission is underscored in Acts (10:1–11:18) and by implication in Paul's rebuke of Peter for withdrawing from table fellowship with gentiles in Antioch (Gal 2:11–14). This latter role of Peter in fostering the gentile mission may well be reflected in the power of the keys and "binding and loosing" given to Peter, which connects with the question of entry into the Christian community. The existence of the Petrine letters, whether authored by Peter or not, also testifies to the standing of Peter in the memory of the early community.

Does the role assigned to Peter in Matthew's Gospel imply a continuing office of a "Petrine ministry" in the church? This question has long been debated along denominational lines, although a more harmonious ecumenical atmosphere has enriched the discussion of a possible place for a "Petrine ministry" in the church in recent times. Obviously, Roman Catholic tradition finds here a biblical basis for the papal office. [9]

---

9. Raymond Brown was the driving force behind the pioneering ecumenical study *Peter in the New Testament: A Collaborative Assessment by Protestant and Roman Catholic Scholars* (ed. Raymond E. Brown, Karl P. Donfried, and John Reumann; New York: Paulist, 1973). More recent works in the same ecumenical spirit would include Martin Hengel, *Saint Peter: The Underestimated Apostle* (trans. Thomas H. Trapp; Grand Rapids: Eerdmans, 2010); Markus Bockmuehl, *Simon Peter in Scripture*

Whatever the trends of later Christian interpretation about the ongoing nature of a Petrine role might be, it is hard not to conclude that Matthew intends by this passage, at the very least, to acknowledge the role of authority within the community. Peter, as the first called, as an early witness of the resurrection, and as a leading voice among the disciples, represents the legitimate role of leadership within the early Christian community. As indicated in the words of Jesus in 16:16–17, that authority must be grounded in faith in Jesus as the Christ and Son of God. As I will note, Peter's fragile faith is also underscored by Matthew (see 16:22–23; 14:28–31, and especially 26:69–75). Thus, the authority given to Peter does not exempt him from failure and the need for admonition and repentance.

The Authority of the ἐκκλησία

A noteworthy characteristic of Matthew's ecclesiology is that the authority of "binding and loosing" given to Peter is also attributed to the church itself. The key text is found in the so-called community discourse of chap. 18 on the issue of how to deal with an errant member of the community (see 18:15–20). The procedure proposed reflects both common sense and a similar procedure found in Qumran's *Manual of Discipline* (see 1QS 5.26–6.2; 1QSa 9.2–3). If a "brother" (Matthew uses the masculine term ἀδελφός) sins against another member, the aggrieved party should take the initiative and seek out the errant member. If that effort at reconciliation fails, then the aggrieved party should bring one or two other members so that "every fact may be established on the testimony of two or three witnesses"—a procedure that echoes Jewish custom (see Deut 19:15). If this effort also fails to persuade the errant member, then the matter is to

---

and Memory: The New Testament Apostle in the Early Church (Grand Rapids: Baker Academic, 2013); also Helen K. Bond and Larry W. Hurtado, eds., *Peter in Early Christianity* (Grand Rapids: Eerdmans, 2015). A recent example of a Catholic perspective is that of Pheme Perkins, *Peter: Apostle for the Whole Church* (Studies on Personalities of the New Testament; Columbia: University of South Carolina Press, 1994). A discordant note is that of Robert H. Gundry, *Peter: False Disciple and Apostate according to Saint Matthew* (Grand Rapids: Eerdmans, 2015), who argues unpersuasively that Matthew's intent was to portray Peter as a negative example. See my critique of Gundry's thesis in "Matthew's Portrait of Peter: Apostle or Apostate?," in *The Figure of Jesus in History and Theology: Essays in Honor of John Meier* (ed. Vincent T. M. Skemp and Kelley Coblentz Bautch; CBQI 1; Washington, DC: Catholic Biblical Association of America, 2020) 145–58.

On the Roman Catholic tradition of the basis for the papal office, see, e.g., *The Catechism of the Catholic Church*, §816, on "Apostolic Succession."

be brought before the ἐκκλησία itself. If the errant brother resists even the assembly, or "church," then he is to be treated "as you would a gentile or tax collector" (18:17). As Brown and others have noted, this formulation—"a Gentile or a tax collector"—reflects the Jewish Christian context of Matthew's community where both of these types would be "outsiders." But, in the context of Jesus's mission portrayed in the Gospel, these individuals are also the objects of Jesus's compassionate ministry (see, e.g., 9:10; 10:3; 11:19; 21:31). Thus, errant members are expelled but not permanently "shunned"—they now become a concern of the church's mission.[10]

To ratify the decision of the community to expel a seriously errant member, Matthew's Jesus extends to the community the same power of "binding and loosing" that had been conferred on Peter (18:18–19). As is probably the case with Peter, "binding and loosing" have to do with determining membership in the community, that is, on the part of Peter, the decision to incorporate gentiles; on the part of the church assembly, the power to excommunicate someone who resists resolving a serious offense. The source of that ecclesial power is the presence of the risen Christ in the midst of the community: "For where two or three are gathered together in my name, there I am in the midst of them" (18:30; see also 28:20). The foundation for this community empowerment also parallels that of Peter, whose authority is rooted in his God-given faith in Jesus as the Christ and the Son of God (16:16–17).

"You are all brothers [and sisters]"

The egalitarian perspective of Matthew's ecclesiology found in chap. 18 is reaffirmed in chap. 23, where Jesus excoriates the false leadership of his opponents. The disciples are not to imitate their example; Jesus cites their failure to practice what they preach (23:3), their lack of compassion (23:4), their hypocrisy ("All their works are performed to be seen," 23:5), and their seeking marks of honor and prestige (23:6–7). Jesus's disciples are to avoid titles of honor such as "rabbi" or "father" or "master," remembering that they have one teacher and one father "in heaven" and one master, the Messiah" (23:9–10). The "greatest" among the disciples is to be "your servant" (23:11–12).

---

10. The procedure outlined in 18:15–17 protects the injured member of the community. While the aggrieved party is asked to take the initiative in seeking reconciliation (see also 5:23–26, 38–42, 43–48, and the petition of the Lord's Prayer, 6:12), the community itself ultimately sets a limit to its tolerance and thereby protects the innocent member.

These admonitions against arrogance and hypocrisy on the part of religious leaders were also taken up in Jesus's teaching in the Sermon on the Mount. There, too, leaders who seek adulation and places of honor are branded as "hypocrites," performing "works of righteousness for people to see them" (6:1). To illustrate such behavior, the Sermon refers to the classic expressions of Jewish piety: almsgiving, prayer, and fasting. Those who give alms should "not blow a trumpet... to win the praise of others" (6:2); those who pray should not make a show of it "so that others may see them" (6:5); and those who fast should "not look gloomy... or neglect their appearance" to impress others that they are fasting (6:16).

Thus, Matthew's vision of the church emphasizes both the role of leadership and the authority of the community's corporate decisions. Leaders are blessed through the grace given them, but they are also fragile and must avoid the pitfalls of arrogance and hypocrisy that such prominence can lead to. The disciples of Jesus are to follow Jesus and share in his mission of salvation, yet they remain human and their faith is frail, characterized by Matthew as "little faith" (see 6:30; 8:26; 14:31; 16:8; 17:20).

In his critiques of false religious leadership, Matthew consistently uses the Pharisees, scribes, and priests as foils. Coupled with their unyielding opposition to Jesus throughout the narrative, the end result is a decidedly negative and stereotyped portrayal of the Jewish religious leaders no doubt reflecting the polemical atmosphere of the post-70 era in which Matthew's Gospel was composed. (Matthew's view of Jewish civil leaders such as Herod the Great and Herod Antipas is also negative.) The pitfall here is, as history has tragically demonstrated, that such descriptions of the Jewish leaders provide an opening to anti-Semitism. As Matthew is a first-century author, it is anachronistic to accuse Matthew himself of the kind of racial and ideological anti-Semitism that is a scourge of the modern era. Matthew, as a follower of Jesus, no doubt considered himself to be authentically and loyally Jewish even though in tension with non-Christian Jews. Yet the Gospel's polemic against the Jewish leaders, read in a different context and time, can pave the way for later forms of anti-Semitism.[11] At the same time, it is important to note that, although the polemic of Matthew's Gospel is directly addressed to the Jewish leaders themselves, it is a rhetorical warning to his own community leadership about the corruptions of power.

---

11. On this, see Francois P. Viljoen, "Matthew, the Church and Anti-Semitism," in Senior, *Gospel of Matthew at the Crossroads of Early Christianity*, 653–82.

*Pastoral Care and Forgiveness as Primary Qualities
of the Church*

The examples in Matthew's Gospel of Jesus's compassion for human frailty, including that of the disciples themselves, point to another fundamental characteristic of the Gospel's ecclesiology, especially evident in the community discourse of chap. 18. As Brown himself astutely noted in his essay on Matthew's ecclesiology, the very structure of the discourse reveals the Gospel's priorities.[12] The segment on internal conflict and the need for discipline (18:15–20) is framed by passages dealing with admonitions about pastoral care for the vulnerable (18:6–14) and the need for limitless forgiveness (18:21–35), with each of these segments concluding with an emphatic statement about the "will of my heavenly Father" (18:14, 35).

The discourse begins with the disciples' question about "greatness in the kingdom of heaven" (18:1)—a passage prompted by Mark 9:33–34, where the disciples argue among themselves about "who is the greatest." Here, as in other passages, Matthew appears to soften the image of the disciples, turning their argument among themselves into a question for Jesus. Jesus's response seems to subvert the question—pointing to a child in their midst, he declares, "Amen I say to you, unless you turn and become like children, you will not enter the kingdom of heaven" (18:3). It should be noted that the entire discourse is directed to the disciples themselves and their way of responding to those in need: children, "little ones who go astray" (not children), and those in need of forgiveness. Thus, in effect, it is the core members of the community—the disciples—who are being instructed on how to treat those who are vulnerable, or on the margins of the community.

This call for repentance (i.e., "turn") and humility, reinforced by Jesus by pointing to the presence of a child (παιδίον), leads into the first segment of the discourse, which cautions against "scandalizing" (σκανδαλίσῃ) "one of these little ones [μικρῶν] who believe in me" (18:6). There is a significant shift in vocabulary here. While the opening segment (18:1–5) referred to "children" (παιδία) as a sign of humility, the next segments (18:6–9, 10–14) refer to "one of the little ones who believe in me" (ἕνα

---

12. Brown comments, "Many times when I have heard chap. 18 of Matthew cited, attention was concentrated on the binding and loosing power to excommunicate. Both before and after the chapter, Matthew has hedged that power by indications that care for one's brother or sister is more important. His goal is not to protect or emphasize the authority but to prevent its misuse" (*Churches the Apostles Left Behind*, 145).

τῶν μικρῶν τούτων τῶν πιστευόντων εἰς ἐμέ). It is no longer a matter of "children" but now adult disciples or believers who are designated as "little ones"—that is, subject to "scandal" (18:6–9) or liable to "go astray" (18:10–14). This concern for the "little ones" coincides with other passages in Matthew where Jesus teaches care for the "least" (ἐλαχίστων, which in fact is the superlative form of μικρός), as in the mission exhortation of 10:42 and in the parable of the sheep and the goats (25:31–46; esp. 25:40, 45).

The precise meaning of the verb σκανδαλίζω ("scandalize") is not defined. Literally it means to "place an obstacle" or block someone. In Matthew's Gospel the verb is used several times and has the connotation of someone's actions causing another to sin or to fail to understand. For example, in 5:29–30, looking at a woman with lust can "scandalize" someone in the sense that the "eye" leads one astray. But, in other instances, observers who fail to understand Jesus's own actions can be "scandalized" by him, that is, find him an obstacle, as in 11:6 or 15:12. Jesus tells Peter to pay the temple tax for himself and Peter so as not to "scandalize" the collectors of the temple tax (17:27). In the context of 18:6–9, the source of "scandal" seems to be some action that causes the "little ones" to go seriously astray. (The NABRE translates the verb as "causes one of these little ones . . . to sin.") Given the serious tone of Jesus's admonition about the consequences for those who cause such "scandal"—namely, that it is better they maim themselves than to be thrown into Gehenna intact—it is probable that the nature of the actions is such that they lead the vulnerable into serious sin or apostasy.[13] The reader is left to consider what sort of actions on the part of leaders or core members of the community could have such an effect on those whose faith is frail.

The next segment, 18:10–14, continues to urge special pastoral care for the "little ones" in the community. First of all, the core members are not to "despise" the "little ones" (18:10). The verb καταφρονήσητε literally means "to look down upon" in the sense of "despise" or consider another inferior, a verb that reinforces the impression that the discourse is directed to the core group or the "strong" within the community who might be tempted to despise the weaker members likely to be led "astray." The term πλανώμενον ("go astray") is used in the illustrative parable of

---

13. "The verb . . . means to pervert and mislead, intellectually and morally. Here, in view of the consequent punishment, it must signify causing others to lose their faith and fall away from God" (W. D. Davies and Dale C. Allison Jr., *A Critical and Exegetical Commentary on the Gospel according to Saint Matthew* [3 vols.; ICC; Edinburgh: T&T Clark, 1988–97] 2:761–62).

the lost sheep, 18:12. In Matt 24:4, 5, 11, 24 the same verb is used to describe those "led astray" or "deceived" (NABRE) by false prophets as the end-time nears.

While some in the community may "despise" such apparently weak and vulnerable members, in fact their "angels in heaven always look upon the face of my heavenly Father" (18:10). The notion of individuals having protective angels has roots in earlier Jewish literature such as Tobit, and angels take a protective or guiding role in other parts of the New Testament, including in Matthew's infancy narrative (1:20; 2:13, 19).[14] Here in Matthew, the implication is that those despised by the arrogant within the community have a privileged place in the court of heaven, gazing directly on the face of God, a note of prophetic reversal sounded elsewhere in the Gospel.[15]

The entire opening section concludes with the parable of the lost sheep (18:10–14). In Luke's version, the parable is the first of three such parables presented by Jesus as justification for his association with outcasts and sinners (see Luke 15:1–32, esp. vv. 1–2). In Matthew the parable is applied to relationships within the community. Far from being despised in the eyes of God, the "little ones" who go astray are to be the object of the community's special care and a source of rejoicing when they are brought home. The emphatic saying of 18:14 underscores the lesson to the pastoral leaders of the community: "In just the same way, it is not the will of your heavenly Father that one of these little ones be lost."

Limitless Forgiveness

The concluding segment of the discourse (18:21–35) serves as the other part of the pastoral inclusion framing the section on conflict and discipline. Assuming once again his role as spokesperson for the disciples, Peter approaches Jesus and asks the "limits" for forgiving someone in the community (literally, a "brother," ἀδελφός) who "sins against me." Peter suggests the limit of "up to seven times" (ἕως ἑπτάκις), with the number "seven" often used in ancient literature as a symbolic number understood to imply an abundant and undefined number of occasions—thus already a generous proposal on Peter's part.[16] Yet Jesus shatters even that generous

---

14. See also, for example, the role of the angel Raphael in Tobit or of the angel who guides Cornelius to send messengers to Peter (Acts 11:13).

15. See, for example, the beatitudes at the beginning of the Sermon on the Mount, 5:3–12, and the parable of the two sons in 21:28–32.

16. The number seven is used throughout ancient Near Eastern literature in this fashion, including in the Bible itself; see Jöran Friberg, "Numbers and Counting," *ABD* 5:1143–45. Davies and Allison note that it is frequently used in contexts

"limit:" "I say to you not seven times, but seventy-seven times" (18:22). Most interpreters see Jesus's words as both evoking and nullifying the oath of Lamech, a descendent of Cain, who in Gen 4:24 swears to increase the sevenfold blood vengeance of his ancestor "seventy-seven times."[17] Jesus's teaching—which will be illustrated in the following parable—is that the disposition to forgive someone who has offended you should be without limits.

The language and moral lesson of the parable of the unforgiving servant (18:23–35) have strong Matthean characteristics and appear only in this Gospel, suggesting that this parable is a Matthean composition. Some consider the parable as a narrative elaboration of the petition regarding forgiveness in Matthew's version of the Lord's Prayer: ". . . and forgive us our debts as we forgive our debtors" (6:12); in both instances the root words "debt" (ὀφείλημα) or "debtor" (ὀφειλέτης) or "to owe" (ὀφείλω) are used.[18]

The point of the parable is clear. A king settles his accounts with his servants and confronts a "debtor" who owes a staggering debt of "10,000 talents" (which the NABRE renders as "a huge amount"). Some estimate that this would be equivalent to 60,000,000 "denarii"—100 of which will be the debt the merciless servant is owed by a fellow servant (18:28, cited as "a much smaller amount" by the NABRE).[19] When the servant is threatened with having himself, his family, and all his possessions sold to pay the debt, he pleads unrealistically "for more time" to pay his sovereign. Yet, amazingly, the king takes pity on the servant and releases him from the entire debt! This act of extraordinary mercy contrasts radically with the action of this same servant when he confronts a fellow servant

---

of "vengeance, expiation, and forgiveness," pointing to such biblical examples as Gen 4:15; Leviticus 16; Lev 26:18; Prov 24:16 (*Gospel according to Saint Matthew*, 2:792).

17. Some translations render the Hebrew number in Gen 4:24 as "seventy times seven times"; in either case, Jesus's words imply limitless forgiveness.

18. See Matt 6:12; 18:24, 28, 30, 32, 34. The codicil that follows the Lord's Prayer in Matt 6:14–15 repeats the call for forgiveness but uses the Greek word meaning "failure" or "trespass" (παραπτώματα).

19. Estimating the relative amount of these figures is not a sure science. A "talent" was a measurement of weight and "10,000" was the largest sum used in ancient accounting. Some estimate that a "talent" was a weight of approximately seventy-five pounds. If the "talent" was in gold, then "10,000 talents" would be a staggering sum in the range of hundreds of millions of dollars in modern terms. The Jewish historian Josephus estimates that the annual tax revenue collected by Herod the Great was between 600 and 800 talents (*War* 2.6.3 §§100–193; *Ant.* 17.11.4 §§317–20). In any case, the sum of "10,000 talents" represents an impossible debt for anyone to handle—which is the point of the parable.

who owes him a relatively small debt, apparently equivalent to 100 days' wages. Completely oblivious to the lavish mercy he had just experienced from his king, he rejects his fellow servant's identical plea "for more time"—a far more realistic prospect given the moderate size of the second servant's debt—and throws the man in prison. His fellow servants are "deeply saddened" (ἐλυπήθησαν σφόδρα) by the actions of the merciless servant and report it to the king (18:31). For failing to act out of the realization of his own experience of the king's compassion and forgiveness of his debt, the servant is condemned to be "tortured" until he pays back the whole debt—a terrible prospect.

Similar to the conclusion of the parable of the lost sheep (18:14), this parable, too, ends with a statement of the heavenly Father's will that anyone who aspires to life within the kingdom of heaven (see the opening statement of 18:2) must be willing "to forgive his brother from his heart" (18:35).

Thus, the overwhelming thrust of Matthew's community discourse is active pastoral care for the vulnerable, avoiding putting in their way any obstacle that might harm them, seeking them out when they go astray, and being willing to offer limitless forgiveness to those who cause injury. Even in an extreme case where a member of the community refuses to cease their destructive behavior and accept reconciliation, the community will treat that person as an object of earnest search, even as it must take the radical disciplinary action of expelling the individual from the community.

▪ III. Conclusion

As Raymond Brown noted, Matthew's Gospel presents a remarkable vision of the church, a community whose characteristics reflect the authority and qualities of Jesus's own person and mission—thus, a church rooted in faith in Jesus as the Christ, the Son of the Living God; a church that is obedient to the will of God; a church whose leaders are animated by faith, avoid arrogance and hypocrisy, and who care for the vulnerable, the "strays," and those in need of forgiveness; a church community conscious of its own authority and whose inner life reflects the reconciling and compassionate spirit of Jesus; a church that is thoroughly missionary in nature and outward directed; a church remaining faithful to its roots in Judaism and yet open to all nations; a church aware of its frailties and challenges yet confident in living in the presence of the risen Christ until the end of time.

In attempting to summarize Matthew's ecclesiology, I became aware of how similar is the vision of the church proclaimed by Pope Francis, particularly in his exhortation, "The Joy of the Gospel." It is all there: the foundation of the church in a personal encounter with Jesus Christ; a church not turned in on itself but outward directed; a church that avoids clericalism and arrogance; a church that is steeped in mercy, forgiveness, and compassion, particularly for the poor and vulnerable. In his own words:

> *I dream of a "missionary option"—that is, a missionary impulse capable of transforming everything, so that the Church's customs, ways of doing things, times and schedules, language and structures can be suitably channeled for the evangelization of today's world rather than for her [own] self-preservation. The renewal of structures demanded by pastoral conversion can only be understood in this light: as part of an effort to make them more mission-oriented, to make ordinary pastoral activity on every level more inclusive and open, to inspire in pastoral workers a constant desire to go forth and in this way to elicit a positive response from all those whom Jesus summons to friendship with himself. (§27)*

There Shall Be No Poor among You: The Lucan Solution

BARBARA E. REID, O.P.
Catholic Theological Union
Chicago, Illinois

In his book *There Shall Be No Poor among You: Poverty in the Bible*,[1] Leslie Hoppe took on the monumental task of sketching out what every section of the Bible and the rabbinic tradition has to say about poverty. His conclusions at the end of his comprehensive study were these: "First of all, the tradition is unanimous in asserting that material, economic poverty is an outrage, that it should not exist, that it is not in accord with the divine will."[2] He observes further that, according to the Scriptures, poverty does not just happen; it results from decisions that people make, mostly wealthy persons who act out of avarice and greed. His second conclusion is that "the biblical tradition finds the experience of the poor to be an apt metaphor for the universal need for salvation."[3] Even so, the injustice of material poverty is never out of sight; nor is there any idealization of the poor as having some sort of special access to God.[4]

From these conclusions flow these consequences: since material poverty is against the divine will, believers must act to eradicate it. For people who are not poor, this includes personal conversion, transformation of lifestyle, and going beyond benevolence to the poor by modeling solidarity with them. Hoppe observes, "The Scriptures do not demand that

---

1. Leslie J. Hoppe, *There Shall Be No Poor among You: Poverty in the Bible* (Nashville: Abingdon, 2004) is a revision of his previous work, *Being Poor: A Biblical Study* (Wilmington, DE: Michael Glazier, 1987).
2. Ibid., 171.
3. Ibid.
4. Ibid., 172.

believers adopt any one economic system whose principles are applicable to every age. What the Bible does expect of believers is that they respond with imagination, creativity, and generosity" in every situation to eradicate the evil of poverty.[5]

Since Hoppe's clear call to believers to end poverty by living according to the values in Torah and the gospel, the level of global poverty has not abated. The United Nations' number 1 Sustainable Development Goal is still to end poverty in all its forms everywhere. More than 700 million people—that is, 10 percent of the world's population—still live in extreme poverty. Although there has been much progress (in 1990, 36 percent of the world's people lived in extreme poverty), the global pandemic raging at the time of this writing threatens to increase global poverty by as much as half a billion people.[6] As Hoppe asserted, there is no universal biblical prescription for how to eradicate poverty, but there is one answer that comes to the fore in the Gospel of Luke and the Acts of the Apostles that bears our continued consideration: communal solidarity and distribution according to need.

In what follows I will sketch briefly Luke's emphasis on the poor and on the danger of riches, then the variety of ways in which followers of Jesus in Luke and Acts deal with their possessions. I will then explore six Lucan parables that illustrate what is needed for solidarity among believers, which ensures that there will be no poor.

■ Good News to the Poor and the Dangers of Riches

There is more emphasis on the poor and on the danger of possessions in Luke than in any other Gospel.[7] From the opening declaration of his mission onward, Jesus shines a spotlight on the poor to whom he brings good news (Luke 4:18; cf. Mark 1:14–15; Matt 4:23). The poor are in prime place in the Sermon on the Plain, "Blessed are you who are poor" (6:20),[8]

---

5. Ibid., 174.
6. Statistics from United Nations report on Sustainable Development Goals: https://www.un.org/sustainabledevelopment/sustainable-development-goals/.
7. See John Gillman, *Possessions and the Life of Faith: A Reading of Luke-Acts* (Zacchaeus Studies, New Testament; Collegeville, MN: Liturgical Press, 1991); Luke Timothy Johnson, *The Literary Function of Possessions in Luke-Acts* (SBLDS 39; Missoula, MT: Scholars Press, 1977); Christopher M. Hays, *Luke's Wealth Ethics: A Study in Their Coherence and Character* (WUNT 2/275; Tübingen: Mohr Siebeck, 2010); idem, *Renouncing Everything: Money and Discipleship in Luke* (New York: Paulist, 2016).
8. Cf. Matt 5:3: "blessed are the poor in spirit." All Scripture quotations are from the NRSV unless otherwise indicated.

followed by the corresponding "woe to you who are rich" (6:24). Jesus frequently speaks about the danger of riches, warning that a person cannot serve both God and mammon (16:13) and how difficult it is for a rich person to enter the kingdom of God (18:25). He tells the crowds, "none of you can become my disciple if you do not give up all your possessions" (14:33). He praises a poor widow who gives two small coins, her whole life, to the temple (21:1–4).

■ Various Models of Dealing with Possessions

Despite the admonition in 14:33, giving up all one's possessions is not the only way that followers express their commitment to Jesus in Luke and Acts. Indeed, Simon Peter, James, John, and Levi do leave everything to follow Jesus (5:11, 28). Another model is exemplified by Mary Magdalene, Joanna, Susanna, and other Galilean women, who place their financial resources at the service of Jesus's mission (8:3).[9] Other well-to-do supporters include Mary, the mother of John Mark, who had a house large enough to host the disciples in Jerusalem (Acts 12:12); Lydia, a dealer in luxury items (Acts 16:14);[10] prominent women in Thessalonica (Acts 17:4); influential Greek women and men in Beroea (Acts 17:12); Prisca and Aquila, who hosted Paul in Corinth (Acts 18:1–11) and who had the means to travel with Paul to Ephesus to establish a new mission base there (Acts 18:18–28). Still another way is that of Zacchaeus, a chief tax collector, who gives half his possessions to the poor (Luke 19:1–10). Yet another model appears in Acts: "All who believed were together and had all things in common; they would sell their possessions and goods and distribute the proceeds to all, as any had need" (2:44–45). And

---

9. The expression διηκόνουν αὐτοῖς ἐκ τῶν ὑπαρχόντων αὐταῖς ("who provided for them out of their resources") indicates that the ministry of the women involved their possessions, property, money, or goods, which is the consistent meaning of ὑπαρχόντων in Luke and Acts: Luke 11:21; 12:15, 33, 44; 14:33; 16:1; 19:8; Acts 4:32. See BDAG, s.v. ὑπάρχω.

10. There is debate over whether Lydia was a poor woman who produced luxury goods (Luise Schottroff, "Lydia: A New Quality of Power," in *Let the Oppressed Go Free: Feminist Perspectives on the New Testament* [trans. Annemarie S. Kidder; Louisville: Westminster John Knox, 1993] 131–37; Ivoni Richter Reimer, *Women in the Acts of the Apostles: A Feminist Liberation Perspective* [trans. Linda M. Maloney; Minneapolis: Fortress, 1995] 98–130) or whether she herself was well off (Shelly Matthews, *First Converts: Rich Pagan Women and the Rhetoric of Mission in Early Judaism and Christianity* [Contraversions; Stanford, CA: Stanford University Press, 2001] 85–89). Given Luke's predilection for rich patrons, I find Matthews's position most convincing.

again: "Now the whole group of those who believed were of one heart and soul, and no one claimed private ownership of any possessions, but everything they owned was held in common.... There was not a needy person among them, for as many as owned lands or houses sold them and brought the proceeds of what was sold. They laid it at the apostles' feet, and it was distributed to each as any had need" (4:32–35).[11]

According to Luke, the ideal voiced in Deut 15:4, "There will, however, be no one in need among you," has become a reality in the early community of disciples in Jerusalem. Their oneness of heart and soul was not only a spiritual reality but took concrete form in the economic system they embraced of collective ownership and distribution according to need. Critical for this system to work is for believers to be committed to solidarity with one another, regarding one another as brother and sister in the family of disciples. Jesus points toward this attitude in Luke 8:21 when he calls those who hear the word of God and do it his mother and brothers and sisters. In Acts, there are frequent references to the community of believers as οἱ ἀδελφοί, "the brothers [and sisters]" (14:2; 15:1, 7, 13, 22, 23; 16:40; 21:17, etc.).

I want to explore next how Luke paints vivid pictures in six parables of what this kind of solidarity and its opposite can look like. Three parables illustrate communal solidarity and three depict isolation and greed that impede oneness. All but one of these parables are unique to Luke and the one shared with Matthew (Luke 14:15-24 // Matt 22:1-10) has unique details that highlight Luke's emphasis on commensality across status differences.

■ Parables of Solidarity

A Friend in Need (11:5–8)

This brief parable involves three friends and shows the lengths to which one would go for a friend in order to fulfill the obligations of hospitality. One man is asleep with his family, when his friend comes at midnight to ask him for bread because another friend has arrived unexpectedly. Jesus sets the scene with the interrogative: Τίς ἐξ ὑμῶν, "which one of you," followed by one long question in vv. 5–7 that can be understood this way: "Can you imagine having a guest and going to a neighbor to borrow bread and the neighbor offers ridiculous excuses about a locked door and sleep-

---

11. Such an ideal was not unique to the first Christians. For example, Aristotle said, "Among friends everything is common" (*Eth. nic.* 9:8 §1168B).

ing children?" The expected response is: "No, I cannot imagine such a thing!"[12] It is unthinkable that a friend would not help a friend in a time of need. Using a *qal wahomer* argument, Jesus then compares the way a friend would respond to a request for bread to the way God reacts to one who asks, searches, and knocks (vv. 9–13). If the sleeping friend supplies bread to his needy friend without hesitation, how much more eager is God to give to those who ask.

Because this parable is sandwiched between the prayer Jesus teaches his disciples (11:1–4) and the assurance that God responds to petitions (11:9–13), it is often understood as a lesson on persistence in prayer. This interpretation is fueled by translations of ἀναίδεια in 11:8 as "persistence": "I tell you, even though he will not get up and give him anything because he is his friend, at least because of his persistence [τὴν ἀναίδειαν αὐτοῦ][13] he will get up and give him whatever he needs."[14] However, in every other known occurrence of ἀναίδεια, it always has a negative connotation: "shamelessness, lack of sensitivity to what is proper, impudence."[15] The Latin translations from the fifth century on render ἀναίδεια as *importunitatem*, which is what led to its English rendering "importunity," or "persistence." Not only is "persistence" an inaccurate translation of ἀναίδεια, but in the parable itself, as explained above, the sleeping friend does not need to be persuaded to give the bread; the petitioner asks only once.[16]

It is better to understand ἀναίδεια as "shamelessness" in this way: both the petitioner and the sleeping friend are "shameless," in that they

---

12. Alan F. Johnson, "Assurance for Man: The Fallacy of Translating *anaideia* by 'Persistence' in Luke 11:5–8," *JETS* 22 (1979) 123–31, here 124; similarly Klyne Snodgrass, *Stories with Intent: A Comprehensive Guide to the Parables of Jesus* (Grand Rapids: Eerdmans, 2008) 437.

13. There is ambiguity about the referent of αὐτοῦ: Is it the shamelessness of the petitioner or of the sleeping friend? Some translations leave it ambiguous; others decide that it refers to the friend requesting bread and translate ἀναίδεια variously: "his friend's harshness" (CEB); "your shameless audacity" (NIV); "because you are not ashamed to keep on asking" (CEV). I think it can refer to both, as I will show below.

14. So NRSV; similarly NABRE, NKJV, and many others.

15. BDAG, s.v. ἀναίδεια. It appears only here in the New Testament. The noun, adjectival, and adverbial forms of ἀναίδεια occur fifteen times in the LXX: Sir 23:6; 25:22; 26:11; 40:30; Deut 28:50; 1 Kgs 2:29; Prov 7:13; 21:29; 25:13; Eccl 8:1; Isa 56:11; Jer 8:5; Bar 4:15; Dan 2:15; 8:23, where it always has this negative connotation. The same is true of all the other references in Greek literature from classical times until the fifth century C.E. Nowhere does the word connote "persistence." See Johnson, "Assurance for Man," 123–31; Klyne Snodgrass, "*Anaideia* and the Friend at Midnight (Luke 11:8)," *JBL* 116 (1997) 505–13.

16. Snodgrass, *Stories with Intent*, 446.

each act in a way that avoids shame[17] and upholds honor by fulfilling the expectations of hospitality. The sleeper does the honorable thing in giving his friend bread; the petitioner overcomes his shame at being caught short and at inconveniencing his friend and his family to maintain honor with his unexpected guest. It is their solidarity in friendship that enables both the petitioner and the sleeper to go to the necessary lengths to make sure all are fed. What the parable does not recount, is that the wife of the sleeping friend is even more inconvenienced that her husband, as she will have to sacrifice sleep to bake more bread for her family during the night. Such is the kind of selflessness and commitment to one another that underlies the ability to redistribute goods and to ensure that there is no one in need.

All Are Invited to the Table (14:15–24)

Jesus tells this parable while he is dining at the home of a Pharisee. He has just advised his host not to invite his friends, relatives, or rich neighbors when giving a banquet, but rather "the poor, the crippled, the lame, and the blind," those who cannot reciprocate. Jesus assures him that he will be repaid at the resurrection of the righteous" (14:12–14). One of the guests then exclaims, "Blessed is anyone who will eat bread in the kingdom of God!" (14:15). The ensuing parable (14:15–24) is a vivid illustration of a banquet hall filled with the guests Jesus listed in 14:13.

The parable envisions who will be present at the eschatological banquet: those who answer the call.[18] As Luke stresses elsewhere (e.g., 9:57–

---

17. Anton Fridrichsen was apparently the first New Testament scholar to suggest that in this parable ἀναίδεια is the avoidance of shame ("Exegetisches zum Neuen Testament," *SO* 13 [1934] 38–46, here 42). Others who interpret ἀναίδεια with a similar positive connotation include Joachim Jeremias, *The Parables of Jesus* (2nd rev. ed.; New York: Scribner, 1972) 158; Kenneth Bailey, *Poet and Peasant: A Literary Cultural Approach to the Parables in Luke* (Grand Rapids: Eerdmans, 1976) 125–33; Bernard Brandon Scott, *Hear Then the Parable: A Commentary on the Parables of Jesus* (Minneapolis: Fortress, 1989) 89–92; Johnson, "Assurance for Man," 123–31; John Nolland, *Luke 9:21–18:34* (WBC 35B; Dallas: Word, 1993) 624–26. Klyne Snodgrass insists that ἀναίδεια always has a negative connotation except in "those places early Christian writers have assigned a positive use in dependence on Luke 11:8" ("*Anaideia* and the Friend at Midnight," 506. For him, ἀναίδεια applies only to the petitioner, and the parable simply says, "If a human will get up in the middle of the night to grant the request of a rude friend, will not God much more answer your requests?" (513). In my estimation, however, this interpretation does not adequately deal with the assertion in v. 8 that it is ἀναίδεια, not friendship, that prompts the sleeper to respond to the request.

18. The image of an abundant feast is often used to envision messianic times, for example, Isa 25:6–8. Although the parable is set in the house of a Pharisee, there is

62; 12:13–21; 14:25–33), preoccupations with possessions and family often stand in the way of responding to the call to discipleship. This parable is not illustrating a reversal of fortunes, as with the rich man and Lazarus, but rather is pointing toward meal practices that followers of Jesus are to embrace in the present time (14:12–14) that anticipate the eschatological banquet (14:15–24). In the Jesus movement, all, despite differences in status, are brother and sister to one another, eating at the same table. Those who are richer are to become siblings, not simply benefactors, of those who are poorer.[19]

All Count (15:8–10)

This short parable, sandwiched between the parable of the lost sheep (15:3–7) and the lost sons (15:11–32), makes the same point as the other two: the value of each one is such that the shepherd, the woman, and the father go to extraordinary lengths to seek out and find and welcome back the lost. The parable begins with a question that presumes the response: of course one would do everything possible to find the lost coin. Just as a shepherd cannot afford to lose one sheep even if there are ninety-nine more, and a father would not let a wandering son stay adrift because he has another at home, so a woman would not content herself with nine drachmas and let the tenth go missing. Most likely she is poor and needs that tenth drachma to feed her family.[20]

---

nothing in it that points toward Pharisees or Jews in general as the ones who refuse the call. All the characters in the parable are Jews; some Jews refused Jesus's invitation and others accepted (Snodgrass, *Stories with Intent*, 314). Moreover, the parable is not an allegory of salvation history, with the first invited, who refuse, being Israel and its leaders; the second group, "the lost sheep of the house of Israel"; and the third, gentiles (so, e.g., François Bovon, *Luke* [trans. Christine M. Thomas; 3 vols.; Hermeneia; Minneapolis: Fortress, 2002–13] 2:372). For references to early Church Fathers and contemporary scholars who advance this interpretation, see Louise A. Gosbell, *"The Poor, the Crippled, the Blind, and the Lame": Physical and Sensory Disability in the Gospels of the New Testament* (WUNT 2/469; Tübingen: Mohr Siebeck, 2018) 172–75. Another difficulty with the allegorizing approach is that if the host is thought to be God or the Messiah, then it is problematic that people who are poor, who have disabilities, and who are of low social status are invited as a second choice (Luise Schottroff, *The Parables of Jesus* [trans. Linda M. Maloney; Minneapolis: Fortress, 2006] 49–56).

19. Schottroff, *Parables of Jesus*, 54.
20. See Susan Marie Praeder, *The Word in Women's Worlds: Four Parables* (Zacchaeus Studies, New Testament; Wilmington, DE: Michael Glazier, 1988) 37–38, on the varying weights and value of drachmas. She concludes, "[T]en drachmas amounted to a small sum of money important only to people of modest means and the poor" (38). Luise Schottroff thinks that the ten drachmas are the woman's entire property and that the situation depicted is one in which people have no land of their own

With this parable, along with those of the lost sheep and lost son, Luke emphasizes again oneness in community. The parable calls attention to the equal value of and the need for every member. None is less valuable than another, and the community of believers is not complete if one goes missing.[21] The final verse underscores the solidarity among the women friends and neighbors who join the happy finder in her joy.

■ Parables of Isolation and Greed

A Solitary Rich Man (12:13–21)

This parable vividly illustrates the isolation that comes from preoccupation with riches. Jesus begins with a warning against greed and then tells about a rich man with an unexpected bountiful harvest. The soliloquy in vv. 17–18 reveals both the man's greed and his isolation.[22] Rather than consult with family members or others in the village, as one would ordinarily do when making important decisions, he asks *himself,* "What

---

and are dependent on money to buy food: "The woman needs the money to survive, even more than the shepherd needs his hundredth sheep" (*Parables of Jesus,* 154). By contrast, Amy-Jill Levine sees the woman as relatively well-off, having her own home and her own set of friends, and she may possibly have other kinds of coins in addition to the ten drachma (*Short Stories by Jesus: The Enigmatic Parables of a Controversial Rabbi* [New York: Harper One, 2015] 42).

21. A popular interpretation is that the lost coin was part of a piece of jewelry, such as a bridal headdress or necklace and that the missing coin ruins its value (see, e.g., "What Is the Meaning of the Parables of the Lost Sheep and Lost Coin?," Got Questions. Your Questions. Biblical Answers, https://www.gotquestions.org/parable-lost-sheep-coin.html). This interpretation, however, cannot be substantiated by archaeology. Of all the myriad coins that have been excavated in Galilee and Judea, none has been found with holes for decorative use; this is a practice of modern Bedouin women, not of women in antiquity. Furthermore, there is no basis in the text for creating a reason why the woman must search for the coin. The reason for her search is the same as that of the sheep owner and the father: because of the high value of what is lost.

22. See Melissa Harl (née Philip) Sellew, "Interior Monologue as a Narrative Device in the Parables of Luke," *JBL* 111 (1992) 239–53, who shows how interior monologue was used in Greek tragedies and epic poetry to paint vivid and poignant characters. In Lucan parables, characters who talk to themselves all exhibit foolish thinking. In addition to the rich man (12:17–18), they include the unfaithful servant (12:42–46), the prodigal son (15:18–19), the steward who was accused of squandering his master's property (16:3–4), the unjust judge (18:4–5), and the owner of the vineyard with the violent tenants (20:9–16). See also Michal Beth Dinkler, "The Thoughts of Many Hearts Shall Be Revealed: Listening in on Lukan Interior Monologues," *JBL* 134 (2015) 373–99.

should *I* do . . . *I* have no place . . . *I* will do this: *I* will pull down *my* barns and build larger ones, and there *I* will store all *my* grain and *my* goods. And *I* will say to *my* soul, Soul, you have ample goods laid up for many years; relax, eat, drink, be merry.'" The rich man has in mind only himself, his pleasure, and how to increase his wealth.

The wrongness of the man's thinking is exposed when God interrupts, posing the critical question: To whom do all his possessions and even his very life belong? The biblical answer is that everything belongs to God: the earth and all that is in it (Ps 24:1). There is an echo of Wis 15:8, which warns against the misspent toil of one who fashions gods out of his own produce, when shortly "the life that was lent him is demanded back" (NABRE).

In Jesus's day, hearers of the parable would have viewed the rich man's greediness from the perspective of limited good; that is, there is a limited amount of any good thing, and whatever one person gains is someone else's loss. Unlike capitalist notions that everyone can increase in wealth, the operating assumption of the first hearers of this parable would have been that if this man's share gets larger, someone else's decreases. The rich man's disregard for how his hoarding is diminishing the life of others is an attitude entirely destructive of community.

Not My Brother (16:19–31)

This parable starkly contrasts the sumptuous life of a nameless rich man with the misery of a destitute beggar, Lazarus. Equally strong is the contrast between their eternal fates, where there is a reversal of fortunes (as elsewhere in Luke, e.g., 1:46–55; 13:30). The repetition of the words "father" and "brother" calls attention to the fact that both men are children of the same father. The rich man repeatedly calls Abraham "father" (16:24, 27, 30) and Abraham addresses him as "child" (16:25), while Abraham also embraces Lazarus as his child (16:22). The image of Lazarus at the bosom of Abraham, εἰς τὸν κόλπον Ἀβραάμ, in the afterlife (16:22) evokes that of a child at its mother's breast.[23] The rich child of Abraham, however, is in torment. He has not emulated his rich father's renowned generosity and hospitality (Gen 18:1–5; Gen 24:35 describes Abraham's

---

23. As in Num 11:12; Ruth 4:16; Lam 2:12; 1 Kgs 17:19; 2 Sam 12:3; see also John 1:18. It is also the posture of the guest of honor reclining against the breast of the host at a banquet as in John 13:23. See Alexey Somov and Vitaly Voinov, "'Abraham's Bosom' (Luke 16:22–23) as a Key Metaphor in the Overall Composition of the Parable of the Rich Man and Lazarus," *CBQ* 79 (2017) 615–33. This image is lost in many translations. The NRSV, for example, renders εἰς τὸν κόλπον Ἀβραάμ as "to be with Abraham."

wealth). And although he sees Lazarus at the breast of their shared father,[24] he does not perceive him as his brother (16:23). He sees Lazarus only as a servant who could take a message to the only brothers in his view: his five siblings in his father's house (16:27–28).[25] If the rich man could have seen poor Lazarus as his brother, then perhaps there could have been equitable sharing both in life and in the inheritance beyond death.

Despising Others (18:9–14)

In this parable, a Pharisee and a tax collector go to the temple to pray. The Pharisee prays with gratitude to God that he has been able to keep the law and even go beyond its stipulations.[26] He appears to be an upright person. But there is a problem: he distances himself (σταθεὶς πρὸς ἑαυτόν)[27] from others who are not like him (οἱ λοιποὶ τῶν ἀνθρώπων). He labels them rapatious (ἅρπαγες), unjust (ἄδικοι), adulterers (μοιχοί), and despises the tax collector. In so judging others, he has usurped what is God's prerogative. His elitism blocks his ability to recognize all other persons as his brothers and sisters to whom he is inextricably connected.

The tax collector, by contrast, acknowledges that he is a sinner and simply prays for mercy, echoing Ps 51:1. Like the Pharisee, he also stands apart (μακρόθεν ἑστώς, v. 13), but we do not know whether it is because he wants to pray privately or because he knows others despise him. Jesus concludes the parable with the assertion that the tax collector has been justified (δεδικαιωμένος, v. 14a).

While most interpreters understand only the tax collector to be justified, Amy-Jill Levine offers another way of seeing both characters as righteous, although flawed. The Pharisee is exemplary in his prayer, fasting, and tithing but is flawed in his judgmentalness. The tax collector is also exemplary in his prayer but may be unable to act on the mercy and justification he has been given. If he has wronged people, it may not be

---

24. The expression ἐν τοῖς κόλποις αὐτοῦ ("at his breast") recurs in 16:23. Again, this is lost in many translations, such as the NRSV: "by his side."
25. William R. Herzog II, *Parables as Subversive Speech: Jesus as Pedagogue of the Oppressed* (Louisville: Westminster John Knox, 1994) 123.
26. It is akin to prayers found in Ps 17:4–5; Jdt 8:25; 2 Macc 1:11; and Thanksgiving Psalms from Qumran, e.g., 1QH 2.20, 21; 3.19, 37; 4.5; 7.34, and prayers found in the Talmud, e.g., *b. Ber.* 28b and in the Tosefta, *t. Ber.* 7.18.
27. Alternatively, σταθεὶς πρὸς ἑαυτόν may simply indicate that he is praying a personal, not communal, prayer (Amy-Jill Levine and Ben Witherington III, *The Gospel of Luke* [NCBC; Cambridge: Cambridge University Press, 2018] 491).

possible for him to make restitution to all of them, nor resist corrupt practices in the future if he continues to work as a tax collector.[28]

As Levine observes, the dichotomy between the characters is not so clear. Further, the concluding verse can be read, "This man went down to his home justified alongside the other [παρ' ἐκεῖνον]." Rather than indicate a comparison—"rather than that other" or "not the former"—παρά with the accusative can mean "because of" or "on account of."[29] The logic is that the excess good deeds of the Pharisee redound to the tax collector, so the latter is justified on account of the former. Levine explains, "Judaism is a communitarian movement . . . in which each member of the community is responsible for the other. . . . This concern for community responsibility means that the sin of one person can negatively impact everyone else. At the same time, it means that the good deeds of one person can have a positive impact on the lives of others."[30]

Understood this way, the parable exposes an attitude that is destructive of community: thinking oneself better than others and keeping apart from them. If the Pharisee had let his initial gratitude lead him to acknowledge that all his righteous deeds were possible due to God's graciousness to him, he could see others, including the tax collector, as his siblings who all equally depend on God's mercy.[31]

■ WHAT THEN SHOULD WE DO? (3:10)

As contemporary believers struggle with what to do to eradicate poverty, lessons from Luke and Acts can supply some of the answers. In the texts we have examined, we have seen that giving away all or some of one's

---

28. Levine, *Short Stories by Jesus*, 193.
29. Timothy A. Friedrichsen, "The Temple, a Pharisee, a Tax Collector, and the Kingdom of God: Rereading a Jesus Parable (Luke 18:10–14a)," *JBL* 124 (2005) 89–119, here 116, citing BDAG, s.v. παρά. Eta Linnemann points out that παρ' ἐκεῖνον cannot be understood as "more justified than," since one is either justified/forgiven or not; there are no degrees of justification (*Jesus of the Parables: Introduction and Exposition* [trans. John Sturdy; New York: Harper & Row, 1966] 62 n. 1). Robert Doran counters, "If one interprets the passive perfect participle as 'having been pronounced δίκαιος,' however, then one can compare who is more upright, more properly observant of his/her duty to God" ("The Pharisee and the Tax Collector: An Agonistic Story," *CBQ* 69 [2007] 259–70, here 262).
30. Levine, *Short Stories by Jesus*, 192–93.
31. Ibid., 192.

possessions, avoiding greed, and living in solidarity with one another as brothers and sisters are key.[32]

From the beginning of the Gospel, Luke emphasizes equitable sharing and being wary of greed in all its forms. After John the Baptist's fiery call to repentance (3:7–9), three different groups ask, "What then should we do?" To the crowds John says, "Whoever has two coats must share with anyone who has none; and whoever has food must do likewise" (3:11). To the tax collectors he advised, "Collect no more than the amount prescribed for you" (3:13). And to soldiers, "Do not extort money from anyone by threats or false accusation and be satisfied with your wages" (3:14). The themes of sharing and avoiding greed introduced in 3:10–14 are further developed in the parables showcasing solidarity among friends (11:1–13), depicting rich and poor dining together (14:15–24), and seeking out all (15:8–10). The parables of the solitary rich hoarder (12:13–21), the rich man blind to his brother Lazarus (16:19–30), and the judgmental Pharisee (18:9–14) provide a contrast, showing what not to do.

The Lucan Jesus places the poor at the center, with what Latin American liberation theologians call a "preferential option for the poor."[33] Gustavo Gutiérrez explains that this does not mean that there is competition for God's love between rich and poor. "[I]n fact, the concept displays the *universality* of God's love for all—a love that, in a world structured to the benefit of the powerful, extends *even* to the least among us. . . . Like a mother who tends most tenderly to the weakest and threatened of her children, so it is with God's care for the poor."[34] A love for those who are poor and prioritizing their needs is necessary to be able to eradicate poverty.

What can lead to a conversion of heart for "lovers of money" (16:14) to become lovers of those who are poor? Beyond threats of reversal of fortune and eternal torment (which might work only with those at a rather low level of moral development), the parable of the rich man and Lazarus suggests that one step is to learn to see poor persons as individuals with names, not an anonymous group "the poor." It is notable that in the parable the name of the rich man is not known, while that of the poor

---

32. Of course there can also be sibling rivalry over money or inheritance, as featured in Luke 12:13; 15:11–32.

33. See, e.g., Gustavo Gutiérrez, *A Theology of Liberation: History, Politics, and Salvation* (Maryknoll, NY: Orbis Books, 1973). The Latin American bishops' conferences at Medellín (1968) and Puebla (1979) strongly endorsed this perspective.

34. As quoted in Michael Griffin and Jennie Weiss Block, eds., *In the Company of the Poor: Conversations with Dr. Paul Farmer and Fr. Gustavo Gutiérrez* (Maryknoll, NY: Orbis Books, 2013) 28–29 (italics original).

man is.³⁵ In real life, the reverse would be true. Coming to know real people who are poor also prevents romanticizing their goodness; like all people, they are both saintly and sinful. The same is true of rich people.

Reflecting on the solitary rich hoarder (12:13–21) can lead us to face the truth that we are all interconnected in this planetary web of life and that one person's excess or one country's greed causes deprivation for others. When it comes to global food supply, for example, staple crops like corn, wheat, soybeans, and rice are plentiful enough to feed everyone in the world. Yet one in nine people is hungry, or 820 million people worldwide. The inequities in the present time are becoming even more extreme, due in part to richer countries stockpiling food during the coronavirus pandemic.³⁶

The parable of the poor woman searching for her lost coin (15:8–10), along with the episodes of the poor widow who gives her two small coins (21:1–4) and the Galilean women followers who helped finance Jesus's ministry (8:1–3), can help us see that women in our world are the ones most severely affected by poverty. The United Nations has recognized that eradicating poverty is intimately linked to gender equality.³⁷ Working on behalf of equity for women is another way to contribute toward eliminating poverty.

It is difficult to know the degree to which the snapshots of life in the community of believers in Jerusalem in Acts 2:44–45 and 4:32–35 reflected historical reality. We do not know whether holding all things in common meant that the community members pooled all they owned or whether they kept their own property with all being able to use it.³⁸ Nor do we know the degree to which common ownership was obligatory or

---

35. The rich man is popularly known as "Dives," which comes from the opening phrase of the parable in the Latin Vulgate, *"Homo quidam erat dives"; dives* means "rich" in Latin. The name Lazarus is a shortened Greek form of the Hebrew or Aramaic name *'Elʿāzār*, "God has helped."

36. Isis Almeida and Agnieszka de Sousa, "Countries Starting to Hoard Food, Threatening Global Trade," Bloomberg News, March 24, 2020, https://www.bloomberg.com/news/articles/2020-03-24/countries-are-starting-to-hoard-food-threatening-global-trade; Farm Policy News, Illinois, "Despite Ample Global Supplies, Concerns about 'Food Nationalism,' and Supply Chain Restrictions Amid COVID-19 Outbreak," March 26, 2020, https://farmpolicynews.illinois.edu/2020/03/despite-ample-global-supplies-concerns-about-food-nationalism-and-supply-chain-restrictions-amid-covid-19-outbreak/.

37. United Nations Entity for Gender Equality and the Empowerment of Women, "The Beijing Platform for Action Turns 20," http://beijing20.unwomen.org/en/infocus/poverty.

38. Joseph A. Fitzmyer, *The Acts of the Apostles: A New Translation with Introduction and Commentary* (AB 31; New York: Doubleday, 1998) 272.

voluntary or how widespread this arrangement was. The very next chapter of Acts shows a breakdown in the system when Ananias and Sapphira keep back some of the proceeds of a sale of land and lie about it to the community (5:1–11). Still, the idealized picture of sharing possessions distributed to each according to need stirs our imagination about how that might be lived today. There continue to be Christian communities of women and men religious who pool their monetary resources and distribute to each according to need. Certain voluntary associations of laypersons also have tried to embody these ideals. In Israel, *kibbutzim*, collective communities, also have a similar aim.

The Gospel of Luke and Acts give no uniform way to respond, nor does the Bible propose a comprehensive economic system. But, as Leslie Hoppe concluded his book, when "[b]elievers recognize that poverty is a creation of those who refuse to live according to the ideals of Torah and the gospel" and "are confident that, with God's help, they can overcome human selfishness and sin so that these ideals will one day give shape to human existence," then "'there shall be no poor' among them."[39] I am most grateful to Leslie for his work on this topic and his forthright challenge to believers to put an end to poverty. May we take it to heart and make Deut 15:4 a permanent reality.

39. Hoppe, *There Shall Be No Poor*, 174.

Reconstructing the Cultural Horizon for Lucan Soldiers: Texts and Artifacts in Conversation

LAURIE BRINK, O.P.
Catholic Theological Unoin
Chicago, Illinois

"Archaeology makes us sensitive to the incarnational aspect of revelation."[1]

Standing nearly ten feet high, the Lions Gate at the ancient acropolis of Mycenae is a silent witness to the once brilliant civilization of the Middle Bronze Age. And standing under the iconic capstone, Leslie Hoppe, OFM, professor of Old Testament studies, regales us with the mystery of Mycenae, the hunt for Homer's golden city, and the archaeological remains that tell only part of the story. That memory is more than two decades old and yet it remains the spark that ignited my interest in archaeology and its potential to illuminate the biblical text. Later, Leslie would recommend that I participate in an archaeological dig at Caesarea Maritima, a site at which he himself had dug. And further down my intellectual road, I would find myself at my doctoral exams searching my memory for the answer to a question posed by the panel of distinguished scholars. "The Canaanite bull"—an answer drawn not from my doctoral courses but from a short course on the Deuteronomistic History that Leslie taught in a small sweltering classroom in the Convent of the Comboni Sisters in East Jerusalem. To say I owe a debt of gratitude to Leslie

---

1. Leslie J. Hoppe, *A Guide to the Lands of the Bible* (Collegeville, MN: Liturgical Press, 1999) 14.

Hoppe would be an understatement. This article is my attempt to integrate artifact and text. In my own way, to follow in Leslie's footsteps.

Ever since William Foxwell Albright traversed the Judean Wilderness using the Bible as his map, archaeologists and biblical scholars alike have been suspicious of any facile attempt to correlate the findings of archaeology with the canonical text.[2] As Margaret M. Mitchell has noted, the use of archaeology in the study of Christian origins is further complicated because of

> the self-conscious hermeneutical program of the earliest Christians, who did not, remarkably, root their religious lives in a tomb cult or fixed shrine to dedicated objects, but instead in telling and retelling a spoken message Paul called *to euangelion,* "the good news." . . . Mark in turn enshrined this *euangelion* in a narrative form.[3]

If we are to "retrieve" the earliest stratum of emergent Christianity, we must begin with the texts. However, if we hope to understand the backdrop against which those texts were written and read, we turn to the material evidence and archaeological finds, which provide a multidimensional access to the ancient world. As Hoppe has well noted, "Archaeology fills a void where literary sources are insufficient or nonexistent."[4]

But engaging archaeology and New Testament studies is no easy task since we have only a few explicitly "Christian" artifacts before the fourth century. But the "good news" of Paul and the apostolic teams took root in a very fertile, very concrete world. Those who would be known as "Christians" might not have been of the world, but they were certainly in it (2 Cor 10:3). We turn, then, from the hunt for explicitly Christian realia toward the myriad archaeological remains from the first- to second-century Mediterranean world. But how might this bevy of material culture contribute to our understanding of New Testament texts? I propose that we have recourse to what Hans-Josef Klauck calls the "horizon of cultural knowledge."

> Our aim is only to construct a horizon to which Luke's story may be linked. We are asking for the cultural script or the lexicon he is sharing with his addressees.[5]

---

2. We need only remember the debacle of the ossuary of James, which pitted archaeologist against biblical scholar in the fight over greater proximity to the realia of Jesus. See Margaret M. Mitchell, "Does the 'James Ossuary' bring us closer to Jesus?" (Feb. 2003) [on-line edition, https://divinity.uchicago.edu/sightings/articles/does-james-ossuary-bring-us-closer-jesus].
3. Ibid.
4. Hoppe, *Guide to the Lands of the Bible,* 14.
5. Personal correspondence, July 13, 2007.

Readers—or, in the case of an ancient audience, auditors—must have knowledge of the cultural context so as to make sense of the text.[6] This horizon of cultural knowledge is constructed from what Wolfgang Iser calls the extratextual reality,[7] which is composed of all the skills and knowledge that readers of a particular culture need in order to read or hear with comprehension. In the process of characterization, this "extra text" has been variously categorized to include (1) language, (2) social norms and cultural scripts, (3) classical or canonical literature, (4) literary conventions, and (5) commonly known historical and geographical facts.[8]

As John Darr and others have proposed, the very stuff that surrounded the first-century readers or auditors provided the interpretive tools by which they made sense of the text. This is particularly true in the process of building character in which readers plays an active role. The author leaves unstated what readers already know or can supply for themselves. Though the author initiates the process of characterization through the creation of textual images, it is readers who interpret, evaluate, and build upon those images through the narrative process. In order to participate in the activity, readers or auditors must draw upon their own horizon of cultural knowledge.

I propose that archaeological evidence, which is, indeed, "extratextual," contributes to our efforts to reconstruct the horizon of cultural knowledge particularly in the process of characterization.[9] In this article, I intend to explore the extra text with which Luke could presume his audience was familiar by comparing contemporaneous literature, analyzing

---

6. Modern literary theorists describe this as "cultural literacy, the network of information that all competent readers possess. It is the background information, stored in their minds that enables them to take up a newspaper and read it with an adequate level of comprehension, getting the point, grasping the implications, relating what they read to the unstated context which alone gives meaning to what they read" (Eric D. Hirsch, *Cultural Literacy: What Every American Needs to Know* [Boston: Houghton Mifflin, 1987]) 2.

7. Wolfgang Iser, *The Act of Reading: A Theory of Aesthetic Response* (Baltimore: Johns Hopkins University Press, 1980) 69.

8. John Darr, *On Character Building: The Reader and the Rhetoric of Characterization in Luke-Acts* (Literary Currents in Biblical Interpretation; Louisville: Westminster John Knox, 1992) 22.

9. More recently, archaeological extra text has been explored beyond its use for characterization. Alan Cadwallader notes that "attention to the cultural currency in the particularities of time and space, period and location, available to an audience to 'think with,' . . . provides an essential comparative grid for Pauline literary usage" ("Assessing the Potential of Archaeological Discoveries for the Interpretation of New Testament Texts: The Case of a Gladiator Fragment from Colossae and the Letter to the Colossians," in *The First Urban Churches*, vol. 1: *Methodological Foundations* [ed. L. L. Welborn and James R. Harrison; WGRWSup 7; Atlanta: SBL Press, 2015] 41).

coinage, and exploring inscriptions. From this we can reconstruct a general portrait of the imperial Roman soldier with whom first-century auditors might have been familiar. It is against this horizon of cultural knowledge that ancient auditors compared the soldiers in Luke-Acts and thus participated the character-building process.

■ I. Excavating the Extra Text

While a comparison of the portrayal of soldiers in Luke-Acts with those found in Greco-Roman literature demonstrates that Luke knew of various military stereotypes and deliberately used them in his construction of characters,[10] what might an exploration of the archaeological extra text contribute to our understanding of Luke's rhetorical agenda? Certainly, soldiers make several significant appearances in Luke-Acts. In the Gospel of Luke, soldiers are found in four pericopes:

- Soldiers seek baptism from John (3:14)
- Centurion of Capernaum sends emissaries to Jesus (7:1–10)
- Herod's soldiers mock Jesus (23:11, 36)
- Centurion pronounces Jesus innocent (23:47)

In the Acts of the Apostles, the military appears at strategic moments in the text:

- Cornelius the centurion sends for Peter (chap. 10)
- Soldiers guard Peter in prison (12:4–10)
- Cohort commander Claudius Lysias rescues Paul (21:31–23:32)
- Centurion guards Paul in Herod's praetorium (24:23)
- Centurion Julius of Augustan cohort escorts Paul to Rome (27:1–43)
- Soldier guards Paul in Rome (28:16)

Several different military units are represented in Luke-Acts: auxiliary cohorts (Acts 10:1; 21:31; 27:1), Herodian soldiers (Luke 3:14; 23:11), and Roman legions (Luke 8:31). The military characters are of various ranks: foot soldiers (Luke 3:14; 7:8; Acts 10:7; 28:16), centurions (Luke 7:2; 23:47; Acts 10:1; 22:25; 27:1), and tribunes (Acts 21:31). Unlike other Gospel writers, Luke demonstrates a penchant for distinguishing among the branches, though without an explanation as to their importance. To

---

10. Laurie Brink, *Soldiers in Luke-Acts: Engaging, Contradicting, and Transcending the Stereotypes* (WUNT 2/362; Tübingen: Mohr Siebeck, 2014) 92–164.

understand the cultural horizon against which Luke is situating his soldiers, we must consider aspects of the Roman military of which a first-century audience might have been aware.[11]

The Professional Roman Soldier

Augustus began his *Res gestae* noting that his greatest accomplishment was bringing freedom to the Republic, an act that he acknowledged had resulted from his raising an army for the task.[12] According to Augustus's own reckoning, the expanse of the empire and the *Pax Romana* were the result of his brilliant leadership and his ability to command a military force par excellence, the largest standing military during peacetime that for the first time in history could be called "professional."[13]

Under Augustan reforms, a Roman citizen with no land and little opportunity for advancement could enlist in the legion or, at various times, be conscripted and begin a lengthy career. A legion held ten cohorts, composed of six centuries. Ten squads (*contubernia*) made up the century.[14] The legate served as the legion's commanding officer and had six tribunes on his staff. Centurions supervised each century. Based on literary and archaeological evidence, the size of the legions has been variously estimated to be between 4,800 and 6,000 men.[15] Auxiliary units generally consisted of one cohort of five centuries. Once entered onto the century role, the recruit then recited the *sacramentum*, only parts of which have survived. Generally, the oath, which was renewed annually, obliged the soldier to follow his general, honor the emperor, and not desert the

---

11. For an overview of the Roman military in the New Testament, see Christopher B. Zeichmann, *The Roman Army and the New Testament* (Lanham, MD: Lexington Books/Fortress Academic, 2018); and Alexander Kyrychenko, *The Roman Army and the Expansion of the Gospel: The Role of the Centurion in Luke-Acts* (BZNW 203; Berlin: de Gruyter, 2014).

12. See Hans Volkmann, *Res gestae divi Augusti: Das Monumentum Ancyranum* (Kleine Texte für Vorlesungen und Übungen 29/30; Berlin: de Gruyter, 1964) 11.

13. Marius is often credited with creating a "professional" Roman army through his various reforms, but Augustus established length of service and retirement benefits and maintained the largest standing army yet known. See Lawrence Keppie, *The Making of the Roman Army: From Republic to Empire* (1984; repr., Norman: University of Oklahoma Press, 1998) 146–47.

14. Jonathan Roth, "The Size and Organization of the Roman Imperial Legion," *Historia* 43 (1994) 346–62, here 346.

15. Pseudo-Hyginus estimates a century of 80 men but also states that a cohort has 600. This suggests a legion strength of between 4,800 and 6,000 soldiers (*De mun castr.* 1.4). Ramsey MacMullen argues that the legions were 10 percent depleted at most times considering retirement and the slow replenishment with fresh recruits ("How Big Was the Roman Imperial Army?," *Klio* 62 [1980] 451–60, here 454).

battlefield, the only exception being to save the life of a citizen.¹⁶ Augustus set the limit of service at sixteen years for those in the ranks with an additional four as a veteran. However, inscriptions attest to soldiers serving as long as fifty years. Veterans were then organized into a separate unit having its own standard and reduced workload (Tacitus, *Ann.* 1.78).

Within the legions, state religion prevailed, but the soldiers were free to worship various gods as long as the state religion was not neglected. Until the edict of Septimius Severus in 197, soldiers were restricted from marrying. The ban might have been imposed by Augustus to shore up the discipline of the army, but it did not prevent the soldiers from creating unions with local women and fathering children. The effect of the ban was to deny legitimacy to the soldiers' children and to prevent the soldiers from including their children in their wills. Claudius attempted to mediate the effects of the ban by granting the rights of married men to retiring soldiers.¹⁷

By the beginning of the first century, Rome controlled the Mediterranean basin, either through its provinces or through its client kingdoms. In the next hundred years, the empire would expand even further reaching is territorial zenith under Trajan. By the second century, the empire included an area of nearly five million square kilometers and an estimated population of fifty-five million.¹⁸ But, though the territory expanded, the army, the strong arm of Roman control, did not dramatically increase. At

---

16. Dionysius of Halicarnassus, *Ant. rom.* 10.18.2; 11.43; Livy 22.38; Polybius 6.33.1; Vegetius 1.8.

17. Chris Thomas, "Claudius and the Roman Army Reforms," *Historia* 53 (2004) 424–52.

18. Population estimations in the ancient world vary greatly. Depending on the method of estimation, numbers between fifty and one hundred million have been proposed. Both the estimated size and the population given here are cited from the OCD (Graham Paul Burton, "Rome (History): 2. From Augustus to the Antonines [31 BC–AD 192]," in *The Oxford Classical Dictionary* [ed. Simon Hornblower and Anthony Spawforth; Oxford: Oxford University Press, 1996] 1327–31, here 1329). For various other estimates and methods of estimation, see K. J. Beloch, "Die Bevölkerung im Altertum," *Zeitschrift für Sozialwissenschaft* 2 (1899) 500–514; P. A. Brunt, *Italian Manpower* (Oxford: Oxford University Press, 1971); E. Lo Cascio, "The Size of the Roman Population," *JRS* 84 (1994) 23–40; Keith Hopkins, "Rome, Taxes, Rents and Trade," in *The Ancient Economy* (ed. Walter Scheidel and Sitta von Reden; New York: Routledge, 2002) 190–230; and Walter Scheidel, "Roman Population Size: The Logic of the Debate," in *People, Land, and Politics: Demographic Developments and the Transformation of Roman Italy, 300 BC–AD 14* (ed. Luuk de Ligt and Simon J. Northwood; Mnemosyne 303; Leiden: Brill, 2008) 17–70. Augustus claimed to have increased the number of registered Roman citizens from 4,063,000 to nearly 5 million in forty years (*Res gestae* 8.1–4).

its apex, the Roman military numbered approximately 380,000 soldiers in legions, fleets, and auxiliary.[19] Tacitus reported the number and locations of twenty-five legions during the reign of Tiberius, with fleets at the Italian ports of Misenum and Ravenna. The city of Rome was protected by three urban cohorts, and nine praetorian cohorts guarded the imperial family (*Ann.* 4.5). By the end of the first century, five more legions had been created. That number remained unchanged until the Principate of Septimius Severus, when an additional three legions were raised.

The Role of Auxiliary

While the number of legions seems disproportionate to the vastness of the empire, and the possibility of one encountering a legionary soldier seems slight, nonetheless provincials would be familiar with the face of the Roman military through the visage of the local militia. As their name suggests, the *auxilia* supplemented the work of the legions and were often used as "cannon fodder."[20] In fact, Tacitus once boasted that victories were achieved without the loss of Roman blood, for the non-Roman auxiliary troops would form the first line of battle (*Agr.* 35.2). The provincial auxiliary retained the name of the region from which the cohort had been originally recruited (*Ann.* 2.17). But by the mid-first century, the cohort's ranks were replenished with new recruits from where it was currently stationed and not necessarily from its place of origin.

Rank-and-file members of the provincial auxiliary, for the most part, did not possess Roman citizenship.[21] Claudius granted citizenship upon retirement after twenty-five years and also gave the right of *conubium*, or legal Roman marriage, to auxiliary veterans (Dio Cassius, *Hist.* 76.15.2).[22]

---

19. Mark Hassall, "The Army," in *The Cambridge Ancient History*, vol. 11: *A.D. 70–192* (ed. Alan K. Bowman and Peter Garnsey; Cambridge: Cambridge University Press, 2000) 320–43, here 320.

20. Denis Saddington, "The Development of the Roman Auxiliary Forces from Augustus to Trajan," *ANRW* II.3 (1975) 176–201, here 180. Josephus, however, credits the auxiliary with much of the success in the campaign against Jerusalem (J. E. Lendon, *Soldiers and Ghosts: A History of Battle in Classical Antiquity* [New Haven: Yale University Press, 2005] 242–47).

21. T. R. S. Broughton, "The Roman Army," in *The Beginnings of Christianity: The Acts of the Apostles* (ed. F. J. Foakes-Jackson and Kirsopp Lake; 5 vols.; London: Macmillan, 1920–33; repr., Grand Rapids: Baker, 1979) 1:429.

22. The granting of citizenship gave rise to the creation of *diplomatae*, or discharge papers, actually carved on two bronze plates on which the discharge formula, the recipient's name, commanding officer, date, and witnesses were engraved. The veteran could purchase the bronze tablets, but the originals were placed in the temple of the Deified Augustus and Minerva in Rome (Graham Webster, *The Roman Imperial*

The possibility of citizenship might have motivated voluntary enlistment, but, unlike their legionary brothers, auxiliary veterans may not have received an allotment of land upon retirement.[23]

From the time of Augustus until Trajan, auxiliary cohorts were not stationed permanently outside their home province,[24] which bore the cost and burden for its auxiliary. While some cohorts might have always retained local leadership, the majority of auxiliary troops were under the command of Roman officers who were to encourage and enforce military discipline (Tacitus, *Agr.* 28). In the region of Judea, auxiliary troops were recruited from among its non-Jewish residents.[25] The cohort, Sebastēnoi (Σεβαστηνοί), was composed of gentile residents from Caesarea and its sister city, Sebaste. The auxiliary was stationed in Caesarea, where Josephus recorded that its inappropriate response to the death of Agrippa nearly cost its removal to Pontus.[26]

In Acts 10:1, Cornelius the centurion is said to be a member of a specific cohort of the auxiliary, called the Italian cohort (σπείρης τῆς καλουμένης Ἰταλικῆς). The *cohors II militaria Italica civium romanorum voluntariorum* is mentioned in various inscriptions and was stationed in Syria in the mid-first century.[27] The title *civium Romanorum* in the cohort's title may indicate a band of Roman citizens who formed an auxiliary

---

Army of the First and Second Centuries A.D. [3rd ed.; Norman: University of Oklahoma Press, 1998] 143).

23. See P. A. Brunt, "Pay and Superannuation in the Roman Army," *Papers of the British School at Rome* 18 (1950) 1–71, here 66.

24. Saddington, "Development of the Roman Auxiliary Forces," 198. The emergence of the permanent frontiers "resulted in more and more units being assigned to the virtually permanent occupation of a particular fort unless transferred."

25. Jews were exempt from military duty and were not obliged to quarter soldiers (*Ant.* 14.10.6 §§204–5).

26. While the local troops were able to stay their immediate removal from Judea, Vespasian transferred them later (*Ant.* 19.9.1–2 §§354–65).

27. Referring to Acts 10:1, Speidel wrote, "[O]bviously, a citizen cohort originally raised in Italy, a *cohors Italica civium Romanorum*, must be meant here" (Michael P. Speidel, "The Roman Army in Judaea under the Procurators," in idem, *Roman Army Studies* [2 vols.; Mavors Roman Army Researches 1, 8; Stuttgart: Franz Steiner, 1984–92] 2:224–32, here 224). Inscriptional evidence attests to at least two cohorts called Italica. The *cohors I Italica civium Romanorum voluntarioru*m (CIL 14.171) and the *cohors II Italica civium Romanorum* (CIL 3.13483a; 16.106), also known as *cohors II Italica* (CIL 6.3528) and *cohors miliaria Italica voluntariorum quae est in Syria* (CIL 11.6117). However, Jonathan P. Roth notes that "the unit is not mentioned by Josephus nor is there epigraphical evidence for it at Caesarea or anywhere in Judea" ("The Impact of the Roman Army in the Province of Judaea/Syria Palestina," in *Impact of the Roman Army (200 BC–AD 476): Economic, Social, Political, Religious and Cultural Aspects; Proceedings of the Sixth Workshop of the International Network*

cohort rather than join an existing legion. After the Flavian period, the title *civium Romanorum* could also indicate a grant of citizenship given to the whole cohort for outstanding service rendered.²⁸

A tomb inscription for a member of the *cohors II Italica*, found in Carnuntum on the Danube, sheds light on where this cohort was stationed.

> Proculus | Rabili f. Col. | Philadel., mil. | optio coh. II | Italic. c. R. 7 Fa[us] tini, ex vexil. sa| git. exer. Syriaci, | stip. VII, vixit an. |XXVI, | Apuleius frater | f. c.²⁹

While his first name, Proculus, was Roman, his father's, Rabilus, was a common Nabatean name. The inscription identified the soldier as a native of Philadelphia, one of the cities of the Decapolis, and was set up by his brother, Apuleius, who may also have been in the cohort.³⁰ According to the inscription, the II Italian cohort formed part of a detachment of archers from the Syrian army. This cohort might have been sent to the Danube in 69 C.E. by Vespasian, who hoped to secure his bid for emperor, while he was fighting the Jewish War (Tacitus, *Hist.* 2.83). That Proculus died after seven years of service indicates that the Italian cohort existed at least as early as 62 C.E. The cohort probably originated in Italy and might have begun with the enrollment of freedmen, though, as is evident with Proculus, recruitment then occurred locally among Roman citizens in the province in which the cohort was stationed.³¹

Indeed, it would seem that Luke's description of the presence of the Italian cohort (Acts 1:1) and the Sebastian cohort (Acts 27:1) in the province of Syria is corroborated by first-century inscriptions³² and texts (*War* 2.52, 58, 63, 74, 236; *Ant.* 19.365, 20.122, 176), though the dating of the narrative events is earlier than the evidence of the cohorts.

Impact of Empire (Roman Empire, 200 B.C.–A.D. 476), Capri, March 29–April 2, 2000 (ed. Lukas de Blois and Elio Lo Cascio; Impact of Empire 6; Leiden: Brill, 2007) 412.

28. See Michael P. Speidel, "Citizen Cohorts in the Roman Imperial Army: New Data on the Cohorts Apula, Campana, and III Camestris," *TAPA* 106 (1976) 339–48.

29. Hermann Dessau, *Inscriptiones latinae selectae* (3 vols. in 5; Berlin: Weidmann, 1892–1916) no. 9168.

30. See Emil Schürer, *The History of the Jewish People in the Age of Jesus Christ (175 B.C.–A.D. 135)* (ed. Geza Vermes, Fergus Millar, and M. Black; 3 vols. in 4 parts; Edinburgh: T&T Clark, 1973–87) 1:365 n. 54; and Benjamin W. Bacon, "Some 'Western' Variants in the Texts of Acts," *HTR* 21 (1928) 113–45, here 141 n. 7.

31. Broughton, "Roman Army," 442.

32. Maurice Dunand, *Le Musée de Soueida: Inscriptions et monuments figurés* (Bibliothèque Archéologique et Historique 20; Paris: Paul Geuthner, 1934) no. 168; and Speidel, "Roman Army in Judaea under the Procurators," 238.

The Roman Centurion

To a late first-century audience, the centurion was *the* face of the Roman military that most provincials would have occasion to see. As the title centurion (ἑκατοντάρχης, "leader of a hundred") indicates, the centurion supervised one of the centuries in a cohort. Centurions held significant power both over their men and over any civilians they encountered, and their salary evidenced their elevated status.[33] A centurion's stipend was more than three times that of a foot soldier[34] and was supplemented by the bribes extracted from the soldiers under his command who hoped for lighter duty (Tacitus, *Ann.* 1.17).

Most centurions were in their thirties by the time they received their staff, the symbol of the centurionate, and most served an average of twenty years. A centurion had a one-in-three chance of promotion to the coveted primipilate—if he lived long enough—which was strong incentive to remain in the military service past his initial enlistment period. Retirement as a *primus pilus* assured a substantial grant, enough to elevate a citizen to equestrian status.[35] In fact, Augustus's intent was that his soldiers should strive for advancement.[36]

Within the Roman auxiliary, centurions were also the primary promoters of discipline and supervision among the ranks. When a vexillation, or detachment of troops, was dispatched for provincial service, the centurion would be the senior military official in charge. These vexillations performed three essential tasks at the provincial level: mediation between the governor and the provincials, tax protection and/or gathering, and police work. Egyptian papyri testify to the use of soldiers for protection during the collection of taxes or, in some cases, for actual

---

33. Xavier Rubio-Campillo, Pau Valdés Matías, and Eduard Ble, "Centurions in the Roman Legion: Computer Simulation and Complex Systems," *Journal of Interdisciplinary History* 46 (2015) 245–63, here 249.

34. Henry C. Boren, "Studies Relating to the Stipendium Militum," *Historia* 32 (1983) 427–60, here 429.

35. "The *primipilares* in fact formed a new military aristocracy, the obvious and virtually only route into the equestrian order for the soldiers of Rome" (Brian Dobson, "The Significance of the Centurion and 'Primipilaris' in the Roman Army and Administration," *ANRW* II.1 [1974] 392–434, here 432).

36. Augustus "wanted the army to be a ladder to higher position for everyone from the auxiliary who coveted the citizenship, the legionary who wanted preferment (often to the Guard), the Praetorian who wished to become a member of the *primi pili* of the legions or something more, as well as the *nobiles*, who wanted to reach high command such as *legatus pro praetore*" (Boren, "Studies Relating to the Stipendium Militum," 450).

collection of the taxes themselves.[37] In addition to protecting the collection and delivery of taxes and customs, soldiers were used to gather vital information. Documents from the Babatha archive found in the Judean desert "show that in A.D. 127 what was clearly a province-wide census was carried out in which the commanders of the auxiliary units stationed in the province served as local or regional *censitores*."[38] The prefect of the auxiliary cavalry unit, Priscus, received and signed Babatha's census registration.[39]

Vexillations of soldiers were also frequently engaged in policing the provinces.[40] Ostraca found near watchtowers on the eastern desert attest to the presence of both local Egyptians and soldiers guarding the desert road (*P. Amst.* 8, 9, 10). Centurions in the rural areas not only provided security for the residents but also acted as de facto judges in civil matters. In August 198 C.E., Gemellus wrote to the *epistratēgos* Calpurnius Concessus and included a copy of an earlier petition to and the response from the prefect.[41] The petitioner claimed to have been abused by a local tax collector who not only injured both him and his mother but also destroyed the doors of his house. The final subscription indicates that Concessus referred the matter to the centurion of the nome as Gemellus had requested. Evidently Gemellus believed that the centurion would be able to adjudicate his claim. If Gemellus's trust was not in vain, then perhaps, "far from being a remote and specialist military, the Roman army would have a real influence on village life, not merely as a vague threat of overwhelming violence which could destroy any challenge to the established

---

37. A second-century papyrus lists soldiers from three cohorts—*I Flavia Cilicia*, *II Ituraeorum* and *I Lusitanorum* and one *ala*—as the collectors of a salt tax (*ChLA* 4.264 [*Chartae Latinae antiquiores: Facsimile Edition of the Latin Charters prior to the Ninth Century* (Olten: Graf, 1954–2019)]).

38. Werner Eck, "Provincial Administration and Finance," in Bowman and Garnsey, *Cambridge Ancient History*, 11:266–92, here 288.

39. See Naphtali Lewis, ed., *The Documents from the Bar Kokhba Period in the Cave of Letters: Greek Papyri* (Judean Desert Studies 2; Jerusalem: Israel Exploration Society, 1989) 65–70.

40. For a detailed analysis of the Roman army used as a policing agent, see Christopher J. Fuhrmann, *Policing the Roman Empire: Soldiers, Administration, and Public Order* (Oxford: Oxford University Press, 2012).

41. *P. Mich.* 6. 425, inv. 2979 probably originated in Karanis in the Arsinoite nome of Egypt and is one of several papyri in the Gemellus family archive. See Herbert Chayyim Youtie and Orsamus Merrill Pearl, *Papyri and Ostraca from Karanis* (2 vols.; Michigan Papyri 6, 8; Ann Arbor: University of Michigan Press, 1944) 118.

order, but as a real and active presence in the local administrative and power structures."[42]

Return to Civilian Life

Following his years of service, a veteran of the legion retired either to his native homeland, his current location, or a land allotment provided to him.[43] Unlike the legionary recruits, the auxiliary forces of the Roman army were noncitizens from various provinces throughout the Roman Empire. In all likelihood, since the veterans of these auxiliary *cohortes* and *alae* did not receive land grants upon retirement, they would have returned to their province of origin or settled near their location of service.

With a sizable pension, the retired soldier had the potential of becoming a significant member of his community. These veterans never forgot the source of their wealth or their military exploits, as evidenced on numerous funerary monuments. In the Museo archeologico nazionale di Aquileia near Ravenna, several epitaphs enumerate the military accomplishments of veterans. Standing 5.5 feet with a width of 2.5 feet, the burial stele of L. Pellartius Celer can barely contain all of the deceased's accomplishments.

> L(ucius) Pellartius C(ai) / Lem(onia) Celer Iulius Mon/tanus stipendior(um) XLIII / missus ex evocato et / armidoctor leg(ionis) XV Apol(linaris) / ab Imp(eratore) Domitiano Caesare Aug(usto) / et accepit pro commodis HS XXX(milia) / quod ante illum nemo alius ac/ce<p>it ex hac militie item bello / Iuda{e}ico donis donatum et co/rona aurea ab

---

42. Richard Alston, *Soldier and Society in Roman Egypt: A Social History* (London: Routledge, 1995) 87.

43. More than forty tombstones uncovered in Asia Minor bear witness to the presence of legionary veterans. These tombstones indicate that recruitment occurred in the province of Galatia and that many soldiers, rather than settle where they had been stationed, returned to their place of origin. According to Speidel, during the first three centuries, "[h]omecoming veterans rose to positions of social prominence, and as we now see, service in the legions was so highly regarded that even local aristocrats enrolled, cementing the bond between Rome and Asia Minor in a particular way" ("Legionaries from Asia Minor," *ANRW* II.8 [1977] 730–46, here 744).

Regarding land allotments, Julius Caesar recognized that the creation of veteran colonies was a way to quickly disperse potentially mutinous soldiers. Augustus continued his policy (*Res gestae* 27), and legionary soldiers could anticipate resettlement in a veteran colony until the reign of Hadrian. Such colonies were located either in depopulated areas of Italy (Tacitus, *Ann.* 14.27) or in newly acquired Roman territories, where they were often a "civilizing" influence and a ready paramilitary force should barbarians cross the borders. For a discussion of the creation of veteran colonies for border defenses, see A. N. Sherwin-White, *The Roman Citizenship* (2nd ed.; Oxford: Clarendon, 1973) 243–44.

divo Tito tulit / annos secum LXXIII hoc sepulcr/um suo titulo donavit et filiab(us) / L(ucius) Pellartius Anthus / cui et aditus datur / loc(us) mon(umenti) in fr(onte) p(edes) LV in ag(ro) p(edes) XLV[44]

After forty-three years of service, Pellartius received a monetary award from Domitian and boasted a golden crown from Titus, awarded for his bravery during the First Jewish War. He was an *evocatus*, or veteran, which meant he had voluntarily reenlisted after his initial sixteen years. He then served as an instructor (*armidoctor*) under Domitian. His unit was the 15th Legion Apollinaris, which, under the direction of Titus, had captured Jotapata during the First Jewish War. He died at seventy-three and was commemorated by his brother.

The Symbolic Military Presence in Coinage[45]

Rome's reputation afforded it the maximum benefit of its military. A moderate military force was able to uphold the *Pax Romana* in outlying provinces largely due to the reputation of the army for swift and thorough retaliation. In some cases, the memory of such havoc remained vivid in the minds of the conquered peoples (Josephus, *War* 2.345–401). While many residents of the empire might never encounter a soldier, they were nonetheless inundated by images of military prowess frequently embossed on Roman coinage and widespread in the markets of the empire.[46]

The propagandistic value of coinage served to make it both a medium of economic exchange and a political tool. "The Roman world found on

---

44. Giovanni Lettich, *Itinerari epigrafici aquileiesi: Guida alle epigrafi esposte nel Museo archeologico nazionale di Aquileia* (Antichità altoadriatiche 50; Trieste: Editreg SRL, 2003) no. 92.

45. Scholars acknowledge that the use of coinage to interpret texts is fraught with methodological difficulties. Responding to Richard Oster's description of coins as "numismatic windows" ("Numismatic Windows into the Social World of Early Christianity: A Methodological Inquiry," *JBL* 101 [1982] 195–223), Bradley J. Bitner argued, "[I]f New Testament scholars insist on regarding coins as 'numismatic windows,' we should at least acknowledge that they are ancient windows indeed, and will almost always provide us with a refracted and restricted view of our objects of inquiry" ("Coinage and Colonial Identity," in Welborn and Harrison, *First Urban Churches*, 1:151–87, here 154).

46. According to C. J. Howgego, "The medium- and long-distance movement of goods on a considerable scale, over and above the localized peasant economy, was a feature of the Roman world," enhancing the possibility that coins traveled beyond their region of origin ("Coin Circulation and the Integration of the Roman Economy," *JRS* 7 [1994] 5–21; quotation from 5). Indeed, the *vici* outside the camp with its mobile markets, the movement of troops, and the retirement of veterans all allowed for the potential spread of coins.

its current coinage that which the modern world finds in its public press, the announcement of important affairs that had recently taken place, of victories, treaties, social and economic changes and the like."[47] Promoting the agenda of the emperor was, however, a secondary benefit in the use of coins. Much of the impetus for the widespread minting and use of coinage in the Principate is attributed to the need to pay the military, since salaries, retirement rewards, and donatives were given to the soldiers in the form of coins.[48] So it is not surprising that military motifs including victory, valiancy, *capta, adlocutio,* loyalty, or concordia are frequent on the reverse of imperial coinage.[49] The Flavians, hoping to promote their ascension via military prowess rather than adoption, replicated the coin types of the Republican and Augustan eras.[50] The most frequent motif they carried over from the Republican period was that of the *capta* type, depicting the personification of the defeated country. Struck to commemorate the Roman victory at the close of the First Jewish Revolt, a denarius of Vespasian shows the emperor in military attire standing over Judea, personified as a woman.[51]

---

47. Jocelyn Toynbee, "Some 'Programme' Coin-Types of Antonius Pius," *Classical Review* 39.7/8 (1925) 170–73, here 170.

48. E. Lo Cascio comments, "Money was created in Rome by the state and functioned, from its beginning as a weight unit, for the state's needs"—the largest state expense being the military ("How Did the Romans View Their Coinage and Its Function?," in *Coin Finds and Coin Use in the Roman World: The Thirteenth Oxford Symposium on Coinage and Monetary History, 25.–27.3.1993; A NATO Advanced Research Workshop* [ed. Cathy E. King and David G. Wigg; Studien zu Fundmünzen der Antike 10; Berlin: Gebr. Mann, 1996] 273–87, here 275). The pay of military inadvertently fostered the use and spread of coinage. According to Richard Reece, "Thus coins supplied to the military are almost bound to find their way into any general circulation in the province that there is, and that general circulation seems to depend on the military for its existence" ("Mints, Markets and the Military," in *Military and Civilian in Roman Britain: Cultural Relationships in a Frontier Province* [ed. T. F. C. Blagg and A. C. King; BAR British Series 136; Oxford: B.A.R., 1984] 148).

On donatives, see Dio Cassius 59.2. The donative ceremony is depicted on Trajan's column, where the emperor is depicted in military dress and seated on a platform, surrounded by soldiers (Elizabeth Wolfram Thill, "The Emperor in Action: Group Scenes in Trajanic Coins and Monumental Reliefs," *American Journal of Numismatics* [2014] 89–142, here 120).

49. Harold Mattingly, *Roman Coins, from the Earliest Times to the Fall of the Western Empire* (London: Methuen, 1928) 152–54.

50. Jane M. Cody, "Conquerors and Conquered on Flavian Coins," in *Flavian Rome: Culture, Image, Text* (ed. A. J. Boyle and W. J. Dominik; Leiden: Brill, 2003) 103–23, here 103.

51. Harold Mattingly, *Coins of the Roman Empire in the British Museum*, vol. 2, *Vespasian to Domitian* (London: British Museum, 1930) 294, no. 308.

Military symbols on coins might have been noticed and perhaps even admired by the soldier in the field, since they represented not only his pay, but his place of importance within the empire. But how were coins viewed by civilians? "It seems then reasonably clear that in the ancient world it was expected that coin designs would be noticed and this expectation was at least sometimes fulfilled."[52] The actual impact that the imperial and military images may have had on the populace is not retrievable; however, the coins "can provide some indication of the impression an emperor wished to give his reign."[53] Such attention to coin types, whether by the emperor himself or by senate and imperial officials suggests that images on coins were noticed. Given the frequency of military motifs on the reverse, in addition to providing a pocket portraiture of the emperor, coins may also have impressed upon the people the might of the military, without whom the emperor could not remain in power.

Though Augustus might have overstated his role in the development of the professional Roman army, he nonetheless created an effective tool for empire building. But the benefits extended beyond the pacification of peoples. As the inscriptional evidence demonstrates, Augustus's hopes for his veterans were realized. If they endured, they rose in rank and retired with a substantial pension, many becoming civic leaders in newly established Roman colonies. In the early Principate, the auxiliary cohorts supplemented the legions, serving as provincial police forces, guarding the edges of the empire and ensuring that Rome's interests were protected. The extant papyri seem to indicate that, while some soldiers overstepped their mandate and abused the populace, others upheld the *Pax Romana* with some semblance of civility. For the civilians throughout the empire, while they may never have encountered a legionnaire or auxiliary soldier, the coins in their pockets were ever-present reminders of Rome's military reach.

■ II. Lucan Soldiers against the Horizon of Cultural Knowledge

The authorial audience of Luke-Acts would measure the literary soldiers at least in part against this cultural and historical horizon drawn from the extra text. Luke invites the audience's participation in the building of

---

52. Andrew Burnett, *Coinage in the Roman World* (London: Seaby, 1987) 68.
53. J. B. Campbell, *The Emperor and the Roman Army, 31 BC–AD 235* (Oxford: Clarendon, 1984) 143.

character by leaving unstated the information that the audience could provide. This is particularly evident in his use of undefined military terms, his ready identification of military units, and his characterization of the centurions.

Luke inserts military terms without explanation: soldiers (στρατευ– όμενοι, Luke 3:14), centurion (ἑκατοντάρχης, Luke 7:2, 6; 23:47; Acts 10:1, 22; 22:25, 26; 24:23; 27:1, 6, 11, 31, 43), soldier (στρατιώτας, Luke 7:8; 23:36; Acts 12:4, 6, 18; 21:32, 35; 23:23, 31; 27:31–32, 42), throw up a rampart (παρεμβαλοῦσιν ... χάρακα, Luke 19:43), armies (στρατοπέδων, Luke 21:20), to take captive (αἰχμαλωτισθήσονται, Luke 21:24), a company of soldiers (τοῖς στρατεύμασιν, Luke 23:11; Acts 23:10), tribune (χιλίαρχος, Acts 21:33; 22:24, 27–29; 23:10, 19, 22; 24:22), spearmen (δεξιολάβους, Acts 23:23). The first-century Greek speaker could figure out that a centurion (ἑκατοντάρχης) led a hundred soldiers and a tribune (χιλίαρχος) commanded a thousand. But if Luke intended a distinction among στρατιώτας (the most common word for "soldier"), στρατευόμενοι (those doing military service), and στράτευμα (a vexillation of soldiers), his auditors would need to bring that knowledge to their encounter with the text.

Three times cohorts are mentioned and two are named: the cohort called Italica (σπείρης τῆς καλουμένης Ἰταλικῆς, Acts 10:1), the cohort (τῆς σπείρης) located in Jerusalem (Acts 21:31) and the cohort Sebastēs (σπείρης Σεβαστῆς, Acts 27:1). Inscriptions attest to the existence of cohorts by these names, but only Josephus places the Augusta cohort in Caesarea. Luke might have wanted to inject a bit of realism into his narrative or, as some have suggested, these names may have come from his sources. In either case, the expectation is that the auditor would be familiar with the designation of σπεῖρα, a company or cohort of soldiers numbering between 500 and 600. In Acts 23:23, the Tribune Claudius Lysias sends Paul to Caesarea, guarded by 200 soldiers, 70 horsemen, and 200 spearmen (στρατιώτας διακοσίους, ὅπως πορευθῶσιν ἕως Καισαρείας, καὶ ἱππεῖς ἑβδομήκοντα καὶ δεξιολάβους διακοσίους).[54] While the number of troops seems excessive for one prisoner, half the cohort would be still be in Jerusalem.

Interpreting these terms requires that the auditor have some familiarity with the Roman military so as to follow the narrative. But in his portrait of centurions, particularly in Luke 7:1–10 and Acts 10, Luke expects his auditors to do more than simply fill in the blanks of missing

---

54. Interestingly, the NABRE translates στρατιώτας as "soldiers" and δεξιολάβους as "auxiliary." The NRSV translates the latter term more accurately as "spearmen."

information. Here they must bring their knowledge and expectations of centurions drawn from the cultural horizon of the Roman military and actively enter into the character-building process.

Luke 7:2 contains the first mention of a centurion in the two volumes.[55] The narrator gives no explanation of what a centurion is, or why one would be in Capernaum. Thus, the unnamed centurion of Capernaum encourages the auditors to use their own imagination and experience to flesh out this character. Drawing from the extra text, Luke's centurion could have been stationed at Capernaum, on the border between Galilee and Trachonitis, where he was to oversee or protect the customs post there. Such stations for the collection of *portoria*, or customs dues, were often situated on high-volume roadways,[56] and Capernaum was situated near the Via Maris. The auditor learns that this centurion owns slaves[57] and is concerned enough about the welfare of a sick slave[58] to entreat a Jewish healer to come to his home. The centurion's benefactions are not toward Rome's gods but toward the God of the Jews.[59] He sends delegations as ambassadors on his behalf, but one of those embassies is composed of the very people subject to him, whom one would surmise were less loyal. Through his friends, the centurion disclaims any accolades

---

55. Other centurions appear in Luke 7:6; 23:47; Acts 10:1, 22; 22:25, 26; 24:23; 27:1, 6, 11, 31, 43.

56. J. J. Wilkes, "The Danube Provinces," in Bowman and Garnsey, *Cambridge Ancient History*, 11:577–603, here 586.

57. While Individual soldiers could own slaves, some slaves might have belonged to the military unit itself. See Michael P. Speidel, "The Soldiers' Servants," *Ancient Society* 20 (1989) 239–48.

58. As Barbara Reid notes in her commentary on the Gospel of Luke (co-authored with Shelly Matthews; WCS 43A; Collegeville, MN: Liturgical Press, 2021), scholars have recently suggested that, since ἔντιμος ("precious," 7:2) can be read as a term of endearment, the relationship between the centurion and his slave could be of a sexual nature. Others, however, argue that ἔντιμος has a monetary connotation and can refer to something of considerable wealth. For the Matthean version, see Theodore W. Jennings Jr. and Tat-siong Benny Liew, "Mistaken Identities but Model Faith: Rereading the Centurion, the Chap, and the Christ in Matthew 8:5–13," *JBL* 123 (2004) 467–94. See also the rejoinder by D. B. Saddington, "The Centurion in Matthew 8:5–13: Consideration of the Proposal of Theodore W. Jennings, Jr., and Tat-Siong Benny Liew," *JBL* 125 (2006) 140–42; and the critique by Christopher B. Zeichmann, "Rethinking the Gay Centurion: Sexual Exceptionalism, National Exceptionalism in Readings of Matt. 8:5–13 // Luke 7:1–10," *Bible and Critical Theory* 11 (2015) 35–54.

59. The excavations of a shrine at Humayma, Jordan, revealed a Nabatean cult site that was rebuilt by Roman soldiers and incorporated both local and legionary elements, "symbolizing harmony between the garrison and the town" (M. Barbara Reeves, "A Nabataean and Roman Shrine with Civic and Military Gods at Humayma, Jordan," *Arabian Archaeology & Epigraphy* 30 (2019) 134–55, here 134.

made by the Jewish elders. He is not worthy, despite their comments, to receive Jesus.

In Luke's double work, the praiseworthy centurion of Luke 7 is meant to foreshadow Cornelius in the second volume (Acts 10:1–8, 24–33, 44–48), upon whom the Holy Spirit will fall and signal divine approbation of the gentile mission. Having constructed the centurion of Capernaum as a facsimile of their own knowledge and experience of soldiers, the auditors now bring that same information to bear on Cornelius.

After his rank and cohort are named, Cornelius is described directly as "devout and god-fearing together with all of his household, giving many alms to the people and praying to God always" (εὐσεβὴς καὶ φοβούμενος τὸν θεὸν σὺν παντὶ τῷ οἴκῳ αὐτοῦ, ποιῶν ἐλεημοσύνας πολλὰς τῷ λαῷ καὶ δεόμενος τοῦ θεοῦ διὰ παντός, Acts 10:2). The narrative not only describes Cornelius as faithful but gives evidence of his faith. He participates in Jewish cultic acts by praying continually and giving alms. He has a reputation among the Jews, and his own envoys recognize his righteousness. Such religious obeisance to a foreign god of a subject people would likely come to the notice of his superiors. If Cornelius is meant to be on active duty, he is taking great risks to demonstrate his piety or so the auditor might think. Interestingly, Cornelius engages in these acts with all of his household (παντὶ τῷ οἴκῳ αὐτοῦ, Acts 10:2). Generally, οἶκός includes the family and slaves. Is Cornelius meant to be seen as retired and living in Caesarea where he might have been stationed? Or he is on active duty? If the latter, then any "marriage" and children would not be considered legitimate.

Character building is a cumulative process. The auditor brings his or her understanding of the centurion of Capernaum into the creation of Cornelius. Likewise, the auditor's characterization of Cornelius affects his or her interpretation of the last centurion to appear in the narrative. In Acts 27, a centurion of the Augustan cohort named Julius is tasked with taking Paul and the other prisoners by sea to Rome. The narrator states that Julius treats Paul well (φιλανθρώπως τε ὁ Ἰούλιος τῷ Παύλῳ χρησάμενος, Acts 27:3). He allows his prisoner, Paul, to go to his friends so that his needs can be met. Rather than seeing this as a dereliction of duty, the auditor may assume that Paul is under house arrest.

Luke depicts the centurion Julius as responsible for securing transport for Paul and the other prisoners, a common task for centurions on vexillation. In the Sagalassus inscription, dated to the reign of Tiberius, soldiers with appropriate papers could requisition transport and a set fee would be paid.[60] After barely surviving a storm at sea, the ship nears land.

---

60. Written in Latin and Greek, the Sagalassus inscription is the earliest imperial

The soldiers intend to kill the prisoners to prevent their escape, but Julius prevents them. And, like the centurion of Capernaum and Cornelius, the centurion of Caesarea, Julius, the centurion of the Augustan cohort plays a significant role in the narrative. True to the stereotype of an obedient soldier, Julius delivers Paul safely to Rome.

Throughout Luke's two volumes, the author has continually invited his audience to bring their own experience, expectations, and extra text to the creation of characters. In the portrayal of soldiers, it appears that the audience was expected to possess preliminary information about Roman military personnel and how that personnel functioned in the provinces.

■ CONCLUSION

Character construction depends on a relationship between the author who penned the work and the audience who will enflesh the characters from the author's skeleton. To achieve successful characterization, the author anticipates that his authorial audience possesses an "inferential capacity"[61] and will draw on a horizon of cultural knowledge built upon the extra text, so as to fill in the gaps.

In order to construct the possible extra text available to the Lucan auditor, scholars tend to rely on contemporaneous literature, but archaeological evidence can also serve as a source of relevant information. By placing Lucan soldiers within the historical context culled—in part— from papyri, inscriptions, and coinage, we can begin to see the horizon of cultural knowledge available to the auditor. Thus, archaeological evidence is not simply illustrative of a particular point in the text. Material culture can actually help to build the backdrop against which the text can be read and understood. But this conversation between text and artifact is not

---

inscription found that details the regulations for the provision of transport. The local community had to provide up to ten wagons or as many mules for officials passing through the city's territory. In return, the owner was to receive ten asses per schoenum (a unit of distance) for a wagon and four asses per schoenum for a mule. If a mule was not available, two donkeys could be substituted. Access to this service was limited to the procurator, military personnel with provincial authorization, and military personnel passing through from other provinces. A centurion was entitled to one wagon or three mules or six donkeys. The edict also addressed hospitality for those eligible for transport services. Members of the provincial's staff, those on military service from other provinces, freedmen and slaves of the imperial house were to be quartered without payment. See Stephen Mitchell, "Requisitioned Transport in the Roman Empire: A New Inscription from Pisidia," *JRS* 66 (1976) 106–31.

61. Seymour Chatman, *Story and Discourse: Narrative Structure in Fiction and Film* (Ithaca, NY: Cornell University Press, 1978) 29.

simply a historical activity. For the modern reader, bringing archaeological evidence to bear on the New Testament texts is akin to "teaching a stone to talk,"[62] a hermeneutical endeavor that invites our participation in the process of making meaning of the text. By engaging the extra text, we, too, can fill in the blanks in Luke's portrayal of the Roman military and participate in the character-building process for ourselves.

---

62. Annie Dillard, *Teaching a Stone to Talk: Expeditions and Encounters* (New York: Harper & Row, 1982).

Who Was Holy and How Did They Get That Way?

CAROLYN OSIEK, RSCJ
Brite Divinity School (emerita)
Fort Worth, Texas

In the fifth chapter of *Lumen Gentium*, the Dogmatic Constitution on the Church of Vatican II, entitled "The Call of the Whole Church to Holiness," the holiness of the church in its members is affirmed in multiple ways, among them the following:

> Now, this holiness of the Church is unceasingly manifested, as it ought to be, through those fruits of grace that the Spirit produces in the faithful. It is expressed in multiple ways by those individuals who, in their walk of life, strive for the perfection of charity, and thereby help others to grow. (§39)

> All of Christ's faithful, therefore, whatever be the conditions, duties, and circumstances of their lives, will grow in holiness day by day through these very situations, if they accept all of them with faith from the hand of their heavenly Father, and if they cooperate with the divine will by showing every man through their earthly activities the love with which God has loved the world. (§41)[1]

Given this renewed reminder of the vocation to holiness that we have all embraced by fidelity to baptism, let us consider again how this call of holiness came to us and how it was received in times past.

As a New Testament scholar, I have long been fascinated by a rather off-handed comment of Paul in his discussion of marital issues in 1 Cor 7:14:

---

1. Walter M. Abbott, S.J., ed., *The Documents of Vatican II* (New York: Guild Press, 1966) 66–70.

> ἡγίασται γὰρ ὁ ἀνὴρ ὁ ἄπιστος ἐν τῇ γυναικὶ καὶ ἡγίασται ἡ γυνὴ ἡ ἄπιστος ἐν τῷ ἀδελφῷ· ἐπεὶ ἄρα τὰ τέκνα ὑμῶν ἀκάθαρτά ἐστιν, νῦν δὲ ἅγιά ἐστιν.

> For the unbelieving husband is made holy through his wife, and the unbelieving wife is made holy through her husband. Otherwise, your children would be unclean, but as it is, they are holy. (1 Cor 7:14 NRSV; NAB also reads "made holy")

What does Paul mean by asserting that a spouse and children are holy because one—one is enough—of the parents is a believer in Jesus? Paul acknowledges that he has a saying "from the Lord" that husband and wife should not separate. He also realizes that here he is faced with a complication that apparently neither Jesus nor his interpreters had envisioned: a believer and an unbeliever in a marriage in which the belief itself may be causing disharmony (1 Cor 7:12–16). It is one of the questions the Corinthians had put to Paul for answers (7:1).

He is certainly not in favor of dissolving this "mixed marriage" if it can be saved, though, if necessary, because of incompatibility of belief and practice, it can be brought to an end (7:15). But he cannot let this be the last word. He ends the subject by holding out the possibility of the wife saving the husband, or the husband saving the wife, thus introducing the possibility of marriage as mission.[2]

In English, we have three different word groups to express this idea: "holy" from Germanic *heilig*, "sanctified" from Latin *sanctus, sanctificare*, and "consecrated" from Latin *consecratio, consecrare*. Two older English translations of this passage, the KJV and RSV, use "sanctify" and "consecrate," but the newer translation says "make holy."

> KJV: "For the unbelieving husband is *sanctified* by the wife, and the unbelieving wife is *sanctified* by the husband: else were your children unclean; but now are they holy."

> RSV: "For the unbelieving husband is *consecrated* through his wife, and the unbelieving wife is *consecrated* through her husband. Otherwise, your children would be unclean, but as it is they are holy."

These two older translations carry the point of setting aside for God's special use.

Paul's assertion of the holiness of the children of believers, and therefore by extension the holiness of the parents as well, is perhaps an echo of

---

2. Later, the author of 1 Peter partially picks up the same idea; but this time, it is only the wife who may save her husband—through her submissive behavior! (1 Pet 3:1–6).

the Roman ideal of the inviolability of the home. This ideal is famously represented in the well-known statement of Cicero that contributed to the rise of the Victorian adage "A man's home is his castle." The background of Cicero's assertion is that, at the instigation of his rival, Clodius, he had been banished from Rome in 58 B.C.E., but he returned triumphantly the following year. During his exile, his house had been destroyed and a temple erected on the site to the goddess Libertas. Cicero persuaded the *pontifices* to deconsecrate it and allow him to return to his property. He plays on the word groups *religio*, binding duties of the pious person, and *sanctus*, whose primary meaning is inviolability—precisely what his home with its household gods had been denied by Libertas:[3]

> Quid est sanctius, quid omni religione munitius quam domus unius cuiusque civium? Hic arae sunt, hic foci, hic di penates, hic sacra, religiones, caerimoniae continentur; hoc perfugium est ita sanctum omnibus ut inde abripi neminem fas sit.

> What is there more holy, what is there more carefully fenced round with every description of religious respect, than the house of every individual citizen? Here are his altars, here are his hearths, here are his household gods: here all his sacred rites, all his religious ceremonies are preserved. This is the asylum of every one, so holy a spot that it is impious to drag any one from it. (Cicero, *De domo sua*, 41.109)[4]

Paul is thinking not only of the inviolability of the home, as Cicero is, but also of holiness residing even in individual members of the Christ community, because of their incorporation into that community of baptism. If we look at earlier ideas of the holy and holiness, however, we see that it resides primarily in God, in sacred objects, and in the collective group; individual people are latecomers on the scene.

The original idea of the holy has to do with the mystery of God and human experience of the numinous, of encounter with manifestations of cosmic power beyond any human ability to control or interpret.[5] Places and objects connected to that experience are then understood to be holy,

---

3. Joanna Kenty, "The Political Context of Cicero's Oration *De Domo Sua*," *Ciceroniana Online* (II.2.2018) 245–64, http://www.ojs.unito.it/index.php/COL/index.

4. M. Tullius Cicero, *The Orations of Marcus Tullius Cicero* (trans. C. D. Yonge; London: George Bell & Sons, 1891), http://www.perseus.tufts.edu/hopper/text?doc =Perseus%3Atext%3A1999.02.0020%3Atext%3DDom.%3Achapter%3D1.

5. The attempt to understand ideas of cultic holiness and their interaction with those of "aspirational" holiness is complex. See especially Michael B. Hundley, "Sacred Spaces, Objects, Offerings, and People in the Priestly Texts: A Reappraisal," *JBL* 132 (2013) 749–67; Matan Orion, "Josephus's Seven Purities and the Mishnah's Ten Holinesses," *JSJ* 47 (2016) 183–211; Alan L. Mittleman, ed., *Holiness in Jewish Thought*

that is, filled with divine power and therefore characterized by ambiguity, at the same time both attractive and fearsome, to be approached with caution. The holiness of God can be deadly to the unaware, as it was to Uzzah, who reached out to steady the ark. It seems that the very object, the ark, is so fraught with divine power that it is not to be touched. The event so angers and frightens David that he will not have the ark reside close to him; he wants to keep his distance from it (2 Sam 6:6–11). Similarly, in the midst of divine manifestation to Moses and Aaron, the holy mountain Sinai is not to be touched by the people or even their animals, under penalty of death, even though the people as a nation have been declared priestly and holy and have undergone ritual purification by clothes washing and abstinence from sexual relations (Exod 19:6, 9–24).[6]

In Hebrew, the primary semantic domain of this experience, קדש, in the Bible carries the meaning of place or objects invested with divine power. So, for example, Moses must stop approaching the burning bush out of curiosity and remove his shoes because he stands on holy ground (Exod 3:5).[7] In continuity with this idea, an object is withheld from ordinary use, given over exclusively to God's use, and therefore must be treated with special care. The initiative comes from God, who makes something or someone holy because he or it pertains to the sanctuary or is prepared for its use, for example, the sanctuary and later the temple itself (1 Kgs 9:3; Ps 93:5), the altar and other sanctuary objects (Exod 29:37; 30:26–29); the priest and his clothing (Exod 29:21); animals for sacrifice (Lev 27:32; Jer 12:3); and silver, gold, and bronze spoils of war that will be dedicated to God (2 Sam 8:10–11).

The identification of the holy extends to the Sabbath (Deut 5:12) and, by extension, from the temple to the whole city Jerusalem (Isa 48:2; 52:1; Joel 3:17; Ps 46:5; cf. Matt 4:5; 24:15; 27:53). References to the "holy mountain" can refer back to Mount Sinai, but often to the land of Israel and the city Jerusalem (Isa 66:20; Joel 4:17; Zech 8:3; Ps 2:6; Dan 9:16), and even to other cities (Isa 64:9–10) in the whole "holy land." The people Israel are declared a priestly people and a holy nation (Exod 19:6),

---

(Oxford: Oxford University Press, 2018), especially Elsie R. Stern, "Reclaiming the Priestly Theology," 12–34; and Tzvi Novick, "Holiness in the Rabbinic Period," 35–53.

6. On the whole idea of holiness as danger, see Mary Douglas, *Purity and Danger: An Analysis of the Concepts of Purity and Taboo* (London: Routledge & Kegan Paul, 1966).

7. "In the OT, holiness is a positive cultic or moral condition of God, people, things, places, and time. It may be an inherent condition or achieved through ritual means. It is defined on the one hand as that which is consistent with God and his character, and on the other as that which is threatened by impurity" (David P. Wright, "Holiness [Old Testament]," *ABD* 3:237–48, here 237).

therefore belonging not to themselves, but set apart for God's own use.[8] The firstborn male of the people or their animals is set aside for God's use and must be either redeemed or, in the case of animals, sacrificed (Exod 13:2, 12–15; cf. Luke 2:23). Because the prophet is dedicated in a unique way to the work of God, Elisha is called a "holy man of God" (2 Kgs 4:9; cf. Luke 1:70; Acts 3:21; Mark 6:20 of John the Baptist). Jeremiah has this holy identity from the womb: "Before I formed you in the womb I knew you, and before you were born I consecrated you; I appointed you a prophet to the nations" (Jer 1:5).[9]

A number of times, the people are urged to "be holy, as I am holy," usually in a context of cultic purity with regard to food and access to the sanctuary (e.g., Lev 11:45), but in Leviticus 19, the holiness of the people is related to their treatment of one another in the holy community, with regard to parents, the poor, the handicapped, and others. The holiness of God, mediated to the people, requires a response from them as members of the community.

The holiness of God and those God sends continues in the Gospels. Demons and then Peter recognize Jesus as the holy one of God, therefore carrying God's power (Mark 1:24; Luke 4:34; John 6:69). The prayer that Jesus teaches his disciples attests that God's name is holy, to be respected and served (Matt 6:9; Luke 11:12; cf. Luke 1:49). At the same time, the way is shown toward participation in that holiness of God, toward being holy as God is holy: forgiveness of human transgressions as a condition for being forgiven.

The prayer of Jesus in John 17 continues this understanding of holiness. In vv. 17–19, Jesus first asks the Father to "sanctify" (RSV, NRSV) or "consecrate" (NAB, NJB) (ἁγίασον) the disciples in truth, even as Jesus does the same to himself, filling both the role of the priest who accepts the offering and renders it holy, and of the offering itself. He sets himself apart as dedicated sacrifice. In the same way, the disciples will be consecrated or set

---

8. This idea of the holy nation is later picked up by the author of 1 Peter, used as a motive for living an honorable life (1 Pet 2:5–12).

9. For a full study of the word group, see Wright, "Holiness (Old Testament)"; and Robert Hodgson, "Holiness (New Testament)," *ABD* 3:237–54; Dale Launderville, "Holy/Holiness, Old Testament," and Barbara E. Bowe, "Holy/Holiness, New Testament," in *Collegeville Pastoral Dictionary of Biblical Theology* (ed. Carroll Stuhlmueller; Collegeville, MN: Liturgical Press, 1996) 430–34. Current scholarship on Leviticus distinguishes the P (Priestly) source, found mostly in Leviticus 1–16 and concerned largely with cultic holiness, from an H (Holiness) source, located in Leviticus 17–26, in which cultic holiness is more supplemented by "aspirational" holiness or the covenantal model, in which holiness also resides in the nation and its members and carries a code of moral expectation. See Stern, "Reclaiming the Priestly Theology."

apart in truth, yet not kept from the world but guarded from the evil one (John 17:15).

Let us now return to Paul. The prevalent word group that he uses to express what he understands by the holy is ἅγιος, the Greek equivalent of קדש. In Paul's experience, the primary context of the Hebrew semantic domain of קדש is cultic, though extended widely to embrace not only a geographical center of holiness but the community as well. It has to do with what is consecrated, dedicated, given over for sacred use, and therefore must be treated with special care. The understanding of the holy that Paul uses certainly was not acquired by virtuous behavior. Any close reading of 1 Corinthians indicates that Paul did not think there was much virtue in the Corinthian community! Rather, Paul would start from the other side, not that far from the sentiments of Leviticus 19: *because* you are holy, act accordingly! So we are back to the question: What does he mean when he declares his people, even children of a "mixed marriage," holy?

Because of this identification of the people with the holy, Paul can call his congregations "the holy ones" (οἱ ἅγιοι) over and over again, both those to whom he writes and those who are with him and send greetings. In Rom 1:7, the Roman congregations whom he addresses without ever having met most of them are not only holy but are *called* to be holy. It is their vocation. The community of Jerusalem and even the Corinthians are "the holy ones" (Rom 15:25; 2 Cor 1:1; cf. Acts 3:21). It becomes a common title for the communities in which he works (Rom 8:27; 1 Cor 16:15; 2 Cor 13:12; Phil 1:1; 4:22; cf. Col 3:12; Eph 1:1, 18; 3:18). Paul uses the image of the most sacred place in the Jewish world as a metaphor for the community, the temple of God, which is holy (1 Cor 3:17). He disapproves of Corinthian engagement in lawsuits, since the holy ones (and that is you, he says) will judge the world in the eschatological epoch (1 Cor 6:20). He urges the Roman congregation to present their bodies as a holy living sacrifice, pleasing to God, set apart for God's service (Rom 12:1).

The trouble is that the people of Paul's communities are *not* set aside or withdrawn from human society. These people to whom Paul writes are not in monasteries or ascetic communities. They live daily lives, with family and work concerns. They marry, raise children, and try to make a living. They have dinner parties, accept invitations to dinner, take lawsuits to court, and come up with their own ideas of what Paul preaches. My co-author Margaret MacDonald suggested many years ago in conversation that, in early house churches, people could enter a house for the weekly meeting of the community and trip over the children's toys left in the peristyle, or that participants in the Lord's Supper could be distracted by the cries of a woman giving birth in a back room. These kinds of verbal images may be startling, but real life was going on in these houses, the lives of families.

It has been an active area of research in New Testament studies in recent years to attempt to locate these people of the early urban communities on the grid of what we know of life in Mediterranean cities in the first and second centuries.[10] They are not the urban elites, but they are not the poorest residents either. If we look to ordinary life in places where we do have some access to it, notably Pompeii and Herculaneum, we see modest houses, businesses, public services, and how the residents participated in the life of their city. If we can judge by Pompeii, there was a relatively high rate of basic literacy, since the walls were frequently used to write political endorsements for local elections. Residents were mostly organized into some kind of kinship structure, whether by blood, marriage, or informal relationship. Sometimes whole households worshiped in the same religious tradition, but not always. Households of any size had a simple morning ceremony of devotion to the household gods. Beyond that, there were differences of belief and religious practice within marriages, families, and extended households, including slaves. 1 Corinthians 7, among other sources, gives evidence of that.

We are familiar with popular philosophical ideals of the authoritative father who rules over everyone in his household, reproduced in the so-called household codes of Col 3:18–4:1 and Eph 5:21–6:9. We also see patterns of total household conversion in Acts of the Apostles (the house of Cornelius 10:47–48; the house of the jailer at Philippi 16:33–34). Nevertheless, we know that free women as well as slaves, female or male, could and did make their own choices about religious affiliation. This was a problem only if anyone perceived varying religious practices to be mutually incompatible, as was often the case for Jews and eventually for believers in Jesus.

The anonymous author of the *Epistle to Diognetus* argued that Jesus's followers are just like everyone else, with no particular customs or

---

10. The literature on this subject is vast. For recent introductions, see Joel B. Green and Lee Martin McDonald, eds., *The World of the New Testament: Cultural, Social, and Historical Contexts* (Grand Rapids: Baker Academic, 2017); also Dietmar Neufeld and Richard E. DeMaris, eds., *Understanding the Social World of the New Testament* (London: Routledge, 2010); Carolyn Osiek, "What We Do and Don't Know about Early Christian Families," in *A Companion to Families in the Greek and Roman Worlds* (ed. Beryl Rawson; Blackwell Companions to the Ancient World: Literature and Culture; Oxford: Blackwell, 2011) 198–213.

language. They participate in everything as citizens but also as resident aliens, aware of belonging to another citizenship (*Let. Diogn.* 5.1–10). Shepherd of Hermas takes it further: believers live in a foreign land, and they will be unable to return to their true home if they are too invested in this land (*Sim.* 1 [50]). Christians were like everyone else, yet there was supposed to be a difference. The difference is the idea of being *holy*, that is, "set apart for God's use." Paul expresses this most clearly in Phil 3:20: "Our πολίτευμα[11] is in heaven, and it is from there that we await a savior, the Lord Jesus Christ, who will transform our poor bodies into something like his glorious body."

Paul seems to be saying that believing men and women not only *are* holy but convey holiness into their families, to their spouses and children. It is not that you are holy *if* you act this way. It is not your performance that brings holiness but rather the free gift of God's choice. By accepting it, you are holy; *therefore* act this way. Of course Paul has some very definite ideas of what "this way" is, which he spells out throughout the rest of 1 Corinthians, with regard to compromised food, lawsuits, incest, marriage, correct participation in the Lord's Supper, and correct belief about resurrection. It is not that his people are holy because of what they do or how they behave. They are holy because God has offered them the gift of faith in Christ and they have responded to that divine initiative—more or less. Their presence in their everyday world is supposed to make a difference. Seen this way, problem people and problem beliefs and practices in the community obstruct the flow of holiness to their spouse, their children, and to their world.

How were they to navigate this identity and live normal lives? Gradually, over some years, more questions were raised about public conduct. A glimpse into developing differences in Christian practice, and hence difficulties of such mixed marriages, is revealed more than a century later in Tertullian's appeal against a Christian widow remarrying, and especially marrying a husband who does not share her faith, precisely Paul's concern in 1 Cor 7:39. For example, if she is to keep a *statio* (early morning fast and prayer), he will want her to come at daybreak with him to the baths. On a day of fast, he will hold a banquet. If she is called on for a duty of charity, he will have urgent family business that will require her presence. How will he take her offering hospitality to unknown visiting church members, rising at night to pray, and even going out at night to attend nocturnal vigils and feasts? (*Ux.* 2.4–5)

---

11. "Citizenship" (NAB, NRSV); "homeland" (NJB); "commonwealth" (RSV).

Rather early and often, there are references in Christian and contemporaneous Jewish sources excluding the practice of abortion and abandonment of newborns (*Did.* 2.2; 5.2; *Barn.* 19.5; 20.1–2; Justin, *Apol.* 1.27; *Let. Diogn.* 5.6; Tertullian, *Apol.* 9.6–8; *Nat.* 1.15; Minucius Felix, *Oct.* 30.2; Philo, *Spec.* 3.108–15; Josephus, *Ap.* 2.202; Ps.-Phocylides, *Sent.* 184–85). By the time of Tertullian, questions were raised about attendance at the theater, the games, and participation in military service—not, in the first place, because of the incredible violence, which is what would bring us up short, but because of the compromised religious loyalties necessitated by participation in public sacrifice to gods that would now be idolatry for them (*De spectaculis; De corona militis*).

Why did Tertullian think it necessary to write a treatise arguing against Christian attendance at the games? Josephus had asserted, in his account of Herod building Jerusalem into a Roman city complete with theater and amphitheater, that it was not Jewish custom to participate in these kinds of entertainment (*Ant.* 15.268), but he is speaking of home turf, Jerusalem, not of Jewish residents throughout the rest of the Mediterranean world. Though Tertullian argues against Christian participation, we do not know how effective his argument was; he could have been a lone voice. The games were the major sporting events of the Roman world. We can suppose that there were just as many sports addicts then as there are now.

It is very important to remember that the vast majority of believers in Jesus—and they began to increase exponentially by the end of the second century—continued to live rather normal lives, perhaps occasionally experiencing some difficulties with their unbelieving neighbors over their odd practices and lack of civic enthusiasm, but the Jews had already experienced that for several centuries. The rare years of outright persecution of Christians passed quickly (until 303 C.E.) and were usually confined to certain regions. Nevertheless, they did leave scars in the collective memory, producing the stories that blossomed into the gripping and often highly legendary accounts in the martyrdom literature that followed.

The rise of a cult of martyrs might have been one of the most powerful causes of the shift in understanding what happened in the following centuries of Christian life. Without relinquishing the full awareness that the gift of God is primary, the ideal of heroic struggle on the part of the martyr became an important part of the history. It is notable that even in the earliest martyr accounts, the demonstration of heroism was gender neutral. Some of the most outstanding narratives of endurance under torture feature women, such as Blandina in Lugdunum (*Acts of the Martyrs of Lyon and Vienne*, Eusebius, *Hist. eccl.* 5.1.3–2.8) or Perpetua and Felicitas in Carthage.[12]

The martyrs were those who were able to demonstrate heroic character in the face of terrible death. They became the models for life, even for the majority whose lives were outwardly ordinary. The accounts of their heroism were the impetus for the rise of the cult of saints, and thus of a shift in the idea of holiness. Though it had always been present, admiration for the exemplary success of the few gained momentum. Beyond the time of the martyrs, it has long been argued that the rise of the ascetic movements of the fourth century and the popularity of the stories of the Desert Fathers and Mothers owe their success to the continued search for heroism, no longer in the face of violent death but now in the face of prolonged life.

The extended burial areas in central Italy, Sicily, and Malta that we now know as "catacombs" began as burials on private property, above and below ground, but then extended far underground as space became limited in the original areas. The soft volcanic *tufa* made it easy to expand underground. By the late fourth century, most of the catacombs of Rome had at least one tomb of a martyr and a lively business in pilgrimage to martyrs' tombs. What better place to be buried than as close as possible to the holy one? These favored burial areas grew into what we know today, with many miles of underground corridors and thousands of burials. They enabled the faithful in their confrontation with death to access the holy through proximity to the martyrs.

The cult of relics was also on its way. Pieces broken off from burials or other holy places, gold and silver miniature replicas of shrines, and other objects could be taken home and cherished not only as memories of pilgrimage but as means to retain access to the power of the holy.[13] The idea of holiness, however, was now becoming not so much the transcendent power of God, though that was certainly never denied, but reference to the qualities of character shown by faithful followers of Jesus. By the late fourth century, a strong tradition was evolving in favor of the ascetic

---

12. Current scholarship on the martyr literature casts serious doubts on "authenticity" in the accounts and places more emphasis on their function in forming Christian identity at later periods; see, e.g, Bart D. Ehrman, *Forgery and Counterforgery: The Use of Literary Deceit in Early Christian Polemics* (New York: Oxford University Press, 2013); Candida R. Moss, *The Myth of Persecution: How Early Christians Invented a Story of Martyrdom* (New York: HarperOne, 2013); Éric Rebillard, *The Early Martyr Narratives: Neither Authentic Accounts nor Forgeries* (Divinations; Philadelphia: University of Pennsylvania Press, 2021).

13. See, e.g., Nicola Denzey, *The Bone Gatherers: The Lost Worlds of Early Christian Women* (Boston: Beacon, 2008).

life, and the ascription of holiness to those who embraced it. There is ample evidence in the literature for the idealization of holiness in the developing practice of ascesis and celibacy. Athanasius's *Life of Antony* set the tone, the idealization of the lone figure who battled the demons within and without. The stories of the Desert Fathers and Mothers amplified the tradition. The female champions of virginity and consecrated widowhood, names like Macrina, Paula, and the two Melanias, loom large in the landscape of holiness in the late fourth and early fifth centuries. At the same time, a theologian like Gregory Nazianzen could eulogize his sister Gorgonia and praise his mother Nonna for their virtue as faithful wives; he felt the need to defend his high praise of those with a vocation to marriage in the face of the priority of virginity that was now well established by his time (*Orat.* 8; 18.7–12).

Paul had a vision of holiness as inherent in the identity of the baptized believer in Christ, chosen by him to be part of the ἐκκλησία, the community of believers. In keeping with this vision, which placed the risen Christ at the center of God's action, he located divine holinesss in the persons themselves who made up the ἐκκλησία, not because of their virtue but because of their having been chosen by the free gift of God.

In the introduction to his Apostolic Exhortation *Gaudete et Exsultate* of March 19, 2018, "On the Call to Holiness in Today's World," Pope Francis says:

> My modest goal is to repropose the call to holiness in a practical way for our own time, with all its risks, challenges and opportunities. For the Lord has chosen each one of us "to be holy and blameless before him in love" (Eph 1:4).

Pope Francis then goes on to recall that the holy figures narrated in Hebrews 12 and the martyrs of Rev 6:9–10 are forerunners who encourage and accompany us, as well as the "saints next door" who are part of our daily lives. Yet the ultimate call is that of Christ, but in the words of Lev 11:44; 1 Pet 1:16: "Be holy for I am holy" (§10). The vocation to holiness, steeped in the Scriptures and reaffirmed in the tradition, still challenges us.

Greco-Roman καλοκαγαθός in the Pauline and Pastoral Letters

FERDINAND OKORIE, CMF
Catholic Theological Union
Chicago, Illinois

Professor Leslie Hoppe is passionate about the historical context of biblical narratives. With his teaching and excellent volume *A Guide to the Lands of the Bible*, he has inspired my appreciation for how the ancient world contributes to our understanding of the Bible. This essay is my gratitude for his scholarly contribution on the significance of reading the Bible with attention to the cultures and values of the ancient world that produced it. This essay examines the appeal to the Greco-Roman value of doing what is good and noble, namely, the καλοκαγαθός in the Pauline and Pastoral letters. I will examine how the Greco-Roman virtue of doing noble and good deeds, which is commonly associated with the sociopolitical and economic elites of the Greco-Roman world, is recommended to the auditors of the Pauline and Pastoral letters. My investigation of the presence of this virtue in the Pauline and Pastoral letters will reveal that, unlike the Greco-Roman honorific inscriptions that promise the one who does noble and good deeds rewards from beneficiaries in this world, the Pauline and Pastoral letters place the ultimate reward of a good person in the eschatological age, which is given only by God.

In the cultural world of early Christians, the link between the term τὸ ἀγαθός ("good") and the deed or action of an individual to benefit others has led to the combination of τὸ ἀγαθός with the verb ποιέω ("to do") to form the compound verb ἀγαθοποιέω ("doing good"). This compound verb has a noun form, ἀγαθοποιός ("the doer of good deeds").[1] The combinations of the noun τὸ ἀγαθός with the verb ποιεῖν, and also the adjectival noun τὸ κάλος ("what is noble") and the verb ποιεῖν appear in various forms in the New Testament (see Matt 19:16; Mark 14:7; Luke 6:27; 2 Cor 9:8; Jas 4:17).

Another significant combination involves the nouns τὸ καλός and τὸ ἀγαθός. Walter Grundmann observes that τὸ καλός and τὸ ἀγαθός play such an important role in the Greco-Roman world that both terms began to occur variously "in the form of καλός τε καὶ ἀγαθός, καλός κἀγαθός and καλός τε κἀγαθός, and from which there derives the noun καλοκἀγαθός."[2] This formulation is commonly found in the political, economic, and social discourses of the ancient world. The good and noble person (καλοκἀγαθός) is also a good citizen of the *polis*, who embodies the virtue of nobility that leads to the good of the commonwealth.[3] The term καλοκἀγαθός never appears in this form in the New Testament. However, the cultural meaning that the term evokes in the Greco-Roman world does appear in the Pauline and Pastoral letters as it is enjoined on the members of the Christian community. There is evidence to support the point of view that believers in the communities of Paul and the Pastoral letters possess the resources to support the community, and they receive gratitude from those who depend on their good deeds and generosity for the collective survival of the group. Moreover, the epistles show that every believer is exhorted to aspire to do good deeds worthy of the eternal reward that God gives.

---

1. For instance, in the *De Iside et Osiride*, the deity is celebrated as ὁ γὰρ Ὄσιρις ἀγαθοποιός ("the doer of good deeds"). Egyptians experience the power in the divine name of Osiris as both active and beneficent, the doer of good things (ἐνεργοῦν καὶ ἀγαθοποιόν) (Plutarch, *Is. Os.* 42).

2. Walter Grundmann, ἀγαθός, *TDNT* 1:10–18.

3. The term τὸ ἀγαθός receives an extensive exposition in Plato's discourse on the allegory of the cave in the *Republic*. He concludes that the last thing a person beholds in the intelligible world after exiting the cave is the form of the good (ἡ τοῦ ἀγαθοῦ ἰδέα), which is the origin of all that is right and noble in every human activity in the visible or material world. See Plato, *Resp.* 7.517bc. In addition, Plato insists that the goal of every human activity in private or public life is to do the good. He concludes that doing what is good benefits everyone in the commonwealth (7. 519e–520a). Similarly, in the *Nicomachean Ethics*, Aristotle affirms that the goal of human activity in the *polis* is to do good (see *Eth. nic.* 1.1.1). He further suggests that to strive for the good (τὸ ἀγαθός) of the state is a divine achievement (κάλλιον δὲ καὶ θειότερον ἔθνει καὶ πόλεσιν) and a noble deed (τὸ κάλος) (1.2.8). Ultimately, Aristotle speaks about the disposition to do good in society as the highest virtue of the *polis* (1.5.4–5).

■ I. A PERSON DOING GOOD

The auditors of the Pauline and Pastoral letters know that the noble and good person of the *polis*, the καλοκαγαθός, is also a benefactor. As a benefactor of the *polis*, the καλοκαγαθός does every good deed that brings about human flourishing and its preservation and development in the *polis*. A few examples will help illustrate this point. Menelaos, for instance, provides equipment of war to the people of Athens against Chalkidia and Amphipolis. For doing what is noble and good for the security of Athens —in other words, for being a καλοκαγαθός—the council decrees that Athenians should recognize Menelaos as a good man (ἀνὴρ ἀγαθός) because he has done a good deed for the people of Athens (ὅτι ἀνὴρ ἀγαθός ἐστιν καὶ ποιεῖ ὅτι δύναται[ι ἀγ]αθὸν τὸν δῆμον τὸν Ἀθηναίων).[4] Another example is when the people of Dionysopolis erect an inscription in honor of the priest Akornion. They honor him with a golden crown (χρυσῷ στε[φάλν]ω), and a statue at the agora (ἀνάστασιν ἀνδρι[ά]ντος τόlπον τὸν ἐπιφανέστατον τῆ[ς] ἀγορᾶς) because he belongs to the class of those who distinguish themselves by showing unpretentious interest for the good of the commonweal, serving with merits as the priest of the city's deity when the people were in need of a minister in the temple of their local god.[5] I will proceed to examine how the Greco-Roman cultural value of doing good and noble deeds to benefit others is part of the persuasive arguments of the Pauline and Pastoral letters.

Showing Interest for a Good Purpose (Galatians 4:18)

Biblical scholars have been challenged by the argument of Gal 4:12–20. Ernest De Witt Burton calls it a dropping argument, and James D. G. Dunn insists that Paul's argument here is erratic. Franz Mussner adds that it is an emotional argument with no theological enterprise: "Paulus arbeitet in diesem Abschnitt nicht mehr mit sachlich-theologischen Argumentum, sondern mit ganz persönlichen, die seine starke, innere Bewegung nicht verbergen können." But Hans Dieter Betz notices that this section is "entirely in conformity with Hellenistic style" as Paul offers a string of topoi belonging to friendship.[6] Paul's argument here is couched

---

4. SIG 174.14; Charles Michel, ed., *Recueil d'inscriptions grecques* (Brussels: H. Lamertin, 1900) 96.14.

5. SIG 762.42–45; IGR 662.42–45.

6. Ernest DeWitt Burton, *A Critical and Exegetical Commentary on the Epistle to the Galatians* (ICC; New York: Scribner, 1928) 235; James D. G. Dunn, *The Epistle to the*

in a Greco-Roman friendship system that includes the distinction between a good friend and a flatterer. Paul identifies himself as a friend of the Galatians who is doing what is good for their sake.

Paul remembers his initial encounter with the Galatians (4:12–20), and he identifies himself as one who shows interest in a good way for their benefit (καλὸν δὲ ζηλοῦσθαι ἐν καλῷ, Gal 4:18) unlike his Jewish-Christian opponents, who, as Paul would want us to believe, have no good intention for the benefit of the Galatians (ζηλοῦσιν ὑμᾶς οὐ καλῶς, 4:17). Paul arrives in this community with an illness, yet they did not loathe or despise him (4:13–14). Rather, they treat him as a friend by doing every good deed possible to aid Paul's recovery (4:14b–15). On his part, Paul's good deed to the community is his ministry of proclaiming the gospel message of God's gift of salvation through Jesus Christ. Paul expresses his desire to be present again in the community and continues to do good deeds toward them until they experience the favor of God through faith in Christ's self-gift on the cross (4:20). Elsewhere, Paul identifies his ministry of making Christ known in the gentile world as a partnership of doing good that includes God, the community, and himself (Phil 3:3–6). Paul knows that his good deed to the Galatians is as a result of his faith in the self-gift of Christ on the cross.[7]

Although Paul writes about supporting himself financially, and proudly speaks about his self-sufficiency (Phil 4:11), yet he has been a beneficiary of the generosity of communities like the Philippians (Phil 4:15–20) and the Galatians, who took care of him as they would an angel of God or Christ Jesus (Gal 4:14c). Similarly, Paul has benefited from the kindness of individuals like Phoebe (Rom 16:2) and Prisca and Aquila (Rom 16:3–4). Planning his next ministerial venture to Spain, he anticipates the goodwill of the believers in Rome, whose generosity toward him will raise their honor among other believers (Rom 15:24). In fact, calling people by name in his letters and asking that they be acknowledged for their benefaction to him are forms of honor and a show of gratitude and reciprocity.[8]

Galatians (BNTC; London: A. & C. Black, 1993) 231; Franz Mussner, *Der Galaterbrief* (HThKNT 9; Freiburg im Breisgau: Herder, 1974) 304; Hans Dieter Betz, *Galatians: A Commentary on Paul's Letter to the Churches in Galatia* (Hermeneia; Minneapolis: Fortress, 1979) 221.

7. The scholars who have engaged the current debate on divine and human agency in Galatians suggest that in this letter faith is not passive. There is a relationship between faith and doing good deeds. See Nijay K. Gupta, *Paul and the Language of Faith* (Grand Rapids: Eerdmans, 2020) 153–54.

8. Zeba A. Crook, "Economic Location of Benefactors in Pauline Communities" in *Paul and Economics: A Handbook* (ed. Thomas R. Blanton IV and Raymond Pickett; Minneapolis: Fortress, 2017) 183–204. here 202.

The Good Fight of a Leader (1 Timothy 1:18–19)

This section of the letter is about Timothy's calling and the exhortation he received to lead the community against false teachers. He is exhorted to aspire to nobility in his role as the leader of the community (1:18–20). Timothy's choice as a leader in Ephesus is linked to a prophetic statement uttered about him (1:18b). Prophets might have spoken and confirmed Timothy's ability to lead, which provides evidence for the divine choice of Timothy as the leader of the community. The selection of Timothy as a leader is based not only on his personal relationship with Paul but more on his divine calling to lead the community in Ephesus. Elsewhere in the letter, Timothy is identified as a "man of God" (6:11) "who is in God's service, represents God and speaks in his name."[9] The prophets who confirm Timothy's divine calling also participate in his installation as the leader in Ephesus (1 Tim 4:14; 2 Tim 1:6; see Acts 13:1–3).

Timothy's faith is the foundation of his noble fight (τὴν καλὴν στρατείαν, 1 Tim 1:18) and good conscience (τὴν ἀγαθὴν συνείδησιν, 1 Tim 1:19; see also 1:5).[10] The word συνείδησις ("conscience"), a term popular among the Stoics, means one's awareness of the quality of one's moral actions or the lack thereof (see Rom 2:15; 9:1–2; 2 Cor 1:12). Timothy's ability to fight the noble fight (1 Tim 1:18) defending sound teaching calls for a good conscience (1 Tim 1:19).

Timothy recognizes the appeal made to him to fight a noble fight with a good conscience as couched in the cultural values of the Greco-Roman world. I interpret ἔχων πίστιν ("having faith") as a circumstantial participle that reminds Timothy that his faith demands that he fight the noble fight to protect sound teaching and carry out the activity of faith with a good conscience.[11] The responsibility given to Timothy is reemphasized in the demand that he not relent in fighting the noble fight of faith (ἀγωνίζου τὸν καλὸν ἀγῶνα τῆς πίστεως, 1 Tim 6:12a) because he has made the noble confession/commitment (τὴν καλὴν ὁμολογίαν, 1 Tim 6:12c) to lead the church in Ephesus. In the Greco-Roman world of early Christianity, the invitation to engage in a noble fight is commonly addressed

---

9. J. N. D. Kelly, *A Commentary on the Pastoral Epistles: I Timothy, II Timothy, Titus* (HNTC; Peabody, MA: Hendrickson, 1968) 139.

10. The author of 4 Maccabees recounts the martyrdom of seven brothers under the Seleucid king; one of the seven brothers encourages the others "to fight the sacred and noble fight for religion" (4 Macc 9:24). The NRSV translation of 4 Macc 9:24 is different from the LXX: ἱερὰν καὶ εὐγενῆ στρατείαν στρατεύσασθε περὶ τῆς εὐσεβείας. The NRSV translates εὐγενής as "noble."

11. See George W. Knight III, *The Pastoral Epistles: A Commentary on the Greek Text* (NIGTC; Grand Rapids: Eerdmans, 1992) 109.

to those who commit themselves to do good for the benefit of others, especially the military class.

Paul describes his own noble fight of faith against opponents as boldness in proclaiming the gospel message of Christ (2 Cor 10:1–6) with a weapon that destroys opponents' arguments and fortresses (2 Cor 10:4). According to Paul, the weapon for the battle against opponents' arguments is the power that comes from God (δυνατὰ τῷ θεῷ, 2 Cor 10:4). For Timothy, conversely, his noble (καλός) fight against false teachers and their false teachings is with the power of faith and a good (ἀγαθός) conscience. Elsewhere, Timothy is reminded that encouraging sound teaching in Ephesus will make him a noble servant of Christ (καλὸς ἔσῃ διάκονος Χριστοῦ Ἰησοῦ, 1 Tim 4:6b), whose way of life firmly stands as an example of the teaching (τῆς καλῆς διδασκαλίας) he has been chosen to proclaim and defend (1 Tim 4:6). As in 1 Tim 1:18–19, likewise here in 4:6, it is Timothy's conduct as the leader of the Christian community in Ephesus that is being emphasized.[12] Timothy will recognize his leadership in the community as an invitation to do good deeds to the believers he leads just as Anubion was the benefactor of the devotees of Isis in an inscription that honors his service to the goddess, his leadership, and goodwill toward her devotees.[13]

Show Yourself a Model of Good Deeds (Titus 2:7)

The letter to Titus shares the same concern for good leadership and household management as 1 Timothy. The letter's recommendation for good leadership is consistent with the expectation of being a good citizen of the *polis* in the Greco-Roman world. Titus is reminded of his commitment to do good and noble deeds in his position as a leader of the community, a ministerial disposition he shares with Paul (see 2 Cor 8:21). Titus is exhorted (2:1–10) to remain an example of good works (τύπον καλῶν ἔργων, Titus 2:7) to five different groups of people in the community: older men (2:2), older women (2:3), younger women (2:4-5), younger men (2:6), and slaves (2:9–10). In other words, Titus is expected to lead by example in his role as a teacher of Christian faith and/or in his capacity as a defender of doctrine.

---

12. Martin Dibelius and Hans Conzelmann, *The Pastoral Epistles: A Commentary on the Pastoral Epistles* (trans. Philip Buttolph and Adela Yarbro; Hermeneia; Philadelphia: Fortress, 1972) 68.

13. Philip A. Harland and John S. Kloppenborg, *Greco-Roman Associations: Texts, Translations, and Commentary*, vol. 2: *North Coast of the Black Sea, Asia Minor* (BZNW 204; Berlin: de Gruyter, 2014) 61–62.

It is difficult to discern whether the word διδασκαλία in Titus 2:7 refers to Titus's leadership as a teacher of faith or as a defender of doctrine. Whichever nuance is correct, what is being emphasized is Titus's disposition to do good in his capacity as a leader and/or teacher in the community. His noble deeds toward others are the yardstick with which his leadership is measured and rewarded. In Titus's cultural world, leaders of associations are expected to support the association with their resources, and they receive public honor for their benefaction. For instance, a certain Opramoas becomes a leader of the Lycian league and is recognized for his exceptional generosity, "his various contributions and civic acts, [and his service] as archphylax for the Lycian League . . . displaying complete integrity and enthusiasm in the discharge of every responsibility entrusted to him by Julius Frugi, who was governor." In return for his benefaction and leadership, he is honored among others with a crown of gold, a bronze statue, and a gilded portrait.[14]

Choosing a Noble Task (1 Timothy 3:1 and Titus 1:8)

The exhortation to be a good and noble leader in the Pastoral letters is spoken not only to Timothy and Titus but also to those who aspire to the office of ἐπίσκοπος (literally, "overseer"), a term that will later be translated as "bishop" (1 Tim 3:1–7; Titus 1:5–9). Those appointed to this kind of leadership are from the ranks of the πρεσβύτεροι ("elders," 1 Tim 5:17–22). One who desires (ὀρέγω) to be considered for the office of ἐπίσκοπος aspires (ἐπιθυμέω) to a noble task (καλοῦ ἔργου, 1 Tim 3:1). As the church enters a new phase of organization and choosing qualified leaders, 1 Timothy reminds members seeking to oversee the community that they need to display the kind of nobility expected of leaders and benefactors in the ancient world.

Just as those who occupy positions of authority and power in the Greco-Roman world are expected to be good and responsible managers of the *polis* by doing what is good, they are "lovers of what is good." Likewise, the ἐπίσκοπος is identified as a "lover of what is good" (φιλάγαθος, Titus 1:8). The term φιλάγαθος frequently appears in honorific inscriptions of the Greco-Roman world. Nevertheless, this observation does not go far enough to explain the meaning of the term in the context of Titus and his community.

---

14. I depend on the translation provided in Frederick W. Danker, *Benefactor: Epigraphic Study of a Graeco-Roman and New Testament Semantic Field* (St. Louis: Clayton, 1982) 115.

The "lover of what is good," φιλάγαθος, in the Greco-Roman world is a virtuous person and a benefactor. In the *Histories*, Polybius describes the honor Romans give the one who loves to do good in the society, and also how the honor motivates others to aspire to be persons who love to do good in the *polis*. Polybius recounts the funeral rites and the attendant ceremony given to a person of proven kindness and generosity toward others, a lover of what is good (φιλάγαθος). At the lying-in-state of a good person, at the Forum Romanum, the person's feats of kindness and generosity are remembered, eulogized, and celebrated (*Hist.* 6.53.1). In other words, Polybius suggests that the funeral of one who distinguishes himself as a "lover of what is good" is so recognized at a public ceremony. Just as Marc Antony mounts the rostrum at the Forum to eulogize Julius Caesar, likewise a relative of the deceased mounts the rostrum and speaks "on the virtues and successful achievements of the dead during his lifetime" (Polybius, *Hist.* 6.53.3 [Patton, LCL]). On the basis of the achievements of the deceased φιλάγαθος, the public laments his death as a monumental loss to the people and the nation. After interment, the family of the deceased φιλάγαθος immortalizes him and continues to remember him at public sacrifices with lavish and elaborate ceremonial accoutrements. Polybius insists that the ceremonial remembrance of the deceased should motivate others to aspire to a life of nobility through love of doing what is good to others (Polybius, *Hist.* 6.53.6–10). This is the context in which to read the leadership of a Christian ἐπίσκοπος as a "lover of what is good." As such, the overseer should benefit the community and inspire others by his exemplary leadership.

Overseers emerge from a context where leaders or cultic priests become patrons, supporting and sustaining the associations they lead from their resources. For instance, a certain Hermaios "piously served the Gods as treasurer of our association . . . and has frequently met expenses for such purposes out of his own resources": paying for sacrifices to the gods, paying for the burial costs of members, donating money for repairs, and providing for other needs of the association. On account of his benefaction, Hermaios is honored and crowned with *aretē* and piety.[15]

■ II. A Community of Persons Doing Good

In this section, I will show that the Greco-Roman cultural value of doing noble and good deeds is demanded not only of leaders but of all members

---

15. Danker, *Benefactor*, 152–53.

of the Christian communities of the Pauline and Pastoral letters. In the context of the social status of the population of the early church, it is revolutionary to exhort members of the community to aspire to the virtuous life that is commonly associated with the elite of the ancient world. While some members of the community are freeborn Roman citizens with elite status, others are freed slaves, and another group is mostly slaves. These members of the early church are mostly merchants, traders, and families of men, women, children, and their slaves. The majority of these members live at a subsistence level. In almost all of his letters, Paul explicitly exhorts his auditors to do good deeds to others (1 Thess 5:12–22; Gal 6:9–10; Rom 12:9–22; see Rom 13:3; 1 Cor 10:31; 3 *Cor.* 13:7; Phil 3:14).[16] The passages I will examine show that doing good is an essential part of Paul's gospel message to his communities of mostly gentile Christians (1 Thess 5:12–22; Gal 6:9–10; Rom 2:1–10; 12:9–22).

Do Good Always (1 Thessalonians 5:15, 21)

In the paraenetic section of the letter to the church in Thessalonica (1 Thess 5:12–22), Paul admonishes the Thessalonians not to seek retribution; rather, they should seek to do good to members of the community and to everyone else in society (εἰς ἀλλήλους καὶ εἰς πάντας, 1 Thess 5:15b). In place of doing evil (κακόν, 5:15a), Paul enjoins them with a strong adversative conjunction (ἀλλά) to press ahead instead with doing what is good (ἀλλὰ πάντοτε τὸ ἀγαθὸν διώκετε, 5:15b).

In the midst of the troubling uncertainty surrounding "the day of the Lord" (5:2), Paul exhorts the community to shun idleness, support the weary, encourage those who are weak, be patient with all, and show kindness to members of the community (5:14). In the literary style of comparative exhortation, he asks the community to avoid doing evil to anyone, not even to those who have done them wrong; rather they should do good at all times (5:15). Paul continues to exhort the Thessalonians to hold firmly to doing good (τὸ καλὸν κατέχετε, 5:21b) and abstain from evil (5:22). Paul wants them to know that, by practicing this virtue, they will promote tolerance and limit persecution in society because their lifestyle reflects the highest value of Greco-Roman nobility (1:7–9; 2:14b).

Work for the Good of All (Galatians 6:9–10)

Speaking directly to the Galatians, Paul outlines the demands of the life of faith in Christ for anyone who has been called by God and has received

---

16. Betz, *Galatians*, 275; Stephen Westerholm, *Justification Reconsidered: Rethinking a Pauline Theme* (Grand Rapids: Eerdmans, 2013) 39.

God's gift of the "Spirit of the Son of God" (Gal 5:13–6:10). Paul summarizes what it means to walk and to be guided by the "Spirit of the Son of God" (5:16, 25): it demands a life of loving service to others (5:13c). Paul knows that faith in Christ and the gift of the "Spirit of the Son of God" come to fulfillment when the believer is doing good deeds in the community through love (5:13). When analyzing the relationship between law, faith, and grace in Galatians we must also examine the meaning of Paul's invitation to the believer to do good deeds in the community. Paul insists that this disposition is enabled by the gift of the "Spirit of the Son of God" to one who has come to faith in Christ (see 3:1–5).

In Gal 6:9–10, Paul invites the Galatians to do what is noble (τὸ καλὸν ποιοῦντες, 6:9a), and to do what is good (τὸ ἀγαθὸν ἐργαζώμεθα, 6:10b) to one another. By making this exhortation to the Galatians, Paul shows that a life of faith in Christ and the subsequent gift of the "Spirit of the Son of God" demands that believers do good deeds in the community because that is what the life of faith in Christ demands, the fulfillment of the "fruit of the Spirit" (5:22–23).[17] Each person should test the quality of his or her work (τὸ ἔργον ἑαυτοῦ, 6:4) in the community. Boasting is unnecessary because it is the Spirit that makes possible the disposition to do good deeds to one another.

The fulfillment of the "fruit of the Spirit" in the life of a believer who is doing noble and good deeds involves participation in the collection to benefit the poor in Jerusalem (Gal 2:10; 1 Cor 16:1–4), serving one another through love (Gal 5:13), restoring a transgressor (Gal 6:1), bearing the burdens of one other (Gal 6:2), and, finally, sharing "material benefits with those who teach the gospel message" (Gal 6:6). The Galatians would recognize the value of their cultural world in Paul's gospel message of faith in the self-gift of Christ on the cross.

Keep on Doing Good to Others (Romans 12:9, 17)

This section of Romans contains Paul's exhortation to the community to embrace a lifestyle that gives meaning to their faith in Christ's self-gift on the cross. This paraenetic section must be examined in light of the argument Paul makes about finding righteousness with God through faith in Christ. This is because those who seek to be made righteous by God through faith in Christ must be disposed to do good deeds, such as supporting in any way possible Paul's ministry to Spain (Rom 15:24). Paul urges the community to have high regard in doing what is noble before others (προνοούμενοι καλὰ ἐνώπιον πάντων ἀνθρώπων, Rom 12:17b; see Prov 3:4; 2 Cor 8:21). They are to hold steadfastly to what is good

17. Betz, *Galatians*, 310.

(κολλώμενοι τῷ ἀγαθῷ, Rom 12:9c); their sincere love for one another ought to manifest itself in showing mutual affection (Rom 12:9, 10; 16); and Paul urges them to match their honor for one another with their disposition to show hospitality (Rom 12:13). Paul presents this paraenesis to the community because of his conviction that the experience of faith in Christ demands a lifestyle of doing good deeds.

The long-standing assumption that first-century believers were poor, and that the early church was attractive only to people from the lower levels of the social pyramid of the ancient world, now receives diminishing support, as current research shows that a small but significant number of the members of the early church came from the upper social class of the Greco-Roman world.[18] These believers had resources; they were active benefactors of the early church; and they supported the community's survival from their surplus. The texts examined above reveal that first-century believers were a community of persons capable of doing good deeds. Paul believes that everyone in the community is capable of benefaction no matter their socioeconomic status. This is true with regard to his campaign to collect money from the communities in the provinces of the Greco-Roman world to benefit the poor in Jerusalem. Paul exhorts the community members to become patrons of the believers in Jerusalem by providing suggestions on how even the less economically solvent members of the community can make their contribution worth the honor it will ascribe to them (1 Cor 16:1–4). This is because both Paul and first-century believers know that the willingness to give generously to an association or a guild is not limited to the elites; even the poor and slaves are known to give generously from their limited resources, becoming patrons to others. Consider a first-century inscription from Ephesus that honors an association of fishermen and fish dealers that includes slaves who also contributed to build a toll office close to the harbor. The contributors are ranked from highest to the lowest. Slaves who contributed as little as five denarii are mentioned in the honorary inscription that celebrates their benefaction.[19]

She Is Devoted to Good Deeds (1 Timothy 5:10)

1 Timothy lists as a qualification for widows to receive church support that "she must be well attested for her good works [ἐν ἔργοις καλοῖς

---

18. Wayne A. Meeks, *The First Urban Christians: The Social World of the Apostle Paul* (2nd ed.; New Haven: Yale University Press, 2003) 56–73; Gerd Theissen, *The Social Setting of Pauline Christianity: Essays on Corinth* (trans. John H. Shütz; 1982; repr., Eugene, OR: Wipf & Stock, 2004) 69–119.

19. For this information I depend on Crook, "Economic Location of Benefactors," 199.

μαρτυρουμένη]" and "devoted herself to doing good in every way [ἔργῳ ἀγαθῷ ἐπηκολούθησεν]" (1 Tim 5:10). I interpret the Greek to mean that her life is a testimony of good works and that she is a role model for good deeds in the church.

As a role model for good deeds she belongs to the same group of people who do good and noble deeds to others in the *polis*. There is enough evidence from the Greco-Roman world to support the view that doing good deeds to others is honorable and prestigious, which is publicly celebrated with an inscription to honor the one doing good deeds.

In the cultural world of Timothy, some women had influence in the public life of the *polis*, such as women patrons of cities. As patrons, they were expected to do every good deed in their power for their client-city. These patrons of cities had imperial, senatorial, and equestrian influence because of their birth, family, and social connections. Their client cities trusted in their power to influence a positive outcome for them. The inscriptions erected in their honor to celebrate their good deeds are a testament to their benefaction. Alongside men, women also were rewarded with public honor for their noble deeds toward others, as in the example of Domitia Melpis, who was honored in an inscription found in a bath in Tarquinii alongside her husband Quintas Petronius Melior, who was a senator. In her position as the wife of a senator, Domitia Melpis was able to do good things for her client city, which in the spirit of Greco-Roman ethos of reciprocity honored her in a damaged but delicately preserved marble plaque alongside one honoring her husband.[20] Provincial cities scarcely declined the opportunity to benefit from the prestige, authority, and power of women of imperial, senatorial, and equestrian status. In addition, a community of Judeans in Kyme or Phokaia did not decline the opportunity to benefit from the generosity of a Jewish woman, Tation. She contributed a building for her community out of her resources, for which they reciprocated by honoring her "with a gold crown (the right to occupy) the front seats" in the synagogue.[21]

Elisabeth Schüssler Fiorenza proposes that the author of 1 Timothy was aware of the role such women played in the community but tried to

---

20. "For Domitia Melpis, a woman of senatorial rank, wife of the consular Quintus Petronius Melior, the orde decurionum and citizens of Tarquinia <set this statue> for their most deserving patrona (Domitiae Mepidi c(larissimae) f(eminae)/coniugi Q(uinti) Petro/ni Melioris viri/ co(n)s(ularis), /orod et cives Tarquiniensium/patronae dig/nissimae)." See *CIL* 11.3368. I depend on Emily A. Hemelrijk for this insight. See Emily A. Hemelrijk, "City Patronesses in the Roman Empire," *Historia* 2 (2004) 209–45, here 218–20.

21. Harland and Kloppenborg, *Greco-Roman Associations*, 2:96.

place restrictions on them.²² However, the stories of women doing good and noble deeds for cities or individuals can yet be detected in other sources.

Become Rich in Good Works (1 Timothy 6:18)

In the Greco-Roman world, those who typically do noble and good deeds to others are identified as patrons, benefactors; and they belong to the aristocratic class of imperial, senatorial, and to some degree equestrian families. They are the owners of lands and slaves, and they are the sociopolitical and economic elites. In other words, they are the wealthy class of the Greco-Roman world, and some of them have become members of the Christian community in Ephesus under Timothy's pastoral leadership. It is this group that Timothy is expected to instruct on how they should use their wealth to do good things in the community (1 Tim 6:17–19). The warning on the proper use of wealth in the community concludes in v. 17 with a reminder on the source of wealth. For wealth has a benefactor, namely, God, "who richly provides us with everything for our enjoyment" (v. 17c). Therefore, wealthy members of the community should be benefactors to others just as God is the benefactor of their wealth. They are to do good (ἀγαθοεργεῖν, v. 18a) and be rich in doing noble deeds (πλουτεῖν ἐν ἔργοις καλοῖς, v. 18b). By doing good deeds in the community they accumulate reward for themselves in the future (v. 19). In the Greco-Roman world, those doing good things typically receive reward and gratitude in the present age as I will shortly illustrate.

In the Greco-Roman class system, the elites emerge from and perpetually remain at a level that bestows economic privilege on them. The emperor sits at the top of the patronal pyramid as the benefactor of the entire empire. The message in 1 Tim 6:17 upends this cultural order and hierarchy, at least for the Christian community under the leadership of

---

22. Elisabeth Schüssler Fiorenza, *In Memory of Her: A Feminist Theological Reconstruction of Christian Origins* (New York: Crossroad, 1983) xiv, xvi. See also Joanna Dewey, "1 Timothy," in *Women's Bible Commentary* (3rd ed., Twentieth Anniversary ed.; ed. Carol A. Newsom, Sharon H. Ringe, and Jacqueline E. Lapsley; Louisville: Westminster John Knox, 2012) 595–601, here 600; Linda M. Maloney, "The Pastoral Epistles," in *Searching the Scriptures*, vol. 2: *A Feminist Commentary* (ed. Elisabeth Schüssler Fiorenza; New York: Crossroad, 1997) 361–80, here 371. These feminist scholars show that 1 Timothy redefines the place of widows from a ministerial office exercised by independent, celibate women to a group of women who receive support from the church yet are under male authority (1 Tim 5:3–16). The ministries' widows previously exercised in the church as a testament to their good works and leadership have been turned into a prerequisite for a widow to receive social service from the church.

Timothy, by reminding the wealthy members of the community in Ephesus that God is the source of their wealth. Wealthy Christians like Philemon in Colossae are exemplary in using their resources to benefit the community. In addition to the fact that Philemon has a house large enough to host the church, Paul eulogizes him for his "love of all the saints" (Phlm 5), and for the good he is doing to refresh their hearts (vv. 6–7). Perhaps Paul has benefited from Philemon's generosity as his guest during his previous visits to the region, and once again Paul asks to be hosted during his forthcoming visit (v. 22). The evidence points to the fact that Philemon is a model believer who uses his resources to benefit the community, and, by mentioning his acts of benefaction in the letter, Paul publicly recognizes him. Wealthy members of the early church like Philemon know that honor is bestowed on the members of an association who do good and noble deeds to benefit the guild. For instance, a league of artists dedicated to the god Dionysus honored one of their own, Kraton, because he demonstrated his generosity and benefaction by "proving responsible for some good thing" for the guide.[23]

While the author of 1 Tim 6:17–19 exhorts only the wealthy members of the community to do good deeds, the author of Titus tells all in the Christian community to be disposed toward doing good deeds (πρὸς πᾶν ἔργον ἀγαθὸν ἑτοίμους εἶναι, Titus 3:1c). Titus reminds them how they became believers (3:1–7), and that their faith requires them to devote themselves to doing good works (καλῶν ἔργων προΐστασθαι, 3:8b; see also 3:14) because it is good and beneficial to others (ἐστιν καλὰ καὶ ὠφέλιμα τοῖς ἀνθρώποις, 3:8c). They are to slander no one, but to live in peace with everyone; they are to be kind and to demonstrate the virtuous life of the *polis*, which includes placing others' well-being above that of oneself through humility (3:2).

■ III. Rewarding a Noble and Good Person

In the Greco-Roman world, the one doing good and noble deeds usually receives gratitude from those who benefit from his or her benefaction—individuals, groups, communities, or society. The good person is recognized at games or with honorific inscriptions etched in public places, in the Capitol in Rome, and at temples and shrines in the provinces, as some of the examples I have drawn from the Greco-Roman world show. In the Pauline and Pastoral letters, the believer who is committed to doing good

---

23. Danker, *Benefactor*, 167–69.

and noble deeds receives recognition and commendation just like those whom Paul mentioned in his letters who supported his ministry. Be that as it may, the overarching evidence, on the basis of what we know from the Pauline and Pastoral letters, reveals that Paul exhorts believers that their acts of goodwill and nobility toward others will receive a heavenly reward, given by God. For instance, in his autobiographical note, Paul speaks about his noble duty of preaching the gospel of Christ (Phil 1:13, 20b) and the far better reward of being with Christ that awaits him (1:23). Paul is more explicit in Corinthians when speaking about sharing in the blessings that accrue to him for his noble work of preaching the gospel (1 Cor 9:19–23). In a comparative analogy of the honor the runner at the Olympian games receives, Paul refers to the honor believers receive that is imperishable, the heavenly recognition by God (1 Cor 9:24–26).

The Reward at Harvest Time (Galatians 6:7–10)

When Paul exhorts the Galatians to do noble and good deeds to one another, he warns them not to be deceived into thinking that their good deeds lack any eschatological value (Gal 6:7–10). How will a believer reach eternal life? Paul's response is emphatic. It is by faith in the self-gift of Christ on the cross, which leads to the gift of the "Spirit of the Son of God" and the consequent disposition of the believer to harvest the "fruit of the Spirit" by doing what is good.[24] The community should take the opportunity to do good at all times because in due season they will reap the reward of eternal life (6:8–9). Paul reintroduces here the antithesis of flesh and spirit (3:2–3; 4:29; 5:16–24). Sowing in the flesh means giving an opportunity to the desires of the flesh, which yields no reward. But sowing in the spirit (6:8) means harvesting the "fruit of the Spirit" through the believer's good deeds in the community since he or she is being enabled by the "Spirit of the Son of God" (5:25) to do so.[25] By appealing to the agricultural language of sowing and reaping, Paul illustrates how doing good to others leads to a reward of eternal life.

Similarly, Timothy is reminded of the reward that awaits him as the benefactor and leader of the community. His good deeds guarantee eternal reward (1 Tim 6:12). In addition, the wealthy members of the community led by Timothy are encouraged to look beyond the earthly honor

---

24. See Betz, *Galatians*, 310.
25. John M. G. Barclay observes that "the one who 'sows in the Spirit' is the one who will 'reap eternal life' (6:8): already in the present, though most fully at the eschaton, there will be a 'fit' between the gift and the quality of the life evidenced by those who have received it (cf. 1 Thess 3:13)." See Barclay, *Paul and the Gift* (Grand Rapids: Eerdmans, 2015) 440–41.

that the Greco-Roman καλοκαγαθός receives; rather, they should look forward to the reward of "life that is the true life" (1 Tim 6:19b). Their good deeds in the community prepare them for "that life that is true life" that only God will give, eternal life. Furthermore, the author of 2 Timothy describes his life of nobility and good deeds in proclaiming the gospel as a "good fight," finishing the race, keeping the faith thereby identifying himself as a reliable patron of the community and as a dedicated believer in Christ (2 Tim 4:7). He identifies his heavenly honor as a "crown of righteousness," which every good and noble believer will also receive from the Lord (4:8).

Eternal Life for Everyone Doing Good (Romans 2:7, 10)

In Romans, Paul paints an image of God sitting in judgment and adjudicating eternal reward for everyone doing good deeds or eternal damnation for everyone who does evil, whether Jew or gentile (Rom 2:2–8). For eternal damnation, Paul claims that Jews will be punished first and gentiles next (2:9); and, for those who do good (τῷ ἐργαζομένῳ τὸ ἀγαθόν), glory, honor, and peace will be their reward, Jews first and gentiles next (2:7, 10). What is the criterion in Romans for eternal life? Jews and gentiles find righteousness before God only through faith in Christ.[26] But Paul also suggests that finding righteousness before God through faith in Christ requires that the believer live a life of doing good deeds in the community.[27]

The reward for doing good (Rom 2:7) and the exhortation to do good (12:9–22) must be seen to belong to Paul's understanding of the human capacity to do good through the gift of the Spirit, a disposition that is made possible by the believer's faith in Christ (Rom 8:4; Gal 5:25).

In the Greco-Roman world, those who do noble and good deeds receive a public display of gratitude in the form of honorific inscriptions. The Pauline and Pastoral letters ensure eschatological reward for those who do good deeds in the community. The reward for the καλοκαγαθός in the Christian community comes at the end of time, at the inauguration of the reign of God, eternal life that is given only by God.

■ IV. CONCLUSION

The Pauline and Pastoral letters reflect Greco-Roman values as part of the early church's gospel message of Christ, including the virtue of doing

---

26. Westerholm, *Justification Reconsidered*, 9.
27. Barclay observes that eternal life for Paul includes "the completion of a life of good work (2:6–7)" (*Paul and the Gift*, 466).

good and performing noble deeds in the community. Paul's ministry and self-identity as a "servant of Christ" (Gal 1:10) are a testament that his life of faith in Christ includes a lifestyle of doing good. Paul reveals that his good deeds for the sake of the gospel are motivated by his desire to share in its blessings (1 Cor 9:23). Likewise, Timothy and Titus are encouraged to be models of church leadership by doing good and noble deeds to others.

The most important development in the Pauline and Pastoral letters is the invitation to the Christian community of mostly artisans, peasants, and slaves to attain to the virtuous life of a καλοκαγαθός, something that is exclusively associated with the privileged class of the Greco-Roman world. Another feature in these letters that is worthy of note is that, in place of being immortalized in this impermanent world through the reciprocal acts of gratitude in the honorific inscriptions, and so on, the Christian communities are encouraged to aspire to the reward of eternal life in the kingdom of God for their good and noble deeds. In his teaching and service to the church, Professor Leslie Hoppe, OFM, is an exemplary καλοκαγαθός.

The Answer Lies Beneath

BARBARA E. REID, O.P.
Catholic Theological Union
Chicago, Illinois

When I travel with Leslie to the Middle East as part of the Biblical Lands Study and Travel Program of Catholic Theological Union, it is evident that he loves archaeology, having participated in several digs in the region. Archaeology is a primary component for Leslie's study and understanding of the Scriptures.[1] His guideline to archaeological study is "the answer lies beneath." Students heard this phrase many times as Leslie guided them through the Israeli National Archaeological Parks.

As Leslie has advocated, archaeology is an invaluable tool leading to mining the meaning of the biblical text. The aim, however, is not to prove the veracity of biblical stories, however much some biblical archaeologists and fundamentalist believers would like. The goal, as Leslie says, is:

> ... to recreate the world of the Bible using the material remains left by the people of that world. This assumes that the Bible is the product of real people who lived at a real time, had certain values, political, economic and social structures. It also assumes that the more we know about these people, the more we can know about the literature that they produced.[2]

Leslie remains passionately interested in the ways that science and technology have revolutionized the study of ancient remains. Those of us who have benefited from his many years of teaching us to look for the answers that lie beneath, say with deep gratitude *ad multos annos*!

---

1. His book *What Are They Saying about Biblical Archaeology* (New York: Paulist, 1984) is a particularly helpful introduction to newcomers to the field.
2. Leslie J. Hoppe, *A Guide to the Lands of the Bible* (Collegeville, MN: Liturgical Press, 1999) 15.

Publications by Leslie J. Hoppe, OFM: A Partial List

- **BOOKS**

The Rise and Fall of the Israelite Kingdoms. New York: Paulist, 2021.

Zechariah, with Malka Zeiger Simkovich. WCS 40. Collegeville, MN: Liturgical Press. Forthcoming.

Anselm Academic Study Bible. New American Bible Rev. ed. Winona, MN: Anselm Academic, 2013: Associate Editor, Old Testament.

Isaiah. New Collegeville Bible Commentary 13. Collegeville, MN: Liturgical Press, 2012.

Priests, Prophets and Sages: Catholic Perspectives on the Old Testament. Cincinnati, OH: St. Anthony Messenger Press, 2006.

New Light from Old Stories: Hebrew Scriptures for Today's World. New York: Paulist, 2005.

There Shall Be No Poor among You: Poverty in the Bible. Rev. ed. Nashville: Abingdon, 2004.

The Holy City: Jerusalem in the Theology of the Old Testament. Collegeville, MN: Liturgical Press, 2000.

A Retreat with Matthew: Going beyond the Law. Cincinnati, OH: St. Anthony Messenger Press, 2000.

A Guide to the Lands of the Bible. Collegeville, MN: Liturgical Press, 1999.

Preaching from the Scriptures: New Directions for Preparing Preachers, with Barbara E. Reid. Pulaski, WI: Assumption BVM Province Franciscan Publishing, 1998.

The Lands of the Bible: A Guidebook for the Israel Study Program of Catholic Theological Union. Collegeville, MN: Liturgical Press, 1995.

The Churches and Synagogues of Ancient Palestine. Collegeville, MN: Liturgical Press, 1993.

A New Heart: A Commentary on the Book of Ezekiel, co-authored with Bruce Vawter. International Theological Commentary. Grand Rapids: Eerdmans, 1991.

Today's Immigrants and Refugees: A Christian Understanding. Washington, DC: United States Catholic Conference, 1988.

Deuteronomy. Collegeville Bible Commentary 6. Collegeville, MN: Liturgical Press, 1985.

What Are They Saying about Biblical Archaeology? New York: Paulist, 1984.

Joshua, Judges: With an Excursus on Charismatic Leadership in Israel. Old Testament Message 5. Wilmington, DE: Michael Glazier, 1982.

■ Articles and Essays

"The Biblical Landscape," a regular feature on biblical archaeology in *The Bible Today*.

"Biblical Geography." In *The Jerome Biblical Commentary for the Twenty-First Century*, ed. John J. Collins et al., fully revised ed., 1–30. London: Bloomsbury T&T Clark, 2022.

"The History of the Biblical Period I." In *The Paulist Biblical Commentary*, ed. José Enrique Aguilar Chiu et al., 1622–24. New York: Paulist, 2018.

"The Strategy of the Deuteronomistic History: A Proposal." *CBQ* 79 (2017) 1–19.

"A Place for Prayer: Solomon's Prayer at the Dedication of the Temple (2 Kgs 8)." In *Prayer in the Catholic Tradition: A Handbook of Practical Approaches*, ed. Robert J. Wicks, 467–78. Cincinnati, OH: Franciscan Media, 2016.

"The Deuteronomistic History: Joshua, Judges, Ruth, 1 & 2 Samuel, 1 & 2 Kings." In *The Catholic Study Bible*, 3rd ed., 179–228. New York: Oxford University Press, 2016.

"Historicity, Truth, and Inspiration: The Stories of Israel's Origins." *TBT* 54.6 (2016) 383–88.

"Biblical Archaeology: Its Past and Future." *Chicago Studies* 51.3 (2012) 263–75.

"'What House Can You Build for Me?': Prophetic Opposition to the Priestly Restoration Program." *TBT* 50.5 (2012) 293–97.

"The Word of God in the Torah." *TBT* 46.5 (2008) 281–86.

"Israel and Egypt: Relationships and Memory." *TBT* 45.4 (2007) 209–13.

"The Afterlife of a Text: The Case of 1 Kings 8." *Liber Annuus* 51 (2001) 9–30.

"History of Israel in the Monarchic Period." In *The Blackwell Companion to the Bible*, ed. Leo G. Perdue. Oxford: Blackwell, 2001.

"Vengeance and Forgiveness: The Two Faces of Psalm 79." In *Imagery and Imagination in Biblical Literature: Essays in Honor of Aloysius Fitzgerald, F.S.C.*, ed. Lawrence Boadt and Mark S. Smith, 1–22. CBQMS 32. Washington, DC: Catholic Biblical Association, 2001.

"Biblical Interpretation in Ancient Israel." *BR* 35 (1990) 37–43.

"The Death of Josiah and the Meaning of Deuteronomy." *Liber Annuus* 48 (1998) 31–47.

"A Response to Robert Hubbard's 'The Eyes Have It.'" *Ex Auditu* 13 (1997) 73–75.

"A Refuge for the Poor." *TBT* 35 (1997) 210–15.

"Fundamentalism." In *Dictionary of Mission: Theology, History, Perspectives*, ed. Karl Müller et al., 167–71. Eugene, OR: Wipf & Stock, 1997.

"St. Jerome: The Bible Translator." *St. Anthony Messenger*, September, 1997, https://www.franciscanmedia.org/saint-jerome-the-bible-translator/

"Archaeology and Biblical Interpretation," "Biblical Theology," and several other articles in *The Collegeville Pastoral Dictionary of Biblical Theology*, ed. Carroll Stuhlmueller, xxxix–xl , li–lv. Collegeville, MN: Liturgical Press, 1996.

"Israel, History of (Monarchic Period). In *The Anchor Bible Dictionary*, ed. David Noel Freedman, 6 vols., 3:565–76. New York: Doubleday, 1992.

"Deuteronomy on Political Power." *TBT* (1988) 261–66.

"Community and Justice." In *Economic Justice: CTU's Pastoral Commentary on the Bishop's Pastoral Letter on the Economy*, ed. Donald Senior and John Pawlikowski, 11–17. Washington, DC: Pastoral Press, 1988.

"Deuteronomy and the Poor." *TBT* 24.4 (1986) 371–75.

"Jerusalem in the Deuteronomistic History." In *Das Deuteronomium: Entstehung, Gestalt und Botschaft*, ed. Norbert Lohfink, 107–10. BETL 68. Leuven: Peeters, 1985.

"Religion and Politics: Paradigms from Early Judaism." In *Biblical and Theological Reflections on the Challenge of Peace*, ed. Donald Senior and John Pawlikowski, 45–54. Wilmington, DE: Michael Glazier,1984.

"Isaiah 58:1–12: Fasting and Idolatry." *BTB* 13.2 (1983) 44–47.

"The Levitical Origins of Deuteronomy Reconsidered." *BR* 28 (1983) 27–38.

"The Elders and Deuteronomy: A Proposal." *Église et Theologie* 14.3 (1983) 259–72.

"The Meaning of Deuteronomy." *BTB* 10.3 (1980) 111–17.

"Biblical Wisdom: A Theology of Creation." *Listening* 14.3 (1979) 196–203.

■ Electronic Publications

The Book of Isaiah: The Fifth Gospel (NowYouKnow Media, 2016); learn25.com
Jerusalem: The Holy City (NowYouKnow Media, 2015); learn25.com
Biblical Archaeology (NowYouKnow Media); learn25.com
"Caesarea Maritima." In *Oxford Bibliographies,* http://www.oxfordbibliographies.com/view/document/obo-9780195393361/obo-9780195393361-0008.xml

Index of Ancient Sources

HEBREW BIBLE/ OLD TESTAMENT
Gen 1:1–Lev 16:34   150

Genesis
1:1–2:4a	16
1	20–21
1:16	18
1:20	20
1:22	20
1:24	20
1:26–30	20
1:27–28	16
1:26–28	3, 15
1:26, 28	18
1:28	17, 20
2:7	11
2:24	31
3	16
3:5	16
4:15	182 n. 16
4:24	182
10:17	29
12:6, 7	38
14:13	91 n. 3
15:13–16	119
15:13	82, 118
16:6	30
16:11	117–18, 120
17:7	150
18:1–5	193
22:24	100 n. 31
24:35	193
24:58	42
26:1, 8	99 n. 25
27:35	34 n. 44
27:46	28
29:25	34 n. 44
29:32	118, 120
31:42	120
31:50	30
33	28
33:17	28
33:18–19	28, 29
34	3–4, 25–44
34:1–12	28–34
34:2	35 n. 46
34:13–29	34–36
34:30–31	37
35	28
35:5	37, 43
37–50	71 n. 31
38	4, 45–59, 61, 70–73, 75–76
38:1	70
38:5	71
38:12–14	66 n. 16
38:12	71
38:14	71
38:16	49
38:21	71
38:22	71
39:14, 17	91
40:15	91
41:12	91
41:52	117, 120
43:32	91
46:15	37
48:22	42
49:5–7	36, 42

Exodus
1:12	118–19
1:15, 16, 19, 22	91
2:6, 7, 11, 13	91
3:5	222
3:11	101 n. 36
3:18	91
5:3	91
7:16	91
9:1, 13	91
10:3	91
12:40–41	82
12:43–49	34
13:2, 12–15	223
15:20	36 n. 49
15:26	87 n. 34
17:8–12	99 n. 28
19:6	44, 222
19:9–24	222
20:1–17	147
20:7	145, 147
20:22–23:33	146
21:2	91 n. 3, 108
22:15–16	35
23:23	29
29:21	222
29:37	222
30:26–29	222
38:8	116

Leviticus
1–16	223 n. 9
11:44	229
11:45	223
16	182 n. 16
17–26	151, 223 n. 9

18:21	41	16:1–17	148 n. 23	15:15	88		
19	223–24	16:18–18:5	148 n. 23	15:35	71		
19:29	45 n. 1	17:14–20	148–49	15:44	71		
20:2	149	19:2–13	148 n. 23	15:57	71		
20:27	149	19:15–21:23	148 n. 23	19:43	66 n. 16		
24:10–23	143	19:15	176	23:14–24	84		
24:11	143, 152	20:17	29	24:24	38		
24:13–16	152	21:10–13	30				
24:14, 16, 23	149	21:21	149	Judges	4–5		
24:15–16	147	22:1–12	148 n. 23	1:1–36	80		
25:10	160	22:13–29	148 n. 23	1:7–8	81		
26:18	182 n. 16	22:28–29	35, 37 n. 50	1:10	88		
26:40–45	143–44, 151	23:4	35 n. 47	1:11	88		
27:32	222	23:16–26	148 n. 23	1:17	88 n. 40		
		23:18	45 n. 1	1:21	81, 88		
Numbers		24:1–4	148 n. 23	1:22–23	81		
11:12	193 n. 23	24:6–25:4	148 n. 23	1:23	88		
15:35–36	149	24:16	148	1:26	88		
15:38	48	25:5–10	148 n. 23	1:34	81 n. 11		
31:25–26	156	25:11–12	148 n. 23	2:1–5	83, 88 n. 40		
32:13	82 n. 15	26:2–13	148 n. 23	2:10	84 n. 23		
32:22	17	26:5–9	118	2:11–16:31	81, 85		
		26:6–8	120	2:11–23	83–84		
Deuteronomy		26:6–7	118–19	2:11–19	83		
1–3	149	26:7	117	2:11–12	83 n. 22		
1:3	82 n. 15	26:10	118	2:11	84		
5:6–21	147	26:20–44	148 n. 23	2:12–15	83–84		
5:11	145, 147	27:1–8	144	2:13	84		
5:12	222	28	146, 162	2:14–16	83 n. 22		
6:4–5	146	28:25	159, 160 n. 26	2:18–19	83 n. 22		
6:4	141, 148 n. 23	28:36	159	2:18	85		
6:10–19	148	28:50	189 n. 15	3–12	62		
6:13	145	29–30	149	3	80		
6:17	147	29:12	84	3:7–11a	79–80		
7:1–6	39	29:13	84	3:8	81, 83		
7:1–5	38–39	29:19–27	83–84	3:9–11	79		
7:1–4	35 n. 47	30	160–61	3:11b–30	79–80		
7:3	29, 33	30:4–5	159	3:11	81, 85		
11:29–32	144	30:4	158 n. 20, 160–61	3:12–30	79		
12:1–4	144	31:16–29	83–84 n. 22	3:12	83		
12:8	87			3:14	81		
12:13–27	148 n. 23	Joshua		3:29	88		
13	145–46	2	46 n. 1	3:30	81, 85		
13:2–12	148 n. 23	5:6	82 n. 15	3:31	79–80		
14:22–15:23	148 n. 23	14:10	82 n. 15	4–12	80		
15:4	188, 198	14:15	88	4–5	79–80		
15:12	91 n. 3, 108	15:10	71 n. 29	4:2	83		

254 Index of Ancient Sources

Judges (cont.)					
4:3	81	14–16	63–64, 70, 75–76	17:7–9	80
4:4	88	14–15	61, 63, 65–66, 68, 72–73	18:1	87–88
4:5	81			18:2	81 n. 11
5:6	79–80	14	67–68	18:3	80
5:14–18	79	14:1–5	64	18:11–12	80
5:17	79, 81 n. 11	14:1–4	66–67	18:12	80, 88
5:31	81, 85	14:4	88	18:15	80
6–9	79–80	14:5–6	64	18:16	81 n. 11
6:1–6	83–84	14:5, 7	66	18:22–23	81 n. 11
6:1	81	14:10	66	18:25–26	81 n. 11
6:7–10	83	14:11–19	65 n. 13	18:30	81 n. 11, 89
6:24	88	14:11	67	18:31	81 n. 11, 88 n. 40
6:32	88 n. 40	14:15	65, 67–69	19:1–2	80
7:25	88 n. 40	14:16	67	19:1	87–88
8:27b	87	14:17	65, 69	19:10	81
8:28	81, 85	14:19	64	19:18	80
8:29	81	15	65, 68	19:30	88
9:22	81	15:1	67	20:1	81
10:1–3	79–80	15:4–6	68	20:4	80
10:1	79	15:4–5	64, 68	20:18	80–81
10:2	81	15:6	65 n. 13, 67	20:26	81
10:3–5	79–80	15:8	64	20:27–28	88
10:3	81	15:9–13	80	20:31	81
10:4	88	15:9	88 n. 40	21:2	81
10:6–16	83–85	15:10	66 n. 16	21:12	81 n. 11
10:6	84	15:13	65	21:14	88
10:7–12:7	79–80	15:14	64	21:19	81
10:8	81	15:15	64	21:21	81 n. 11
10:10	84	15:16–17	88 n. 40	21:25	87–88
10:17–11:11	85	15:19	88		
11:1–12:6	79	15:20	64, 81	Ruth	
11:34–40	89	15:57	66 n. 16	4:16	193 n. 23
12:6	88	16	61, 63, 65, 68	4:18–22	46 n. 2, 48
12:7	81	16:1–3	65		
12:8–10	79–80	16:3	80	1 Samuel	5
12:9	81	16:4–22	65 n. 13	1:11	117
12:11–12	79–80	16:4	68	2:22	116
12:11	79, 81	16:5	65, 69	3:1	88
12:13–15	79–80	16:11–12	65	4–6	102, 107
12:14	81	16:16	65, 69, 85 n. 26	4:3	107
13–16	4, 62, 64, 79–80	16:19	69	4:4	107
13	64	16:21	70	4:5	107
13:1, 2, 5, 25	64	16:31	64, 80–81	4:6	91–92, 95, 101–2, 106–7
13:1	81, 83	17–21	62, 87–88		
13:24	80	17:6	87–88	4:9	91–92, 95, 101–2, 106
13:25	80 n. 10	17:7–13	80		

4:11, 13, 17, 18, 21, 22	107	29:3	91–92, 95, 99–102, 106	18:1	100 n. 31
5:1, 2	107			27:16	100 n. 31
5:3, 4	107	29:4–5	101		
5:7	102	29:6–7	99	2 Chronicles	
5:8	99 n. 29, 102	30:17	96	28:18	66 n. 16
5:9	107	31	96	29:8	160 n. 26
5:10	102, 107				
5:11	99 n. 29, 102	2 Samuel		Ezra	
6:2	102–3, 106	3:3	100 n. 31	1:11	153 n. 3, 157 n. 14, 157 n. 15
6:3	102–3	5:17–25	108		
6:4	99 n. 29, 102–3	6:6–11	222	2:1	153 n. 3, 157 n. 14, 157 n. 15
6:5	102–3	7:11	87		
6:8	103	7:14	17 n. 20	4:1	153 n. 3, 157 n. 15
6:11, 15, 17	107	8:10–11	222	6:19–21	153 n. 3, 157 n. 15
7:4	84	12:3	193 n. 23		
8:7b	16 n. 19	13	71	6:21	32
9:9	88	13:14	29–30	8:35	153 n. 3, 157 n. 15
10:5	98	18:3	99 n. 28	9	39
10:7	99 n. 28			9:1–2	39
11:1	99 n. 28	1 Kings		9:4	153 n. 3, 157 n. 14, 157 n. 15
12:10	84	2:29	189 n. 15		
13–14	94, 109	2:39–40	100 n. 31	10:6–8	153 n. 3, 157 n. 15
13:3	91–94, 98, 100, 106	2:39	99	10:6	157 n. 14
		3:16–28	46 n. 1	10:16	153 n. 3, 157 n. 14, 157 n. 15
13:5	94	6:1	82		
13:6	93–95	9:3	222		
13:7	91–94, 106	11:33, 38	87 n. 34	Nehemiah	
13:19–23	96	14:8	87 n. 34	1:8–9	160 n. 29
13:19	91–92, 95–96, 101–2, 106	15:2	100 n. 31	1:9	158 n. 20, 160
		17:19	193 n. 23	7:6	153 n. 3, 157 n. 14, 157 n. 15
13:20	95	18:18	84		
13:23	98	22:30	99 n. 28	9:27–31	83
14:11	91–92, 95, 101–2			13:8	39
14:21	91–92, 94, 100–101, 106	2 Kings			
		2:39	100 n. 31	Esther	
14:22	94	4:9	223	7:8	17
18:27	96	10:30	87 n. 34		
19:8	96	13:3–6	84	Job	
21:11, 13	99	23:22	87	7:1	116, 117 n. 30
22:2	105–6	24:14–16	153 n. 3, 157 n. 15	10:17	116 n. 24, 117 n. 30
25:13	96			14:14	116, 117 n. 30
27:2	99	24:17	140		
27:8–12	101 n. 36			Psalms	
27:12	99	1 Chronicles		2:6	222
28	101, 106	2:3–15	46 n. 2, 48	8	20–21
29	109	11:43	100 n. 31	8:5–8	18
29:2	99	17:10	87	9:14	117

Index of Ancient Sources

Psalms (*cont.*)
17:4–5   194 n. 26
24:1   193
25[24]:18   117
31[30]:8   117
33:13–14   11
34:1   100 n. 31
46:5   222
51:1   194
78   80
78:60   89
80:1   11
84:4   160 n. 27
93:5   222
99:1   11
103:1–2   1
106:34–46   83–84
107:39   120
110:2   48
119[118]:50, 92, 152   117
123:1   11
146:2   164 n. 37
147   160–61
147:2   158 n. 20, 161

Proverbs
1–9   67 n. 19
3:4   239
7:13   189 n. 15
21:29   189 n. 15
23:27   45 n. 1
24:16   182 n. 16
25:13   189 n. 15
26:2   160 n. 27
30:16   120

Ecclesiastes
8:1   189 n. 15

Song of Songs
7:6   69 n. 23

Isaiah
2:1–5   44
8–23   113
8:22–9:1   173
22:15–25   175
25:6–8   190 n. 18
40   111–24
40:1–2   116, 121
40:2   5, 115–24
40:26   116
41:16   163 n. 34
42:1–4   161 n. 32, 173
44:6   116
45:12   116
45:13   116
47:4   116
48:2   116, 222
49:1–6   161 n. 32
49:5–6   121
49:6   161–62
50:4–9   121, 161 n. 32
51:15   116
52:1   222
52:9   121
52:13–53:12   161 n. 32
53:5, 6   121
53:8   5, 115, 119–22, 124
53:11   121
54:5   116
54:7–10   151
56:11   189 n. 15
61:1   160 n. 27
64:9–10   222
66:20   222

Jeremiah
1:5   223
7:12   89
8:5   189 n. 15
12:3   222
13:9   157 n. 14
15:1–4   162
15:4   160 n. 26
15:7   162
22:24   48
24:9   160 n. 26
27:2–15   143
28:6   153 n. 3, 157 n. 15
29:1   153 n. 3, 157 n. 15
29:4   153 n. 3, 157 n. 15
29:16   153 n. 3, 157 n. 15
29:18   160 n. 26
29:20   153 n. 3, 157 n. 15
29:31   153 n. 3, 157 n. 15
30:19   157 n. 14
31:7   157 n. 14
34:8   160 n. 27
34:9   91 n. 3, 108
34:14   91 n. 3
34:15   87 n. 34, 160 n. 27
34:17   159–60
35:4, 6   157 n. 14
36:1, 4, 22, 31   157 n. 14
37:3   157 n. 14
39:44   157 n. 14
40:4–5   87 n. 34
40:7, 11   157 n. 14
46:19   153 n. 3, 157 n. 15
47:11   157 n. 14
48:7   153 n. 3, 157 n. 15
48:11   153 n. 3, 157 n. 15
49:3   153 n. 3, 157 n. 15
51:36–44   134

Lamentations
2:12   193 n. 23

Ezekiel
1:1   153 n. 3, 157 n. 15
3:11   153 n. 3, 157 n. 15
3:15   153 n. 3
4:5–6   82
10:3–4   150
10:18–19   150
11:16   150
11:22–23   150
11:24–25   153 n. 3, 157 n. 15
12:3–4   153 n. 3, 157 n. 15
12:7   153 n. 3, 157 n. 15
12:11   153 n. 3, 157 n. 15
16   140, 143, 148–50
16:8–14   148
16:8   150
16:15–43   6, 140–41
16:15–29   141
16:21   148
16:22, 43   143

Index of Ancient Sources   257

16:23–29	148	37:1–14	163 n. 35	Sirach	
16:37	149	43:4–5	150	7:15	116, 117 n. 30
16:38	149	46:17	160 n. 27	19:2	45 n. 1
16:59–63	150–51			23:6	189 n. 15
16:59	143, 149	Daniel		25:22	189 n. 15
16:60	142, 150	2:15	189 n. 15	26:11	189 n. 15
17	140–52	3:19–23	47	40:30	189 n. 15
17:1–24	143–44, 152	8:23	189 n. 15		
17:1–21	141	9:16	222	Baruch	
17:1–2	142	12:2	163	3:7–8	157 n. 14
17:3–8	142, 148			4:15	189 n. 15
17:7	143	Joel			
17:9–10	142, 148	3:17	222	1 Maccabees	
17:11–21	142	4:13	17	1:42	35 n. 45
17:12–21	148	4:17	222	3:51	122
17:12–18	142				
17:12–15	142	Amos		2 Maccabees	
17:12–14	142	1:15	153 n. 3, 157 n. 15	1:10–2:18	164
17:13	140, 147, 152			1:11	194 n. 26
17:15–21	6, 141, 143, 152	Jonah			
17:15–18	143	1:9	91 n. 3, 109 n. 58		
17:15–17	143			**New Testament**	
17:18–19	147	Micah		Matthew	
17:18	147	1:14	71	1:1–18	172
17:19–21	142	4:1–4	44	1:3	46 n. 2, 49–50
17:19–20	142			1:20	181
17:20	143	Zechariah		2:13, 19	181
18:20	148	6:10	153 n. 3, 157 n. 15	4:5	222
20:9, 14, 21	144	8:3	222	4:12–17	173
20:32–44	149	11:8	85 n. 26	4:18–22	174
20:33	144	14:2	153 n. 3, 157 n. 15	4:18	175
20:39	144	14:9	44	4:23–5:1	174
23:46	160 n. 26			4:23–25	174
24	135	Judith		4:23	186
25:3	153 n. 3, 157 n. 15	4:3	122	5–7	174
26–28	5–6, 125, 139	5:11	122 n. 44	5:3–12	181 n. 15
26	135, 139	5:19	164	5:3	186 n. 8
26:2	135	6:19	122	5:17	172
26:7–14	135	7:32	122	5:23–26	177 n. 10
27–28	136, 139	8:25	194 n. 26	5:29–30	180
27:26–36	137	9:2–4	40	5:38–42	177 n. 10
28	137–38	12:14	101 n. 36	5:43–48	174, 177 n. 10
28:2	16–17	13:20	122	6:1	178
28:5–6	139			6:2	178
28:9	17	Wisdom		6:5	178
28:16	139	12:7	157 n. 14	6:9	223
29–32	135	15:8	193	6:12	177 n. 10, 182

Index of Ancient Sources

Matthew (*cont.*)

6:14–15	182 n. 18	18:21–35	179, 181–83	6:20	186
6:16	178	18:21	175	6:24	187
6:30	178	18:30	177	6:27	231
8–9	174	18:35	179	7:1–10	202, 214
8:1	174	19:16	231	7:2	214–15
8:5–13	173	21:15	46 n. 2	7:6	214, 215 n. 55
8:26	178	21:28–32	181 n. 15	7:8	214
9:10	177	21:31	177	8:1–3	197
9:27	46 n. 2	22:1–10	188	8:3	187
9:35–36	174	22:34–40	174	8:31	202
10:1–11:1	174	23	7	9:57–62	190–91
10:3	177	23:3	177	11:1–13	196
10:5	173	23:4	177	11:1–4	189
10:42	180	23:5	177	11:5–8	7, 188–90
11:6	180	23:6–7	177	11:9–13	189
11:19	177	23:9–10	177	11:12	223
12:21	173	23:11–12	177	11:21	187 n. 9
12:23	46 n. 2	24:4, 5, 11, 24	181	12:13–21	7, 191, 192–93, 196–97
14:28–31	176	24:15	222		
14:31	178	25:31–46	180	12:15, 33, 44	187 n. 9
15:12	180	26:69–75	176	13:30	193
15:15	175	27:53	222	14:12–14	190–91
15:21–28	173	28:20	177	14:15–24	7, 188, 190–91, 196
15:22	46 n. 2	**Mark**		14:25–33	191
16:8	178	1:14–15	186	14:33	187
16:13–20	7, 174–76	1:24	223	12:42–46	192 n. 22
16:16–17	177	6:20	223	15:1–32	181
16:16	175	8:31–33	174	15:3–7	191
16:22–23	176	9:33–34	179	15:8–10	7, 191–92, 196–97
17:4	175	14:7	231		
17:20	178	16:7	175	15:11–32	191, 196 n. 32
17:24–27	175	16:19	11	15:18–19	192 n. 22
17:27	180			16:1	187 n. 9
18:1–5	179	**Luke**		16:3–4	192 n. 22
18:1	179	1:46–55	193	16:13	187
18:2	183	1:49	223	16:14	196
18:3	179	1:70	223	16:19–31	7, 193–94, 196
18:6–14	179	2:23	223	18:4–5	192 n. 22
18:6–9	180	3:7–9	196	18:9–14	8, 194–95, 196
18:6	179	3:10–14	196	18:21	188
18:10–14	180–81	3:10	195–98	18:25	187
18:14	179, 183	3:14	202, 214	19:1–10	187
18:15–20	7, 176, 179	3:33	46 n. 2, 50 n. 9	19:8	187 n. 9
18:15–17	177 n. 10	4:18	186	19:43	214
18:17	177	4:34	223	20:9–16	192 n. 22
18:18–19	177	5:11, 28	187	21:1–4	187, 197

Index of Ancient Sources 259

21:20	214	16:33–34	225	12:10	240
21:24	214	16:40	188	12:13	240
23:11	202, 214	17:4	187	13:3	238
23:36	202, 214	17:12	187	15:24	233, 239
23:47	202, 214, 215 n. 55	18:1–11	187	15:25	224
		18:18–28	187	16	240
24:12	175	21:17	188	16:2	233
24:51	11	21:31–23:32	202	16:3–4	233
		21:31	214		
John		21:32, 35	214	1 Corinthians	
1:18	193 n. 23	21:33	214	3:17	224
4	53	22:24	214	6:20	224
6:69	223	22:25, 26	214, 215 n. 55	7	225
7:35	166, 168	22:27–29	214	7:1	220
13:23	193 n. 23	23:10	214	7:12–16	220
17:15	224	23:19	214	7:14	219–20
17:17–19	223	23:22	214	7:39	226
20:1–10	175	23:23	214	9:19–23	244
		23:31	214	9:23	246
Acts of the Apostles		24:22	214	9:24–26	244
1:1	207	24:23	202, 214, 215 n. 55	10:31	238
2:44–45	187, 197			15:5	175
3:21	223–24	27:1–43	202	16:1–4	239–40
4:32–35	188, 197	27:1	207, 214, 215 n. 55	16:15	224
4:32	187 n. 9				
5:1–11	198	27:3	216	2 Corinthians	
8:1, 4	167 n. 41	27:6	214, 215 n. 55	1:1	224
8:33	120 n. 36	27:11	214, 215 n. 55	1:12	234
10:1–11:18	175	27:31–32	214	8:21	235, 239
10	202, 214	27:31	214, 215 n. 55	9:8	231
10:1–8	216	27:42	214	10:1–6	235
10:1	206, 214, 215 n. 55	27:43	214, 215 n. 55	10:3	200
10:2	216	28:16	202	13:12	224
10:22	214, 215 n. 55				
10:24–33	216	Romans		Galatians	
10:44–48	216	1:7	224	1:10	246
10:47–48	225	2:1–10	238	2:10	239
11:13	181 n. 14	2:2–8	245	2:11–14	175
11:19	167 n. 41	2:7, 10	245	3:1–5	239
12:4–10	202	2:9	245	3:2–3	244
12:4, 6, 18	214	2:15	234	3:17	82
12:12	187	8:4	245	4:12–20	232–33
13:1–3	234	8:27	224	4:18	232–33
14:2	188	9:1–2	234	4:29	244
15:1, 7, 13, 22, 23	188	12:1	224	5:13–6:10	239
15:20, 28–29	49 n. 8	12:9–22	238, 245	5:16–24	244
16:14	187	12:9, 17	239–40	5:25	244–45

260 Index of Ancient Sources

Galatians (*cont.*)
6:7–10   244–45
6:9–10   238–39

Ephesians
1:1, 18   224
1:4   229
3:18   224
5:21–6:9   225

Philippians
1:1   224
1:13, 20   244
1:23   244
3:3–6   233
3:5   109 n. 58
3:14   238
3:20   226
4:11   233
4:15–20   233
4:22   224

Colossians
3:12   224
3:18–4:1   225

1 Thessalonians
1:7–9   238
2:14   238
5:2   238
5:12–22   238
5:15, 21   238

1 Timothy
1:5   234
1:18–20   234
1:18–19   234–35
3:1–7   236
3:1   236–37
4:6   235
4:14   234
5:3–16   242 n. 22
5:10   240–42
5:17–22   236
6:11   234
6:12   234, 244
6:17–19   242

6:18   242–43
6:19   245

2 Timothy
1:6   234
4:7   245
4:8   245

Titus
1:5–9   236
1:8   236–37
2:1–10   235
2:7   235–36
3:1–7   243
3:8   243
3:14   243

Philemon
5   243
6–7   243
22   243

Hebrews
12   229

James
1:1   166–67
1:21, 24–25   167 n. 42
2:2, 8–13, 19   167 n. 42
4:4, 11–12   167 n. 42
4:17   231

1 Peter
1:1   166–67
1:16   229
2:5–12   223 n. 8
3:1–6   220 n. 2

Revelation
6:9–10   229

**JEWISH PSEUDEPIG-
RAPHA AND RELATED
TEXTS**

3 *Apoc. Bar.*
0:2–3   157 n. 13

4 *Baruch*
6:19   157 n. 13

Demetrius fragment
6:1   157 n. 13

1 Enoch
89:41   83

2 Esdras
11:8–9   161 n. 30

4 Ezra
5:16–18   157 n. 13
14:21–22   157 n. 13

Jubilees   4
30:2   40–41
30:4–5   41
30:8–10   41
30:18   41
34:14   37 n. 51
41:1–24   46

Lives of the Prophets
12:1–2   157 n. 13
20:1   157 n. 13

3 Maccabees
2:12   122
6:10   157 n. 14

4 Maccabees
9:24   234 n. 10

Psalms of Solomon
2:6   157 n. 13
8:28   158, 166
9:2   158, 166

Testament of Asher
7:2–3   165
7:2   158
7:4   166 n. 40

Testament of Benjamin
7:2   157 n. 12

Index of Ancient Sources

Testament of Dan
5:7–8   157 n. 12
5:11   157 n. 12

Testament of Joseph
1:5   157 n. 12

Testament of Judah   4
4:3   157 n. 12
5:6   157 n. 12
6:3   157 n. 12
7:8   157 n. 12
10:1–12:17   46
23:5   157 n. 12

Testament of Levi
6:4–5   37 n. 51
13:6–7   157 n. 12

Testament of Naphtali
4:2   157 n. 12
5:8   156 n. 11, 157 n. 12

DEAD SEA SCROLLS AND RELATED TEXTS
1QH
2.20, 21   194 n. 26
3.19, 37   194 n. 26
4.5   194 n. 26
7.34   194 n. 26

1QM
1.2, 3   153 n. 3

1QS
5.26–6.2   176

1QSa
9.2–3   176

4QpNah (4Q169)
3–4 iv 1   153 n. 3

4QapocrJerC^a (4Q385^a)
17a–e ii 7   153 n. 3

4Qpap psEzek^e (4Q391)
77.2   153 n. 3

6Qpap apocrSam–Kgs (6Q9)
1.2   153 n. 3

Aramaic Levi Document
3:10, 16–18   40
4   40

OTHER JEWISH TEXTS
Philo
De Abrahamo
66   157 n. 16
68   157 n. 16
72   157 n. 16
77   157 n. 16
85   157 n. 16
De confusione linguarum
17.77–78   158 n. 17
77–78   157 n. 16
197   158
De congress eruditionis gratia
84   157 n. 16
De vita contemplativa
22   157 n. 16
In Flaccum
17.46–47   158 n. 17
46   157 n. 16
De fuga et inventione
36   157 n. 16
95   157 n. 16
Quis rerum divinarum heres sit
98   157 n. 16
Legatio ad Gaium
281   157 n. 16
Legum allegoriae
2.35   156
De migration Abrahami
176   157 n. 16
De vita Mosis
1.71   157 n. 16
1.103   157 n. 16
1.163   157 n. 16
1.170   157 n. 16
1.195   157 n. 16
1.222   157 n. 16
1.233   157 n. 16
1.236   157 n. 16
1.239   157 n. 16
1.254–55   157 n. 16
2.232   157 n. 16
2.246   157 n. 16
2.288   157 n. 16
De opificio mundi
135   157 n. 16
De praemiis et poenis
16   157 n. 16
80   157 n. 16
115   158
Quaestiones et solutions in Genesin
1.27   157 n. 16
De specialibus legibus
2.25   157 n. 16
2.146   157 n. 16
2.150   157 n. 16
2.158   157 n. 16
3.108–15   227
3.111   157 n. 16
4.178   157 n. 16
De virtutibus
77   157 n. 16
102   157 n. 16
219   157 n. 16

Josephus
Antiquities
1.21.1 §338   41
1.21.1 §340   43
1.110–12   158 n. 18
1.210   158 n. 18
1.216   158 n. 18
1.255   158 n. 18
10.223   158 n. 18
14.10.6   204–5, 206 n. 25
15.268   227
17.11.4 §§317–20
                      182 n. 19

Josephus (*cont.*)
Antiquities (*cont.*)
19.9.1–2 §§354–65
     206 n. 26
19.365   207
20.122, 176   207
Contra Apionem
2.38   158 n. 18
2.202   227
Jewish War
2.6.3 §§100–193
     182 n. 19
2.52, 58, 63, 74, 236
     207
2.345–401   211

RABBINIC LITERATURE
Genesis Rabbah
57:4   37 n. 51
80:8   35–36
80:10   36
80:11   37 n. 51
85:8   48
85:9   48

Aggadat Bereshit
64C   48

Babylonian Talmud
Megillah 10b   49
Berakot 28b 194 n. 26
Sotah 10a   49

Tosefta
Berakot 7.18 194 n. 26

Targumim
Neofiti
Gen 38:25   47

Pseudo-Jonathan
Gen 38:25   47
Gen 38:26   47 n. 4

EARLY CHRISTIAN TEXTS
Apostolic Fathers
Barnabas
19.5   227
20.1–2   227

Didache
2.2   227
5.2   227

Letter to Diognetus
5.1–10   226
5.6   227

Shepherd of Hermas
Similitudes
1 [50]   226

New Testament
Apocrypha and
Pseudepigrapha
3 Corinthians
13:7   238

Other Christian Texts
Ambrose of Milan
*Expositio Evangelii
secundum Lucam*
3.17–18   52
3.19   52 n. 15

Augustine
Questions on Genesis
167   42
Contra mendacium
14.30   51

Clement of Alexandria
Stromateis
1.141ff.   157 n. 13

Cyprian of Carthage
Testament
30   51

Ephrem the Syrian
*Commentarium in
Genesim*
34.1   55
34.2   55–56
34.3   54
Hymni de nativitate
1.12   54
9.8, 10–11   54–55
9.9   55
15.7, 8   54
Hymni de virginitate
22.19–21   53
22.20   54 n. 21

Eusebius of Caesrea
Historia ecclesiastica
5.1.3–2.8   228
*Quaestiones evangelicae
ad Stephanum*
7.1   52
7.2   52

Gregory of Nazianzus
Oratio in laudem Basilii
8   229
18.7–12   229

Jerome
*Commemtariorum in
Matthaeum libri IV*
1:15–20   51 n. 12

John Chrysostom
Homiliae in Genesim
62.1   57
62.2   57–58
Homiliae in Matthaeum
3.2   58
3.4   58

Justin
Apologia
1.27   227

Origen
Homiliae in Lucam
27   51 n. 12

Index of Ancient Sources 263

Severus of Antioch
Hom. cath.
94   51 n. 12

Tertullian
Apologeticus
9.6–8   227
Ad nationes
1.15   227
Ad uxorem
2.4–5   226
De cultu feminarum
2.2.12   51
De pudicitia
12   49 n. 8

CLASSICAL GREEK AND LATIN WRITINGS
Aristotle
Ethica nicomachea
1.1.1   231 n. 3
1.2.8   231 n. 3
1.5.4–5   231 n. 3
9:8 1168B   188 n. 11

Augustus
Res gestae
8.1–4   204 n. 18
27   210 n. 43

Cicero
De domo sua
41.109   221

Dio Cassius
Historia
59.2   212 n. 48
76.15.2   205

Dionysius of Halicarnassus
Antiquitates romanae
10.18.2   204 n. 16
11.43   204 n. 16

Livy
22.38   204 n. 16

Minucius Felix
Octavius
30.2   227

Plato
Respublica
7.517bc   231 n. 3
7.519e–520a   231 n. 3

Plutarch
De Iside et Osiride
42   231 n. 1

Polybius
Histories
6.33.1   204 n. 16
6.53.1   237
6.53.3   237
6.53.6–10   237

Pseudo-Hyginus
De mun castr.
1.4   203 n. 15

Ps.-Phocylides
Sentences
184–85   227

Tacitus
Agricola
28   206
35.2   205
Annales
1.17   208
1.78   204
2.17   205
4.5   205
14.27   210 n. 43
Historiae
2.83   207

Thucydides
Peloponnesian War
2.27   154 n. 7

Vegetius
1.8   204 n. 16

PAPYRI
P. Amst.
8, 9, 10   209

P. Mich.
6. 425, inv. 2979   209 n. 41

Index of Authors

Albright, William Foxwell, 200
Allison, Dale C., Jr., 181 n. 16
Alter, Robert, 30 n. 23
Aubet, Maria Eugenia, 133, 137
Auld, A. Graeme, 93 n. 7, 103 n. 37

Bal, Mieke, 69 n. 24
Barclay, John, 169, 244 n. 25
Barker, John, 4
Bergant, Dianne, 3
Berlin, Adele, 89
Berman, Joshua, 145–46
Berry, Thomas, 13
Betz, Hans Dieter, 232
Bitner, Bradley J., 211 n. 45
Blenkinsopp, Joseph, 39 n. 63, 82, 112
Block, Daniel I., 86 n. 28
Blyth, Caroline, 25
Bodi, Daniel, 137
Boer, Roland, 126
Botha, Phil, 56
Bottéro, Jean, 105 n. 42
Brettler, Marc Zvi, 63 nn. 7 and 10, 69 n. 22, 78
Brink, Laurie, 8
Brown, Raymond E., 171–72, 174, 175 n. 9, 177, 179, 183
Brueggemann, Walter, 71 n. 30
Burton, Ernest De Witt, 232

Cadwallader, Alan, 201
Carvalho, Corrine, 5–6
Cascio, E. Lo, 212 n. 48
Chaney, Marvin, 104
Coomber, Matthew J. M., 129
Crenshaw, James L., 64 n. 10

Darr, John, 201
Darwin, Charles, 11
Davies, W. D., 181 n. 16
Davis, Andrew R., 5
Delio, Ilia, 24
Doak, Brian R., 105 n. 49
Doran, Robert, 195 n. 29
Driver, S. R., 93
Dufoix, Stéphane, 154 n. 7, 155, 165 n. 39
Dunn, James D. G., 232

Ekblad, Eugene Robert, 120–21
Elat, Moshe, 131 n. 25
Exum, J. Cheryl, 62, 64 n. 10

Fewell, Danna Nolan, 31
Foucault, Michel, 72
Francis, Pope, 7–8, 18 n. 22, 184, 229
Frankel, David, 32, 39
Fretheim, Terence, 39, 43
Freud, Sigmund, 15
Fridrichsen, Anton, 190 n. 17

Gafni, Isaiah, 169
Gaventa, Beverly Roberts, 50 n. 10
Grafton, Anthony, 78–79
Greenberg, Moshe, 105 n. 42
Groß, Walter, 63 nn. 9 and 10, 83 n. 22
Gruen, Erich, 169
Grundmann, Walter, 231
Gunkel, Hermann, 31–32, 37, 39
Gunn, David M., 31
Gutiérrez, Gustavo, 196

Haak, Robert D., 85 n. 26
Habel, Norman C., 15, 20–21

Halpern, Baruch, 78
Hamilton, Victor P., 29
Harrington, Daniel J., 51 n. 13
Hayes, Zachary, 10 n. 1
Hertzberg, Wilhelm, 96
Hoppe, Leslie J., 111, 172 n. 4, 185–86, 198, 200, 247
Howgego, C. J., 211 n. 46
Huxley, Julian, 22, 24

Iser, Wolfgang, 201

Jaspers, Karl Theodor, 12
Jigoulov, Vadim S., 133
John Paul II, Pope, 11
Joseph, Alison L., 36 n. 50

Kalmanofsky, Amy, 134
Kampen, John, 174 n. 8
Kee, H. C., 165 n. 40
Kelm, George L., 71 n. 29
Klauck, Hans-Josef, 200
Klopper, Frances, 31
Konradt, Matthias, 173
Kooij, Arie van der, 114, 122
Kraabel, A. Thomas, 154
Kratz, Reinhard G., 63 n. 9
Kronholm, Tryggve, 50 n. 10

Launderville, Dale, 6
Law, Timothy, 113
Leonard-Fleckman, Mahri, 4
Leuchter, Mark, 76 n. 42
Levine, Amy-Jill, 50 n. 10, 192 n. 20, 194–95
Levinson, Bernard M., 146
Linnemann, Eta, 195 n. 29
Lonergan, Bernard, 13
Long, Burke, 88
Lopez, Kathryn M., 41
Loretz, Oswald, 105 nn. 42 and 46, 108

MacDonald, Margaret, 224
MacMullen, Ramsey, 203 n. 15
Marx, Karl, 15
Matthews, Shelly, 215 n. 58
Mazar, Amihai, 71 n. 29, 74, 98 n. 20

McCarter, P. Kyle, Jr., 93 n. 7, 103 n. 37
McLaughlin, John L., 5
Meier, John, 172
Miller, Patrick D., Jr., 103 n. 37, 107, 109
Mitchell, Margaret M., 200
Momigliano, Arnaldo, 78
Mussner, Franz, 232

Na'aman, Nadav, 105
Nevader, Madhavi, 136 n. 42, 137
Neville, Ann, 130 n. 24
Nickelsburg, George W. E., 42
Niditch, Susan, 62 n. 5, 64–65
Nietzsche, Friedrich, 15
Nihan, Christophe, 150–51
Noble, Paul, 38

Odell, Margaret S., 128
Okorie, Ferdinand, 8–9
Okoye, James Chukwuma, 3–4
Osiek, Carolyn, 8
Oster, Richard, 211 n. 45
Ottley, R. R., 117 n. 26
Otto, Eckart, 146, 148–49

Parry, Robin, 31
Paton-Williams, David, 121 n. 42
Paul, Shalom, 121 n. 41
Praeder, Susan Marie, 191 n. 20

Rahner, Karl, 13
Reece, Richard, 212 n. 48
Reid, Barbara, 7–9, 215 n. 58
Richter, Sandra, 144
Ricoeur, Paul, 15
Roberts, J. J. M., 103 n. 37, 107, 109
Rofé, Alexander, 39
Roth, Jonathan P., 206 n. 27
Rowton, M. B., 105

Sailhamer, John, 43–44
Santos, Narry F., 167 n. 41
Schneider, Tammi J., 69 n. 22
Schökel, Luis Alonso, 78
Scholtz, Susanne, 31
Scholz, Anton, 113
Schottroff, Luise, 191 n. 20

Schüssler Fiorenza, Elisabeth, 241
Scott, James M., 154 n. 6
Seeligmann, Isac Leo, 113–14, 122
Sellew, Melissa [née Philip] Harl, 192 n. 22
Senior, Donald, 7
Simkovich, Malka Zeiger, 6–7
Singer, Ithamar, 109
Smend, Rudolph, 144
Smith, Mark S., 4–5, 76 n. 43
Snodgrass, Klyne, 190 n. 17
Sparks, Kenton L., 108
Speidel, Michael P., 206 n. 27
Spinoza, Baruch, 87
Stackert, Jeffrey, 146
Sternberg, Meir, 27, 30, 32, 35 n. 47
Stone, Bryan Jack, 98 n. 21

Teilhard de Chardin, Pierre, 3, 13, 21–23
Troxel, Ronald, 114–15, 122

Ulrich, Eugene, 115 n. 19
Unnik, W. C. van, 154

Victor, Royce M., 69 n. 22

Wagner, J. Ross, 114–15, 122
Wainwright, Elaine M., 50 n. 10
Weippert, Manfred, 105
Wellhausen, Julius, 150
Westermann, Claus, 30, 32, 37 n. 51, 39
White, Hayden, 78
Wilcox, Peter, 121 n. 42
Wilson, Ian, 136
Wolfs-Knuts, Ulrika, 89 n. 44

Yasur-Landau, Assaf, 98 n. 24
Younger, K. Lawson, Jr., 62 n. 4, 83 n. 21

Ziegler, Joseph, 112, 118